DYNAMICS OF DIFFERENCE:
CHRISTIANITY AND ALTERITY

DYNAMICS OF DIFFERENCE: CHRISTIANITY AND ALTERITY

A Festschrift for Werner G. Jeanrond

Ulrich Schmiedel and James M. Matarazzo, Jr.

Bloomsbury T&T Clark
An imprint of Bloomsbury Publishing Plc

BLOOMSBURY
LONDON • NEW DELHI • NEW YORK • SYDNEY

Bloomsbury T&T Clark

Imprint previously known as T&T Clark
An imprint of Bloomsbury Publishing Plc

50 Bedford Square	1385 Broadway
London	New York
WC1B 3DP	NY 10018
UK	USA

www.bloomsbury.com

BLOOMSBURY, T&T CLARK and the Diana logo are trademarks of Bloomsbury Publishing Plc

First published 2015

© Ulrich Schmiedel and James M. Matarazzo Jr., 2015

Ulrich Schmiedel and James M. Matarazzo Jr. have asserted their right under the Copyright, Designs and Patents Act, 1988, to be identified as Editors of this work.

All rights reserved. No part of this publication may be reproduced or transmitted in any form or by any means, electronic or mechanical, including photocopying, recording, or any information storage or retrieval system, without prior permission in writing from the publishers.

No responsibility for loss caused to any individual or organization acting on or refraining from action as a result of the material in this publication can be accepted by Bloomsbury or the author.

British Library Cataloguing-in-Publication Data
A catalogue record for this book is available from the British Library.

ISBN: HB: 978-0-5676-5685-8
ePDF: 978-0-5676-5686-5
ePUB: 978-0-5676-5726-8

Library of Congress Cataloging-in-Publication Data
Dynamics of difference : Christianity and alterity : a Festschrift for Werner G. Jeanrond / edited by Ulrich Schmiedel and James M. Matarazzo, Jr.
  pages cm
  Includes index.
  ISBN 978-0-567-65685-8 (hardcover)
 1. Philosophical theology. 2. Other (Philosophy)–Religious aspects–Christianity. 3. Other (Philosophy)–Religious aspects. 4. Other (Philosophy) 5. Bible–Criticism, interpretation, etc.
  I. Jeanrond, Werner G., 1955- honouree. II. Schmiedel, Ulrich, editor.
 BT40.D96 2014
 230--dc23
 2014030990

Typeset by Fakenham Prepress Solutions, Fakenham, Norfolk NR21 8NN
Printed and bound in Great Britain

Werner G. Jeanrond
Photo courtesy of St Benet's Hall, University of Oxford

CONTENTS

Preface ix
Contributors xii

(Instead of the) Introduction: Open to the Other –
The Dynamics of Difference in Werner G. Jeanrond's
Hermeneutical Theology   *Ulrich Schmiedel*   1

Part I
BIBLICAL OTHERS AND OTHER BIBLES

1 Moses: The Significant Other   *Brian Klug*   17
2 Joseph in Egypt: Assimilation and Separation from the
   Other   *Andrew D. H. Mayes*   25
3 Becoming 'Another': Nicodemus and his Relationships in the
   Fourth Gospel   *Mary Marshall*   33
4 The Bible, *Nostra Aetate*, and the 'Good Text-Bad Text'
   Hermeneutics   *Jesper Svartvik*   41
5 The Alterity of the Letter: Revelation in *Dei Verbum*
   Olivier Riaudel   51

Part II
PHILOSOPHICAL OTHERS AND OTHER PHILOSOPHIES

6   Ethics of Vision: Seeing the Other as Neighbour   *Arne Grøn*   63
7   The Outer and Inner Constitution of Human Dignity in Meister
    Eckhart   *Dietmar Mieth*   71
8   The Value of the Other   *Tage Kurtén*   79
9   Love of God and Love of One Another According to
    Paul   *Jeffrey Bloechl*   87
10 Paul Ricoeur as Other   *Bengt Kristensson Uggla*   95
11 The Other of Dialectic and Dialogue   *David Tracy*   105
12 Encountering the Other: The Concept of Encounter in
    Philosophy and Theology   *Matthias Petzoldt*   115
13 In-Between Subjectivity and Alterity: Philosophy of Dialogue
    and Theology of Love   *Claudia Welz*   125

Part III
THEOLOGICAL OTHERS AND OTHER THEOLOGIES

14 The Other Language: Religion in Modernity *Knut Wenzel* — 137
15 Laughing at the Other *Ola Sigurdson* — 145
16 Foreignness as Focal Point of Otherness *Pierre Bühler* — 153
17 Sexual Difference in Christian Doctrine and Symbolism: Historical Impact and Feminist Critique *Kari Elisabeth Børresen* — 161
18 The Other on the Cross *Anne-Louise Eriksson* — 173
19 The Other Within and the Other Without *George Newlands* — 181
20 Augustinian Love *Rowan Williams* — 189
21 Who loves? Who is loved? The Problem of the Collective Personality *Johannes Zachhuber* — 199
22 *Gegenüber* Revisited: 'Thirding-as-Othering' in Karl Barth's Concept of Space *Kjetil Hafstad* — 209

Part IV
RELIGIOUS OTHERS AND OTHER RELIGIONS

23 Empathy and Otherness in Interreligious Dialogue *Catherine Cornille* — 221
24 In the Presence of God – Making Room for the Other: An Autobiographical Approach *Karl-Josef Kuschel* — 231
25 Related Rivals: How Christians and Muslims Might Relate to One Another *Susanne Heine* — 239
26 'Who Practices Hospitality Entertains God Himself' *Mona Siddiqui* — 247
27 Beyond Indifference: Religious Traditions as Resources for Interreligious Toleration *Christoph Schwöbel* — 255

Part V
GOD AS OTHER AND THE OTHERNESS OF GOD

28 Loved by the Other: *Creatio ex nihilo* as an Act of Divine Love *David Fergusson* — 265
29 The Other and the Interruption of Love *Lieven Boeve* — 275
30 The Middle English Poem *Pearl*: A Study in the Unfamiliar *Santha Bhattacharji* — 285
31 Finding the Otherness of God in Literature *David Jasper* — 293

Index of Subjects — 301
Index of Names — 308

PREFACE

Werner G. Jeanrond is a prominent and provocative theologian. With this *Festschrift* in honour of his sixtieth birthday, we investigate the challenge of alterity for Christianity, exploring and elaborating on this core concern in Jeanrond's hermeneutical theology. Blurring disciplinary boundaries, more than thirty of his colleagues and companions from ten countries invite us to track the dynamics of difference driven by the encounter with the self as other, the other as other, and God as the radical other. Who is my other? What do I encounter when I encounter my other? And what responses and responsibilities does the encounter with my other evoke? Questions like these are explored in the following five parts of this compilation, which analyse (1) alterity in the Bible, (2) alterity in philosophy, (3) alterity in theology, (4) alterity in interreligious dialogues, and (5) the radical alterity of God.

The first part touches on Jeanrond's hermeneutical reflections on biblical theologies. It takes us from analyses of others in the Bible – as exemplified by three tricky biblical others – to the Bible as other in intra- and interreligious dialogue. Exploring alterity in philosophy, the second part begins with ethical examinations of connections and disconnections between alterity and morality, concentrating on subjectivity, society and community, before our attention is drawn to the conversation between philosophy and theology. Here, the contributions investigate how encounters with the other are conceptualized in philosophy, critically and creatively drawing on Jeanrond's theology. These investigations lead us to the third part, which examines alterity in theology. It opens with an analysis of the interdependence between religion as an other to secularity and secularity as an other to religion. Tying in with Jeanrond's reflections on Jesus Christ as the other, the following contributions consider the challenge of others and otherness for churches in both the past and the present, from christological, pneumatological and ecclesiological perspectives. Particular attention is paid to the marginalization of female others. The fourth part engages with the dialogues between religious others and other religions, referring to Jeanrond's concept of a 'hermeneutics of love'. Its content stretches from a thorough examination of interreligious empathy, to practical and theoretical discussions of encounters between the Abrahamic religions, to an assessment of religious traditions as resources for interreligious modesty and empathy. Here, the radical otherness of God is stressed, which brings us to the fifth and final part of this compilation. The investigation of alterity in thinking and talking about God starts with a retrieval of the doctrine of the *creatio ex nihilo*, highlighting that alterity is necessary for a relation of love between creator and creation. Subsequently, God's alterity is characterized as the interruption of our attitudes and assumptions about God. Here, Jeanrond's

A Theology of Love is discussed in detail. The *Festschrift* concludes with an analysis of the traces of God's otherness which can be found in literature. Following Jeanrond's explorations of the many faces and facets of the other, all of the contributions to this compilation ultimately aim to advocate openness to the other as a necessity for both religion and reflections on religion.

Editing a compilation by silent-and-stealth research in order to surprise a theologian with a *Festschrift* involves risks. First and foremost, we could not consult Jeanrond for his comments, critiques and counsels. We delved into his writings to identify contributors for our compilation. Following Jeanrond's preference for short and succinct studies, our research resulted in a long list of scholars which continually changed throughout the preparation of this *Festschrift*. We are grateful to all who supported us in approaching the contributors who attest to Jeanrond's network within the continent of Europe, the UK, the US and beyond. Undoubtedly, we will have missed excellent and exciting scholars. We would like to ask for their forbearance: what we have edited is *a* compilation for Werner G. Jeanrond – which is to say that there will be more opportunities to engage with his work. These opportunities bring us to the risk of accidentally announcing the completion or closure of Jeanrond's theology by compiling a *Festschrift*. The peremptory response from one of the scholars we consulted is incisive: 'I would be appalled by a *Festschrift* for my sixtieth birthday' – as if it implied that it was time for the honorand to retire. Since (or in spite of the fact that) Jeanrond was born in the Saarland, we opted to follow the German(ic) tradition to honour a scholar with a compilation for her or his sixtieth birthday. Yet, if this *Festschrift* announces anything, it is that Jeanrond's theology is neither complete nor closed, but that its engagement with the other is a promising point of departure for resistance against any completion and closure of interpretation.

We would like to thank all of those who shared the risks of editing this compilation with us. We are grateful to the Jeanrond Family who supported us from the beginning. Without Betty Jeanrond, there would be neither a compilation nor a surprise compilation. Without Hans-Josef Jeanrond, its cover would look far less enticing. We are grateful that he allowed us to use his photograph *Crabe*, which can be found in Werner Jeanrond's study in St Benet's Hall, Oxford. We wish to thank both staff and students at St Benet's – especially Penelope Lane – who strongly supported us. Brian Klug has exemplified the exciting environment which the University of Oxford affords us. We are grateful for the conversations with him which lurk between the lines of this *Festschrift*. Thanks are due to Marijn de Jong for his careful, critical and constructive review of the complete compilation. Nevertheless, some mistakes might have crept into the contributions – these are obviously our own. We are grateful to Hannah M. Strømmen who helped with both our Swedish and our English. She offered the counsel which reconciled the times when we were of different opinions. Thanks to the generous support by the Right Reverend Cuthbert Madden, OSB, Abbot of Ampleforth, we were able to cover the cost for the indexing of this compilation. We would like to thank Oxford University Press for the permission to reprint the translation of Stéphane Mallarmé's poem 'Brise Marine'. We are grateful to Miriam Cantwell, Dominic

Mattos and Anna Turton at Bloomsbury T&T Clark for their enthusiasm for this *Festschrift*. And, of course, we wish to thank the contributors to this compilation for their patience with us, the inexperienced editors. Finally, we would like to thank Werner Jeanrond, who strongly supports our pursuits and projects both inside and outside academia – without knowing it, he supported the project of this compilation. We could not wish for a more attentive supervisor, which is why we are honoured to honour him with a *Festschrift* for his sixtieth birthday.

Oxford, Easter 2014
Ulrich Schmiedel and James M. Matarazzo, Jr.

CONTRIBUTORS

Santha Bhattacharji is Senior Tutor at St Benet's Hall and a member of the Faculty of English at the University of Oxford. Her research focus is on Old English poetry and the Middle English mystics.

Jeffrey Bloechl is Associate Professor of Philosophy and Director of the Psychoanalytic Studies Program at Boston College. His research concentrates on Emmanuel Levinas, phenomenology, psychoanalysis, philosophy of religion and metaphilosophy.

Lieven Boeve is Professor of Fundamental Theology in the Faculty of Theology and Religious Studies at the Catholic University of Leuven. He is also Director-General of the Office for Catholic Education in Flanders. His research interests include theological epistemology, continental philosophy and neo-Augustinianism in contemporary theology.

Kari Elisabeth Børresen is Professor Emerita in the Faculty of Theology at the University of Oslo. She is a pioneer of religious gender studies, especially ancient and medieval formations of Christian doctrine.

Pierre Bühler is Professor of Systematic Theology at the University of Zürich, where he directs the Institute of Hermeneutics and Philosophy of Religion. His research focuses on Martin Luther, Søren Kierkegaard, theological and philosophical hermeneutics, literary studies and the dialogue between theology, philosophy and natural as well as social sciences.

Catherine Cornille is Professor of Comparative Theology and Newton College Alumnae Chair of Western Culture at Boston College. Her research interests focus on the theology of religions, the theory of interreligious dialogue and intercultural theology.

Anne-Louise Eriksson is Dean of the Church of Sweden Institute for Pastoral Education in Uppsala. An ordained priest in the Church of Sweden and former Associate Professor at the Stockholm School of Theology, her research focus is on practical theology and theological approaches to gender.

David Fergusson is Professor of Divinity and Principal of New College at the University of Edinburgh. His areas of research include Reformed theology, the doctrines of creation and providence and the relationship of the church to society, particularly with respect to political liberalism.

Arne Grøn is Professor of Ethics and Philosophy of Religion as well as co-founder of the Centre for Subjectivity Research at the University of Copenhagen. His research interests include the hermeneutical philosophy of religion, subjectivity and selfhood, and the ethics of vision.

Kjetil Hafstad is Professor of Systematic Theology at the University of Oslo. His research focuses on constructive and contextual theology, theology of civil disobedience and the ethical implications of globalization.

Susanne Heine is Professor Emerita of Practical Theology and the Psychology of Religion in the Faculty of Protestant Theology at the University of Vienna. She is also an ordained Lutheran pastor. Her areas of research include Christian-Muslim theological dialogue, gender studies and the psychology of religion.

David Jasper is Professor of Literature and Theology at the University of Glasgow and Distinguished Overseas Professor at Renmin University of China in Beijing. His broad research interests in theology and literature span from the early church fathers, to medieval mystics, to modern and postmodern philosophy and theology.

Brian Klug is Senior Research Fellow in Philosophy at St Benet's Hall and a Member of the Faculty of Philosophy at the University of Oxford. He is also a Fellow of the College of Arts and Sciences, Saint Xavier University, Chicago, and an Honorary Fellow of the Parkes Institute for the Study of Jewish and non-Jewish Relations, University of Southampton. His research focus includes the philosophy of Ludwig Wittgenstein as well as contemporary Jewish identity, racism and Islamophobia.

Bengt Kristensson Uggla is Amos Anderson Professor of Philosophy, Culture and Management at Åbo Akademi University. He is also Professor at the Stockholm School of Theology. His areas of research include hermeneutics, education theory and communication theory. He is an expert on the philosophy of Paul Ricoeur.

Tage Kurtén is Professor of Systematic Theology, Theological Ethics, and Philosophy of Religion at Åbo Akademi University. His research concentrates on the philosophy of Ludwig Wittgenstein, contextual theology, epistemology, ethics and Nordic theological studies.

Karl-Josef Kuschel is Professor Emeritus of the Theology of Culture and Interreligious Dialogue in the Faculty of Catholic Theology at the Eberhard Karls University of Tübingen. His research focus spans the areas of theology and literature, ecumenical theology, interfaith studies and globalization.

Mary Marshall is Tutorial Fellow and Director of Studies in Theology at St Benet's Hall and Departmental Lecturer in the Faculty of Theology and Religion at the

University of Oxford. Her primary research interests concern the gospels and gospel tradition in its Jewish contexts.

Andrew D. H. Mayes is Erasmus Smith's Professor of Hebrew Emeritus at the University of Dublin, and a Fellow of Trinity College, Dublin. His research is on the Hebrew Bible, ancient Israelite history and religion and methodology in historical reconstruction and religious understanding.

Dietmar Mieth is Professor Emeritus of Theology in the Faculty of Catholic Theology at the Eberhard Karls University of Tübingen. He is also a Fellow of the Max Weber Center for Advanced Cultural and Social Studies at the University of Erfurt. His areas of research include human dignity in social ethics, and the theology of Meister Eckhart.

George Newlands is Professor Emeritus of Divinity at the University of Glasgow. He was University Lecturer at the University of Cambridge and Dean of Trinity Hall. His broad research interests include the doctrine of God, the theology of love, human rights and intercultural theology.

Matthias Petzoldt is Professor Emeritus of Fundamental Theology, Dogmatics and Hermeneutics in the Faculty of Protestant Theology at the University of Leipzig. He is an ordained Lutheran pastor. His areas of research include fundamental theology, language philosophy, theology of religion and the dialogue between theology and natural as well as social sciences.

Olivier Riaudel is Professor of Fundamental Theology at the Catholic University of Louvain in Louvain-la-Neuve. His current research explores contemporary systematic theology, Wolfhart Pannenberg, the analysis of theological language and the rational requirements of the Christian faith.

Christoph Schwöbel is Professor of Systematic Theology and Director of the Institute of Hermeneutics and Cultural Dialogue in the Faculty of Protestant Theology at the Eberhard Karls University of Tübingen. His main research focus is in the area of fundamental theology. An expert on Trinitarian theology, he has written widely on Christianity and contemporary culture.

Mona Siddiqui, OBE, is Professor of Islamic and Interreligious Studies at the University of Edinburgh. Her primary research is in classical Islamic law (*fiqh*) and juristic arguments at the interface with contemporary ethical issues.

Ola Sigurdson is Professor of Systematic Theology at the University of Gothenburg. His research interests include the intersection between traditional systematic theology and continental critical theory, theology of culture and the relationship between theology and Marxism.

Jesper Svartvik is Krister Stendahl Professor of Theology of Religions at the Centre for Theology and Religious Studies at Lund University and the Swedish Theological Institute in Jerusalem. His current research explores interreligious aspects of the Bible, the intersection between christology, science, and non-Christian religious traditions and both early and contemporary Jewish-Christian relations.

David Tracy is Andrew Thomas Greeley and Grace McNichols Greeley Distinguished Service Professor Emeritus of Catholic Studies and Professor of Theology and the Philosophy of Religions at the University of Chicago. His research interests span the field of contemporary theology and include philosophical and systematic theology, hermeneutics and the relations between religion and modern thought.

Claudia Welz is Professor with special responsibilities in Ethics and Philosophy of Religion at the University of Copenhagen. Her research is on hermeneutics, the theology of the Reformation, Søren Kierkegaard, theories of subjectivity, German and French phenomenology, philosophy of psychology, memory studies and modern Jewish thought.

Knut Wenzel is Professor of Fundamental Theology and Dogmatics in the Department of Catholic Theology at the Goethe-University Frankfurt. His research interests include the hermeneutics of Paul Ricoeur, narrative theology, the history and theology of secularity as well as the relationship between theology and contemporary culture.

Rowan Williams is Master of Magdalene College, University of Cambridge, and former Archbishop of Canterbury. Prior to his episcopal tenure as Bishop of Monmouth, Archbishop of Wales, and then Archbishop of Canterbury, he was Lady Margaret Professor of Divinity at the University of Oxford. His broad research interests include the early church fathers, systematic and practical theology and literature.

Johannes Zachhuber is Associate Professor of Modern Theology in the Faculty of Theology and Religion and Fellow and Tutor in Theology at Trinity College, University of Oxford. His research focuses on patristic theology, modern and postmodern theology and continental philosophy.

(INSTEAD OF THE) INTRODUCTION
OPEN TO THE OTHER: THE DYNAMICS OF DIFFERENCE IN WERNER G. JEANROND'S HERMENEUTICAL THEOLOGY

Ulrich Schmiedel[1]

'Religion is relation'.[2] According to Werner G. Jeanrond, theology revolves around relations: to oneself as other, to the other as other, and to God as the radical other.[3] Since these inter-related relations are established inside as well as outside Christianity, theology cannot be confined to Christianity – let alone, confessional Christianity – but investigates relationality in today's communities, societies and academies.[4] The centrality of relationality is neither ahistorical nor acultural for Jeanrond. In contrast to the anxieties which characterized both premodern and modern contexts, postmodern contexts are arguably characterized by 'relational anxiety'.[5] Since relations are always already relations to the other, it is *the* challenge of postmodernity to engage with experiences of alterity.[6] In response to this challenge, Jeanrond explores the praxis of love. Love – as Jeanrond argues – is *in-between* the lovers: it is a web of inter-related relations. Lovers are embedded,

---

1. I am grateful to Marijn de Jong, Brian Klug, James M. Matarazzo, Jr., and Hannah M. Strømmen (who improved both my English and my Swedish) for their critical and constructive comments to this introduction.

2. Werner G. Jeanrond, *Guds närvaro: Teologiska Reflexioner I* (Lund: Arcus, 2006 [1998]), p. 113 (my translation). Cf. idem, *Kirkans Framtid: Teologiska Reflexioner III* (Lund: Arcus, 2012), pp. 114–15.

3. Cf. ibid., where Jeanrond refers to theology as 'relationsvetenskap' as opposed to 'religionsvetenskap'.

4. Cf. ibid., pp. 107–17, particularly pp. 107–8.

5. Cf. the critical conversation with Paul Tillich's theology in Werner G. Jeanrond, 'Ecclesia Semper Reformanda: Protestant Principle and Church Renewal', *Dansk Teologisk Tidsskrift* 37 (2010), pp. 271–81 (277). Also cf. idem, *Guds närvaro*, p. 45.

6. Cf. ibid., pp. 47–62. Also cf. idem, *Gudstro: Teologiska Reflexioner II* (Lund: Arcus, 2001), p. 178; idem, 'Zur Hermeneutik postmoderner Öffentlichkeit', in Edmund Arens and Helmut Hoping, eds, *Wieviel Theologie verträgt die Öffentlichkeit?* (Freiburg/Breisgau: Herder, 2000), pp. 82–100 (89).

enmeshed and entangled in this web in which alterity – the otherness of the other – opens them to transformation and transcendence: 'love lives off the very otherness of the other lovers'.[7] Hence, Jeanrond conceptualizes alterity not substantially but functionally: the other is the one who transforms and transcends me. Strictly speaking, the other is always already *my* other: actual and acute, never abstract.

In what follows, I argue that, throughout his hermeneutical theology, Jeanrond construes alterity and relationality as *complementary* concepts. In his combination of alterity and relationality, the other functions as resistance to the closure of interpretation. I explore the significance of the other's relational resistance by concentrating on alterity in the relation between textual and non-textual others, in the relation between Christian and non-Christian others and in the relation to God as the radical other. Of course, my exploration cannot completely cover Jeanrond's reflections on relationality and alterity. Yet, it is pertinent and promising to track his engagement with the complementary concepts of alterity and relationality in order to point to what I call the dynamics of difference which drives Jeanrond's hermeneutical theology.

In-Between the Textual and the Non-Textual Other

Interpretation is rooted in the relation between the interpreted and the interpreter – the text and the reader of the text.[8] Qualifying the relation of interpretation, Jeanrond stresses the correlation between the genres and styles of text-production and the genres and styles of text-reception.[9] Through this correlation, an adequate interpretation can be achieved. But what makes an interpretation adequate?

---

7. Werner G. Jeanrond, 'Subjectivity and Objectivity in Theological Hermeneutics: The Potential of Love for Interfaith Encounters', *Al-Bayān: Journal of Qurʾān & Hadīth Studies* 11/2 (2013), pp. 71–92 (87). Throughout his publications, Jeanrond stresses the significance of alterity for the praxis of love. Cf. Werner G. Jeanrond, *Call and Response: The Challenge of Christian Life* (New York: Continuum, 1995), pp. 117–19; idem, *Guds närvaro*, pp. 27–8; 68–71; idem, 'Love', in Adrian Hastings, ed., *The Oxford Companion to Christian Thought* (Oxford: Oxford University Press, 2000), pp. 394–7; idem, *Gudstro*, pp. 141–3; idem, *A Theology of Love* (London: Continuum/T&T Clark, 2010); idem, *Kyrkans Framtid*, pp. 13–94; or idem, 'Love', in Nicholas Adams, George Pattison and Graham Ward, eds, *The Oxford Handbook for Theology and Modern European Thought* (Oxford: Oxford University Press, 2013), pp. 233–53.

8. Cf. Werner G. Jeanrond, *Theological Hermeneutics: Development and Significance* (London: SCM, 2002 [1991]), pp. 6–7; 93–119.

9. Cf. Werner G. Jeanrond, *Text und Interpretation als Kategorien theologischen Denkens* (Tübingen: Mohr Siebeck, 1986), pp. 94–118. Cf. the English translation, *Text and Interpretation as Categories of Theological Thinking*, trans. T. J. Wilson (New York: Crossroad, 1988), pp. 94–119.

Following Friedrich Schleiermacher, Jeanrond assumes that interpretation is characterized by 'approximation' (*Annäherung*).[10] When interpretation aims for approximation, it continues to cultivate the critical and creative tension between the interpreted and the interpreter. Since the tension between the interpretative object and the interpretative subject is what drives interpretation, it cannot be reduced to either objectivism or subjectivism. Thus, no adequate interpretation can claim to have exhausted the opportunities for transformation and transcendence which are offered through the relation between the textual and the non-textual other. To capture these opportunities, Jeanrond refers to David Tracy's concept of the classic. What a classic (be it textual, musical or personal) exemplifies is that any adequate interpretation is open and open-ended: adequate interpretation is approximate interpretation.[11]

Examining the tension between the text and the reader of the text, Jeanrond describes and defines reading as an 'existential activity'.[12] The reader opens herself to the text in order to be changed by her reading. Crucially, her openness must not override critical and self-critical explanations of the text as change is ambiguous, allowing for disclosures and distortions of meaning. Jeanrond points to Paul Ricoeur who highlighted the distinction between primary and secondary naïveté: interpretation involves an existential pre-understanding (primary naïveté) which is followed by explanation which is then followed by an existential understanding (secondary naïveté).[13] Here, the secondary naïveté becomes the primary naïveté as

---

10. Friedrich D. E. Schleiermacher, 'Hermeneutik und Kritik', in idem, *Hermeneutik und Kritik: Mit einem Anhang sprachphilosophischer Texte Schleiermachers*, ed. Manfred Frank (Frankfurt: Suhrkamp, 1977), pp. 69–306 (168). Also cf. the English translation *Hermeneutics and Criticism: And Other Writings*, ed. Andrew Bowie (Cambridge: Cambridge University Press, 1998), pp. 225–68 (235). For Schleiermacher's hermeneutics cf. Werner G. Jeanrond, *Theological Hermeneutics*, pp. 44–50. Idem, 'Biblical Criticism and Theology: Toward a New Biblical Theology', in Werner G. Jeanrond and Jennifer L. Rike, eds, *Radical Pluralism and Truth: David Tracy and the Hermeneutics of Religion* (New York: Crossroad, 1991) pp. 38–48 (47), points to Schleiermacher who – long before Emmanuel Levinas – discovered the significance of the relation between other and other through his reflection on linguisticality.

11. Cf. David Tracy, *The Analogical Imagination: Christian Theology and the Culture of Pluralism* (London: SCM, 1981), pp. 99–153. Also cf. the critical conversation in Werner G. Jeanrond, *Text und Interpretation*, pp. 131–40; ET, pp. 133–42.

12. Werner G. Jeanrond, *Theological Hermeneutics*, pp. 93–119 (110).

13. Cf. Paul Ricoeur, 'From Existentialism to Philosophy of Language', in idem, *The Rule of Metaphor: The Creation of Meaning in Language*, trans. R. Czerny (London: Routledge, 2003), pp. 372–81 (376–7). For Ricoeur's hermeneutics cf. Werner G. Jeanrond, *Theological Hermeneutics*, pp. 70–6. Jeanrond highlights how Ricoeur re-worked the distinction between primary and secondary naïveté through the concepts of 'prefiguration', 'configuration' and 'refiguration' (pp. 191–2n. 92). For Jeanrond's conversation with Ricoeur cf. idem, 'Hermeneutics and Revelation', in Maureen Junker-Kenny and Peter Kenny, eds, *Memory, Narrativity, Self and the Challenge to Think God* (Münster: LIT, 2004),

the process of interpretation begins again and again. In critical conversation with Ricoeur, Jeanrond stresses the inter-relation of these moments within the process of interpretation, where the existential and the explanatory cannot be nicely and neatly distinguished. Jeanrond also invokes the ethical responsibility which is involved in interpretation: the ideologies of both the interpreted and the interpreter must come under critique in every interpretation. Interpretation, therefore, combines existential, explanatory *and* ethical dimensions.[14]

When Jeanrond applies his three-dimensional concept of interpretation to theology, the application immediately implies that he opts for what Schleiermacher called a general philosophical as opposed to a special theological hermeneutics.[15] Jeanrond defends the need for a hermeneutics which is not automatically absorbed by theological agendas and approaches, criticizing what could be called neo-orthodox and neo-neo-orthodox theologies (both construing 'orthodoxy' through a critique of theological liberalisms). These theologies reduce the tension between the textual and the non-textual other either to objectivism or to subjectivism.

Karl Barth rejected philosophical as opposed to theological hermeneutics because of its 'totalitarian claim' (*Totalitätsanspruch*)[16] which allegedly polices the absolute alterity of God. While Jeanrond agrees with both Barth and Barthians that one's hermeneutical critique needs critique, he exposes the objectivism within neo-orthodox hermeneutics. According to Jeanrond, Barth attempted to evade or escape the process of interpretation by referring to revelation – directly, not indirectly.[17] He demanded 'obedience' to revelation which is why his hermeneutics is marked by 'subordination': the reader of the biblical text is subordinated to the biblical text.[18] Subordination appeals to the objectivity (not necessarily the objectivism) of the text. But according to Jeanrond, the objectivity of the text rests on the subjectivity of the text's reader. By referring to revelation, Barth objectified his own reading experience.[19] He identified his interpretation of the text with the

---

pp. 42–57 and the response by Paul Ricoeur, 'Comments after Jeanrond's "Hermeneutics and Revelation"', pp. 58–62.

14. Cf. Werner G. Jeanrond, *Theological Hermeneutics*, pp. 113–17.

15. Cf. Friedrich D. E. Schleiermacher, *Kurze Darstellung des theologischen Studiums zum Behuf einleitender Vorlesungen* (Berlin: Reimer, 1830), pp. 59–61. Also cf. the English translation *Brief Outline of the Study of Theology*, trans. W. Farrer (Edinburgh: T&T Clark, 1850), pp. 142–5. Cf. Werner G. Jeanrond, *Theological Hermeneutics*, pp. 7–9; 159–64.

16. Karl Barth, *Kirchliche Dogmatik*, vol. I/2 (Zürich: Theologischer Verlag, 1983), p. 523. For the English translation cf. *Church Dogmatics*, vol. I/2, trans. G. W. Bromiley (London: Continuum, 2004), p. 472. Cf. Werner G. Jeanrond, *Theological Hermeneutics*, pp. 127–36.

17. Cf. Werner G. Jeanrond, 'Subjectivity and Objectivity', p. 73.

18. Cf. Werner G. Jeanrond, *Theological Hermeneutics*, pp. 130–4.

19. Cf. ibid., pp. 133–5.

text, which is why the text could not resist instrumentalization(s).[20] Jeanrond traces the instrumentalization of biblical and non-biblical texts by theological and non-theological discourses throughout the history of hermeneutics. His defence of a general philosophical as opposed to a special theological hermeneutics could be called a critique of the totalitarian claims of both theological and non-theological interpreters – which is to say, Jeanrond turns Barth and Barthians from their heads onto their feet.

Turning from the neo-orthodox to the neo-neo-orthodox theologies which loosely (or not so loosely) follow George R. Lindbeck's study on the nature of doctrine, Jeanrond exposes the subjectivism in their hermeneutics.[21] Comparing religion to a language or a language game, Lindbeck advocated the 'intratextual' interpretation of biblical texts. Here, texts are to be understood inside as opposed to outside the language or language game of Christianity.[22] Jeanrond clarifies that Lindbeck's concept of intratextual interpretation runs the risk of reductionism – not of the reader to the biblical text, but of the biblical texts to the reader.[23] The tension between the interpreted and the interpreter is dissolved in favour of a community of interpreters.[24] However, if the texts are identified with the community's interpretation of the texts, the texts cannot resist their instrumentalization. The theologian knows what the text says before she starts reading it.[25]

20. Cf. Jeanrond's reflections on biblical theology, Werner G. Jeanrond, 'Biblical Criticism and Theology', pp. 38–48; idem, 'After Hermeneutics: The Relationship between Theology and Biblical Studies', in Francis Watson, ed., *The Open Text: New Directions for Biblical Studies* (London: SCM, 1993), 85–104; idem, 'Criteria for New Biblical Theologies', *The Journal of Religion* 2 (1996), pp. 233–49.

21. Cf. George R. Lindbeck, *The Nature of Doctrine: Theology and Religion in a Postliberal Age* (London: SPCK, 1984), particularly pp. 15–29. Jeanrond discusses the debate between George Lindbeck and David Tracy in relation to the debate between Karl Barth and Rudolf Bultmann in Werner G. Jeanrond, 'The Problem of the Starting-Point of Theological Thinking', in John Webster, ed., *The Possibility of Theology: Eberhard Jüngel in his Sixtieth Year* (Edinburgh: T&T Clark, 1994), pp. 70–89. Also cf. idem, 'Correlational Theology and the Chicago School', in Roger A. Badham, ed., *Introduction to Christian Theology: Contemporary North American Perspectives* (Louisville: Westminster John Knox Press, 1998), pp. 137–53.

22. Cf. George R. Lindbeck, *The Nature of Doctrine*, pp. 113–23.

23. Cf. the concise critique of Stanley Fish in Werner G. Jeanrond, *Text und Interpretation*, pp. 110–12; ET, pp. 110–13.

24. Cf. Werner G. Jeanrond, *Theological Hermeneutics*, pp. 161–3.

25. Building on Stanley Fish's theory of interpretive communities, Stanley Hauerwas argued in *Unleashing the Scripture: Freeing the Bible from Captivity to America* (Nashville: Abingdon, 1993), p. 9 that the Bible 'should only be made available to those who have undergone the hard discipline of existing as part of God's people'. Hence, Hauerwas attempted to restrict access to the biblical texts to those who have been disciplined by a community of interpreters. As a consequence, however, the biblical text cannot resist the potential or actual distortions in the discipline of what Hauerwas construes as God's people.

In opposition to the reduction of alterity to the boundaries of particular linguistic communities, Jeanrond stresses that it is possible to blur these boundaries. As a theologian who has written monographs in three different languages, he exemplifies the possibility of moving from this to that linguistic community. For Jeanrond, the fact that one cannot dispose of one's linguisticality (temporality or spatiality) does not imply that one is determined and defined by one's language.[26] Because of the possibility of blurring boundaries, linguistic communities are not fully fixed. They can be changed from the inside as well as from the outside. Accordingly, 'theology must not be limited to a positivistic or pragmatic explication of … customs' within a clear-cut language or a clear-cut language game.'[27] If theology fails to recognize the internal and external opportunities for change, it reduces the alterity of the other, thus cutting off the experience of transformation and transcendence. Jeanrond sharply suggests that the reduction of theology to a particular community could 'contain a seed of … sectarian terror' – irrespective of whether the community is ecclesial or non-ecclesial.[28]

Overall, it is in response to the reduction of the alterity of either the interpreter (objectivism) or the interpreted (subjectivism) within theology that Jeanrond emphasizes the creative tension in-between textual and non-textual others. Although he does not use the terminology of alterity – the other and the otherness of the other – in his reflections on the theory of interpretation, the significance of alterity in relationality cannot be underestimated. Jeanrond stresses the autonomy (not autarchy) of both the interpreted and the interpreter in order to cultivate a tension – a tension which drives the dynamics of difference, keeping interpretation open and open-ended. Hence, already at the outset of Jeanrond's career, the complementary concepts of alterity and relationality function as resistance to the closure of interpretation. Such relational resistance is crucial for Christianity: only through resistance to closure, can theology point to transformation and transcendence.

In-Between the Christian and the Non-Christian Other

In *Theological Hermeneutics* – a study which should have been entitled 'Hermeneutical Theology', as he himself has indicated – Jeanrond turns from the interpretation of texts to the interpretation of traditions. He analyses how Christians construed what is Christian at the expense of what is non-Christian. Today, the context for the construction of the identity of Christianity is changing radically. The processes summarized in the catchy category of globalization

---

26. Jeanrond refers to spatiality, temporality and linguisticality as the core conditions of humanity's being throughout his writings. Inter alia cf. Werner G. Jeanrond, *Gudstro*, p. 75; idem, 'Zur Hermeneutik postmoderner Öffentlichkeit', p. 84; 96; idem, *A Theology of Love*, p. 2; 7; 9; 259; idem, 'Subjectivity and Objectivity', p. 80; 85.

27. Werner G. Jeanrond: 'The Problem of the Starting-Point', p. 87.

28. Ibid., p. 89.

multiply the opportunities for encounters between Christian and non-Christian others.²⁹ But since the otherness of the other continues to stir controversy, these opportunities run the risk of provoking polemical identity politics – Christianity *versus* non-Christianity.³⁰ Jeanrond traces Christianity's identity politics from the past to the present, stressing the shift in the identification of Christianity's other to Islam.³¹ For Jeanrond, hermeneutical theology has to criticize any identity politics rooted in explicit or implicit exclusions which turn my other into a total (which is to say, non-related and non-relational) other. The imagination of identity is 'dialectically related' to the imagination of alterity;³² and both imaginations are to be continually criticized through a hermeneutics of suspicion.

Hermeneutically, Jeanrond acknowledges the relevance of theories of interreligious translations according to which representatives of the one religion translate their beliefs and behaviours for representatives of the other religion.³³ Yet, he points to philosophical and sociological deficits in these theories. Philosophically, they have to reduce (or even reject) the otherness of the other. Whenever the other cannot correspond or conform to my categories, her otherness is 'lost in translation'.³⁴ Here, Jeanrond extends the critique to Jürgen Habermas' project of translating the religious into the non-religious.³⁵ Sociologically, the theories of mutual translation come – plainly put – 'too late'.³⁶ The actual or virtual encounter with the other always already shapes both Christian and non-Christian religions which is why identities are syncretistic: heterogeneous as opposed to homogeneous. Ultimately, Jeanrond's critique of polemical identity politics aims for recognition and respect for Christian and non-Christian others. In order to remain open to the other, Jeanrond rejects universalism and relativism in the reflection on interreligious encounters (a parallel to his rejection of objectivism and subjectivism in the reflection on interpretation).³⁷ Both critiques can be conceptualized with the complementary concepts of alterity and relationality. But

---

29. With recourse to Zygmunt Bauman, *Globalization: The Human Consequences* (Cambridge: Polity Press, 1998) cf. Werner G. Jeanrond, *A Theology of Love*, pp. 217–20.

30. Cf. Werner G. Jeanrond, 'Belonging or Identity? Christian Faith in a Multi-Religious World', in Catherine Cornille, ed., *Many Mansions? Multiple Religious Belonging and Christian Identity* (Maryknoll: Orbis, 2002), pp. 106–20 (107–11).

31. Cf. Werner G. Jeanrond, 'Toward an Interreligious Hermeneutics of Love', in Catherine Cornille and Christopher Conway, eds, *Interreligious Hermeneutics* (Eugene, OR: Wipf and Stock, 2010), 44–60 (47).

32. Ibid.

33. Cf. ibid., pp. 46–52.

34. Ibid., p. 49.

35. Cf. Jürgen Habermas, *Die Zukunft der menschlichen Natur* (Frankfurt: Suhrkamp, 2001). Also cf. the English translation, *The Future of Human Nature*, trans. W. Rehg et al. (Cambridge: Polity Press, 2003).

36. Werner G. Jeanrond, 'Toward an Interreligious Hermeneutics of Love', p. 50.

37. Cf. ibid., pp. 51–2. Also cf. Werner G. Jeanrond, 'Interkulturalität und Interreligiösität: Die Notwendigkeit einer Hermeneutik der Liebe', in Thomas Schreijäck

how can a critique aim for recognition and respect of alterity in relationality? How can the others meet each other?

Jeanrond turns the problem into the solution of the problem. Building on Rowan Williams' concept of 'conversations of charity', he points to the praxis of love.[38] Love is not the outcome of intra- or interreligious encounter – as if I had to reject the otherness of my other before I could both love her and be loved by her. Instead, love is the origin of intra- and interreligious encounter. Again and again, Jeanrond stresses that to love my other is not the same as to like my other: to love each other, Christian and non-Christian others do not have to agree with each other.[39] Hence, love comes in *before* one starts the conversation about intra- and interreligious agreement and disagreement – which is to say, recognition and respect for alterity in relationality forms and informs the praxis of love.

Nonetheless, even the praxis of love has to be assessed critically and self-critically since the concept of love has been (ab)used for turning the other into a total other. Jeanrond points to a theological trajectory which facilitated and fostered what could be called a 'Christianization' of love according to which whoever is non-Christian is incapable of love.[40] Here, my other is incapacitated by me: love is turned topsy-turvy. Jeanrond stresses the necessity for openness to otherness: 'Christian approaches to love share with other religious and non-religious approaches the understanding that love seeks the other'.[41] When Christianity is open to both Christian and non-Christian others, it is open to transformation and transcendence which is vital if it is not to be turned into a museum or mausoleum. 'God's gift of love cannot be exclusively claimed by Christians. Rather, the Christian praxis of love has been made possible through the proclamation of God's gift of love' – both inside and outside Christianity.[42] Consequently, Jeanrond distinguishes between the primary theological and the secondary ecclesiological belonging of Christians.[43] The identity of Christianity

---

and Knut Wenzel, eds, *Kontextualität und Universalität: Die Vielfalt der Glaubenskontexte und der Universalitätsanspruch des Evangeliums* (Stuttgart: Kohlhammer, 2012), pp. 156–73.

38. With what he calls 'conversations of charity', Rowan Williams, *Lost Icons: Reflections on Cultural Bereavement* (London: Continuum, 2000), pp. 80–1, draws 'attention to recognitions or possibilities of recognition *prior* to any agreement about what we have in common'. Cf. Werner G. Jeanrond, *A Theology of Love*, pp. 224–5; idem, 'The Ambiguous Power of Prejudice and Love', in Jesper Svartvik and Jakob Wirén, eds, *Religious Stereotyping and Interreligious Relations* (New York: Palgrave Macmillan, 2013), pp. 45–55 (49–50).

39. The distinction between 'love' and 'like' follows from Jeanrond's interpretation of Thomas Aquinas' systematic theology of love. Cf. Werner G. Jeanrond, *A Theology of Love*, pp. 77–83. Also cf. idem, 'Subjectivity and Objectivity', pp. 86–8.

40. Cf. Werner G. Jeanrond, *A Theology of Love*, pp. 105–34. Also cf. idem, 'Love', pp. 243–6.

41. Ibid., p. 233.

42. Werner G. Jeanrond, 'Ecclesia Semper Reformanda', pp. 279–80.

43. Cf. Werner G. Jeanrond, 'Belonging or Identity', pp. 106–7.

is not the end of belonging, but a means to the end of belonging – belonging to God. Christians are not called to secure the identity of Christianity, they are called to God.[44] Traditions cannot offer ultimate belonging. But by offering penultimate belonging, they can offer structures of support for the ultimate belonging to God.

According to Jeanrond, Jesus Christ's praxis clarifies that ecclesiological belonging is temporary and transient, whereas eschatological belonging is transformative and transcendent.[45] Hence, theology cannot be confined to christology.[46] Jeanrond emphasizes that – ironically – Jesus Christ can only be accessed through the tradition(s) which he transforms and transcends. He retrieved the double commandment of love (Mt. 22.35–40) from traditions and institutions as a critique against the oppression caused by traditions and institutions.[47] According to Jeanrond, Jesus Christ taught me how to love my others – not how to fit into traditional or institutional categories.[48] Christology, therefore, cannot identify Jesus Christ with Christianity's interpretation(s) of Jesus Christ. Instead, it has to relate to 'Jesus Christ as the other'.[49] Jeanrond pushes the otherness of Jesus Christ to the extreme when he refers to his 'foreignness'.[50] Thus, christology allows for the retrieval of 'tradition in spite of tradition'[51] which insists that christological statements remain open to revision.[52]

Overall, Jeanrond stresses that 'to be transformed by God, human beings … need to expose themselves critically and self-critically to the other'.[53] Consequently, it is both alterity and relationality which run through Jeanrond's studies on intra- and interreligious encounters. Christianity is not interpreted as the restoration of tradition, but as the creation and re-creation of tradition through communication with others. If it is freed from oppression,[54] communication might allow

44. On the concept of the identity of the church cf. Werner G. Jeanrond, *Gudstro*, pp. 164–71.

45. Cf. Werner G. Jeanrond, 'Belonging or Identity', pp. 106–7. For Jeanrond's concept of the discipleship which follows from Jesus' praxis and preaching, cf. *Call and Response*, particularly pp. 24–44.

46. Jeanrond follows David Tracy's *Blessed Rage for Order: The New Pluralism in Theology* (Chicago: The University of Chicago Press, 1996), pp. 22–63. Cf. Werner G. Jeanrond, 'Theology in the Context of Pluralism and Postmodernity: David Tracy's Theological Method', in David Jasper, ed., *Postmodernism, Literature and the Future of Theology* (London: Macmillan, 1993), pp. 143–63.

47. Cf. Werner G. Jeanrond, *Theological Hermeneutics*, pp. 177–9.

48. Cf. Werner G. Jeanrond, *Gudstro*, p. 74.

49. Ibid., p. 35 (my translation).

50. Ibid. (my translation).

51. Werner G. Jeanrond, *Theological Hermeneutics*, p. 177. Also cf. Jeanrond's extensive exploration of christology in *Gudstro*, pp. 32–71.

52. Cf. ibid, p. 52.

53. Werner G. Jeanrond, 'Belonging or Identity', p. 117.

54. Cf. Werner G. Jeanrond, *Call and Response*, pp. 32–6. Also cf. idem, 'Der christliche

for the approximation (*Annäherung*, not *Anpassung*) to the other. A dynamics of difference, therefore, runs through Jeanrond's reflections on both texts and traditions. With the help of religious and non-religious others, theology might be able to resist the identification and instrumentalization of God.

In-Between the Other and the Radical Other

Regarding the relation to the radical other, Jeanrond points to the 'dynamics of encounter' which includes 'eschatological openness to transcendence and transformation'.[55] Eschatology 'grounds' the inter-related relations to the other.[56] According to Jeanrond, *the* theme of theology – God – is always already connected to both how I see my other and how I see myself as other. Yet, can the relationship to the radical other be qualified by the complementary concepts of alterity and relationality? Would such a qualification reduce the radicality of God's alterity? Would it confine God within my concept of God?

Stressing the absolute alterity of God, past and present theologies have reflected on God outside of humanity's spatiality, temporality and linguisticality. Again, Jeanrond points to the neo-orthodox theologies of Barth and Barthians. He explores how the concept of God construed in these theologies made it impossible to conceive of a theology which offered resistance to the totalitarianism in the history of Germany.[57] The transcendent was elevated and exalted above the immanent so that any project of political theology was called into question before it could even begin. Although what holds for Barth's theology does not hold for Barth's personality, Jeanrond argues that, voluntarily or involuntarily, 'the anti-ideological and anti-institutional theology' of God's absolute alterity might aid and abet totalitarianism.[58] For Jeanrond, theology is inevitably and inextricably public and political. The incapacity of Barth and Barthians to construe a theological critique of totalitarianism cautions him against conceptions of the absolute alterity of God, for a God who is conceived of as total or totalized other is non-related and non-relational.[59]

Gottesglaube und die Erneuerung der Kirche', in Ferdinand R. Prostmeier and Knut Wenzel, eds, *Zukunft der Kirche – Kirche der Zukunft* (Regensburg: Friedrich Pustet, 2004), pp. 23–42.

  55. Werner G. Jeanrond, 'Toward an Interreligious Hermeneutics of Love', p. 52.
  56. Cf. Werner G. Jeanrond, *Gudstro*, p. 19 (my translation).
  57. Cf. Werner G. Jearnond, 'From Resistance to Liberation Theology: German Theologians and the Non/Resistance to the National Socialist Regime', *The Journal of Modern History* 64 (1992), pp. 187–203 (188–99).
  58. Ibid., p. 190.
  59. Cf. Werner G. Jeanrond, 'Subjectivity and Objectivity', p. 85. Also cf. the critique of Emmanuel Levinas' conception of the other by Paul Ricoeur, *Soi-même comme un autre* (Paris: Éditions du Seuil, 1990), pp. 221–2. Cf. the English translation *Oneself as Another*, trans. K. Blamey (Chicago: The University of Chicago Press, 1992), pp. 188–9.

Similarly, Jeanrond criticizes the contemporary turn to God's absolute alterity as exemplified by Jean-Luc Marion's phenomenology.[60] Radicalizing Barth's theology, Marion not only seeks to secure the transcendent against instrumentalization and identification with the immanent, but he also construes a concept of God which lies above the world, drawing a distinction between 'idol' (*idole*) and 'icon' (*icône*) which points to 'the play between the self's constitution of the object and the self's constitution by the object'.[61] Jeanrond appreciates Marion's distinction,[62] but he criticizes the purely pragmatic function language has for Marion since it denies and destroys any possibility for analogy.[63] Jeanrond argues that the world of spatiality, temporality and linguisticality is '*co-constitutive*' for the experience of the encounter with God.[64] It is not enough to emphasize the alterity of God. Such emphases are to be accompanied by a constructive interpretation of the experience of the encounter with God in both the past and the present. Following Jeanrond, one could argue that apophatic theology alone runs the risk of denying God's relationality, while cataphatic theology alone runs the risk of denying God's alterity. If the one is separated from the other, God cannot be thought of as alterity in relationality. Hence, Jeanrond stresses that 'relationality' complements 'alterity' and 'alterity' complements 'relationality'. God's alterity cannot be interpreted as absolute alterity. Only the complementary combination of alterity and relationality offers the opportunity to reflect on experiences of God in God's creation.

Expectedly, for Jeanrond, the praxis of love offers the opportunity for the revelation of God.[65] But as Jeanrond's critique of Marion's phenomenology highlights, the concept of love is not immune against ideologies. If God is conceived of as the pure 'gift' or the pure 'giving' of love which hovers before, behind or beyond the world, political theologies are incapacitated. Jeanrond echoes those feminists who warn theology not to retreat into apolitical meditations on God's love.[66] Christianity's emphasis on God's incarnation challenges theology to think of God's love inside as opposed to outside the world – *without* reducing the creator to the creation. Accordingly, Jeanrond interprets love as a praxis (not as a

---

60. Cf. Jean-Luc Marion, *Dieu sans l'être* (Paris: PUF, 1982). Cf. the English translation *God without Being*, trans. T. A. Carlson (Chicago: The University of Chicago Press, 1991). Also cf. the concise contextualization of Jean-Luc Marion by Graham Ward, 'Introducing Jean-Luc Marion', *New Blackfriars* 76 (1995), pp. 317–24.

61. Ibid., p. 319.

62. Cf. Werner G. Jeanrond, 'Der christliche Gottesglaube und die Erneuerung der Kirche', pp. 37–8; idem, *Guds närvaro*, p. 88; idem, *Gudstro*, p. 160.

63. Cf. Werner G. Jeanrond, *Guds närvaro*, pp. 47–62; idem, 'Zur Hermeneutik postmoderner Öffentlichkeit', pp. 91–5.

64. Ibid., p. 98 (my translation).

65. Cf. Werner G. Jeanrond, *Guds närvaro*, p. 75.

66. Werner G. Jeanrond, 'Zur Hermeneutik postmoderner Öffentlichkeit', p. 89–99. Also cf. Pamela S. Anderson 'The Other', in Nicholas Adams, George Pattison and Graham Ward, eds, *The Oxford Handbook for Theology and Modern European Thought*, pp. 83–104 (99–102).

principle) which combines actions and reflections on actions.[67] Since the praxis of love is rooted in the engagement with the other, it is open and open-ended. God cannot be confined to Christianity:[68] God is not the God of a Christian 'tribalism'.[69] Jeanrond criticizes theologies which try to decode inner-Trinitarian love in order to deduce criteria for the praxis of love from their decodings.[70] Instead, he advocates the exploration of the inter-related relations of the praxis of love in order to assess the potential for transformation and transcendence in these relations: a relation to the other allows for a relation to God.[71] The exclusion of others is tantamount to the elimination of love, because if love involves recognition and respect for the otherness of the other, the other cannot be excluded.[72]

Drawing the consequences from his interpretation of the relation to God, Jeanrond affirms a 'dialectics between ecclesiology and eschatology'.[73] Eschatology is crucial for the retrieval of the potential of love since the praxis of hope points to God as love – a love which leads to reconciliation.[74] Again, hope cannot be reduced to Christian hope which is why Jeanrond adds 'inter-hope dialogue' to intra- and interreligious dialogues.[75] Within the inter-hope dialogue, the hopes of non-religious and religious others – both Christian and non-Christian – can be criticized by radical hope. Attention to the 'radical hope' which fuels every eschatological expectation opens hope for alterity within relationality.[76] Radical hope is the resistance to interpretative closure, because who or what one hopes for differs from one's hope.[77]

Overall, Jeanrond's reflections on the relation to God as the radical other are characterized by the complementary concepts of alterity and relationality.

67. Cf. Werner G. Jeanrond, *A Theology of Love*, pp. 4–5; 169–71; 235–7.

68. Cf. Werner G. Jeanrond, 'Ecclesia Semper Reformanda', p. 273.

69. Ibid., p. 281. Also cf. Werner G. Jeanrond, 'Thinking about God today', in Werner G. Jeanrond and Aasulv Lande, eds, *The Concept of God in Global Dialogue* (Maryknoll: Orbis, 2005), pp. 89–97.

70. Werner G. Jeanrond, *A Theology of Love*, p. 241. Also cf. idem, 'Revelation and the Trinitarian Concept of God: Are they Key Concepts for Theological Thought?', *Concilium* 1 (2001), pp. 120–30.

71. Cf. Werner G. Jeanrond, *A Theology of Love*, pp. 241–2.

72. Cf. ibid., p. 233.

73. Ibid., p. 228. Also cf. Werner G. Jeanrond, *Kyrkans Framtid*, pp. 29–46.

74. Cf. Werner G. Jeanrond, 'Love and Eschatology', *Dialog* 50/1 (2011), pp. 53–62.

75. Here Jeanrond follows Anthony Kelly, *Eschatology and Hope* (Maryknoll: Orbis, 2006), pp. 16–18. Cf. Werner G. Jeanrond, 'Ecclesia Semper Reformanda', pp. 280–1.

76. Cf. ibid. Also cf. Jeanrond's summary of Kelly's eschatology, Werner G. Jeanrond, 'Individuum und Gemeinschaft: Eschatologische Positionen in der gegenwärtigen Dogmatik', in Hermann Deuser and Saskia Wendel, eds, *Dialektik der Freiheit: Religiöse Individualisierung und theologische Dogmatik* (Tübingen: Mohr Siebeck, 2012), pp. 217–37 (231–6).

77. For the concept of radical hope cf. Jonathan Lear, *Radical Hope: Ethics in the Face of Cultural Devastation* (Harvard: Harvard University Press, 2006).

Without relationality, God becomes 'too' transcendent; without alterity, God becomes 'too' immanent. The dynamics of difference which result from the tension between alterity and relationality keep interpretation open and open-ended. Such a dynamics is constitutive of any political theology which aims to resist past, present and potential totalitarianisms.

In-Between: The Dynamics of Difference

I have analysed Jeanrond's hermeneutical theology, concentrating on the relations between the textual and the non-textual other, the Christian and the non-Christian other, and the other and the radical other. For Jeanrond, religion entails the engagement with what I characterized as the complementary concepts of alterity and relationality. The critical and creative tension between these concepts is cultivated throughout Jeanrond's hermeneutical theology in order to resist the closure of interpretation. This relational resistance evokes the dynamics of difference which is a catalyst for transformation and transcendence.

There is a tendency, however, within religions – Christian and non-Christian alike – to avoid engagement with the other by denying either alterity or relationality. If the complementarity of these concepts is dismissed, there is no need for interpretation: the dynamics of difference is blocked; interpretation is confined, curtailed and closed. Jeanrond rarely explores the reasons for the repeated blockage inside and outside Christianity. But it seems to me that such an exploration is needed to further reflect on the praxis of love. Arguably, most persons – again Christian and non-Christian alike – do not think or talk of recognition and respect for the otherness of the other when they think or talk about love. The engagement with the other (who could be vile and violent) is seen as frightening. Jeanrond points to a 'trivialization' according to which the praxis of love has been deprived of 'its full force of otherness'.[78] But is it enough to introduce a prescriptive as opposed to a descriptive concept of love to reverse the blockages of the dynamics of difference? Jeanrond is undoubtedly correct when he denies that hermeneutical theology has to follow the 'trivialization' of love. However, to follow this trivialization neither practically nor theoretically is difficult – perhaps much more difficult than his appeal to 'choice' suggests.[79] If it was a matter of choice, it would be baffling as to why anyone would choose the 'trivialization' of love after reading Jeanrond's theology. A psychological, sociological and

---

78. Werner G. Jeanrond, 'Love', p. 250.

79. For Jeanrond's appeal to the theologian's choice cf. inter alia Werner G. Jeanrond, 'The Problem of the Starting-Point', pp. 87–9; idem, *Call and Response*, p. 134; idem, 'Criteria for New Biblical Theologies', 242–5; idem, 'Vertrautheit und Fremdheit als Kategorien theologischen Interpretierens', in Hendrik Johan Adriaanse and Rainer Enskat, eds, *Fremdheit und Vertrautheit: Hermeneutik im europäischen Kontext* (Leuven: Peeters, 1999), pp. 175–88 (186–7); idem, 'Zur Hermeneutik postmoderner Öffentlichkeit', p. 99; idem; *A Theology of Love*, pp. 217–18; 245; and idem, 'Subjectivity and Objectivity', p. 81.

theological exploration of the roots and reasons for the trivialization of love would be necessary to avoid the consequence that the concept of love loses touch with human and all-too-human lovers.

Nonetheless, Jeanrond makes a convincing case for the cultivation of the dynamics of difference within the inter-related relations to oneself as other, to the other as other, and to God as the radical other. His hermeneutical theology is open to the others who might trigger transformation and transcendence. In conversation with Werner G. Jeanrond, this *Festschrift* contributes to the cultivation of the creative tensions between others in relationality and alterity. In what follows, Jeanrond's colleagues and companions track the dynamics of difference to which the engagement with others gives rise.

Part I

BIBLICAL OTHERS AND OTHER BIBLES

1

MOSES: THE SIGNIFICANT OTHER

Brian Klug

I am a stranger on the earth; do not hide from me your commandments.

(Ps. 119.19)

Preamble

In September 1913, on a trip to Rome, Sigmund Freud visited the church of San Pietro in Vincoli. This was not his first visit to the church that houses Michelangelo's *Moses*. (The first was in 1901.) But on this occasion he kept returning to the spot. He wrote about the visit to his disciple Edoardo Weiss: 'Every day for three lonely weeks in September of 1913 I stood in the church in front of the statue, studying it, measuring it and drawing it until there dawned on me that understanding which in the essay I only dared to express anonymously'.[1] The essay to which he alludes, 'The Moses of Michelangelo', appeared the following year.[2] In it he says that 'no piece of statuary has ever made a stronger impression on me than this'.[3] I doubt that he would have felt this way were it not for the fact that he found Moses the man so mesmerizing.[4]

As do I. I shall discuss neither Michelangelo's statue nor Freud's essay (though I touch on them again in an afterword). But the way Freud situates himself in relation to his subject strikes a chord with me and gives me an opening. His essay

---

1. Harald Leupold-Löwenthal et al., eds, *Sigmund Freud Museum*, trans. T. Roberts (Wien: Christian Brandstätter, 1995), p. 66, item 186. Freud kept his authorship of the essay anonymous until 1924.

2. It was published in German in the third volume of the journal *Imago*, April 1914, under the title 'Der Moses des Michelangelo'.

3. Sigmund Freud, 'The Moses of Michelangelo', in James Strachey, ed., *Totem and Taboo and Other Works*, trans. J. Strachey, *The Standard Edition of the Complete Psychological Works of Sigmund Freud*, vol. 13 (London: The Hogarth Press and the Institute of Psychoanalysis, 1955), pp. 210–38 (213).

4. There is no obvious connection between the view of Moses in this essay and the later view in *Moses and Monotheism*.

begins with a confession: 'I may say at once that I am no connoisseur in art, but simply a layman'.[5] Similarly, I may say at the outset that I am no biblical scholar and despite my education at an Orthodox Jewish school I am far from being a *talmid chochem*, someone steeped in Jewish learning. Nor am I a theologian. I am 'simply a layman'. I am writing about Moses because no figure in the *Tanakh* 'ever made a stronger impression on me'. But what impression does he make exactly and why? This is the itch that, for a reason similar to the one Freud gives, I need to scratch: 'Some rationalistic, or perhaps analytic, turn of mind in me rebels against being moved by a thing without knowing why I am thus affected and what it is that affects me'.[6] Furthermore, the textual Moses – the Moses of scripture – like the marble Moses sculpted by Michelangelo is enigmatic. What Freud says about the latter applies to the former: 'so many different readings of it are possible'.[7] And if Freud kept coming back to the statue, 'studying it, measuring it and drawing it', so I have returned time and again to the figure in the text, studying him, connecting the dots in the biblical narrative, trying to take his measure. There came a moment, says Freud, when understanding 'dawned' on him. I have had my Eureka moment too, when I saw Moses in a new light, reflected in the title of this essay: Moses as the quintessential other whose otherness is profoundly significant. What that otherness consists in and what it signifies: this is the topic of my essay.

I offer, in short, a *reading* of Moses. It is, to be sure, a *selective* reading, but in a sense this is what is called for when reading a text, certainly a complex text, especially a text that is seen as sacred, as the Torah is seen in both Judaism and Christianity. Sacred texts never tire of being read: being interpreted or elucidated so as to fathom their meaning – which by definition is inexhaustible. They are *available* to the reader but they are never simply there for the taking. As Werner G. Jeanrond observes, 'there is no such thing as a neutral, innocent, a-historical reading'. He continues: 'every reader already makes a selection – whether consciously or unconsciously – between possible reading attitudes, which he/she then applies to the text'.[8] At the same time, a reading 'must do justice to the text'.[9] That is to say, it must not do *in*justice; for no single exegesis can do *full* justice to a text like the Torah. It is a matter of giving a 'responsible interpretation'.[10] My reading of Moses is a response to the biblical text. It is a reading that I find *suggested* by the text; and in this *Festschrift* for Werner Jeanrond, I harbour the hope that he will not deem it irresponsible.

The edition of the Torah to which I shall refer is the Masoretic text, mainly in English translation, primarily the 1999 translation produced by the Jewish

---

5. Sigmund Freud, 'The Moses of Michelangelo', p. 211.
6. Ibid., p. 211.
7. Ibid., p. 215.
8. Werner G. Jeanrond, *Text and Interpretation as Categories of Theological Thinking*, trans. T. J. Wilson (Eugene, OR: Wipf & Stock, 1986), p. 120.
9. Ibid.
10. Ibid., p. 153.

Publication Society (JPS).¹¹ For my purposes, historical questions about incidents, places and persons in the text are neither here nor there. Likewise, I bracket out questions about authorship raised by the so-called Higher Criticism and Documentary Hypothesis: they belong to another kind of enquiry. How the text evolved does not interest me, but how it works on the reader does. In short, I treat the Torah as given.¹² What follows is my take.

The argument does not proceed by way of premises to a conclusion. It is heuristic rather than syllogistic. It is no more linear than the progress of the Israelites from Egypt to Canaan. Moreover, like the wilderness terrain, it is rough and full of holes. Hence I present it under the heading 'meanderings'. So much by way of preamble.

Meanderings

Freud refers to Moses as a 'hero'.¹³ No one would dispute that Moses is the hero of the exodus saga, the story that occupies four of the five books that go by his name. Unless, of course, the hero is God. Over and again, God claims the credit for the deeds that might lead us to regard Moses as a hero. He¹⁴ introduces himself to the people of Israel at Sinai saying, 'I the LORD¹⁵ am your God who brought you out of the land of Egypt, the house of bondage' (Exod. 20.2), reminding them of this over and again throughout the narrative. It is God who leads them to a land of milk and honey, God who guides them by day (the pillar of cloud) and by night (the pillar of fire), God who ensures they win their battles and God who gives them their laws. Yet Moses is ubiquitous in the performance of each and every feat. So, who is the hero of the exodus saga: God or Moses? God *and* Moses? God *through* Moses? Let us not quibble over a preposition when the essential point

---

11. JPS, *Hebrew-English Tanakh* (Philadelphia: The Jewish Publication Society, 2000). Unless I indicate otherwise, all translations are from this source.

12. I treat the Torah as 'given' in two respects. First, as with a William Shakespeare play, what interests me is the final product, even if it is jointly written by Francis Bacon, the 6ᵗʰ Earl of Derby and Christopher Marlowe (plus a redactor). Second, seeing the Torah as sacred means seeing it as gifted, in some sense, from heaven (*Torah min HaShamayim*). The Torah is literature raised to a higher power.

13. Sigmund Freud, 'The Moses of Michelangelo', p. 213.

14. God, of course, is neither male nor female. I refer to God as 'he' for want of a pronoun that is neither gendered ('he', 'she') nor impersonal ('it'). 'It' turns God into a mere force whereas God in the Hebrew scriptures has a personality. 'She' has the merit of disrupting the conventional association between God and male. But 'he', precisely because it is conventional, is less conspicuous. In this essay, I opt for the less conspicuous and use 'he'. It is an unsatisfactory solution to an intractable problem.

15. The noun is no less problematic than the pronoun. How do you translate יהוה (the Tetragrammaton: yod, heh, waw, heh)? The JPS translation uses 'LORD' – initial capital followed by small capitals – and I follow suit.

is this: two persons and one relationship dominate the story: Moses, God and the closeness between them. They act together. This is my point of departure. In a way, the rest of the essay is an attempt to bring this point into focus – and to bring it home.

Who is Moses? The final word on him is this: 'Never again did there arise in Israel a prophet like Moses – whom the LORD singled out, face to face (Deut. 34.10).[16] He is a singular figure; and the more you look at him the more singular he becomes. A thread of otherness runs through his biography. If he is a hero then he is a hero with a difference – with the accent on difference. He barely belongs to the people he champions, but nor does he belong to some other people: he belongs nowhere. What nationality would have been stamped in his passport? Born a Hebrew, he is cast upon the waters of the Nile at the age of three months. Nursed by his birth mother, he is adopted by Pharaoh's daughter, who gives him an Egyptian name: Mosheh (Moses).[17] As a young man he leaves – or rather flees – the country in which he grew up, settling in Midian, where he marries Zipporah, the daughter of Jethro, an idolatrous priest, and to all intents and purposes lives the life of a Midianite shepherd.[18] Then, at the age of eighty, he returns to Egypt, not to take up residence again but to reconnect to his Hebrew roots in his old age. Would the Israelites have accepted him as one of their own if Aaron, who had stayed in Egypt and lived among them, had not accompanied his brother on his return and spoken for him and performed the 'signs' that convinced the people that God had not abandoned them and that they should listen to Moses (Exod. 4.27-31)?[19] They listen, but they do not exactly embrace him. They leave their homes and follow him out of Egypt but repeatedly rebel against him, seeing him as the very opposite of a hero: an enemy of the people who is leading them on a wild goose chase into a desert where they will die for want of food and water (Exod. 16.3 and passim). As for Moses, he is as exasperated with them as they are discontented with him, protesting to God that they are not his problem: 'Did I conceive all this people, did I bear them, that You should say to me, "Carry them in your bosom as a nurse carries an infant," to the land that You have promised on oath to their fathers?' (Num. 11.12). *Whose* fathers? Theirs, not ours: Moses uses the third person even though he shares the same ancestry. Even in the midst of the people he calls his kin (Exod. 4.18) he is, in his own eyes and in theirs, an outsider. The Torah ends with a parting of the ways, the people proceeding to Canaan to complete their journey, Moses at the end of his tour of duty, gazing at

16. יְדַעְתִּיו, the word translated as 'singled out', literally means 'knew'. The JPS translation makes the same word-choice in Gen. 18.19 (regarding Abraham) and in Exod. 33.12 and Exod. 33.17 (both times regarding Moses). This captures the implication of the word in context.

17. The text suggests a Hebrew derivation for Moshe (Exod. 2.10), but secular and rabbinic commentators alike generally agree that the name is Egyptian.

18. Zipporah refers to Moses as an Egyptian (Exod. 2.19).

19. There is an ambiguity in the Hebrew as to whether Aaron or Moses performed the signs, but the text states explicitly that it was Aaron who spoke to the elders of the Israelites.

their destination from the summit of Mount Nebo in the land of Moab, excluded and alone. He dies there, away from the people. He is not even buried by them: God himself inters him in an unknown grave (Deut. 34.6). The text explains his exclusion from Canaan as if it were a contingent matter, a punishment for his behaviour (Num. 20.12) or perhaps theirs (Deut. 3.26). But, given who Moses is, it is the only ending that makes sense. Moses *must* remain outside – he *cannot* arrive – because he *is* an outsider. He is excluded by the inner logic of his being. He is excluded by who he is.

Aaron, it is true, shares a similar fate: he is barred from entering the land and dies on top of a mountain (Mount Hor) in the wilderness (Num. 20.28). But who is Aaron? Not Moses: taken on his own, he is quite a different character. Far from being an outsider, he is, if anything, too close to the people, as the episode with the golden calf demonstrates: he colludes with them while Moses, alone on the summit of Sinai, communes with God. Aaron also joins with Miriam in speaking against their brother 'because of the Cushite woman he had married: "He married a Cushite woman!"' (Num. 12.1). It is possible that they mocked her on account of her blackness (a Cushite being an Ethiopian), though the text does not say this. It does not elucidate, leaving us to speculate. Nor is it clear whether the woman in question is Zipporah or a second wife. But this much we know: Moses 'married out', once if not twice. Moreover, there is no mention of his entering into matrimony with a Hebrew woman. Thus, marriage is another mark of Moses' difference, his distance from the people of Israel, his growing away from them in his private life. But I digress. I was saying that Aaron is not Moses. On the other hand, in a way he is: when the text couples him with Moses, rather than taking him on his own, he becomes almost an extension of his brother. At the burning bush God says to Moses: 'You shall speak to him and put the words in his mouth' (Exod. 4.15). From this point on, whenever they act together they act as one – but always it is Moses acting (or speaking) through Aaron. Sometimes their complicity is implicit, as with the incident of the striking of the rock. 'Moses and Aaron assembled the congregation in front of the rock' but only Moses strikes it (Num. 20.10-11). They act as one and they are punished as one. It is this identity that is reflected in the fate they share at the end. If Moses cannot enter Canaan, nor can the man who *represents* him. Aaron, in the end, is also governed by the inner logic of Moses' being.

Speaking of the burning bush, it is worth taking a closer look at the arrangement that God sets up between himself, Moses and Aaron. Aaron is to act as Moses' 'spokesman' (Exod. 4.16) or 'prophet' (Exod. 7.1), with Moses 'playing the role of God' (Exod. 4.16). It is an odd arrangement if not unique in the annals of prophecy: God is to speak through a prophet who speaks through a prophet. Why is this necessary? (The conundrum is too large for this essay but too conspicuous to ignore.) The arrangement is necessitated by Moses' reluctance to play the part that God assigns him: 'Who am I that I should go to Pharaoh and free the Israelites from Egypt?' (Exod. 3.11). This is an instance of a trait for which Moses is celebrated: 'Now Moses was a very humble man, more so than any other man on earth' (Num. 12.3). Perhaps he was being more timid than humble. At any rate, despite God's best effort to reassure him, he resists, pleading a speech impediment (Exod. 4.10), which God considers a lame excuse and brushes aside. Moses still demurs and thus incurs the wrath of the divine (Exod. 4.13-14). For a first date in a forty-year relationship, it is not an auspicious start. In fact, it is remarkable that the relationship survived its inception. God, exasperated by Moses, had the option of appointing Aaron instead. In other words, the odd arrangement that God instituted was not necessary at all – or would not have been if God had not wanted to persevere with Moses. God chose Moses, the man with a speech and language disorder.[20] Either he disregarded his disability or (as I prefer to think) it caught his fancy. Either way, Moses emerges from the interview at the burning bush not only as an unlikely national hero but as an improbable prophet: a spokesperson 'slow of speech and slow of tongue' (Exod. 4.10). The more you look at him the more singular he becomes.

If God's choice of Moses is surprising, his choice of words is astonishing: Moses is to be 'God' and Aaron is to be his 'prophet'. Let us, to begin with, be clear that this is not a paraphrase or loose translation from the Hebrew. God uses the selfsame word that from Gen. 1.1 onwards refers to himself: אֱלֹהִים (*elohim*). Let us also be clear that there is not the slightest hint here (nor elsewhere) of the divinization of Moses. How, then, is God using the word 'God'?[21] Metaphorically, of course. But it is a telling metaphor: putting Moses in the position of God tells of their closeness. Nor is it the only intimation of intimacy between them. 'The LORD would speak to Moses face to face, as one man speaks to another' (Exod. 33.11; see also Deut. 34.10). And when Miriam and Aaron protest that God has spoken through them as well as through Moses (Num. 12.2), God replies: 'With him I speak mouth to mouth, plainly and not in riddles' (Num. 12.8). Mouth to mouth: could the text dare to use a more vivid phrase to express the closeness between Moses and God: God who, from day one, precisely *speaks*?

God, who speaks the world into existence, imparts a word to Moses that is the making (or remaking) of an entire people. But who is God? Moses gives his answer in the *Shema*, the rousing declaration that he makes to the people shortly before his death: 'Hear, O Israel! The LORD is our God, the LORD alone' (Deut. 6.4).[22] That is to say, the LORD, as God, is alone. No one could be more singular, for God is not of this world. He is the original outsider, 'the radical and eternal other', to borrow a phrase from Jeanrond.[23] This is what draws Moses and God together:

---

20. His impediment is mentioned again twice: at Exod. 6.12 and Exod. 6.30.

21. I owe the formulation of this question to Reva Klein in conversation about this passage.

22. The *Shema* is the cornerstone of Judaism. It is translated variously, often with 'one' instead of 'alone'. The JPS version is the same as the translation by Rashbam, the grandson and student of the renowned Medieval biblical commentator Rashi (1040–1105): see the comment on Deut. 6.4 in Joseph H. Hertz, ed., *The Pentateuch and Haftorahs* (London: Soncino Press, 1961), p. 769.

23. Werner G. Jeanrond, *A Theology of Love* (London: Continuum/T&T Clark, 2010), p. 259.

their difference. Hence, with a touch of irony mingled with affection, God calls Moses 'God'. The attraction is mutual: each singles out the other. The Psalmist says 'deep calls to deep' (Ps. 42.8).[24] Here other calls to other.

This calling becomes the calling of a people, the Israelites, who go from one extreme of otherness to another: from being abject slaves in Egypt to becoming a nation of priests (Exod. 19.6); an 'other people' and not just *another* people.[25] God, through Moses, gives them a code of ethics in which he lays peculiar emphasis on 'the stranger' (גֵּר, *ger*). 'You shall not oppress a stranger, for you know the feelings of the stranger, having yourselves been strangers in the land of Egypt' (Exod. 23.9). According to a *baraita* in the Talmud, the Torah repeats this commandment (or words to similar effect) between thirty-six and forty-six times, depending on how you count.[26] The widow and the orphan, two other marginalized groups, are frequently mentioned in the same breath as the stranger (Deut. 14.29). It is not just a matter of refraining from oppression. God *loves* the stranger (Deut. 10.18) and commands the people: 'you shall love him [the stranger] as yourself' (Lev. 19.34; see also Deut. 10.19).[27] In short, God takes a marginalized people and makes a double move: he moves them to the centre and he places the marginalized at the heart of their ethics. Who better to mediate these moves than the speech-impaired outsider, Moses (who is also an orphan of sorts)?

The emphasis on the outsider goes still deeper. Not only does God keep reminding the people that they were strangers in Egypt, but they will be strangers in their own land too. As he points out (through Moses): 'the land is Mine; you are but strangers resident with me' (Lev. 25.23; compare Ps. 39.13).[28] This is one of the most unsettling lines in the whole of the Torah.[29] It is, in a way, the bottom line, for 'all the earth is Mine' (Exod. 19.5; compare Deut. 10.14 and Ps. 24.1). Resident stranger: it is the human condition.

So, who is Moses? He is the human partner of the universal God. He is the out-and-out outsider who, for this very reason, is a universal figure; for who is

---

24. Ps. 42.8 is numbered 42.7 in different versions of the Bible.

25. On their place in the world – their universal role as a particular people – see Brian Klug, 'A People Apart?', *Jewish Quarterly* 217 (2011), pp. 54–8.

26. Norman Solomon, ed., *The Talmud: A Selection* (London: Penguin, 2009), p. 472.

27. The command to love your *neighbour* as yourself appears earlier in the same chapter: Lev. 19.15.

28. Ps. 39.13 is numbered 39.12 in different versions of the Bible.

29. Among other things, it unsettles the promise of the land to the descendants of Abraham. In Genesis this promise is categorical (except perhaps for a hint given in Gen. 18.19). With Moses, it becomes conditional: the people have to merit the land (though it is understood in advance that they will lose it [Deut. 4.25-7; 31.16]). Moses is no patriarch. And when God offers to create a new people through him he refuses (Exod. 32.10, Num. 14.12). Once again, this is an expression of the inner logic of his being: his role is not to bring a new people into the world but to lift an existing people onto a higher plane. No significant bloodline runs through the singular Moses.

not a stranger on the earth?[30] Love the stranger, love the other, love the marginalized: ultimately, this love is what is signified by Moses, God's significant other. No wonder God buries him himself.

Afterword

The reading I have given goes against the grain of a familiar view of Moses as a figure of law as distinct from – even opposed to – love, a view often transferred to Judaism and to the Jews as a people. However, the love for the other that I highlight and associate with Moses should not be understood in a mawkish way. It implies respect, concern and care, not sentimental attachment. It entails a code of conduct, an ethics, rather than a beautiful feeling.

I would not want my conclusion to appear to deprive Moses of his all-round humanity by changing him into a milksop or an angel. I prefer to close by recalling Michelangelo's impassioned figure, supporting the tablets of stone with his right arm, his head turning to his left. Freud notices 'the angry scorn of the hero's glance'. He continues: 'Sometimes I have crept cautiously out of the half-gloom of the interior as though I myself belonged to the mob upon whom his eye is turned – the mob which can hold fast no conviction, which has neither faith nor patience, and which rejoices when it has regained its illusory idols'.[31] Haunting words: the words of Freud, the iconoclast, looking into the eye of Moses, reading his mind.

---

30. The implications of this thought are far-reaching, but that is an essay for another day.
31. Sigmund Freud, 'The Moses of Michelangelo', p. 213.

2

JOSEPH IN EGYPT:
ASSIMILATION AND SEPARATION FROM THE OTHER

Andrew D. H. Mayes

The acknowledgement of the otherness of the other and the implications of that recognition for human relationships is an issue thoroughly rooted in biblical thought: it was in that context that Israel marked out its self-understanding, a self-understanding that was dynamic in its recognition of the tension that exists between integration and isolation, between assimilation and separation. The Joseph story is an extended treatment of that theme in vivid narrative form. It is a pleasure and a privilege to offer this study as a tribute to Werner G. Jeanrond. It is offered in celebration of an enriching friendship rooted in collegiate proximity during his years in Trinity College, Dublin, but regularly refreshed in succeeding years.

The Story of Joseph

The story of Joseph (Gen. 37–50) performs a clear function in its present context: it forms the bridge between the patriarchal and the exodus traditions, explaining how Israel came to find itself in a situation of oppression from which it was delivered by Yahweh. In terms of genre too, as a short story, it marks a transition from the saga-like material of the patriarchal stories to the longer narrative of the exodus. It is this which is also a first pointer to the fact that the connection now established between all three is a deliberate construct, designed to bring together heterogeneous materials and to create a continuous account of Israel's origins. Without the linkage of the Joseph story, the patriarchal and exodus stories form no continuity, but rather stand parallel: each is complete in itself, the patriarchal tradition being stories told by those already settled in the land and tracing their origins to Mesopotamia, the exodus tradition tracing Israel's origin to Egypt. It is the Joseph story that makes the continuity, so that the residence in Egypt is now an episode in an ongoing history rather than the beginning of that history. Thus, it is to the creation of the Pentateuch that the Joseph story has made its distinctive contribution.[1]

---

1. For the original independence of the Pentateuchal themes cf. Martin Noth, *Überlieferungsgeschichte des Pentateuch* (Stuttgart: Kohlhammer, 1948); ET: *A History of*

That the Joseph story was not composed for this purpose is indicated by a number of considerations: its genre is distinct; there are significant discontinuities in terms of content. The death of Joseph's mother Rachel, recorded in Gen. 35.19, is not presupposed in the story (37.10); the racial exclusiveness of the patriarchal stories, presupposed in Gen. 24, is a minor feature of the Joseph story (43.32; 46.34), but contradicted by Joseph's marriage to the daughter of an Egyptian priest (41.45); the dominance of 'Elohim' as the divine designation throughout the story fits with the absence of reference to visions, covenant or promise, a binding feature of the patriarchal sagas. The independence of the Joseph story is then confirmed by the fact that the story, uniquely in the Pentateuch, finds parallels and connections with, in addition to the Tale of Sinuhe to be discussed below, motifs, vocabulary and other stories deriving from Egypt.[2]

Interpretations of the Story

The interpretation of the Joseph story is a matter of ongoing discussion. Older views[3] emphasized the Hyksos period of the Egyptian fifteenth dynasty as a time when Semites could credibly have risen to positions of power in Egypt, and so as a suitable context within which to understand Joseph, and similar concerns with a historical interpretation continue to engage Egyptologists such as Kenneth A. Kitchen and James K. Hoffmeier.[4] Common to these views is a narrow interpretation of the story as if its significance were to be determined, and indeed exhausted, by its 'historicity', understood as a reliable account of what actually happened. Even if it were acceptable – a highly improbable proposition – that the story was composed in the thirteenth century BC, its historicity would not thereby be decided, nor would the question of its historicity exhaust the question of its meaning. In any case, the Joseph story is undoubtedly of much later date. Whatever the Egyptological parallels, which certainly do not preclude even if they do not require a late seventh to sixth century date, these parallels fit with what may be concluded from the Hebrew of the story, which Donald B. Redford has demonstrated to be late, deuteronomic or priestly.[5] This is not, however, the issue.

Pentateuchal Traditions, trans. B. W. Anderson (Englewood Cliffs, NJ: Prentice Hall, 1972); but especially Rolf Rendtorff, *Das überlieferungsgeschichtliche Problem des Pentateuch* (Berlin: De Gruyter, 1977); ET: *The Problem of the Process of Transmission in the Pentateuch*, trans. J. J. Scullion (Sheffield: JSOT Press, 1990).

2. Cf. John D. Currid, *Ancient Egypt and the Old Testament* (Grand Rapids, MI: Baker Books, 1997), pp. 74-82; and especially James K. Hoffmeier, *Israel in Egypt* (Oxford: Oxford University Press, 1996), pp. 77-106.

3. Cf. especially John Van Seters, *Prologue to History: The Yahwist as Historian in Genesis* (Louisville: Westminster John Knox, 1992), pp. 20-30.

4. Cf. Kenneth A. Kitchen, 'Review of Redford, *A Study of the Biblical Story of Joseph*', *Oriens Antiquus* 12 (1973), 223-42; James K. Hoffmeier, *Israel in Egypt*, p. 98.

5. Donald B. Redford, *A Study of the Biblical Story of Joseph* (Leiden: Brill, 1970), pp. 55-72, has noted over fifty examples.

Early date does not decide historicity, nor does late date preclude it, and in neither case is significance determined.

Gerhard von Rad, while still accepting standard Pentateuchal source criticism, moved beyond it to argue that the Joseph story is a *novella*, and that it derived from the wisdom school associated with the royal court in the time of Solomon.[6] One should not be diverted by the point that this argument was probably incompatible with source criticism from the recognition that this signalled a significant move away from traditional scholarly preoccupations towards offering an important response to the question of the point and purpose of the story. Von Rad's argument that the story showed a high level of literary and psychological skill in its portrayal of an ideal scribe who could give good counsel, speak well, resist the temptation of women and be magnanimous, was indeed open to serious criticism, not least on the grounds that wisdom influences in the story are not as pervasive as von Rad argued, but also because the characterization of Joseph as an ideal scribe is scarcely compatible with his naïve reporting of his dreams to his father and brothers.[7] Yet, von Rad's view was based on an approach which has continued to be fruitful since his work appeared.

Von Rad's view of the Joseph story as a product of the Solomonic Enlightenment was accepted by Frank Crüsemann,[8] but for the latter the question the story set out to answer was not that of the ideal scribe but rather a political question relating to the constitution of Israel: should one man rule over his brothers? The story culminates in Joseph's reconciliation with his brothers, a reconciliation based on their acceptance of his rule. This involves acknowledgement of its necessity for their survival. Had it not been for Joseph's foresight in setting aside food through taxes then starvation would have ensued. It is not for itself that the monarchy imposes taxes but for the welfare of the people.[9] So the story is in general aimed at an alienated Israel, advocating reconciliation between sovereign and subject on the basis of the recognition of the life-preserving power of centralized rule. Yet the fact that Joseph is not king indicates a subtle dimension of this purpose. Joseph, as eponym of the northern tribes of Israel, represents those for whom the highest office in the Davidic state was not attainable. The problem is that of reconciling high officials in that state, who derived from the north, with their northern brethren. The task of Joseph in Egypt is that of northern officials in the

---

6. Gerhard von Rad, 'The Joseph Narrative and Ancient Wisdom', in idem, *The Problem of the Hexateuch and Other Essays*, trans. E. W. Trueman Dicken (Edinburgh: Oliver & Boyd, 1966), pp. 292–300.

7. Cf. Claus Westermann, *Genesis 37–50: A Commentary*, trans. J. J. Scullion (Minneapolis: Fortress Press, 1986), pp. 26–7; and, on the exegetical tendency to 'beatify' Joseph, cf. George W. Coats, *From Canaan to Egypt* (Washington: Catholic Biblical Association of America, 1976), p. 44n. 50.

8. Frank Crüsemann, *Der Widerstand gegen das Königtum* (Neukirchen-Vluyn: Neukirchener Verlag, 1978), pp. 143–55.

9. Thus, as Crüsemann notes, the story answers point for point the objections raised against the monarchy in 1 Sam. 8.

Solomonic kingdom in 1 Kgs 4: the laying aside of provisions derived from taxes. So the Joseph story is Davidic monarchic propaganda, aimed at the north and the officials deriving from there.

This undoubtedly represents in principle the right approach. Whatever else it is, the Joseph story is not a historical report; it is in the first instance a story, and as such, the first question to be addressed to it is the question of theme. What is the story about? It is only through that question that we are liberated from the sterile preoccupation with issues of truth understood in terms of that which is historically verifiable. Yet it must be doubted, even if the correct question is asked, that in this instance the correct answer, though of course there may be more than one correct answer, has been given. Crüsemann's interpretation has anchored the story in a quite specific historical period, and tied it to a quite specific political issue. Its significance is thus tied to a set of historical and political circumstances that are problematic. The 'Davidic/Solomonic empire' is now clearly understood to be the retrojection to this time of the aspirations of a much later time, while the age of Solomon can no longer be seen as having been the age of enlightenment that this view presupposes.[10] Moreover, the story depends upon a sense of Egypt which for this period of Israelite life is not only indemonstrable, but is excluded by archaeological finds relating to cultural contact between Palestine and Egypt in this time.[11] The Joseph story, in other words, does not make sense within this context.

An alternative possibility, which better accounts also for the manifestly late linguistic features of the story, is proposed by Bernhard Lang.[12] While recognizing that the story is an adaptation of an older form, Lang argues that it is in its present form a diaspora novella, which, through being set in the remote age of the patriarchs, has been given a timeless quality. It is a novella deriving from and addressed to the Egyptian diaspora which gives a very distinctive presentation of the possibilities for Jewish life outside the land. The story depicts Egypt in glowing terms as a welcome home for Jews. Egypt is rich in pasture, and intermarriage is not a problem. If you come as a new immigrant there will be fellow Jews to welcome you. Even though society in Egypt is structured according to a patron-client relationship, Jews can live within such a society even while maintaining their kinship solidarity. In return for the benefits that Egypt offers, Jews contribute to the pagan state. Joseph is an ideal role model for diaspora Jews. In this way, Jewish society in the Egyptian diaspora is open rather than closed, preserving its distinctiveness while living a life of participation in the pagan state. So Joseph

---

10. Cf. e.g. J. Maxwell Miller and John H. Hayes, *A History of Ancient Israel and Judah* (Louisville: Westminster John Knox Press, 2006), pp. 148–220; Israel Finkelstein and Neil A. Silberman, *David and Solomon* (New York: Free Press, 2006); and the various essays in Lowell K. Handy, ed., *The Age of Solomon: Scholarship at the Turn of the Millennium* (Leiden: Brill, 1997).

11. Cf. Bernd U. Schipper, *Israel und Ägypten in der Königszeit* (Göttingen: Vandenhoeck & Ruprecht, 1999), pp. 111–16.

12. Bernhard Lang, 'Joseph the Diviner: Careers of a Biblical Hero', in idem, *Hebrew Life and Literature: Selected Essays of Bernhard Lang* (Aldershot: Ashgate, 2008), pp. 93–109.

presents a starkly different model of Judaism to the Mosaic model of separation and strict adherence to the law.

This is an attractive reading of the Joseph story, all the more remarkable for being appropriate to the situation of Jewish communities in different diaspora contexts. Indeed the figure of Joseph, the wise scribe and interpreter of dreams who can accurately predict the future, finds its best parallel in the figure of Daniel in the courts of Nebuchadnezzar and Belshazzar, who is also wrongfully imprisoned and there finds rehabilitation.[13] Yet, while it is most likely that the exilic/post-exilic period is the time to which the Joseph story is best suited, Lang's very positive interpretation of the story leaves some fundamental questions unanswered. In particular, it does not take adequate account of the negative attitude towards life in Egypt that the story increasingly expresses. Egypt is a place of danger; it is 'the land of my affliction';[14] it is the place where Joseph, even as ruler, realizes his longing for his family and desires to be buried in Canaan (50.24-26). Egypt, in the end, is a place from which one departs.

The Joseph Story and the Tale of Sinuhe

In significant ways Lang's interpretation of the Joseph story fits with what has been taken to be the conclusion of that story in Gen. 47.27.[15] This verse corresponds with the opening of the story (37.1) in grammatical structure, and so delineates the scope of the story as an account which goes from Jacob in Canaan to Israel in Egypt. Yet it is doubtful that these verses can be seen as marking the limits of the original Joseph story as an entity independent of the patriarchal narrative. That original independence is, as noted above, quite clear. The beginning and end in 37.1 and 47.27 are markers in the Joseph story not in its original form but at a certain stage in its history, particularly when it came to provide the explanation for how it was that Israel came to be in Egypt. The Joseph story as part of that wider history is a different entity, with a different purpose, from the Joseph story as originally conceived. Gen. 47.27 clearly points forward to the beginning of the exodus tradition and is taken up immediately in Exod. 1.7.[16]

This distinction between the Joseph story in its original composition and the Joseph story as part of the wider history is obviously significant. By means of it, several sections of Gen. 37–50 may be recognized as part of the later development of the story. This is obviously the case with Gen. 38 and 49, which are part of that process of integration of the Joseph story, but it must also be true of 46.1-27 and 48, for both of which the patriarchal narrative framework is determinative,

---

13. Dan. 2 and 5; cf. especially Donald B. Redford, *Egypt, Canaan and Israel in Ancient Times* (Princeton: Princeton University Press, 1992), pp. 422-9.

14. Gen. 41.52; the same term is used by Jacob of his service to Laban (Gen. 31.42) and of Israel's slavery in Egypt (Exod. 3.7).

15. Cf. George W. Coats, *From Canaan to Egypt*, pp. 8-9.

16. Cf. Claus Westermann, *Genesis 37–50*, p. 172.

and indeed in the main the late priestly redaction of the patriarchal narrative.[17] The conclusion of the story in Gen. 50 presents an account which has clearly undergone major modification in the interests of fitting it into the wider context. In its present form the story tells how, on the death of Jacob, Joseph and his household, accompanied by the servants and elders of Egypt, brought his body for burial in Canaan in the cave of the field at Machpelah, which had earlier been bought by Abraham. Then they returned to Egypt where Joseph eventually died. Having earlier made his brothers swear to bring his body home, Joseph was embalmed and put in a coffin in Egypt.

What is necessary for the Joseph story in its wider setting is that Joseph and his brothers should remain in Egypt, for it is the secondary function of the Joseph story to explain the presence of Israel in Egypt and the exodus; and so, at the end of the present story, Joseph and his household return to Egypt where Joseph dies and is put in a coffin. It is likely, however, that an older and very different ending has been preserved, but is here modified. The elaborate account of the return of Jacob's body to Canaan is an unnecessary and unexpected constituent of the older Joseph story, but forms a fitting account of the death and burial of Jacob when that Joseph story came to form the conclusion of the patriarchal narrative. Behind the present conclusion we can recognize the older conclusion to the Joseph story, in which indeed the death of Jacob is related to the return of his body to Canaan, but within the context of the return of Joseph himself to his homeland. Such an ending would be a fitting conclusion to a narrative in which the arrival in Egypt of Joseph's brothers and their father is a major element in bringing home to Joseph the fact that Egypt cannot be his final resting place. The dynamic of the story requires the return of Joseph to Canaan.

Our understanding of the Joseph story is considerably assisted by a comparison with the Egyptian Tale of Sinuhe,[18] a story whose popularity through Egyptian history from the time of its composition in the Middle Kingdom is attested by the

---

17. It is not possible to take up at this point the detail of new developments in Pentateuchal criticism. For an outline of the position adopted here see my *The Story of Israel between Settlement and Exile* (London: SCM Press, 1983), pp. 139-49. See also especially the essays by Rolf Rentdorff and Konrad Schmid in John W. Rogerson, ed., *The Pentateuch* (Sheffield: Sheffield Academic Press, 1996). As far as the Joseph story in particular is concerned, it is now evident that the older attempt to trace J and E sources here does not work, and that the only adequate explanation for the characteristics it exhibits is to understand it as an artistic unity which was, through the work of a late (priestly) editor, incorporated into the Pentateuch. See Robert Alter, *The Art of Biblical Narrative* (New York: Basic Books, 1981), pp. 157-76; Claus Westermann, *Genesis 37-50*, pp. 19-26; 245-7.

18. According to James K. Hoffmeier, *Israel in Egypt*, p. 80, 'it is inappropriate to compare two pieces of literature in order to identify the genre of the one from the other unless there is good evidence that the texts in question are indeed commensurate'. In light of the parallels to be adduced below, it is clear that these texts are indeed 'commensurate'. It is noteworthy that Hoffmeier, *Israel in Egypt*, p. 100n. 47, says of Sinuhe that 'He could have been the invention of the writer for purely propagandist ends. On the other hand, Sinuhe

numerous copies of it.[19] The story relates that Sinuhe, in the service of Princess Nefru, the wife of Sesostris, was with Sesostris on an expedition against the Libyans at the time of the death of the latter's father, the Pharaoh Amenemhet. Sesostris immediately set off home, but Sinuhe, disturbed by an overheard conversation, fled. Avoiding the Residence, which he expected to be in turmoil that he would not survive, he made his way south, east across the Nile, and then northwards reaching the Walls of the Ruler built to guard Egypt against Asiatic incursions. He eventually encountered an Asiatic ruler who assisted him, headed for Byblos, but was carried off and befriended by Amunenshi, the ruler of Upper Retenu, who had Egyptians in his service. Questioned by Amunenshi, Sinuhe was unable to give a clear account of the reason for his flight ('it is like a plan of God'), and went on to sing the praises of the new Pharaoh, Sesostris I. Amunenshi kept Sinuhe with him, married him to his daughter, gave him the best of the land and made him chief of a tribe. Sinuhe lived many years there, entertaining messengers to and from the Residence, and assisting Amunenshi in many missions as army commander. Apparently becoming an object of envy, Sinuhe was challenged to combat, overcame the challenger and further enriched himself with his enemy's plunder. But the fight marked a turning point: overcome by the thought of death and burial in a foreign land, Sinuhe was filled with longing to return to Egypt, praying that the God who brought him there should bring him home, and that the Pharaoh himself might receive him back to the Residence. The Pharaoh sent word to Sinuhe, inviting his return, in response to which Sinuhe once more sang the praises of Sesostris, assuring him that his flight was not planned. Having handed over all his possessions to his children, he departed south to the Residence. At the frontier of Egypt he was left by his Asiatic escort and then proceeded to the palace where he prostrated himself before the Pharaoh. Sinuhe was welcomed, re-introduced to the Queen and family. The princesses sang a hymn of praise to the Pharaoh begging forgiveness. Sinuhe was then fully restored to royal favour, and provided with food, and with a pyramid tomb, 'as is done for a Chief Friend'.

A relationship between this Egyptian tale and the story of Joseph has long been noted.[20] J. Robin King's particular contribution is to put the stories structurally into the wider ancient near eastern context, but it is the detailed points of contact between the Joseph and Sinuhe stories in particular that are remarkable here. In both the hero rises to an exalted status in his homeland;[21] flight follows in both

---

might have been an historical figure around which the story was embellished'. The same is surely the case with Joseph.

19. For the text, cf. Miriam Lichtheim, *Ancient Egyptian Literature I* (Berkeley: University of California Press, 1975), pp. 222-35. See especially Richard B. Parkinson, *The Tale of Sinuhe and other ancient Egyptian Poems 1940-1640 BC* (Oxford: Oxford University Press, 1997), pp. 21-53; idem, *Poetry and Culture in Middle Kingdom Egypt* (London: Continuum, 2002), pp. 149-68.

20. Cf. especially J. Robin King, 'The Joseph Story and Divine Politics: A Comparative Study of a Biographic Formula from the Ancient Near East', *JBL* 106/4 (1987), pp. 577-94.

21. For Sinuhe cf. Robert B. Parkinson, *Tale of Sinuhe*, p. 43n. 1.

instances; after a journey to a different country the fugitive rises to prominence in the adopted country and marries into the adoptive family; the hero is endangered in the adopted country and eventually seeks to return home; an escort is given to the border of the homeland to which the hero returns for burial.

This extensive correspondence justifies a conclusion already reached, that the Joseph story in its original independence related the actual return of Joseph to Canaan; it is its secondary context as a bridge between the patriarchal and exodus traditions, and in particular the need to provide a background to the exodus story that has brought about the change to its present form. Like the tale of Sinuhe so that of Joseph told of his return to his homeland. Moreover, just as the tale of Sinuhe is in genre a modified form of a funerary autobiography,[22] modified in order to become propaganda for the homeland as a home for all Egyptians, so also the story of Joseph is best understood as propaganda for the homeland. However good life may be in Egypt, this is not home. Both Goshen and Iaa, the land granted to Sinuhe by Amunenshi, are geographically unknown, fictional quantities, liminal locations where there can be no final resting place. If Sinuhe is addressed to Egyptian exiles in Palestine calling them home, so Joseph is addressed to the exilic community in Egypt, to persuade them that their real security lies in their reconciliation with their brothers within the borders of their true home.

---

22. Modified in the sense that such autobiographies generally expressed exclusively praise for the subject, emphasizing especially his high ethical and moral character; cf. Robert B. Parkinson, *Tale of Sinuhe*, pp. 21-2.

3

BECOMING 'ANOTHER': NICODEMUS AND HIS RELATIONSHIPS IN THE FOURTH GOSPEL

Mary Marshall

When Werner G. Jeanrond and I met as new colleagues in 2012 he remarked, with what I think was only partial levity, that we two had been afforded an unusual opportunity to make conversation between the fields of biblical studies and systematic theology. Any reader of Jeanrond's own work will acknowledge that in his case, such a special opportunity is quite unnecessary. His published work displays careful attention to biblical texts as well as modern biblical scholarship, giving every suggestion that he is well practised in such conversations. In my own case, however, these promptings had been sadly neglected and I have welcomed with relief this timely opportunity to engage more closely with Jeanrond's work and his field more generally. I have revisited areas of my research in conversation with Jeanrond's exposition of the significance of difference for love. The conversation has enabled me to illuminate the Fourth Gospel from new angles by applying Jeanrond's ideas and borrowing liberally from his vocabulary. Although this essay is unashamedly concerned with analyzing the Gospel text, I hope it will be clear to Werner Jeanrond that his kind and generous welcome, as well as his invitation, was not in vain.

In several published works Jeanrond has highlighted the problematic presentation of love in the Johannine literature.[1] In this essay I propose to draw out some further implications of this, with particular reference to the figure of Nicodemus. Nicodemus inhabits the margins of the Gospel world, exciting persistent debate among exegetes as to whether Nicodemus is included in or excluded from the category of disciple, abiding in Jesus and possessing eternal life. I shall argue, in harmony with Jeanrond's account of the significance of the praxis of love, that

---

1. See for example Werner G. Jeanrond, 'Biblical Challenges to a Theology of Love', *BibInt* 11 (2003), pp. 640–53; idem, 'The Future of Christianity in Europe', in Werner G. Jeanrond and Andrew D. H. Mayes, eds, *Recognising the Margins: Developments in Biblical and Theological Studies* (Dublin: Columba, 2006), pp. 182–200 (196–7); idem, *A Theology of Love* (London: Continuum/T&T Clark, 2010) pp. 25–44.

our assessment of Nicodemus, rather than resting on an evaluation of his understanding of, or faith in Jesus, is best measured according to his relationships. In other words, Nicodemus is understood in terms of the other with whom he is associated and who associates with him.

The Narrowing of Love's Horizon in the Gospel of John

Jeanrond has expounded a prevailing view among biblical scholars that the Johannine Gospel and epistles offer a distinctive understanding of love as limited to the Johannine community. Whereas the Jesus of the Synoptic Gospels enjoins his hearers to love their neighbour (Mt. 19.19; 22.39 and parallels) and their enemies (Mt. 5.44); the Johannine Jesus commands his disciples to 'Love one another' (Jn 13.34-35; 15.12, 17). For a reader in a society which prizes inclusivity and outreach, nurtured on the Good Samaritan as a model for the universal scope of love in Christianity, John's version seems at best incomplete and at worst offensive. Jeanrond observes that John's presentation allowed 'the unholy alliance between Christian love, unity and uniformity to emerge that still throws its long shadow over much of the Christian discourse of love'.[2] In Johannine literature love is an 'inward looking praxis' designed to shore up the harmony and identity of the Johannine community and to preserve it from what lies beyond. What is more, love is a 'Christian' quality which marks the identity of the disciples, 'By this everyone will know that you are my disciples, if you have love for one another' (Jn 13.35). For the fourth evangelist, therefore, the loving and loved other is '*another*' one like the loving subject. The disciples of Jesus and John's community (now as much as in the early centuries of the church) are instructed to 'love one another' and thus build a communal identity at the expense of a simultaneously constructed 'totally other'. Since this 'totally other' represents what the disciples are not, it is neither a loved nor loving other, because love is the hallmark of a disciple (that by which disciples are recognized as disciples).[3] The 'totally other' is beyond any potential for engagement with the disciples – that which is 'totally other' cannot be authentically encountered or understood – and so by thus constructing the community, John is able to isolate the disciples from external challenge or threat.[4]

So Johannine love has casualties; although the world is sometimes a 'loved subject' (3.16-17 cf. 4.42; 6.33), it is often characterized as a hated subject to be hated in return. 'If the world hates you, be aware that it hated me before it hated you. If you belonged to the world, the world would love you as its own. Because you do not belong to the world, but I have chosen you out of the world – therefore

---

2. Werner G. Jeanrond, 'The Future of Christianity', p. 197.

3. See Werner G. Jeanrond on the continuation of this theme in the history of Christian theologies of love in 'Toward an Interreligious Hermeneutics of Love', in Catherine Cornille and Christopher Conway, eds, *Interreligious Hermeneutics* (Eugene, OR: Wipf and Stock, 2010), pp. 44-60 (57).

4. I am grateful to Ulrich Schmiedel for his helpful insights on this point.

the world hates you' (15.18-19 cf. 7.7; 16.33; 17.14-16). That the Fourth Gospel exhibits many 'sectarian' characteristics is not a new observation and will not be rehearsed here.[5] However, those elements of John which hint at isolation and animosity towards those outside the community bolster the impression of an inward looking community where inside and outside are clearly and fiercely demarcated. Yet the parameters of love, and therefore of the evangelist's community, are not entirely free from ambiguity. As has already been noted, 'the world' is both loved and hated. The question of boundaries between, what in the context of this essay we term, 'another' (who is to love and be loved) and 'totally other' (excluded from love) is also prompted by figures like Nicodemus, who is not a disciple, yet not explicitly marked for exclusion.

The Ambiguity of Nicodemus' Portrayal

Much of the discussion surrounding Nicodemus' three appearances in John (Chapters 3, 7 and 19) has focused on discerning whether he may be considered a 'true' disciple, that is 'another' of the loved and loving in-group, or whether he remains outside the boundaries of the evangelist's conception of community and relationship and is, therefore, 'totally other'. The resolution of this issue has usually centred on an evaluation of Nicodemus' faith in and understanding of Jesus, but any attempt at such an evaluation is, I shall demonstrate, fraught with ambiguity. In what follows I shall select a sample of Nicodemus' words and actions for analysis, in order to highlight the problematic potential for double meaning and ambiguity which persists in John's presentation of Nicodemus.[6]

An initial and obvious example is found in John's introduction of Nicodemus as one who 'came to Jesus by night' (3.2). From this it might be concluded that because Nicodemus walks at night, he stumbles because the light is not in him (11.10) and he does not know where he is going (12.35). Jesus comes as a light to a dark world (1.5; 12.35) to do the Father's work while it is day (9.4).[7] The timing of Nicodemus' visit may align him with Judas, who does Satan's work at night (13.30 cf. 13.27), and others overtaken by the darkness of Jesus' absence (12.35).[8] Yet this is not the only plausible interpretation of the timing of Nicodemus' visit and risks

---

5. See existing analyses in Wayne A. Meeks, 'The Man from Heaven in Johannine Sectarianism', *JBL* 91 (1972), pp. 44–72.

6. A more thorough exegesis of the passages may be found in Mary Marshall, *The Portrayals of the Pharisees in the Gospels and Acts* (Göttingen: Vandenhoeck & Ruprecht, 2014).

7. Craig R. Koester, *Symbolism in the Fourth Gospel: Meaning, Mystery and Community* (Minneapolis: Fortress Press, 1995), pp. 5–6.

8. This kind of interpretation is supported by Michael D. Goulder, 'Nicodemus', *SJT* 44 (1991), pp. 153–68 (154); cf. Wayne A. Meeks, 'Man from Heaven', p. 54 and Jerome H. Neyrey, *The Gospel of John* (Cambridge: Cambridge University Press, 2007), p. 76.

a naïve application of Johannine symbolism.⁹ It is Jesus' presence as 'light of the world' which determines both day and night (8.12; 12.35-6, 46) and so by coming to Jesus Nicodemus has emerged from the darkness of night into the light of Jesus' presence. The significance of a nocturnal visit is, in and of itself, ambiguous and may only be clarified by an analysis of what follows in order to determine whether Nicodemus approaches Jesus *qua* light of the world.

Nicodemus next appears in John's narrative at 7.50-2 where he reminds the Pharisees 'Our law does not judge people without first giving them a hearing to find out what they are doing, does it?' (7.51) yet it is unclear to whose case he refers. The Pharisees have sent the police to arrest Jesus (7.32, 45), whom they also accuse of deceit (7.47) and it could be that Nicodemus here cautions the Pharisees against a hasty condemnation of Jesus. However, he does not mention Jesus by name and the Pharisees have not passed any judgement as such on Jesus, rather, their plan to arrest him suggests their intention to give him a hearing. Alternatively Nicodemus' intervention follows closely on a condemnation of the crowd as 'accursed' (7.49) and a castigation of the Temple police (7.47), so may be read as a defence of either or both of those groups.[10] In any case, it is possible that Nicodemus interferes not out of concern for any injured party (Jesus, crowd or police) but from a sincere regard for a legal principle (Deut. 1.6 cf. 13.14; 19.18-19). In other words, Nicodemus' actions need not convey a concern for (let alone a belief in) Jesus or Jesus' teaching 'Do not judge by appearances but judge with right judgement' (7.24), but for the same Torah to which the Pharisees appeal in 7.49.[11] Yet does it follow that his interjection is incorrect or unwelcome?[12]

Nicodemus' final appearance is alongside Joseph of Arimathea at Jesus' burial (19.38-42). The burial of Jesus may be considered in some ways parallel to the anointing of Jesus at Bethany by Mary (12.3). Jesus greets Mary's action with approval and seems to envisage a second anointing after his death (12.7). It is possible, therefore, that Nicodemus and Joseph are due the same praise as that granted to Mary. Viewed in parallel to the Bethany anointing, the burial of Jesus might be judged appropriate to the situation and a gesture of discipleship. On the other hand, it could be that Mary's proleptic anointing of Jesus for his burial

---

9. A further alternative to the interpretations offered here is that the function of the night-time setting is purely chronological cf. Jn 21.3 or represents the rabbinic practice of nocturnal discussion. See Francis P. Cotterell, 'The Nicodemus Conversation: A Fresh Appraisal', *ExpTim* 96 (1985-6), pp. 237-42 (238-9) and Raymond E. Brown, *The Gospel according to John*, 2 vols (New York: Doubleday, 1966/1970), vol. 1, p. 130.

10. Severino Pancaro, 'The Metamorphosis of a Legal Principle in the Fourth Gospel: A Closer Look at Jn 7.51', *Bib* 53 (1972), pp. 340-61 (342).

11. Jouette M. Bassler, 'Mixed Signals: Nicodemus in the Fourth Gospel', *JBL* 108 (1989), pp. 635-46 (640); Michael D. Goulder, 'Nicodemus', p. 155.

12. Marines de Jonge argues that there has been no development in Nicodemus' attitude since Chapter 3, *Jesus: Stranger from Heaven and Son of God. Jesus Christ and the Christians in Johannine Perspective* (Missoula, MT: Scholars Press, 1977), p. 36.

renders Nicodemus' actions unnecessary, it is, in the words of Michael Goulder, 'an extravagant error'.[13] Do Joseph and Nicodemus bring Mary's act to completion or should they instead have rendered this service to Jesus while he was still 'with them' (12.8)? Is there sufficient similarity between the anointing and the burial to infer approval for one from the other? In her action, Mary demonstrated her awareness of Jesus' impending death, that she would not always have him. In their action, do Nicodemus and Joseph demonstrate that they neither expect nor understand that Jesus will rise again? Yet if so, are they no more ignorant than the disciples (2.22), Mary Magdalene (20.13), Simon Peter and the Beloved Disciple (20.9), all of whom are confused by the resurrection?

Proposal for a New Measure

My examination of John's presentation of Nicodemus' faith, understanding and motivations has been brief and treated only three small aspects of his portrayal. It has, however, clearly exemplified the difficulties which pertain to the interpretation of these episodes and the evaluation of the status of Nicodemus. John's presentation of Nicodemus is replete with ambiguity. Following the interpretations offered above, it is possible to tend one way or another on the assessment of Nicodemus' character at certain points. For example, Jesus' conversation with Nicodemus suggests that he does not understand heavenly things (3.12), does not receive Jesus' testimony (3.11) and has no right to teach Israel (3.10). He approaches Jesus but his spirit of enquiry does not lead to understanding; he visits at night and remains in darkness. Thus one might favour a particular assessment of Nicodemus on a given point, yet still fail to demonstrate a consistent trend or irrevocable indication concerning Nicodemus' status overall. We might condemn Nicodemus out of hand or give him the benefit of the doubt but the fruitfulness of this method of evaluation is limited. Without a decisive argument in either direction it can only result in stalemate and a reaffirmation of the evangelist's ambiguity in this regard.[14]

13. Michael D. Goulder, 'Nicodemus', pp. 155-6; cf. Andrew T. Lincoln, *The Gospel according to Saint John* (London: Continuum, 2005), p. 486.

14. I therefore agree with Wayne A. Meeks that 'ambiguity is doubtless an important and deliberate part of the portrait of this obscure figure' ('Man from Heaven', p. 54) and with Margaret Davies, 'Nicodemus is the only named Character who fails to make a decision' (*Rhetoric and Reference in the Fourth Gospel* [Sheffield: JSOT, 1992], p. 37). *Pace* Michael D. Goulder, 'John's writing is notoriously ambiguous but about Nicodemus I do not think it is as ambiguous as that. An overall view suggests rather that John's attitude to him is solidly negative ...' ('Nicodemus', p. 153) and Colin G. Kruse, '[Nicodemus is] an example of the sort of belief that the evangelist hoped his gospel would evoke in its readers', (*The Gospel According to John* [Leicester: InterVarsity Press, 2003], p. 174). Jouette M. Bassler issues a vital reminder that ambiguity is an aspect of many of the characterizations in John's Gospel and does not make Nicodemus a *tertium quid* in 'Mixed Signals', pp. 635-46.

Against this background, I propose an alternative path to discerning Nicodemus' status with regard to Jesus and those abiding in his love. Although Nicodemus' choices and actions are shrouded in mystery, the evangelist does provide clear descriptions of Nicodemus' identity and location in terms of to whom he relates and who relates to him, that is, the 'others' in his relationships.

Nicodemus is introduced in terms of his relationship as ἄνθρωπος ἐκ τῶν Φαρισαίων (3.1). Note that he is not called ὁ Φαρισαῖος but is identified precisely as a *member* of the Pharisaic group. This description is given even before Nicodemus' name is mentioned and so might be considered a significant aspect of his identity. He is also a leader *with respect to* the Jews (3.1). These same groups will be identified as objects of the disciples' fear, i.e. as 'totally other', in 7.13, 12.42 and 20.19. In their exchange both Jesus and Nicodemus adopt plural pronouns and verbs; this is most starkly illustrated at 3.11 where Jesus says ὃ οἴδαμεν λαλοῦμεν καὶ ὃ ἑωράκαμεν μαρτυροῦμεν, καὶ τὴν μαρτυρίαν ἡμῶν οὐ λαμβάνετε. Jesus and Nicodemus thus become the representatives of two opposing groups; the one speaks about what it knows, the other is ignorant.[15] The former, represented by Jesus, is clearly aligned with the evangelist's own confession (summarily expounded in 3.13-18), whereas the latter, represented by Nicodemus, does not understand and is placed at odds with Jesus and his group. Therefore Jesus questions Nicodemus' status not simply as a teacher but a teacher of *Israel* (3.10). Nicodemus' role as a member of a group again takes precedence over his identity as an individual.

In Chapter 7, Nicodemus is again identified as εἷς ὢν ἐξ αὐτῶν [the Pharisees] but his interaction with them on this occasion drives a wedge between Nicodemus and the Pharisaic group. His question implies the Pharisees' neglect or transgression of the law and, although, as shown above, it is difficult to ascertain how Nicodemus relates to Jesus at this point, it is clear that Nicodemus' question distinguishes him from the Pharisees. The Pharisees themselves confirm this when they ask Μὴ καὶ σὺ ἐκ τῆς Γαλιλαίας εἶ; (7.52). They use 'Galilean' to denote something distinct from themselves and so they expect a negative answer; it is unthinkable that εἷς ὢν ἐξ αὐτῶν is a Galilean. Nicodemus does not represent their opinion but that of a Galilean, i.e. one sympathetic to Jesus. However, just as at 4.12 and 9.40 the evangelist implies an affirmative response to the questions, to which the speakers expect a negative answer; it is possible that Nicodemus, although a Pharisee, may be considered a Galilean. 'Galilean' has *replaced* εἷς ὢν ἐξ αὐτῶν (7.50 cf. 3.1) in the eyes of the evangelist.[16]

---

15. So Raymond E. Brown, *John*, vol. 1, p. 131; Ernst Haenchen, *John*, vol. 1, trans. R. Funk (Philadelphia: Fortress Press, 1984), p. 199; and Andrew T. Lincoln, *Saint John*, pp. 148–9. *Contra* Colin G. Kruse, *John*, p. 109n. 1, who argues that Jesus' plural pronoun denotes him and his father.

16. The respective function and significance of Judea and Galilee or Judeans and Galileans has prompted a good deal of discussion which cannot be rehearsed here. Note, however, the arguments of Jouette M. Bassler, 'The Galileans: A Neglected Factor in Johannine Community Research', *CBQ* 43 (1981), pp. 243–57 (254 and 257), who suggests

Finally in Chapter 19, what is unambiguous is Nicodemus' *association* with a secret disciple. John does not state that he is *himself* a secret disciple but that he accompanies Joseph. The corollary of this is that Nicodemus may certainly not be counted among the Ἰουδαιοι whom Joseph fears (19.38). His relationship with Joseph now prevails over the relationship he had with the Ἰουδαιοι in 3.1 when he was introduced as one of their leaders. It is not clear, however, that becoming a 'secret disciple' (if such Nicodemus is) brings him within the scope of the community subject to Jesus' commandment to 'love one another'. He may be liable to the criticism of 'secret believers' in 12.42-3 that 'they loved human glory more than the glory which came from God' (cf. 7.13 and 9.22).[17] However, Nicodemus and Joseph engage in what must be, to at least some degree, a public act and so have overcome their fear to a greater extent than the disciples who lock their door for fear (20.19). Although, from the evangelist's perspective, it might be overstating the case to claim that Nicodemus is 'one of us', he is now one with Joseph and consequently must have ceased to be 'one of them'.

Concluding Remarks

If the reading I have proposed were translated into the terms concerning love in the Fourth Gospel with which this essay began, we might say that Nicodemus begins as 'totally other', that subject which the Johannine disciples fear; to whom they deny the capacity to love and be loved and with whom they could not or would not engage. In his final appearance, Nicodemus himself has become cut off from these objects of fear; hated and hating subjects. His own fear is now the disciples' fear of the same 'totally other' which, once upon a time, he had related to as 'another' like him. This perspective on John admits the suggestion that, although the categories of 'another' and 'totally other' are stark, they are not static. As one of the Pharisees, Nicodemus represented the 'totally other' which John excluded from love and relationship with the disciples. Yet he was able to leave that category and ally himself with others for whom the Jews remain totally other and the object of fear.

I do not here pretend to do anything as ambitious as to suggest how these observations may contribute to a theology of love but I have been concerned to analyse how the 'otherness' of Nicodemus is to be characterized. Nicodemus' identity in relation to other figures in the gospel is not static. Over the course of his three appearances his human encounters demonstrate, and to some extent *effect*, how he permeates the boundaries between different kinds of 'other'. John's characterization of love would seem at first sight to contradict Jeanrond's claim

---

that in Jn 7.52, 8.48 and 18.5 the epithets 'Galilean', 'Samaritan' and 'Jew' convey primarily symbolic information concerning an individual's response to Jesus. Although 'Galilean' should not be equated with 'disciple' or 'believer', it is generally associated with a positive response to Jesus.

17. So Michael D. Goulder, 'Nicodemus', p. 155.

'Love meets the other where the other is right now and not where we would ideally prefer the other to be'.[18] The recipients of Jesus' command prefer 'another' like them. The figure of Nicodemus, I would tentatively suggest, demonstrates the dynamics of difference: the potential for transforming relationship beyond this sphere of preference. Nicodemus finds relationships beyond others both like and unlike himself, which result in his transformation from identification with John's 'totally other' to recognising a 'totally other' in common with John, and thereby the problematic nature of this very category. It is possible that Nicodemus reflects the potential, as yet unfulfilled, to complete the transformation from John's 'totally other' to 'another' loved and loving recipient of Jesus' new commandment. The figure of Nicodemus perhaps provides a different angle on John's narrowed horizon of love.

---

18. Werner G. Jeanrond, *A Theology of Love*, p. 246.

4

THE BIBLE, *NOSTRA AETATE*, AND THE 'GOOD TEXT-BAD TEXT' HERMENEUTICS[1]

Jesper Svartvik

Werner G. Jeanrond served as Professor of Theology at Lund University from 1995 to 2007. It is a pleasure and a privilege to contribute to this *Festschrift* in honour of him. I have chosen a topic that combines two interests of his (and mine): hermeneutics and post-Vatican II theology.

It is often asserted that what makes the seventeen sentences in the fourth paragraph in *Nostra Aetate* – the Roman Catholic declaration on interreligious relations, adopted 28 October 1965 – so different from Christian declarations previously addressing the topic of Jews and Judaism is that it refers to Rom. 9–11.[2] Previously, allusions to passages in Hebrews had dominated a supersessionist

---

1. An earlier version of this chapter was summarized at the Society of Biblical Literature in Chicago, 17 November 2012. Heartfelt thanks are due to John Borelli, Philip A. Cunningham, Mary C. Boys, Craig R. Koester, Göran Larsson, Svante Lundgren, Michael McGarry, Inger Nebel, Anna Frydenberg, John T. Pawlikowski, Joseph Sievers, and Jakob Wirén for their comments. Many thanks also to Jaya Reddy who has improved my English. I profited considerably from the impressive commentary of Craig R. Koester on Hebrews, especially the extensive introduction, cf. idem, *Hebrews* (New York: Doubleday, 2001), pp. 19–131.

2. Joseph Sievers, '"God's Gifts and Call are Irrevocable": The Interpretation of Rom 11:29 and Its Uses', *Society of Biblical Literature 1997 Seminar Papers* (Atlanta, GA: Scholars Press, 1997), pp. 337–57 (347) asserts that Rom. 11.29 had never been cited in any official Catholic pronouncements before Vatican II. For the turn to Romans, cf. idem, '"God's Gifts and Call are Irrevocable": The Reception of Romans 11.29 through the Centuries and Christian-Jewish Relations', in Cristina Grenholm and Daniel Patte, eds, *Reading Israel in Romans: Legitimacy and Plausibility of Divergent Interpretations* (Harrisburg, PA: Trinity Press International, 2000), pp. 127–73 (158); Petra Heldt, 'Protestant Perspectives after 40 Years: A Critical Assessment of *Nostra Aetate*', in Neville Lamdan and Alberto Melloni, eds, *Nostra Aetate: Origins, Promulgation, Impact on Jewish-Catholic Relations* (Berlin: LIT Verlag, 2007), pp. 163–74 (169); John Connelly, *From Enemy to Brother: The Revolution in Catholic Teaching on the Jews 1933–1965* (Cambridge, MA: Harvard University Press, 2012), pp. 3; 243; 256; 299.

discourse which had presented Christianity as the *verus Israel* that had superseded the *vetus Israel*. Hence, inherently, *verus Israel* was also *versus Israel*: anti-Jewish.[3] Joseph Sievers emphasized the importance of the shift from a discourse of supersessionism to one inspired by Paul's Epistle to the Romans: 'Only under the impact of the onslaught of antisemitism in this century were [the] eyes of Christian theologians … opened to the possibility that Rom. 11.29 … rather than e.g. Heb. 8 might provide a hermeneutical key to better understanding the Jewish people's relations with God and with the Church'.[4] In what follows, I shall address the reception history of Heb. 8.13 ('In speaking of "a new covenant", he has made the first one obsolete. And what is obsolete and growing old will soon disappear'), especially in relation to the remarkable return of Rom. 9–11 in Christian theological treatises on Jews and Judaism.

Romans versus Hebrews: The 'Good Text-Bad Text' Paradigm?

We see here the contours of a phenomenon in the hermeneutical landscape that we might call 'the good text-bad text' paradigm. Like two police officers who choose to play different roles ('good cop-bad cop') in an interrogation, different biblical texts are referred to by different people because they have divergent agendas. When interreligious interactions are debated, some refer to Rom. 9–11 (especially Rom. 11.29), while others prefer to quote Heb. 8 (especially Heb. 8.13).

Unquestionably, Hebrews has often been a stumbling block. The examples are legion, but one may suffice here: Earl S. Johnson, Jr., who in his commentary on Hebrews opens his analysis of Heb. 8 by stating that it 'serves as a kind of center point for the letter', concludes his analysis by pronouncing a surprisingly stern verdict on the covenantal commitment:[5] 'The old covenant that demanded absolute obedience to the Hebrew law … is no longer operative. It is *obsolete* … God will make all things new (Isa. 43.19; Rev. 21.5). Do you not see it?'[6] What is striking is that Johnson is referring to the penultimate chapter in the last book of the Bible, a chapter which is discussing eschatological expectations. Hence what is being compared in the book of Revelation is obviously not the old covenant

---

3. On the history of Christian anti-Judaism, cf. Edward H. Flannery, *The Anguish of the Jews: Twenty-Three Centuries of Antisemitism* (New York: Stimulus, 1995); James Carroll, *Constantine's Sword: The Church and the Jews* (Boston: Houghton Mifflin, 2001); Robert Michael, *A History of Catholic Antisemitism: The Dark Side of the Church* (New York: Palgrave Macmillan, 2008) and also Paul O'Shea, *A Cross Too Heavy: Pope Pius XII and the Jews of Europe* (New York: Palgrave Macmillan, 2011), pp. 27–51.

4. Joseph Sievers, '"God's Gifts and Call are Irrevocable": The Interpretation of Rom 11:29 and Its Uses', p. 356.

5. Earl S. Johnson, Jr., *Hebrews* (Louisville: Westminster John Knox Press, 2008), p. 38.

6. Ibid., p. 43. It would be interesting to explore whether a touch of a disconcerting theological *Schadenfreude* is discernible here.

and the new covenant, nor the Old Testament and the New Testament.[7] What the author of Revelation is comparing is this world and the world to come. Although Johnson seems to think that he is describing the old covenant when using words like 'obsolete' or 'old', he is actually referring to this world. We will return to this observation below. Suffice it now to point out that it is rewarding to seek to unveil veiled eschatological motifs in the interpretations of Hebrews.

The Entstehungsgeschichte *of* Nostra Aetate

Nostra Aetate is the shortest of the documents of Vatican II, but its genesis is the most tortuous of them all. The story of how *Nostra Aetate* was written has been told many times.[8] Many contributed to the writing, but at the very centre we find three people: Jules Isaac, a Jew who lost his family in the *Shoah*; the Jesuit Cardinal Augustin Bea; and Angelo Giuseppe Roncalli, Pope John XXIII.

Elected Pope, in 1959 John XXIII proclaimed that there would be a Second Vatican Council. In 1960, he formed a Secretariat for Christian Unity as a preparatory body for this Council. Cardinal Bea was elected president.[9] John Borelli argues that it was only after Jules Isaac visited John XXIII on 13 June 1960 that the Pope was convinced Vatican II should address Catholic-Jewish relations.[10] In other words, we have reason to assert that the month of June in 1960 was *the* decisive moment for a Catholic *Decretum de Judaeis*, which is to say the turning point for Christian theology in general.

---

7. For illuminating perspectives on the expression 'Satan's Synagogue' in Revelation, cf. David Frankfurter, 'Jews or Not? Reconstructing the "Other" in Rev 2:9 and 3:9', *Harvard Theological Review* 94 (2001), pp. 403-25.

8. Cf. Augustin Bea, 'The Church and the Non-Christian Religions', *The Month* (January 1966), pp. 10-20; Guiseppe Alberigo, *A Brief History of Vatican II*, trans. M. Sherry (Maryknoll, NY: Orbis, 2006), pp. 105-6; Thomas Stransky, 'The Genesis of *Nostra Aetate*: An Insider's Story', in Neville Lamdan and Alberto Melloni, eds, *Nostra Aetate*, pp. 29-53; John Connelly, *From Enemy to Brother*, pp. 239-72. Cf. Thomas Stransky, 'The Foundation of the Secretariat for Promoting Christian Unity', in Alberic Stacpoole, ed., *Vatican II by Those Who Were There* (London: Geoffrey Chapman, 1986) pp. 62-87; Johannes Willebrands, 'Christians and Jews: A New Vision', in Alberic Stacpoole, ed., *Vatican II by Those Who Were There*, pp. 220-36. Also cf. Edward I. Cassidy, *Ecumenism and Interreligious Dialogue: Unitatis Redintegratio, Nostra Aetate* (New York: Paulist Press, 2005), pp. 126-8.

9. Cf. Thomas Stransky, 'The Foundation of the Secretariat for Promoting Christian Unity', pp. 62-87. Connelly argues that Augustin Bea was 'an instrument of change and not a source of ideas', John Connelly, *From Enemy to Brother*, p. 268.

10. John Borelli, 'Vatican II: Preparing the Catholic Church for Dialogue. Reflections Approaching the Fiftieth Anniversary of the Council'. (www.nwcu.org/2012%20 Workshop/2012Documents/JohnBorelli-NWCU2012Keynote.pdf, accessed 26 September 2014), p. 14. Cf. Marco Morselli, 'Jules Isaac and the Origins of *Nostra Aetate*', in Neville Lamdan and Alberto Melloni, eds, *Nostra Aetate*, pp. 21-8.

What made June 1960 the decisive moment in time? Borelli points out that there were only a few writings on Jews and Judaism in the first fifteen years after the *Shoah*. However, that would change drastically with the trial of Adolf Eichmann.[11] The trial was widely broadcast; Eichmann's role and responsibility in the *Shoah* were vigorously discussed, as was Hannah Arendt's report on 'the banality of evil'.[12] Hence, the earliest stages of the Catholic document on Jewish-Christian relations coincided with the Eichmann trial. Is the simultaneity of the trial and the preparations for Vatican II at least part of the answer to the question of the *Entstehungsgeschichte* of *Nostra Aetate*? There were six drafts of *Nostra Aetate*. When the first five versions were discussed, the political corollaries were a recurring feature. In the Middle East all politics are theological and all theology is political. Hence, there was pressure from Arab countries that were apprehensive about a statement that might recognize the State of Israel.[13] This was the reason for the document's avoidance of the word 'Israel'. Instead of 'Israel', the expression 'Abraham's stock' (*stirps Abrahae*) is used. It is a phrase that had been common for a long time in Christian texts. However, this term unquestionably has its deficiencies, as numerous Muslims also see themselves as the stock of Abraham.

We have no indications that Heb. 8.13 was ever at the centre of the discussions when drafting *Nostra Aetate*. Borelli, who has been extraordinarily helpful when this contribution was drafted, recently wrote to me:

> In none of the materials available ... was there ever any mention of the Letter to the Hebrews, especially as a passage that needed to be addressed. ... I actually think what happened was more along the lines of the development that John Connelly has outlined in his recent book, *From Enemy to Brother*, that a growing number of theologians ... began to see during the course of the war ... the grave effects of the church's teaching.[14]

Hence, in the preparations for *Nostra Aetate*, Hebrews was seen as a stumbling block, not a stepping stone for improved interreligious relations.

The Return of Hebrews in Contemporary Nostra Aetate *Assessments*

The polarization of biblical usage that we have described seems to be growing in intensity. One example is a series of articles by the late Avery Cardinal Dulles, in which he argued in favour of a mission to the Jews – based on Hebrews. The *Sitz*

---

11. John Borelli, 'Vatican II', p. 16.
12. Hannah Arendt, *Eichmann in Jerusalem: A Report on the Banality of Evil* (New York: Penguin, 1963). Cf. Seyla Benhabib, 'Arendt's *Eichmann in Jerusalem*', in Dana Villa, ed., *The Cambridge Companion to Hannah Arendt* (Cambridge: Cambridge University Press, 2000), pp. 65–85.
13. Cf. John Connelly, *From Enemy to Brother*, p. 249.
14. John Borelli in private correspondence (24 September 2012).

im Leben for his articles was the release of *Reflections on Covenant and Mission* in 2002.[15] The document was part of the consultations between the National Council of Synagogues and the Catholic Bishops' Committee on Ecumenical and Interreligious Affairs in the USA.[16] In 'Covenant and Mission' Cardinal Dulles criticized *Reflections on Covenant and Mission* for not stating what he took to be 'the Christian position on the meaning of Christ for Judaism'. He refers to Heb. 8.13:

> The most formal statement on the status of the Sinai covenant under Christianity appears in the Letter to the Hebrews, which points out that in view of the new covenant promised by God through the prophet Jeremiah, the first covenant is 'obsolete' ... Christ, we are told, 'abolishes the first [covenant] in order to establish the second' (Heb. 10.9).[17]

Three years later, the Cardinal stated that the Vatican II 'left open the question whether the Old Covenant remains in force today'.[18] Once again, his proof text is Hebrews:

> The Letter to the Hebrews contains ... a lengthy discussion of the two covenants based on the two priesthoods ... The Old Law, with its priesthood and Temple sacrifices, has been superseded and abolished by the coming of the New. ... The Letter to the Hebrews, which is essentially a treatise on priesthood, teaches that with the cessation of the Levitical priesthood and the Temple sacrifices, the Old Testament is to that extent superseded.[19]

One is taken aback when the Cardinal describes his theological musings in the following way: 'Without any pretence of giving a final solution [*sic!*] I shall try to indicate some elements of a tenable Catholic position'.[20] It is indeed baffling that

---

15. 'Reflections on Covenant and Mission: Consultation of the National Council of Synagogues and the Bishop's Committee for Ecumenical and Interreligious Affairs', https://www.bc.edu/dam/files/research_sites/cjl/texts/cjrelations/resources/documents/interreligious/ncs_usccb120802.htm, accessed 26 September 2014.

16. Connelly wrongly asserts that the study document was drafted by three members of the Christian Scholars group on Christian-Jewish Relations: Mary C. Boys, Philip A. Cunningham, and John T. Pawlikowski, cf. John Connelly, 'The Catholic Church and Mission to the Jews', in James L. Heft, ed., *After Vatican II: Trajectories and Hermeneutics* (Grand Rapids: Eerdmans, 2012), pp. 96–133 (116–17). Far from being a text written by three individuals, *Reflections on Covenant and Mission* was a product of the Secretariat for Ecumenical and Interreligious Affairs.

17. Avery Dulles, 'Covenant and Mission', *America* 187/12 (2002), pp. 8–11 (9).

18. Avery Dulles, 'The Covenant with Israel', *First Things* 157 (2005), pp. 16–21 (16).

19. Ibid., p. 18. Less baffling but still surprising is that he refers to Adam and Eve as 'our first parents', p. 16.

20. Ibid., p. 20.

he actually used those two notorious words when addressing the issue in a way that cannot be described as anything but a disparaging of Judaism.

Mary C. Boys, Philip A. Cunningham and John T. Pawlikowski responded. Stating that they are 'troubled by Cardinal Dulles's assertion that the Letter to the Hebrews offers "the most formal statement of the status of the Sinai Covenant under Christianity"', they argue that 'official Catholic teaching today has, in the Biblical Commission's 1993 formulation, "gone its own way" and "set aside" the opinion of the author of Hebrews about Israel's covenant'.[21] In other words, they maintain that it is not in accordance with Catholic hermeneutics to appeal to Hebrews in this way when discussing Jewish-Christian relations. They describe Hebrews as a stumbling block.

Hebrews: Is it really the 'Bad Text'?

We have seen that Hebrews is hardly ever referred to by Christians who want to promote a genuine dialogue with Jews and Judaism. However, I would like to challenge the interpretation that Hebrews cannot serve as a facilitator for constructive conversations. I argue that by presenting Romans as the solution to the plight of Jewish-Christian relations, the polyphony in Hebrews has been silenced far too often. Hence, I seek to demonstrate that Hebrews might *also* – or should we say *instead*? – be understood as a stepping stone. I wish to assert that the Romans-versus-Hebrews dichotomy prevents a renewed perspective on Hebrews to flourish, similar to the renowned and recognized 'new perspective' on Paul. In fact, one easily sees the similarities between the Romans-versus-Hebrews tensions and 'the Jewish Jesus who remained within second temple Judaism' versus 'the Christian Paul who converted to Christianity' assumptions in twentieth-century scholarship.[22] The new perspective on Pauline scholarship could thrive only when this false bipartition was abandoned.

The debate between Dulles, on the one hand, and Boys, Cunningham and Pawlikowski, on the other, on Heb. 8.13 is of course not the only instance where Hebrews has played a predominant role in discussions on how Christian theology is to be articulated. Might one say that, in many circles, Hebrews is still understood as the oldest systematic theological treatise – as the first church statement

---

21. Mary C. Boys, Philip A. Cunningham and John T. Pawlikowski, 'Theology's "Sacred Obligation": A Reply to Cardinal Avery Dulles on Evangelization', *America* 187/12 (2002), pp. 11–16 (13).

22. Cf. Daniel R. Langton, 'Paul in Jewish Thought', in Amy-Jill Levine and Marc Z. Brettler, eds, *Jewish Annotated New Testament* (Oxford: Oxford University Press, 2011), pp. 585–7; and also idem, *The Apostle Paul in the Jewish Imagination: A Study in Modern Jewish-Christian Relations* (Cambridge: Cambridge University Press, 2010). On the issue of Paul, cf. John G. Gager, 'Paul, the Apostle of Judaism', in Paula Fredriksen and Adele Reinhartz, eds, *Jesus, Judaism, and Christian Anti-Judaism* (Louisville: Westminster John Knox Press, 2002), pp. 56–76 (56 and 64).

– rather than as a text written within a specific historical context, the fall of the second temple?[23] Eventually, the 'good text-bad text' hermeneutics prevents the emergence of post-supersessionist readings of Hebrews.

Two Trajectories in the Reception History of Hebrews

Hebrews, described by Pamela Eisenbaum as 'the most mysterious text to have been preserved in the NT canon', has had a most interesting *Wirkungsgeschichte*.[24] I cannot possibly do justice to twenty centuries of interpretations here. Hence, I will focus on two very distinct and different readings of Hebrews: the *polemical* trajectory and the *parenetical* trajectory.

The first Trajectory: Polemics and Supersessionism

In *Die Mystik des Apostels Paulus* Albert Schweitzer uses the expressions *Hauptkrater* and *Nebenkrater* when describing two motifs in Pauline theology: *Erlösungsmystik*, which Schweitzer argues is the centre of Paul's thinking, and the motif of justification, which is similar to a subsidiary crater within the main crater.[25] As I have been using the expression 'trajectory', the word *Hauptkrater* might be fitting when describing the consequences of the first trajectory, which was launched early on in the history of Christianity. It is fuelled by the interest of the anonymous author of Hebrews in comparing reality and shadows of reality. As a matter of fact, the word 'better' occurs nineteen times in the New Testament, and thirteen of these instances we find in Hebrews. Hebrews uses the word more often than all other New Testament texts together. John F. A. Sawyer concludes that Hebrews 'seeks to demonstrate the superiority of Christianity to all other varieties of Judaism'.[26]

We all know the damage this trajectory has caused, so it may suffice to quote but one text. This passage can be found in the commentary on Hebrews by Erik Heen and Philip D. W. Krey.[27] The example is taken from *Homilies on the Gospels* written by the Venerable Bede (672–735):

23. The apocalyptical context of the text is noticed in Robert P. Gordon's, *Hebrews* (Sheffield: Sheffield Phoenix Press, 2008), p. 114. Cf. Morna D. Hooker, 'Christ, the "End" of the Cult', in idem, *The Epistle to the Hebrews and Christian Theology* (Grand Rapids: Eerdmans, 2009), pp. 189–212 (207).

24. Pamela Eisenbaum, 'Locating Hebrews within the Literary Landscape of Christian Origins', in Gabriella Gelardini, ed., *Hebrews: Contemporary Methods, New Insights* (Leiden: Brill, 2005), pp. 213–37 (213).

25. Albert Schweitzer, *Die Mystik des Apostels Paulus* (Tübingen: Mohr Siebeck, 1930).

26. John F. A. Sawyer, 'Hebrews, Letter to the', in idem, ed., *A Concise Dictionary of the Bible and Its Reception* (Louisville: Westminster John Knox Press, 2009), p. 110.

27. Erik Heen and Philip D. W. Krey, *Hebrews* (Downers Grove, IL: InterVarsity, 2005), pp. 123–30.

For 'what is becoming obsolete and growing old is ready to vanish away [Heb. 8.13]'. And what does it mean that our Lord's precursor came from a father who was mute, a leader of the priests of that time? Is it not that, by the time our Lord appeared, the tongue of the ancient priesthood had to large extent become mute as regards the spiritual sense of the law's teaching, since the scribes and those learned in the law were only concerned with teaching the keeping of the letter of the law? Moreover, in a number of instances, they were even falsifying the letter of the law by substituting their own traditions, as is proven by our Lord's having rebuked them more than once in the Gospels. And what does it mean that he was born to a barren mother? Is it not that the law, which was ordered to beget spiritual issue for God with the help of the priestly office, led no one to perfection, undoubtedly because it was unable to open up the gates of the kingdom to its followers?[28]

Still using the belligerent metaphors, we see here how Heb. 8.13 serves as a launching pad for a teaching of contempt. We need not dwell on this interpretation of Hebrews, as the reading and the reading's consequences are notorious. Suffice it to assert that it has shaped Christian teaching on Jews and Judaism over two millennia. What about the alternative?

The Second Trajectory: Parenesis and Pilgrimage

The second reading is not as well-known, which might strike us as somewhat peculiar since its adherents are distinguished. It is quite different in tone and tenor, describing life as a pilgrimage toward the City of God.[29] Although it has not been so prominent in history, we see it surfacing from time to time. What makes such a surfacing possible? One interesting example is Origen's *On the First Principles*:

The apostle says with reference to the law that they who have circumcision in the flesh 'serve as the copy and shadow of heavenly things [Heb. 8.5]'. And in another place, 'is not our life on earth a shadow? [Job 8.9]' If then both the law that is on the earth is a 'shadow' and all our life that is on earth is the same, and we live among nations under the 'shadow of Christ', we must consider whether the truth of all these shadows will be learned in that revelation when, no longer 'through a mirror and darkly', but 'face to face [1 Cor. 13.12]' all the saints

---

28. Beda Venerabilis, *Homilies on the Gospels* 2.20, quoted in Erik Heen and Philip D. W. Krey, *Hebrews*, p. 128.

29. The pilgrimage motif is discussed by Andrew Lincoln, *Hebrews: A Guide* (London: Continuum/T&T Clark, 2006), p. 107 and Craig R. Koester, *Hebrews*, p. 29. For exegetical surveys of the pilgrimage terminology in Heb., cf. Jon Laansma, *'I Will Give You Rest': The Rest Motif in the New Testament with Special Reference to Mt 11 and Heb 3–4* (Tübingen: Mohr Siebeck, 1997); and Judith Hoch Wray, *Rest as a Theological Metaphor in the Epistle to the Hebrews and the Gospel of Truth: Early Christian Homiletics of Rest* (Atlanta, GA: Scholars Press, 1998).

shall be counted worthy to behold the glory of God and the causes and truth of things. And the pledge of this truth being already received through the Holy Spirit, the apostle said, 'Even if we have known Christ after the flesh, yet now henceforth we know him no more'.[30]

When quoting Job 8.9 Origen does not apply it to Israel as a theological rival but includes himself. The foci in this interpretation are Heb. 11.13 and 13.14: we are *all* pilgrims upon earth. In the words of Marie E. Isaacs, 'the promised land (see 6.5; 12.22), the new covenant remains part of our author's vision of the future. However imminent, that future has yet to be achieved. For the present it is experienced by the believer as hope'.[31]

In 'Reading Hebrews without Presupposing Supersessionism', I discuss this future-oriented interpretation of Hebrews, which has been proposed by Ernst Käsemann, William G. Johnsson, and more recently also by Richard B. Hays.[32] The implied readers of Hebrews are no less a wandering people than the people of Israel.[33]

Many interpreters read the New Testament through the lens of a limited number of verses, which are understood to be programmatic. One of these paradigmatic statements is Heb. 8.13, which, according to most interpreters, declares that with the advent of Christianity God has terminated the old covenant with the Jewish people. However, in 'Reading the Epistle to the Hebrews without Presupposing Supersessionism', I show that there are no grounds for such sweeping statements. It is possible and plausible that what the author of Hebrews actually compares and contrasts are the earthly world and the heavenly world, and – to a middle Platonist such as the author of Hebrews – heaven always trumps earth. The metaphorical discourse of Hebrews is directed towards the future. What is being compared is not the new covenant and the old covenant, but rather the old world and the new world, heaven and earth. These circumstances should be taken into consideration by those who refer to Hebrews to find arguments in favour of a supersessionist understanding of Christianity.

---

30. Origen, *On the First Principles* 2.6.7, quoted in Erik Heen and Philip D. W. Krey, *Hebrews*, p. 125.

31. Marie E. Isaacs, *Reading Hebrews and James: A Literary and Theological Commentary* (Macon, GA: Smyth & Helwys, 2002), p. 109.

32. Ernst Käsemann, *The Wandering People of God: An Investigation of the Letter to the Hebrews*, trans. R. A. Harrisville and I. L. Sandberg (Minneapolis: Augsburg, 1984); William G. Johnsson, 'The Pilgrimage Motif in the Book of Hebrews', *Journal of Biblical Literature* 97/2 (1978), pp. 239–51; Richard B. Hays, '"Here We Have No Lasting City": New Covenantalism in Hebrews', in Richard Bauckham et al., eds, *The Epistle to the Hebrews and Christian Theology* (Grand Rapids: Eerdmans, 2009), pp. 151–73; and Jesper Svartvik, 'Reading the Epistle to the Hebrews without Presupposing Supersessionism', in Philip A. Cunningham et al., eds, *Christ Jesus and the Jewish People Today: New Explorations of Theological Interrelationships* (Grand Rapids: Eerdmans, 2011), pp. 77–91.

33. Richard B. Hays, '"Here We Have No Lasting City"', p. 166-7.

Conclusion: 'A New Vision for Christian-Jewish Relations'

In an unsurpassed way, *Nostra Aetate* tackled the sources of Christian teaching of contempt, the consequences of which had afflicted the Jewish people in the Christian world. By voting in favour of *Nostra Aetate* the Council Fathers allowed themselves to be inspired by the covenantal language of Rom. 9–11 rather than a notoriously polemical reading of Heb. 8. Pawlikowski asserts that thereby they stated that 'everything that had been said about the Christian-Jewish relationship since Paul moved in a direction they could no longer support'.[34] Few would disagree with Pawlikowski: *Nostra Aetate* is the result of a journey on a road less travelled in history. However, one might ask, if by choosing to ignore the legacy of Heb. 8, the council fathers facilitated the wandering for those who prefer to keep following the road *more* travelled in history, those who programmatically question the validity of the Jewish covenant.[35]

In short, by saying nothing, the Council Fathers made it possible for others to keep on saying something – and many would argue that that 'something' is different from what the Council wanted.[36] This is why Connelly writes that the prehistory of *Nostra Aetate* is a 'lost story worth recovering, because the theologians at Vatican II rehearsed many of the points that have been debated in recent years'.[37] Connelly has pointed out that what is still lacking in Jewish-Christian relations is what he calls 'a new vision'.[38] I suggest that a non-polemical and parenetical reading of Hebrews and its pilgrimage motif might foster such a new vision. Nothing suggests that the readers of the epistle are any less a wandering people than the people of Israel.

---

34. John T. Pawlikowski, 'Reflections on Covenant and Mission Forty Years after *Nostra Aetate*', *Crosscurrents* 56/4 (2007), pp. 70–94 (71).

35. Ibid., p. 94n. 49.

36. Philip A. Cunningham, 'Official Ecclesial Documents to Implement Vatican II on Relations with Jews: Study Them, Become Immersed in Them, and Put Them into Practice', *Studies in Christian-Jewish Relations* 4 (2009), pp. 1–36.

37. John Connelly, 'The Catholic Church and the Mission to the Jews', in James L. Heft and John O'Malley, eds, *After Vatican II: Trajectories and Hermeneutics* (Grand Rapids: Eerdmans, 2012), pp. 96–133 (97).

38. Ibid., p. 132.

5

THE ALTERITY OF THE LETTER REVELATION IN *DEI VERBUM*

Olivier Riaudel

My reflections are born out of astonishment. As a student, I was astonished to discover that the First Vatican Council was the first council to use the concept of revelation, and that the term was only employed once at the Council of Trent. The astonishment which caused me to wonder – naïvely, but sincerely – how it was possible to do theology without 'revelation' has remained with me since my first year of theology.[1] This very astonishment has recently found a more elaborated expression thanks to François Nault's 'Révélation sans théologie, théologie sans révélation' which exposes the alternative between the 'two possibilities that the very text of *Dei Verbum* contains …, and in relation to which one seems obliged to *choose*: the possibility of a (theo*logical*) revelation without hermeneutics and the possibility of a (hermeneutical) theo*logy* which can do without the concept of revelation'.[2] Nault suggests a switch to the question of *text*.[3] 'Moving from a *revelational* paradigm to a *textual* paradigm, to put it rather briefly, does not necessarily mean to reject the logic of *Dei Verbum*, but certainly calls for an awareness of the limits of that conciliar document'.[4]

The following study essentially consists of a commentary on Nault's suggestion to move on to a *textual* paradigm. I argue that *Dei Verbum* does not leave enough room for a reflection on the letter when examining the Word of God. Yet, underlining the importance of the letter does not necessarily lead us to move on to a textual paradigm. By taking up the terms of Nault's alternative (the possibility

---

1. For a critique of the ubiquitous utilization of the concept of revelation in theology cf. Werner G. Jeanrond, 'Revelation and the Trinitarian Concept of God: Are they Key Concepts for Theological Thought?', Concilium 1 (2001), pp. 120–30.

2. François Nault, 'Révélation sans théologie, théologie sans révélation', in Philippe Bordeyne and Laurent Villemin, eds, *Vatican II et la théologie: Perspectives pour le XXIe siècle* (Paris: Éditions du Cerf, 2006), pp. 127–52 (128). If not stated otherwise, translations from the French are my own.

3. Ibid., p. 147.

4. Ibid., pp. 147–8.

of a theological revelation without hermeneutics and the possibility of a hermeneutical theology without revelation), it seems to me that the difficulty we may encounter when comparing the text of *Dei Verbum* with the practice of theology as it exists today consists precisely in the development of a hermeneutics for the theology of revelation which *Dei Verbum* proposes. Whatever else the excellent developments of *Dei Verbum* in interpreting the scriptures may be, the theology of revelation which it develops does not acknowledge the problem raised by the interpretation of scripture, because it does not take the hermeneutical questions of the letter, the text, and the interpreter of the text sufficiently into account.[5]

The Bipartition of Dei Verbum

The first clue to the difficulty of *Dei Verbum* lies in its structure. The text's bipartition has often been noted, a symptom of its management by two sub-commissions: one dealing with revelation, one dealing with scripture. In my view, the bipartition is telling as to the difficulty of this text because it leads to a reflection on revelation without dealing immediately with scripture. Fictional theology is not a very reassuring genre, but if we were allowed a moment of indulgence into fiction, we could very well imagine what questions would have been answered by a dogmatic constitution which would have dealt with the interpretation of the Bible. What would such a constitution have asked about what we call 'revelation'? But let us stop fiction here. Christoph Theobald explains how the bipartition was organized: 'In October 1964, Monsignor van Dodewaard summarized the relationship of the two parts: after having treated the relations between scripture and tradition, attention was focused on scripture *itself*, "which, according to the council's orientation, must be approached not only from the doctrinal angle, but also ... in its pastoral aspect"'.[6] It is the question of the relation between scripture and tradition. Hence, the centre of the constitution involves overcoming a theory of two sources through a new approach to revelation.

The Bible as Literature

However, there is a fundamental question which the constitution not only does not approach, but also does not allow us to approach: what is the hermeneutical principle of our interpretation of the Bible? We can of course cite *Dei Verbum* 12: 'Holy Scripture must be ... interpreted in the sacred Spirit in which it was written'. Yet this assertion, quite right in itself, is more an explanation of what the

---

5. These questions are addressed in Werner G. Jeanrond, *Theological Hermeneutics: Development and Significance* (London: SCM Press, 2004), pp. 78–119.

6. Christoph Theobald, 'L'Église sous la Parole de Dieu', in Giuseppe Alberigo, ed., *Histoire du Concile Vatican II (1959–1965)*, vol. 5 (Paris: Éditions du Cerf, 2005), p. 342.

interpretation of the Bible seeks to be than an explanation of the principle which organizes such an interpretation.

Noting that *Dei Verbum* provides no criteria for determining the sense of scripture,[7] Eugen Schlink regretted the hasty integration of scripture into the Church's Magisterium because of the absence of any reflection on a counterpoint between scripture and church: 'For a non-Catholic, it thus seems that the Council's principles concerning the relationship between Scripture, Tradition and Magisterium are in many regards a more apologetic than a dogmatic presentation'.[8] Accordingly, the presentations describe more what ought to be than what is: 'They are established in order to defend the Roman Church's identity with itself and its possibilities of future development. But, at the same time, in a way which does not appear clearly and distinctly, they subject the Church and its Magisterium to a normative "counterpoint", namely the historical apostolic tradition'.[9] The absence of the letter, however, signals a lack of alterity in the conception of revelation: nothing reminds us of what – by definition – resists a harmonization of the letter and the meaning. Consequently, nothing reminds us of the difference between revelation and church, between scripture and magisterium. Yet, beyond the ecumenical difficulty, three other problems arise.

First of all, concern for a canonical interpretation supposes the idea that all scripture is a symphony. However, modern criticism insists on plurality: the plurality of the theologies in-between and even in each book. Any interpretation which considers the Bible to be *one* book is likely to be seen as an authoritarian power play. For example, Northrop Frye wrote that

> 'the Bible' has traditionally been read as a unity, and has influenced Western imagination as a unity. It exists if only because it has been compelled to exist. Yet whatever the external reasons, there has to be some internal basis even for a compulsory existence. Those who do succeed in reading the Bible from beginning to end will discover that at least it has a beginning and an end, and some traces of a total structure.[10]

The Bible's unity is affirmed in advance, masking the alterity of the texts composing it.

The second difficulty can be seen in rereading the first paragraph of *Dei Verbum* 12: 'However, since God speaks in Sacred Scripture through men in human fashion, the interpreter of Sacred Scripture, in order to see clearly what God wanted to communicate to us, should carefully investigate what meaning

---

7. Eugen Schlink, 'Écriture, Tradition et Magistère selon la constitution *Dei Verbum*', in Bernard D. Dupuy, ed., *Vatican II La Révélation divine*, vol. 2 (Paris: Éditions du Cerf, 1968), pp. 499–511 (506).

8. Ibid., p. 507.

9. Ibid.

10. Northrop Frye, *The Great Code: the Bible and Literature, Collected Works of Northrop Frye*, vol. 19, ed. A. A. Lee (Toronto: University of Toronto Press, 2006), pp. 6–7.

the sacred writers really intended, and what God wanted to manifest by means of their words'.

It seems to me that we must contest the identification of 'what God wanted to communicate to us' and what 'the sacred writers really intended' with what is authentically interpreted by the Church's Magisterium. What is absent here is the letter of the biblical text. According to *Dei Verbum*, we are to reduce the sense of a text to the writer's intention, and we are to determine this sense by ignoring the alterity of the letter and the plurality of its interpretations. Moreover, the *Catechism of the Catholic Church* goes further in developing a possible interpretation of *Dei Verbum* 12, stating that 'Sacred Scripture is written principally in the Church's heart rather than in documents'.[11] Accordingly, the sense of sacred scripture would be accessible without the letter. Ignorance of the Bible as literature could not be better expressed. 'Literature', comes from *littera*, letter, a discourse in which the resources of language are implemented to produce effects on the recipient, thus exceeding the function of communicating information. Hence, to call for the letter of God's Word to be taken into account means to stress the literary quality of the Bible.

Thirdly, it seems to me that what is underlying these difficulties is what has been marked as a major advancement in *Dei Verbum*: a theology of self-revelation, God's revelation of God's self. But the insistence on the *Selbst* of the *Selbstoffenbarung* ignores the *différance* which delays the identification of self with self, as Jacques Derrida stresses.[12] How can we talk about a *Selbstoffenbarung* of God in the biblical texts, read in human (and often all too human) institutions, if not by reflecting on what *is given in the sign*, in the letter, in the institution?

The Limits of Interpretation

What is the hermeneutical principle of our interpretation of the Bible? What leads theologians to prioritize *these* texts over *those* texts? Is the principle for such a priority provided by the Bible? If so, is the principle provided by the unity of meaning produced by the closing of the canon, its articulation, between the Old and the New Testament? Or is it provided by a canon within the canon? What leads us to prioritizing such a canon? Or does the principle of interpretation lie outside of the text? Is it a referent to which we are sent by the text? Is the referent provided by the Christian community, by its tradition or traditions?[13]

Through the concept of tradition, capitalized or decapitalized, *Dei Verbum* avoids the theory of the two sources of Revelation. However, it cannot answer the question of the principle of our interpretation. Both the text and the reader of the text are absent from the constitution. The fact that *Dei Verbum* construes

---

11. *Catechism of the Catholic Church* (London: Continuum, 1994), p. 31.
12. Cf. Jaques Derrida, *De la grammatologie* (Paris: Editions de Minuit, 1967).
13. These questions are addressed in Werner G. Jeanrond, *Theological Hermeneutics*, pp. 159–82.

'revelation' first and foremost under the category of 'word' makes its articulation in terms of a reflection on the letter difficult. As Christoph Theobald points out: '*Dei Verbum* provides no indications as to the *concrete access of man today to Revelation or the Word of God*'.[14] Theobald reflects on the plausibility and the credibility of the category of revelation, stressing the *relationship* which can be established between the Nazarene and the women and men whose paths he crossed.[15] However, hermeneutically, the mediations by which 'revelation' is perceived and received are crucial. Yet, these mediations are indeed the reason for controversy.[16] Not only did these mediations cause difficulty in the formulation of the document, but the Constitution also struggled to articulate the relation between theology and history. In *Dei Verbum* 8/2, history is evoked to state that 'there is a growth in the understanding of the ... words which have been handed down', demonstrating that the question was much more one of developing and defining dogma than one of the development of interpretations according to their respective historical contexts.

A theology of self-revelation runs the risk of taking the letter of the scriptures as a pure mediation, a pure mediation which would preserve the identity of the giver and the gift. However, we cannot afford to ignore Georg F. W. Hegel's reflections on mediation. Hegel is undoubtedly *the* thinker of mediation. In the introduction to *The Phenomenology of Spirit*, he affirms that the absolute cannot be captured by means of thought, like a bird can be caught by a lime stick.[17] For Hegel, mediation does not introduce a third; rather, it is the internal and immanent deployment of a thing's identity to itself. Talking about mediation is to deny immediacy (not equality) to the self. Accordingly, mediation never constitutes an obstacle to identity – identity instead of alterity.

Here, Derrida's reflections on scripture come in. Classically, the sense of scripture would be to represent the language, the spoken language. Hence, the sign is allotted the function of referral: the sign replaces the thing in its absence, awaiting the thing's return. This is where Derrida's concept of *différance* intervenes. Because mediation is always mediatized by a sign, presence is deferred

---

14. Christoph Theobald, '*Dans les traces...*' *de la constitution* 'Dei Verbum'*... du concile Vatican II: Bible, théologie et practiques de lecture* (Paris: Édition du Cerf, 2009), p. 12.

15. Ibid., p. 27.

16. Today, the question of the 'the spirit' of the Second Vatican Council is asked again and again, sometimes with sarcasm as to the existence of such a 'spirit'. For interpreters of my generation, born after the Council, it seems to me that a useful way of approaching the 'spirit' consists in studying the drafting and the drafts of the texts. Studying the history of texts allows us to shed light on the processes of articulation and formulation, and these processes provide us with a relatively clear assessment of what might have been the Council's 'spirit'. However, if we approach the 'spirit' of the Second Vatican Council through the history of the drafting of the texts, we must recognize that there is more in the history of the text than in the text itself.

17. Georg F. W. Hegel, *Phänomenologie des Geistes, Gesammelte Werke*, vol. 9, ed. W. Bonsiepen and R. Heede (Hamburg: Meiner, 1980), p. 53.

again and again. 'The epoch of the sign is essentially theological' states Derrida, critiquing the classical distinction of the sign into signifier and signified.[18] Why? Because such a clear-cut distinction between signifier and signified supposes the possibility of thinking of a signified as a signified – pure presence – *before* the signified's 'fall' into a system of signifiers. Derrida problematizes the hermetic distinction between signifier and signified, and the sign's function of referral and representation of the referent. He proposes a concept of writing which captures the impossibility of stopping the chain of signification: stopping with a signified which is not a signifier. We are referred from sign to sign, with each signified being a signifier for a signified – *'différance'*. What the detour through Derrida allows us to see is the risk involved in any interpretation.[19] Writing is abandoned by its author, deprived of the assistance of a word which might specify what the author wanted to say. It is subjected to various interpretations. As Martin Luther lamented, scripture has a wax nose.[20]

The Limits of Divine Condescension

Theobald concisely and cogently presented the key question which is at the origin of the crisis in biblical interpretation since the Enlightenment:

> As for *interpretation*, first and foremost it should be noted that the biblical 'crisis' of modernity appeared at the weak point of the patristic and medieval system of spiritual interpretation of the Scriptures. Whereas the Fathers had a quiet conviction as to the literal sense of the text, critical exegesis opens a rift in the relation between the *facts* and the *writings*.[21]

Hence, the crisis of interpretation was triggered by calling the literal sense into question. However, the crisis cannot be solved by conceptualizing the relationship of facts, of accounts of facts, and of scriptures as explained in *Dei Verbum*. For not only have we realized that 'History with a capital H ... does not exist' but also that what the medievals called the literal sense is itself a composed sense.[22] As Paul Beauchamp writes: '*Littera* is not the "literal sense", but only the letter. ... Hence the literal sense is itself allegorical, following the etymology of this word to the letter: saying something else. The literal sense, if it is sense, is already itself a game'.[23]

18. Jaques Derrida, *De la grammatologie*, p. 25.
19. Werner G. Jeanrond discusses Derrida's significance for theological and philosophical hermeneutics in *Theological Hermeneutics*, pp. 102–5.
20. Cf. Martin Luther, *Select Works of Martin Luther: An Offering to the Church of God*, trans. H. Cole, vol. 1 (London: W. Simpkin and R. Marshall, 1826), p. 73.
21. Christoph Theobald, '*Dans les traces...*' *de la constitution* 'Dei Verbum', p. 93.
22. Paul Veyne, *Comment on écrit l'histoire: essai d'épistemologie* (Paris: Seuil, 1971), p. 37.
23. Paul Beauchamp, *Le récit, la lettre et le corps* (Paris: Éditions du Cerf, 1982), p. 61.

Does that not lead us to thinking of inspiration not as based on the representation of God, who speaks, who authors, and who writes, but as a rule of interpretation, a practicing of biblical texts? It is the practice of exposition to the text in the sense which Paul Ricoeur intended when he wrote: 'Consequently, understanding is *to understand oneself before the text*. Not at all in imposing one's own finite ability to understand on the text, but in exposing oneself to the text and receiving a greater self from it'.[24] Exposing ourselves to the text in its alterity means exposing ourselves to its letter:

> For us, the letter too comes from God. We cannot understand this traditional *data* while remaining in a perspective where the relation with God is altogether commanded, or rather absorbed, by the dimension of the Word, reducing any other dimension to being unimportant or inoperative. The category of 'now', or the instant of the Word's impact is, correlatively, too exempt from really confronting those from the beginning and the end. Yet it is the letter which, by its repetition as a sign of memory and desire, reveals itself as an opening, a passage from the beginning in the end.[25]

The Textual Paradigm?

Finally, I would like to respond to François Nault's suggestion. Should we shift to a 'textual' paradigm? We cannot make such a shift, for we are not dealing with doctrines, but with God. Taking the difficulties of the conciliar text into account should not lead us to return to a doctrinal position on revelation. Faith is a theological act: there exists a form of homologation of the theological experience of Christ by the believer. And this leads us to distinguish between the intersubjective processes of the homologation of tradition (namely experience); the source of the tradition (namely the experience of Christ); and the echo of the source (namely the model as well as the matrix of the believers' experience which the scriptures represent).

A personalist theology like the one of *Dei Verbum* tends to distinguish the Word of God from the written words in the scriptures. Hence, the distinction Word of God versus scriptures overlies the distinction between the oral and the written. Evidently, such a theology of revelation as word leaves aside all the difficulties related to the letter; however, it is particularly problematic as to the difference between the written and the oral. As François Martin emphasizes, 'the difference between the oral and the written is patent: phonetic systems are not those of transcription, and those of transcription are secondary compared to the phonetic.

---

24. Paul Ricoeur, 'La fonction herméneutique de la distanciation', in idem, *Du texte à l'action. Essais d'herméneutique II* (Paris: Seuil, 1986), pp. 116-17. Also cf. Werner G. Jeanrond, *Text und Interpretation als Kategorien theologischen Denkens* (Tübingen: Mohr Siebeck, 1986), pp. 42-65.

25. Paul Beauchamp, *Le récit, la lettre et le corps*, p. 39.

Writing in fact transfers into visual form what is structured by sounds'.[26] Literature brings out a difference, a difference which writing undoubtedly makes more apparent, but which also touches the spoken – a difference which does not separate the spoken from the written, but which cuts across all discourse, be it phonetic or graphic. This difference occurs 'between *communication* and *enunciation*'.[27] The gap here involves implementing the work, written or oral, which is a literary work, distinguished from other types of discourse, written or oral, whose sole purpose is transmitting information. Seen from this angle, any expression, written or oral, results in a text, but not every text is a literary work. But in literary works appears what is the culmination of human speech: to be a speech act, precisely before being an act of communication. Poetry is the best example. Like a declaration of love, that no one would dream of reducing to a transmission of information!

What is paradoxical is that the culmination of the word occurs through the power of language to discreetly form an obstacle to the clear-cut transmission of a message: to be able to turn words from their obvious meaning. It is not in disappearing, but indeed in affirming its alterity that the text produces a sense.

Is this the kind of squall-inviting mast
that storm winds buckle above shipwrecks cast
away – no mast, no islets flourishing?
Still, my soul, listen to the sailor sing![28]

Obviously, it would have been more precise to say that Stéphane Mallarmé will not leave, that he will leave neither his work nor his family. But that would be to forget the heuristic power of the metaphor, to be mistaken about the referent of the work. For what do literary works talk about? We might imagine that the referent is the real world, hidden under the cover of fiction. The text would be aiming at a referent which it would be tasked with representing and reproducing. Thus, in an exegetical commentary, one can explain the sense of a biblical text through a series of references to a given historical event, a given place, and a given social group which produced the text. But one could not reduce *La Comédie humaine* to a successful representation of the French society of the Restoration. Hence, in addition to the reference, we must acknowledge the enunciation, the interaction of the text with the reader. Accordingly, to refuse a textual paradigm is to say that we face not only the question of the interpretation of scripture, but the question of its accomplishment, or – as 2 Pet. 1.16-21 puts it – of ἐπίλυσις, of *dénouement*. The *dénouement* is of the order of the encounter the apostles had with the Son of God made flesh. They recognized the Son in the flesh, they in whose eyes 'Jesus Christ

---

26. François Martin, *Pour une théologie de la lettre: l'inspiration des Ecritures* (Paris: Éditions du Cerf, 1996), p. 103.

27. Ibid., p. 104.

28. Stéphane Mallarmé, 'Sea Breeze', in idem, *Collected Poems and Other Verse*, trans. E. H. and A. M. Blackmore (Oxford: Oxford University Press, 2006).

was openly set forth crucified' (Gal. 3.1). The arrival of the Word in the flesh, that is what scripture announced, but could not contain. And that accomplishment took place in an alterity of the flesh, an alterity still clearer than that of the letter.

Should we move from a revelational paradigm to a textual paradigm? It seems to me that the textual paradigm cannot allow us to account for what is at the centre of the Christian faith: the birth in the flesh of God's children. That does not mean (and this is the point of the distinction between a statement and the stating) that we have to appeal to another concept with no relation to the text like a personalist theory which would emphasize that faith is not the business of texts, but of personal encounter. The flaw in such a theory is that it is developed in independence from a reflection on the texts, the texts of the scriptures, which are for us the only texts which allow us to speak about the Word of God. Scripture must be not only the soul, but the flesh of any theology, if it is true that the Church, as *Dei Verbum* 21 states, 'especially in the Sacred Liturgy … unceasingly receives and offers to the faithful the bread of life from the table both of God's word and of Christ's body'. That is one of the forms of a dynamics of difference.

Part II

PHILOSOPHICAL OTHERS AND OTHER PHILOSOPHIES

6

ETHICS OF VISION: SEEING THE OTHER AS NEIGHBOUR[1]

Arne Grøn

Seeing the Other?

'He saw me. Nobody has seen me as much as William did. He could almost see more than there is'.[2] This is a quote from an interview with Else Lidegaard, a Danish journalist, looking back trying to explain her relation to William Heinesen, the author from the Faroe Islands. Her words indicate the significance inherent in seeing the other. But what does it mean to see another as the other, making it possible for *her* to say: 'He saw me'?

In seeing, we can give significance to what we see. We do not first have to decide to do so – in order then to see accordingly. Rather, the very act of seeing is a matter of paying attention. On this account, the significance inherent in seeing is the significance *we* give to what we see. However, it does not simply let us emerge as the source of signification. It also turns us outward. Something matters to us and this comes to the fore in how we see.

In seeing another who sees us, we more or less manifest ourselves in the eyes of the other. This means that seeing is not only a matter of paying attention to what is important to oneself. The fact of seeing – and being seen – is itself of significance. In seeing the other who sees us we may tell her what she means to us. But does this not imply that we give significance to her as the other? In the very gesture of seeking to tell the other what she means to us, however, she already figures as the other. Yet, even when we turn ourselves to the other, telling her what she means to us, the question is whether we actually see *her*. Do we not just see what she means to us? This question is disturbing, putting us – oneself

---

1. This contribution is a revised version of the Robertson Lecture which I delivered at the University of Glasgow, 18 October 2011.
2. In Danish: 'Han så mig. Ingen har set mig så meget som William. Han kunne næsten se mere, end der er', Marianne Krogh Andersen, 'Sjælevenner', *Weekendavisen*, 14 October 2011.

seeing the other – into question. What do we see in the other we see? Do we see *the other*?

This brief line of reasoning – to be developed in the following – leads us back to the opening question: what does it mean to see another as the other, making it possible for *her* to say 'He *saw* me'? Let us call this sense of seeing the other emphatic. It contrasts other ways of seeing in which we see each other without being able to say that we really see the other (although we may pay a lot of attention to each other). The quote suggests an answer: 'Nobody has seen me *as much as* William did. He could almost see *more* than there is'. Is seeing another as the other a matter of seeing more – than there is to see?

Let me give another quote:

> It is written, 'Why do you see the splinter in your brother's eye but do not see the log that is in your own?' A pious man has piously interpreted these words as follows: The log in your own eye is neither more nor less than seeing and condemning the splinter in your brother's eye. But the most rigorous like for like would of course be that seeing the splinter in someone else's eye becomes the splinter in one's own eye. But Christianity is even more rigorous: this splinter, or seeing it judgingly, is a log. And even if you do not see the log, and even if no human being sees it, God sees it. Therefore a splinter is a log!³

This is a quote from the end of Søren Kierkegaard's *Works of Love*. Reading or listening to the words from Mt. 7.3, we may be both puzzled and caught by the image. We can imagine what it would be like to have a splinter in one's eye, but the image of a log in the eye is grotesque. It runs counter to what we expect and imagine. Probably, we have a sense of what it is about, without fully realizing what it means. Reading or listening to the interpretation given in the quote, we may come to see what it is about: seeing the splinter in the brother's eye *is* the log in one's own eye. This may strike us as a sudden and deep insight: 'Yes, this is what it means!' But that still leaves us with the task of explaining for ourselves the implications.

Seeing the splinter in the other's eye *is* a log in one's own: what does this claim do? It redirects our vision, but it can only do so by confronting us with that fact that we are already seeing. We are reflected *in* seeing, not just reflecting *upon* seeing. As the one seeing, we are questioned. Indirectly, the text leaves us, the readers and listeners, with the question: '… and how do you see?'

Put differently, the claim re-situates us in a field of vision which is already ethically imbued. It reminds us that in seeing, we are not placed in a free position. But this is what we easily overlook. For in seeing, our attention goes outwards. Thereby, we can make ourselves blind to the fact that we are ourselves doing

---

3. Søren Kierkegaard, 'Works of Love', *Kierkegaard's Writings*, vol. 16, trans. H. V. Hong and E. H. Hong (Princeton: Princeton University Press, 1995), p. 382; idem, 'Kjerlighedens Gjerninger', *Søren Kierkegaards Skrifter*, vol. 9, ed. Niels Jørgen Cappelørn et al. (Copenhagen: Gad, 2004), p. 375.

something in seeing the other. But is it fair to say that we make ourselves blind? Probably, we are not aware of any act of self-blinding. Yet, we may later come to see that we did make ourselves blind to what we were doing towards others.[4] The critical insight, then, is that we, *in seeing*, can make ourselves blind to our own seeing. This may also be the case when we are occupied by what the other means to us.

My argument in what follows is twofold: first, seeing the other in the emphatic sense ('He saw me') draws upon the possibility of *not* seeing her, and, secondly, it is not adequately described in terms of seeing *more* of the other. Changing one's way of seeing the other demands us as the one already seeing her. We only come to understand what it means to *see* the other if we realize that we can fail to do so. This is a possibility we already have *in* seeing the other – and not a possibility next to seeing her. We can only come to see differently in *seeing*, as the one who can be caught in seeing. What it means to see the other concerns us in how we already see her. It requires us to see differently – to see the other *as the other*. But how should we account for this 'as the other'? Does seeing the other *as neighbour* offer an answer?

Ethical Reversal

Let us take our point of departure in the context of the second quote. What kind of ethics is at work here? Kierkegaard's *Works of Love* is a sustained reflection on what it means to love one's neighbour. It consists of discourses, addressing its reader as someone listening to *and* seeing others. Accentuating the duty to love one's neighbour, *Works of Love* turns the reader into a subject who is to change her ways of seeing the other. Our view of the other is to be reversed – but how?

The reversal required is ethical. It has to do with what I will call the ethics of vision which is not just one form of ethical position but pertains to what the ethical means. Ethics concerns us in what we are to do. Yet, this does not exhaust the ethical. There is a second question which intensifies the ethical concern: *how* we do what we are to do. This sounds as if there were two questions – the first about what to do and the second about how to do it. But we do not have a choice between the 'what' and the 'how'. Rather, the second question qualifies the first. How we do what we ought to do may change the ethical character of what we do. The intricacy of the two questions can be seen in a distinction between benevolence and mercy made in one of the discourses in *Works of Love*.[5] An act of benevolence may point to itself – making itself visible to the other as an act of

---

4. This point can be made in reading, for example, Kierkegaard's 'upbuilding' discourse on Paul: Søren Kierkegaard, 'The Thorn in the Flesh', in idem, *Kierkegaard's Writings*, vol. 5, trans. H. V. Hong and E. H. Hong (Princeton: Princeton University Press, 1990), pp. 315–30; idem, 'Pælen i Kjødet', in *Søren Kierkegaards Skrifter*, vol. 5, ed. Niels Jørgen Cappelørn et al. (Copenhagen: Gad, 1998), pp. 7–34.

5. 'Mercifulness, a Work of Love Even If It Can Give Nothing and Is Able to Do

benevolence, thereby placing *her* in a position that defines her as being dependent on what one gives to her. Works of love can be done in ways that even humiliate the other.

Thus, ethically, 'how' qualifies 'what'. This is reflected in a distinction introduced in the very beginning of *Works of Love*: 'There are indeed only some works that human language specifically and narrowly calls works of love [*Kjerlighedsgerninger*], but in heaven no work can be pleasing unless it is a work of love [*en Kjerlighedens Gjerning*]'.[6] The locution *Kjerlighedsgerninger* implies that prior to engaging in action we are able to make a list of specific kinds of actions so that to perform an action belonging to one of the types listed would be to perform a work of love. But *every* action should be a work of love. This requirement is woven into the insight that 'there is no work, not one single one, not even the best, about which we unconditionally dare to say: The one who does this unconditionally demonstrates love by it. It depends on *how* the work is done'.[7]

How then is it possible to recognize love? On the one hand, love must manifest itself in works of love, on the other its visibility or recognizability remains an open question. Who is the addressee of this question? If we only ask whether love can *be seen or recognized* we are looking in the wrong direction. For who is 'doing the seeing'? The critical point is that love itself is a matter of seeing. Therefore, love can only be recognized by *itself* recognizing or seeing love in the other. This inversion – love's recognizability through its *own* recognition of love in the other – is unfolded in the opening discourse of the second series of discourses in *Works of Love*: 'Love Builds Up'.[8] Love *is* to presuppose and thus to see love in the other.

These two steps – the ethical concern being intensified in the question of how we do what we are to do and the recognizability of love reversed in the love's recognition – re-situate us in a social world of seeing and being seen, as a field of vision already ethically imbued. We are questioned as to how we see the other in what we are doing. The 'act of seeing' implied in what we do towards the other can be edifying, seeking to build up, but it can also be an act of self-assertion. Through what we do we may seek to tell the other how she should see herself.

The other is exposed to us seeing her. However, this does not exhaust the power inherent in seeing. In seeing we are also affected – to the point of being ourselves questioned. The question concerning us comes to us – from the other although she may not voice the question. She is not only exposed to but also beyond what we can do to her. She is not just part of a social world in which 'we' are seeing and being seen. This comes to the fore in the question that strikes us when being ourselves questioned: how is the other to see herself in and through what we do to her? When we, in doing an act of benevolence, point to ourselves doing this

Nothing', Søren Kierkegaard, 'Works of Love', pp. 315–30; 'Kjerlighedens Gjerninger', pp. 312–26.

6. Søren Kierkegaard, 'Works of Love', p. 4; 'Kjerlighedens Gjerninger', p. 12.

7. Søren Kierkegaard, 'Works of Love', p. 13; 'Kjerlighedens Gjerninger', p. 21.

8. Søren Kierkegaard, 'Works of Love', pp. 209–24; 'Kjerlighedens Gjerninger', pp. 212–26.

act, the other is placed in a position where she is to see herself as being defined as the recipient of our act. In being ourselves questioned we can be struck by the fact that the other already sees herself – also in being exposed to what we do to her. Ethically, our vision is reversed in how we are to see the other seeing herself. In that sense we are not 'doing' the reversal.

Seeing – and Yet Not Seeing

If we define the power inherent in seeing as that of giving significance to or depriving someone of significance, seeing appears simple: either we see the other or we do not. However, the inversion of perspective just outlined – from love as something we can look for and maybe recognize, to love itself as a matter of seeing and recognizing love – leads us back to the question: what does it mean to see the other *as the other*? Love is indeed a matter of seeing the other, but inherent in seeing is the possibility of seeing *without* seeing, or seeing *and yet not* seeing. What is implied in this more complex, if not complicated, alternative?

There are ways of seeing which consist precisely in not seeing the other. If one ignores or overlooks the other, one has in fact seen her. This can happen in passing by in the city or on the road. The road we take, we also walk with our eyes.

One can even make the other understand that she does not exist for oneself. But how does this work? It requires not only that one has seen the other, but also that one – by the way one sees her – tells her how *she* should see herself: as inferior to oneself. One *makes* her see oneself as superior. The implication, however, is that the self-conception of the arrogant is dependent on others seeing themselves as inferior. This is an example of seeing *and yet not* seeing. Arrogance only functions by ignoring the other, but for all that, ignoring remains a mode of seeing the other. It even presupposes that the other sees for herself.

The other is not simply there, before our eyes, just to be observed and identified. Yet, she is visible beyond our seeing. The visibility of the other is not only to be defined in terms of seeing but turns seeing the other into a demand on us. This is the ethical reversal of perspective.

As the Neighbour?

What does it mean then to see the other in the emphatic sense ('He saw me')? Rather than facing the alternative either to see or not to see the other, we are questioned as to whether we see the other when seeing her. Seeing the other as the other draws on and responds to our possibilities of seeing and yet not seeing her. We can see each other in ways so as to not see the other – to the point of that being the point in seeing her. Human beings are social beings also in the sense that they are capable of making others invisible. But what is made invisible in this sense is already seen. Seeing the other as the other is a countermove: seeing the other *despite ourselves*.

This first, more negative, part of my argument delineates the second, more positive which concerns the demand to see the other *differently*: as the other. How is this possible? Can we find an answer in seeing the other as the neighbour? The neighbour is not there to be seen in the sense of grasping what the other is (seeing as identifying). Also, it is not about seeing more of the other. What then is the reversal of perspective implied in: 'seeing the other *as neighbour*'?

It should be easy to see the other closest to oneself, the neighbour. Yet it is difficult. Why? What is closest to oneself is ambiguous. It not only indicates the neighbour in a direct sense but also who is important for oneself. In *Works of Love*, Kierkegaard contrasts neighbourly love and preferential love. The neighbour is not a matter of choice. She is given to oneself. Therefore, Kierkegaard insists on reading the passage in Lk. 10.36 accurately.[9] The answer Jesus offers to the question: 'Who is my neighbour?' is a second question reversing the first: 'Which of these three seems to you to have been the neighbour to the man who had fallen among robbers?' This means that the one asking is addressed – as the neighbour of the neighbour. The implication is that one is to see differently in order to see the other as neighbour. The question is not where to find my neighbour but whether I show myself to be the neighbour of the neighbour. This is an open, disturbing question. But maybe this is what we need in ethics, making us reflect upon our own ways of seeing in acting.

Seen in this light, it makes sense to turn love into a duty – in the commandment to love your neighbour as yourself. The duty catches one in seeing, redirecting one's vision. What then does it mean to see the other as neighbour? The other is not simply the other. Seeing the other as the other implies seeing that she is *other than the other I see*. That is – she is beyond my seeing. But *this* changes the way I should see her. It is seeing the other with a sense of limits: limits to what one is to see of the other, limits to what one has seen of the other. In that sense there is always more to be seen. But this means: the other is still to show who she is. In other words, seeing the other as neighbour breaks off identification. It is to see her as invisible in her visibility.

Seeing and Understanding

Yet, is it possible to *see* the other differently – that is: differently from how we see her? It is still we who see the other. Does seeing the other not lead us back to seeking to comprehend her?

'The notion of the face', Emmanuel Levinas claims, 'brings us to a notion of meaning prior to my *Sinngebung* and thus independent of my initiative and my power'.[10] Apparently, the face is a matter of seeing the other. We face the other in seeing her. In a critical sense, however, the face of the other is *not* to be seen. The

---

9. Søren Kierkegaard, 'Works of Love', p. 22; idem, 'Kjerlighedens Gjerninger', p. 30.
10. Emmanuel Levinas, *Totality and Infinity: An Essay on Exteriority*, trans. A. Lingis (Pittsburgh, PA: Duquesne University Press, 1969), p. 51.

face is the trace of the other. It bears her alterity. She is exterior to me, and exteriority is 'true in a face to face that is no longer entirely vision, but goes further than vision'.[11] The face is not there, before our eyes, to be grasped. Rather, the face of the other stands out from the visible. But does it not still concern us seeing the other?

Levinas' move against vision links seeing to taking at hand or grasping. Seeing turns what is seen into something at hand, observable, knowable. It bears the paradigm of knowing – in the history of Western philosophy, from Plato to Martin Heidegger. But this move, still dependent on Heidegger, reduces what it means to see.

In seeing the other, something is at stake – it is a matter of actually seeing her. In the claim that seeing the other is to comprehend, turning her into something to be known, seeing means: *having seen* what we see (likewise, comprehending is understood as having comprehended what we are to understand). But in seeing and understanding the other, we face the other as the other *still to be seen and to be understood*.

Remarkably, when we see the face of the other such as to observe its features, the colour of the eyes, we do not see the other. We see without seeing her. But this does not mean that the face is something behind the invisible. Rather, it shines or breaks through the visible, and does so in speaking or being silent. 'The face speaks. The manifestation of the face is already discourse', Levinas notes.[12] 'Speech refuses vision, because the speaker does not deliver images of himself only, but is personally present in his speech, absolutely exterior to every image he would leave'.[13] But the other speaking is the other still to be seen. More than that, it is the other seeing us. The eyes of the other can speak silently.

The face of the other is not there, just to be seen. But neither is it just not to be seen. Rather, the invisibility of the other – that the face of the other is not to be seen – is a demand put on us seeing her. We are to see her so as not to see (observe) her face. We are to understand in what sense the face of the other is not to be seen. But this means that the other is there – still to be seen, beyond us seeing her. The other is in-visible: She is invisible *in* her visibility. 'Seeing and yet not seeing' is turned around. We shall see the other in such a way that we, for ourselves, realize that she is beyond what we see. She is not simply there to be seen – that means that she is still to be seen.

Seeing in the Accusative?

Face-to-face does not mean that we can place ourselves in the relation between the other and oneself. We are not 'in' the relation. Rather, the face of the other already withdraws from us, leaving us behind, exposed to the other before relating to her. 'The neighbor', Levinas claims, 'excludes himself from the thought

11. Ibid., p. 290.
12. Ibid., p. 66.
13. Ibid., p. 296.

that seeks him, and this exclusion has a positive side to it: my exposure to him, antecedent to his appearing, my delay behind him, my undergoing, undo the core of what is identity in me'.[14] This refusal of the appearing of the other 'makes me his neighbor'.[15]

How do I see the other as neighbour? The neighbour only appears to me in that I am exposed to her. In this sense I am made the neighbour of the neighbour. In contrast to Levinas, we could speak of 'appearing *as* exposure'. Seeing the other as neighbour is to see in the accusative.

What then does it mean that the neighbour is 'the absolutely other'?[16] She is absolutely other *for me*. This changes *my* position. She is beyond me who sees her. To see the other as the neighbour is to see her as the other, but 'as the other' designates me as the one to see her. I am to see her 'beyond me': as this other she is not an instance of 'the other'. She is other than the other I see her as, beyond what I see. But this is how *I* shall see her.

This way of understanding 'seeing the other as neighbour' goes against Levinas' critique of seeing and comprehending. Levinas refers to a response that answers 'to a non-thematizable provocation', a response that answers 'before any understanding'.[17] But is there no understanding in this response? The accusative – being addressed and questioned in the proximity of the neighbour – 'derives from no nominative'.[18] We do not lead ourselves from nominative into the accusative. Yet, in the accusative we are in the nominative. We are the one to respond, as the one already seeing and yet not seeing the other.

Alterity and Asymmetry

Seeing the other is about an ethical reversal which is not a perspectival exchange (in German: *Perspektivenwechsel*). Seeing the other as neighbour means seeing in the accusative, as the neighbour of the neighbour.

Alterity implies asymmetry. That a difference in perspective – to the point of asymmetry – is crucial for love's recognition can be seen when we reflect a bit on the passage: 'He almost saw more than there is to see'. I have argued that seeing the other is not a matter of seeing more than there is to see. Still, there is a truth to what Else Lidegaard says. This is how she sees William: in gratitude. The critical point is that this is, at the same time, what *he* cannot say. Imagine that he responded: 'Yes, I saw almost more than there is to see'. If he said that, *he would not see her*.

---

14. Emmanuel Levinas, *Otherwise than Being or Beyond Essence*, trans. Alphonso Lingis (Pittsburgh, PA: Duquesne University Press, 1998), p. 89.
15. Ibid., p. 11.
16. Ibid., p. 91.
17. Ibid., p. 12.
18. Ibid., p. 11.

7

THE OUTER AND INNER CONSTITUTION OF HUMAN DIGNITY IN MEISTER ECKHART

Dietmar Mieth[1]

The Exodus Metaphysic

Meister Eckhart was revolutionary in his influence, even if it was not his intent. He laid the groundwork for the conception of freedom in the self-abnegation of the human being. His re-evaluation of the human being from the inside out did not result in the reform of institutions, but created an unprecedented self-awareness. This self-awareness continued to crop up after Eckhart as it was accessible to everyone – inside and outside Christianity.[2]

First and foremost, Eckhart is interested in God's nature, in its significance for humanity. For Eckhart, God is his being himself (*est suum esse*).[3] He understands *Ego sum qui sum* (Exod. 3.14) as reduplication: the affirmation of positivity and the exclusion of negativity by repetition.[4] Simultaneously, he understands it as a reflected reference to the *ab nihilo* of God: his *bullitio sive parturitionem*, the primary source of everything, including the *bonum bonum*, the good of the good.[5] This primary source of everything comprises the plenitude of beings. God as *primum* is *dives per se*.[6] Accordingly, God's creatures are not defined by themselves, but by categories which are always already later than God is: *Omnis perfectio eget*

---

1. I am grateful for Jo Ann van Vliet's and Naomi van Steenbergen's support with the English translation of my contribution.

2. Cf. Dietmar Mieth, 'Meister Eckhart: The Power of Inner Liberation', in Amatha Kumar Giri, ed., *The Modern Prince and the Modern Sage: Transforming Power and Freedom* (New Dehli: Sage India, 2009), pp. 405–23.

3. Meister Eckhart, *Die lateinischen Werke*, vol. 2, ed. Loris Sturlese (Stuttgart: Kohlhammmer, 2000), p. 27.

4. Ibid., p. 21.

5. Ibid., p. 18. Cf. Markus Vinzent, 'Questions on the Attributes (of God): Four Rediscovered Parisian Questions of Meister Eckhart', *The Journal of Theological Studies* 63 (2012), pp. 156–85.

6. Meister Eckhart, *Die lateinischen Werke*, vol. 2, p. 26.

ipso, qui est ipsum esse, ipsi innititur, ipsi inhaeret, cum quia sine ipso esset nihil et non esset sapientia, nec quidquam aliud, sed purum nihil.[7] Hence, Eckhart assumes the outer constitution of all creatures, including human creatures. God, however, is not outside but inside his creation, transforming its 'realities'. Because he is 'real' in a different sense than everything and everybody he created, his 'reality' can only be conceived of as the reality of an idea. Such an idea might be interpreted as a first metaphor – a first 'word' – which enables language to say more than it says in the empirical description of entities according to the categories of human understanding. God is beyond these empirical descriptions; yet, as a metaphor, he is 'really real', unlike the reality of what is empirically described. However, although God's 'being' cannot be construed in the categories of human understanding, he is not far from his human creatures. He comes – as Eckhart assumes following Augustine – closer to these creatures than these creatures come to themselves.[8] God is not a substance, but a process: the continuous process of God giving Godself.

The Grace of God

For Eckhart, God is *alius, non aliud*. Reality is taken to be a process in which God is a continuous actuality (*actualitas*). This actuality is the 'pure working' which comes from the outside to the inside without temporal difference. Continually, God is working in the soul of the human being: creating it through the participation in the incarnation which means both *creatio continua* and *incarnatio continua*. As Eckhart explains: 'Some simple folk imagine they will see God as if he were standing there and they here. That is not so. God and I are one. Through knowledge I take God into myself, through love I enter into God … God and I are one in this operation: He works, and I come into being'.[9] The density of this union is achieved through God's self-revelation in the continual and actual working which constitutes his being (*actus purus/lûter wirken*). However, it can be reversed: 'And He wants our bliss so badly that He entices us into Himself with every means at His disposal … I will never give thanks to God for loving me, because He cannot help it, whether He would or not: His nature compels Him to it. I will give him thanks because by His goodness He cannot cease to love me'.[10]

7. Ibid., p. 28.
8. Cf. Christine Büchner, *Gottes Kreatur – 'ein reines Nichts'? Einheit Gottes als Ermöglichung von Geschöpflichkeit und Personalität im Werk Meister Eckharts* (Innsbruck: Tyrolia, 2005).
9. Meister Eckhart, *The Complete Mystical Works of Meister Eckhart*, trans. M. O'Connell Walshe (New York: Crossroads, 2009), pp. 331–2 (= Sermon 65). Cf. *Die deutschen Werke*, vol. 1, ed. Josef Quint and Georg Steer (Stuttgart: Kohlhammer, 1936), pp. 113–14 (= Sermon 6).
10. Cf. Meister Eckhart, *The Complete Mystical Works of Meister Eckhart*, pp. 372–3 (= Sermon 73). Cf. *Die deutschen Werke*, vol. 3, pp. 268–9 (= Sermon 73).

Nothing is independent of God. According to Eckhart, God is the only *isticheit*, the only one who can say 'I am'.[11] However, God is an intellectual being (*Deus est intelligere*). If we take the immateriality of intellectuality seriously, God does not *exist*.

In the perspective of his unconditional self-revelation, God is love. How deeply Eckhart's God is involved and included in a correlation with his creatures becomes clear when Eckhart refers to 'God's image'.[12] The concept of image, however, does not capture a reflection of God in the human being, whether distorted or undistorted; it captures a process of imaging or un-imaging. Eckhart refers to the to-and-fro of a movement, in which the image of God arises simultaneously in God and in God's creature. Since it is a process, the image is in flux. Consequently, it is not necessary to prohibit images: images are merely fluctuating and fleeting impressions. The human being cannot create images of God; therefore, she or he must un-image – which is to say, deconstruct – these images. The process of imaging is imageless, since the image cannot be fixed.[13] Evidently, Eckhart assumes a correlation between God and God's creation. Human nature presupposes God's grace, comprehending and continuing his unconditional self-revelation. God's justice, too, is always already present in the self-revelation of God.

The Justice of God

During his trial before the Inquisition in 1326, Eckhart points to his 'efforts for justice' which earned him prosecution.[14] He even refers to God *as* justice.[15]

> The just are so set on justice that if God were not just they would not care a bean for God: they are so firmly established in justice and so thoroughly self-abandoned that they reck not the pains of hell or the joys of heaven or anything at all. Indeed, were all the pains of those in hell, men or devils, and all the pain that has been suffered or ever will be suffered – were all this to be set beside justice, they would not care a jot, so firmly do they stand by God and justice. ... Whoever understands about the just man and justice understands all that I am saying.[16]

---

11. Cf. Meister Eckhart, *Die deutschen Werke*, vol. 1, p. 197 (= Sermon 12). Cf. ET: *The Complete Works of Meister Eckhart*, p. 296 (= Sermon 57).

12. Cf. Meister Eckhart, *Die deutschen Werke*, vol. 1, p. 263 (= Sermon 16b). Cf. ET: *The Complete Mystical Writings of Meister Eckhart*, pp. 114–15 (= Sermon 14b).

13. Mauritius Wilde, *Das neue Bild vom Gottesbild: Bild und Theologie bei Meister Eckhart* (Freiburg/Schweiz: Universitätsverlag, 2000), pp. 288–310.

14. Cf. Eckhart's response to the accusations during the trial, Meister Eckhart, *Die lateinischen Werke*, vol. 5, p. 275.

15. Cf. Kurt Flasch, *Meister Eckhart: Philosoph des Christentums* (München: C. H. Beck, 2010), pp. 49–65.

16. Meister Eckhart, *The Complete Mystical Writings of Meister Eckhart*, p. 329 (= Sermon 65). Cf. *Die deutschen Werke*, vol. 1, pp. 103–4 (= Sermon 6).

Accordingly, the attitude of a just person remains just, irrespective of the person's circumstances. Justice is the expression of the essence of the just; a just person cannot be otherwise than just. However, it is crucial to understand the distinction between justice and a just person. Maurice O'Connell Walshe's translation is not faithful to the original in which the Middle High German concept of *underscheit* captures both a distinction and a relation.[17] With 'justice' Eckhart – who is otherwise very cautious about naming – names God. Justice fulfils the criterion of reason: justice is delegated to the will which holds together what rationally belongs together. According to Kurt Flasch, for Eckhart, God is worthy of the recognition by reason because of God's justice.[18] However, Eckhart's reflections on God might be pushed further: God recognizes human beings through the incarnation. The notion of God's incarnation is central to Eckhart's thought since it captures a correlation. Both parties of the correlation arise from their relation with each other. Theologically, Eckhart answers the question of how a human being becomes a just human being by pointing to the correlation between God's justice on the one hand and God's just creature on the other. The human being becomes just because she or he always already *is* just. As mentioned above, 'God works, and I come into being'.

Consequently, Eckhart's reflection on God entails the question of the human being about his or her own self. God is never the object. Like the human being, God is the subject. The self-revealing God meets the human being. Such a God is liberated from characterizations such as the authoritative legislator or the sovereign represented by ecclesial powers. He is the God of self-opening vastness, the God of trust.[19]

The Homo Divinus

The notion of the *homo divinus* is essential to medieval mysticism, concentrating on the divinity and nobility of the human being.[20] Evidently, the relevance that theological and philosophical notions have for a society is to be checked against reality, in the past as much as in the present. Often it is the case that such notions are met with a response only long after their conceptualization. The notion of equality (Gal. 3.28), for instance, did not result in the elimination of slavery. Yet, it challenged slavery again and again.

17. Ibid., p. 105: 'Swer underscheit verstât von gerehticheit und von gerechtem, der verstât allez, das ich sage'.
18. Kurt Flasch, '*Iusti vivent in aeternum*', in Georg Steer and Loris Sturlese, eds, *Lectura Eckhardi II: Predigten Meister Eckharts von Fachgelehrten gelesen und gedeutet* (Stuttgart: Kohlhammer, 2003), pp. 29–52.
19. Cf. Dietmar Mieth, 'Eckhart's God', in Asa Kasher and Janine Diller, eds, *Models of God and other Ultimate Realities* (Heidelberg: Springer, 2013), pp. 801–10.
20. Cf. Loris Sturlese, *Homo divinus: Philosophische Projekte in Deutschland zwischen Meister Eckhart und Heinrich Seuse* (Stuttgart: Kohlhammer, 2007).

In the Middle Ages, the political and social structure of serfdom diverted from slavery, for the possession of a peasant did not include her or his soul. Nonetheless, serfdom led to the widespread oppression of peasants. In Germany, it resulted in the Peasants' Wars.[21] In Middle High German documents, 'serfdom' (*Leib-Eigenschaft*) was referred to as '*Eigenschaft*'. So when Eckhart preached that human beings should be '*âne* [without] *Eigenschaft*', his preaching was of political and social importance, even if he used the concept metaphorically.[22] 'Serfdom' is a lesser form of the slavery which is denounced by the notion of equality within Christianity. The so-called Memmingen Articles of 1525 demand the abolition of serfdom – indeed, the abolition of '*Eigenschaft*'! – justifying their demand with the equality of all human beings which is established through the redemption by Christ.[23]

Eckhart utilizes '*Eigenschaft*' as a concept which applies to all human beings, concentrating on incarnation instead of redemption. God's divine-human nature must be identifiable in human beings; strictly speaking, in the ethics of human beings. Whatever criteria human beings identify as humane, these criteria might also be applied as criteria for the image of God. Hence, for Eckhart, the ethical recognition of righteousness is relevant as a dogmatical criterion. Theology is not separated from human rationality. On the contrary, faith is to be explained through rationality. Eckhart's commentary on John's Gospel, therefore, conceives of ethics as the relation between faith and reason: 'In the beginning was the word. With respect to morality, we teach that the principle of all our intentions and actions must be God. ... Furthermore, if you wish to know whether or not all of your internal and external actions are in accordance with God, ... see whether the end of your intentions is God. In that case, the action is in accordance with God [*divina*]'.[24] However, Eckhart continues: 'Yet we also teach that our work ought to be rational, and that it ought to be a work that is controlled by ... reason. For "In the beginning was the word" also means: in the beginning was reason'.[25]

Seen in the light of Eckhart's doctrine of justice as the scope of his ethics, a just person is constituted by justice. Hence, the constituent and the constituted coexist in a habitual correlation. Justice is both divine and human; and it is habitualized

---

21. Cf. Peter Blickle, *Der Bauernkrieg: Die Revolution des Gemeinen Mannes* (München: C. H. Beck, 2006). Blickle refers to the critique of serfdom in Eike von Repkow's *Sachsenspiegel*.

22. Frank Tobin notes that the 'word *Eigenschaft* in Meister Eckhart's German sermons ... demonstrates well his creative use of language by uniting in it normally disparate areas of reality', Frank Tobin, 'Eckharts mystical use of language: The context of *Eigenschaft*', *Seminar: A Journal of German Studies* 3 (1972), pp. 160–8 (168). Cf. idem, *Meister Eckhart: Thought and Language* (Philadelphia: University of Pennsylvania Press, 1986), p. 189.

23. Peter Blickle, *Der Bauernkrieg*, pp. 55–60.

24. Meister Eckhart, *Die lateinischen Werke*, vol. 3, p. 42.

25. Ibid.

as a virtue.[26] The correlation between justice and a just person is the original act of morality.[27] This 'archaeological' dimension, in which the origin is more important than the outcome, can only be arrived at through self-abnegation. According to Eckhart, any action of the justified and just person strengthens the correlation of constituent (justice) and constituted (just person), so that the Son is born again and again into the heart of the Father.[28] In this cross-temporal birthing, the human being acts 'without cause' for the sake of freedom. She or he acts rightly and righteously because she or he emanates from absolute goodness. As mentioned above, the question of what is morally right in concrete circumstances, however, is on a different page for Eckhart – the page of reason.[29]

Overall, through mystics such as Eckhart, medieval mysticism cut the path towards a concept of the equality of all human beings.[30] The *homo divinus* is aware of his divine constitution.[31] She or he does not deny the role of ecclesial institutions, but views these institutions not as constitutive of the human being. The subject's sense of her or his self advances.[32] In 1935, Herma Piesch already argued that the reference for medieval mysticism is not ecclesiology.[33] For Eckhart, christology is the reference for the divinity and the nobility of the soul. Hence, Eckhart's *homo divinus* stresses the significance of the individual, yet without applying it to the domain of human rights.[34]

---

26. Cf. Ibid., p. 410.

27. Cf. Theo Kobusch, 'Mystik als Metaphysik des moralischen Seins', in Kurt Ruh, ed., *Abendländische Mystik im Mittelalter* (Stuttgart: Metzler, 1986), pp. 49–62.

28. Cf. Meister Eckhart, *Die deutschen Werke*, vol. 1, pp. 30–1 (= Sermon 2).

29. Cf. Meister Eckhart, *Die deutschen Werke*, vol. 2, pp. 483; 489.

30. Cf. Dietmar Mieth, 'Human Dignity in later medieval spiritual and political conflicts', in Marcus Düwell, Jens Braarvig, Roger Brownsword, and Dietmar Mieth, eds, *The Cambridge Handbook of Human Dignity: Interdisciplinary Perspectives* (Cambridge: Cambridge University Press, 2014), pp. 74–84.

31. Cf. Loris Sturlese, *Homo divinus*. Particularly relevant are pp. 34–45.

32. Werner G. Jeanrond traced this development as a rediscovery of the loving subject in Werner G. Jeanrond, *A Theology of Love* (London: Continuum/T&T Clark, 2010), pp. 67–103.

33. Herma Piesch, *Meister Eckharts Ethik* (Luzern: Vita Nova Verlag, 1935). Piesch argued that the concept of humanity takes the place of 'Christianity' and 'Church'. Eckhart was in doubt as to whether the grace of baptism is necessary for a human being. Clearly, he did not solve this theological problem. However, the fact that he considered sacraments to be the emblematic signs of the grace of God, given in the *creatio continua* and in the *incarnatio continua*, demonstrates that he had a different conception of this theological problem.

34. Also cf. Jan A. Aertsen and Andreas Speer, eds, *Individuum und Individualität im Mittelalter* (Berlin: De Gruyter, 1996).

The Kingdom of God

For Eckhart, the concept of the Kingdom of God captures the richness of the inner human being. It goes together with the concept of 'real' poverty: not knowing, not willing, and not having.[35] Like Martin Luther, Eckhart follows the psychological as opposed to the sociological interpretation of '*regnum Deum intra vos est*' (Lk. 17.21): 'The Kingdom of God is within you' as opposed to 'The Kingdom of God is amongst you'. Accordingly, the concept of the kingdom of God articulates an individualization of the biblical message. This individualization allows distance from institutions, both ecclesial ones and political ones.[36] Here, the door is opened for the so-called mystical interpretation. The distance to institutions follows from the distance to the world (*mundus*), conceived of as society. However, such a distance is not possible for religious communities. Eckhart interprets the presence of Jesus Christ in the soul as a 'communitarian' gift.[37] However, he is not emphasizing communitarianism but universalism. Again, what is at stake is the inner human being – a person's inner being – which indeed is accessible to anyone, independently of her or his confessional status. The radicality of the transformation of the inner human being is expressed in The Lord's Prayer. For Eckhart, the prayer implies the abandonment of one's own will, so that 'when we say "Thy kingdom come, Thy will be done", we are praying to God to deprive us of ourselves'.[38]

Crucially, 'rich' and 'richness' as characterizations of a human being are related to '*adelig*', to the nobility of the human being. Hence, it corresponds to Eckhart's interpretation of the doctrine of grace: grace accompanies a person in becoming a person, while it is always already in the person. There is no distinction between the grace in creation and the grace in salvation;[39] God's love starts before time, 'when we were not'.[40] Particularly in his sermon '*Homo quidam nobilis*', Eckhart demonstrates the relation between 'rich' and 'richness' on the one hand and nobility on the other (which corresponds, as mentioned above, to the divinity of the *homo divinus*). The richness given by God is the anticipation of the being

---

35. Cf. Meister Eckhart, *Die deutschen Werke*, vol. 2, pp. 486–520 (= Sermon 52). Also cf. Dietmar Mieth, 'Meister Eckhart on Wealth', *Medieval Mystical Theology* 21 (2012), pp. 233–54.

36. Markus Vinzent, 'Salus extra ecclesiam? Meister Eckharts Institutionenskepsis', in Dietmar Mieth and Britta Mueller-Schauenburg, eds, *Mystik, Recht und Freiheit: Religiöse Erfahrung und kirchliche Institutionen im Mittelalter* (Stuttgart: Kohlhammer, 2012), pp. 158–68.

37. I have traced Eckhart's 'communitarianism' in Dietmar Mieth, *Christus, das Soziale im Menschen: Texterschließungen zu Meister Eckhart* (Düsseldorf: Patmos, 1972).

38. Meister Eckhart, *The Complete Mystical Works of Meister Eckhart*, p. 102 (= Sermon 12).

39. Cf. Meister Eckhart, *Die deutschen Werke*, vol. 1, p. 367 (= Sermon 21). Cf. ET: *The Complete Mystical Works of Meister Eckhart*, p. 468 (= Sermon 97).

40. Ibid., p. 100 (= Sermon 12).

of the human being. In reaction to this anticipation, the human being becomes richer: she or he is perfected. Eckhart describes the becoming as follows:

> This man returns richer than when he set forth. Whoever had gone out of himself like that would be given back to himself in a truer sense; and all things, just he had fully abandoned them in multiplicity, will be entirely returned to him in simplicity, for he finds himself and all things in the present 'now' of unity. And the man who went forth thus would return much nobler then when he had departed. This man now dwells in unhampered freedom …, for he needs to undertake and take nothing small or great – for whatever belongs to God belongs to him.[41]

Jesus' promises in Mk 10.29-30 and Lk. 18.29-30 form the background of Eckhart's description: the gain of giving without reservation. Such giving is possible in *this* life, not only in the life after this life!

In sum, Eckhart conceptualizes the power of inner liberation.[42] Yet, such inner liberation has social, political, and juridical consequences. Eckhart insists on the equality of all human beings in their relation to God – God's actuality, God's giving of his life to all human beings through creation and incarnation.

> Whoever would exist in the nakedness of this nature, free from all mediation, must have left behind all distinction of person, so that he is as well disposed to a man who is across the sea, whom he never set eyes on, as the man who is with him and is his close friend. As long as you favour your own person more than a man you never have seen, you are assuredly not right and you have never for a single instant looked into this simple ground.[43]

Ultimately, it is Eckhart's christology which leads him to his concept of the human being. When humanity is included in God's incarnation, the dignity of the human being – with its social, political, and juridical implications – is an equal dignity for all human beings. Eckhart was revolutionary as he anticipated Immanuel Kant who conceived of human dignity as the absolute value. But it is, as Eckhart says, even harder.

---

41. Meister Eckhart, *The Complete Mystical Works of Meister Eckhart*, p. 270 (= Sermon 51). Cf. *Die deutschen Werke*, vol. 1, p. 245 (= Sermon 11).

42. Cf. Dietmar Mieth, 'Meister Eckhart: The Power of Inner Liberation', pp. 405–25.

43. Meister Eckhart, *The Complete Mystical Works of Meister Eckhart*, p. 109 (= Sermon 13).

8

THE VALUE OF THE OTHER

Tage Kurtén

Love and the Fragility of Human Worth

Over the past ten years, many shocking events have taken place in the Nordic countries, outrages where human life has been shown to be of no value to certain human beings. It suffices to think of the terror attack in Norway on the 22 July 2011, when Anders Behring Breivik killed 77 people in Oslo and on the island of Utøya. Breivik's acts are unique, but in all their tragic detail they show what persons among us are capable of doing.

Current Christian theology claims that every human life is of equal worth. Cases like the one mentioned above make one ask: what exactly do we mean when we speak of the value of our fellow humans? And how can we guarantee that people will be treated with dignity in our multicultural age? These questions become still more urgent as the support for xenophobic right-wing political parties currently increases all over Europe. These occasionally quasi-fascist parties have seats in most of the European parliaments, and in some countries they are members of the state government. Are there arguments for the equal value of every human being that might convince such people at all?

An important phenomenon in human life with bearings on the way we relate to other persons is love. Werner G. Jeanrond has written a book on the concept of love. In his introduction 'Horizons of Love', he stresses the complexity of love. What he seems to find crucial is the relationality of love.[1] In my contribution, I shall focus on the relation of love between two (or more) persons. I argue that an important aspect of the relation is what in the relation we emphasize. Is a relation of love something that primarily depends on the person expressing love, or on the quality of the person being loved? Or would it perhaps be possible to understand love in some other way? I will discuss what role religion might play in our understanding of the relation of love.

One of the concepts of love which Jeanrond discusses is the concept of *agape* as it has been presented by the Swedish theologian Anders Nygren (1890–1978).

---

1. Werner G. Jeanrond, *A Theology of Love* (London: Continuum/T&T Clark, 2010), p. 21.

Nygren who built upon a contrast between *agape* and *eros* has been criticized in many ways and by many scholars.[2] Jeanrond is somewhat ambivalent towards Nygren's main ideas. I will highlight some of the aspects of Nygren's ideas, aspects that have not received so much attention, in order to convince my readers that Nygren is indeed still able to contribute to our understanding of love. He can, therefore, help us come to grips with the present situation in the multicultural countries of Europe.

The Tacit Moral Demand

The Danish theologian Knud E. Løgstrup (1905–81) situated human morality in the face-to-face encounter between two (or more) persons. His well-known phenomenological idea is that every encounter with another human being involves an ethical dimension. In the encounter, the other person shows some kind of trust in me. For example, an immigrant from Somalia (which is one of the countries from which refugees have arrived in my own country of Finland), who asks me for the way to the railway station, has trust in me not leading him astray. The trust that he shows me represents a demand on me to live up to his trust. This element of the encounter is tacit; it is presupposed in the whole situation involving me and the other person. And I cannot escape it, according to Løgstrup. The other person represents a demand upon me which I cannot pass by. Literally, I could, of course, pass the other person by, but this would cause me a bad conscience. For Løgstrup, this picture expresses something universal.[3]

For a long time I have found this description by Løgstrup quite convincing. However, the late modern development and the discussions concerning a post-secular condition in our multicultural societies have made me more and more suspicious of the universality of the description. It is not that I would not find the relation between trust and an ethical demand convincing. Rather, the issue is our interpretation of the parts played by the different human beings in Løgstrup's picture. Also, I have doubts concerning our ability to reach a common human understanding of the encounter.

The story of my encounter with a refugee from Somalia can of course be met with the question which a philosopher at Åbo Akademi University raised: 'Why should one bother at all if one meets a complete stranger who is in trouble?'[4] There are generally two ways of answering this question. Either, there is something in

---

2. Cf. Charles W. Kegley, ed., *The Philosophy and the Theology of Anders Nygren* (London: Southern Illinois University Press, 1970).

3. Cf. Knud E. Løgstrup, *Den etiske fordring* (Copenhagen: Gyldendal, 1991), pp. 17–33. For the English translation, cf. *The Ethical Demand*, trans. T. I. Jensen (Notre Dame, IN: University of Notre Dame Press, 1997).

4. Hannes Nykänen, *The 'I', the 'You' and the Soul: An Ethics of Conscience* (Åbo: Åbo Akademi University Press, 2002), p. 167.

the other person that causes me to react morally, or there is something in me that makes me perceive the situation in a certain way. What I would like to investigate further is whether there is any point in maintaining the idea that any ordinary human being would indeed see something similar in other human beings, and that this something would be the cause of their moral reaction. If this is true, how can we come to terms with somebody like Breivik?

When it comes to a person with racist beliefs and behaviours, how could Løgstrup's idea of a tacit demand be of any help? If a person does not perceive the expressions of trust from a fellow human, how can she or he come to be aware of an ethical demand in the situation? According to Løgstrup, we *cannot escape* the tacit demand. When a person *does* understand the trust she or he encounters in the other, she or he is morally obliged to respond to that trust. That is Løgstrup's basic point.

Anders Nygren's Agape *takes us further*

Anders Nygren is famous for his distinction between two fundamentally different ways of understanding love. He names them with the Greek words *eros* and *agape*. Understood as relational concepts, the main characteristic of Nygren's two concepts of love is the way they describe two different ways of relating to the object of love. In his schematic presentation of the two kinds of love, Nygren describes the following dichotomies:

Eros is determined by the quality, the beauty and worth of its object; it is not spontaneous, but 'evoked', 'motivated'. Eros *recognizes value* in its object and loves it.	Agape is sovereign in relation to its object, and is directed to both 'the evil and the good'; it is spontaneous, 'overflowing', 'unmotivated'. Agape loves – and *creates value in its object*.[5]

Jeanrond also points to Nygren's comparison between *eros* and *agape*. In describing Nygren's two different views, his emphasis is slightly different than mine. Jeanrond's description of *eros* stresses self-love as one decisive element of Nygren's understanding. Moreover, he describes *agape* as a different kind of love, which, as he writes, 'is spontaneous and unmotivated, indifferent to value, creative, and the initiator of fellowship with God'.[6] Slightly differently from Jeanrond, I find the schematic overview above to be the most central part of Nygren's understanding of the two concepts. It is not primarily *eros* as self-love I would like to stress, but *eros* as love determined by some qualities of its object, the other. Likewise, it is not *agape* as creative in quite general terms that I find

---

5. Anders Nygren, *Agape and Eros: The Christian Idea of Love*, trans. P. S. Watson (Chicago: University of Chicago Press, 1953), p. 210.
6. Werner G. Jeanrond, *A Theology of Love*, pp. 116–17.

important; it is *agape* as it creates value in its object, the other, which ought to be stressed. The relationship coloured by *agape* is constitutive of the worth and dignity of our fellow human beings.

There are two important points I wish to stress in relation to Nygren's presentation. The first point attempts to extend the relevance of Nygren's basic concepts. It concerns the scope of the two ways of understanding love. Historically, Nygren wants to show that the understanding of love as *agape* is Christian – strictly speaking, uniquely Christian.[7] Also, he seems to think that it is possible to come across this idea only in a Christian framework. This, of course, remains to be shown. I do not find it necessary to claim the Christian uniqueness of *agape*. To my mind, the idea put forward by Nygren is primarily heuristic. He presents two different concepts of love, and asks his readers to consider what they imply. There is nothing that would logically exclude the possibility of *agape* being expressed and experienced in all kinds of human contexts, not only in Christian ones. However, another way of understanding Nygren is to presuppose that *agape* represents what Christian faith understands as Christian love. Whenever we meet such expressions of love, these could be called examples of *Christian* love. It is, however, also important to notice that Nygren does not want to make an evaluation of the two kinds of love. The contrast which he describes through his scheme is '*a difference in type, not a difference in value*'.[8] This means that an *eros* love could be valuable in human life, according to Nygren. The important point is that it would be an expression of love in a sense other than *agape*.

The second point that I want to stress I find even more important. When Nygren makes his conceptual distinction he talks about a '*grundmotiv*'.[9] In order to get a deeper understanding of Nygren's idea, we must take into consideration what this concept stands for. The most basic meaning of the concept might perhaps best be understood with the help of his *Meaning and Method*. There, it becomes clear that Nygren connects his discussion of 'basic motifs' with the idea of 'self-evident presuppositions' in history.[10] With 'self-evident presuppositions', Nygren wants to underscore the importance of views, habits and different linguistic understandings which are taken for granted in different kinds of contexts. What such self-evident presuppositions might possibly imply can be illustrated by a story Nygren used in a number of different texts. His aim with the story was mostly to explain how the gospel, the good news, may be understood. However, the story also has the power of illustrating the concept of self-evident presuppositions.[11]

---

7. Cf. Anders Nygren, *Agape and Eros*, pp. 46–8.
8. Ibid., p. 210.
9. Anders Nygren, *Eros och agape* (Stockholm: Verbum, 1966), p. 34.
10. Cf. Anders Nygren, *Meaning and Method: Prolegomena to a Scientific Philosophy of Religion and a Scientific Theology*, trans. P. S. Watson (London: Epworth Press, 1972), pp. 351–71.
11. For the following, cf. Anders Nygren, 'Tro och vetande: religionsfilosofiska och teologiska Essayer', *Luther-Agricola-Sällskapets Skrifter* 6 (1970), pp. 159–70 (163–4).

Nygren's story takes us back to the ending of World War II within Norway: Norway had been occupied by the Germans during the war. Many men and women in the resistance movement had had to live underground. When peace came in 1945, the country of Norway rejoiced. Norway was a free nation again. However, the lives of people living outside of the range of this news were not immediately changed. Their 'self-evident presupposition' was that they still lived in an occupied country, until the good news reached them: Norway has been liberated! Yet, this news was not necessarily immediately accepted at face value: the messenger could be lying. Until these persons had become convinced that they could trust the messenger, their understanding of the situation was coloured by the conviction that they still lived in an occupied country. And all they experienced in the world around them continued to be perceived in that light.

The role of basic motifs in theology must be understood in analogy with this story. In our efforts to come to terms with real examples of love, we ought to take notice of those frames that are taken for granted in order to understand what we see. These frames representing basic understandings of love determine, as a matter of course, the views of the phenomena under study.[12]

One important aspect determining our understanding of human relations is whether we look at them from the point of view of *agape* or of *eros*. Bearing this particular understanding of Nygren's distinction in mind, his two concepts become important tools for finding out and discovering what is going on between persons when love comes to mind and moral questions arise. It is not a question of which words are being used. It is a question of trying to see if a concrete situation reveals a fundamental understanding expressing an underlying basic motif of *eros* or of *agape*.

Both motifs can, of course, be mixed in many situations where, for example, different persons represent different basic motifs. As we already saw, there need not be any absolute value judgements linked to the two motifs. It might be perfectly acceptable to understand sexual love, for example, as a mixture of give and take, of desires and gifts. Both varieties could also be seen as important and valuable. However, looking at the relation between spouses through the lens of *agape* will result in a different perception than looking at it through that of *eros*. A spouse could, from an *eros*-point-of-view, ask her partner why he loves her, wishing to hear reasons stressing her good qualities. From an *agape* viewpoint, a spouse might be totally satisfied with being valuable in the eyes of the person who loves her, whose love might be expressed, for example, in sex.

The above picture makes one ask whether Jeanrond is a little too hasty in his conclusions when he writes: 'Nygren's theology of "Christian love" … does not pay attention to any kind of phenomenology of love, since its chief interest was to rehabilitate the Lutheran doctrine of justification as the only legitimate framework for a Christian understanding of love'.[13] Arguably, one could choose to read Nygren like that. However, one would run the risk of throwing out the baby with

12. Anders Nygren, *Meaning and Method*, pp. 371–5.
13. Werner G. Jeanrond, *A Theology of Love*, p. 120.

the bathwater. I agree that there are problems in the interpretation of the history of theology and theologians in Nygren's presentation. Nonetheless, I argue that his notion of self-evident presuppositions and the contextual understanding of the Christian tradition which followed from it present us with conceptual and methodological tools which lead up to discoveries that otherwise would be hard to make.

During the last decades of his life, Nygren found his own ideas to be congenial with the philosophy of Ludwig Wittgenstein. I think he was on the right track here. His idea of 'motif research' should, as far as I understand, be seen in this light. His interpretations primarily concern an understanding of language. Nygren understood language as embedded in larger or smaller contexts, where different evident presuppositions had their part to play. As far as I can see, this leads to a very dynamic view of history and of the history of ideas. Nygren's reflections on love furthermore come close to Raimond Gaita's thinking on the subject, and to the ideas of philosophers like Camilla Kronqvist and Hannes Nykänen at Åbo Akademi University, where Wittgenstein's legacy has been well defended.[14] I will not deny that Nygren could be said to have a kind of Lutheran apologetics interwoven into some of his studies, something that Jeanrond has noticed.[15] This, however, is no reason to disapprove of the basic ideas underlying Nygren's understanding of human relations.

Eros, Agape, *and the Other*

When we return to the idea of the other, the two basic motifs will also be of heuristic value. In Løgstrup's basic picture of human encounter, we found that a fundamental problem is how to understand the relation between the two persons in his example. What is it that we emphasize, consequently? Is it the other who is standing there as an expression of trust, or is it the one who is presupposed to react upon the trust that has been shown? Interpreted from an *eros*-point-of-view, the emphasis is put on the person expressing trust. Following from this, a cognitive objectively given element becomes important for the person who faces this trustful other. First, he has to establish what exactly it is that he has before his eyes. Is it a person in need? Is it a person showing trust? Then he can perceive the tacit demand of the other and react to that. His final reaction becomes conditioned.

In the early 2000s, the story of the Good Samaritan (Lk. 11.25-36) was being discussed in the philosophical seminar at Åbo Akademi University over an extended period of time. This discussion was inspired by an article by Peter Winch entitled 'Who is my neighbour?'. One of Winch's main points is to highlight the

---

14. Cf. Raimond Gaita, *A Common Humanity: Thinking About Love and Truth and Justice* (London: Routledge, 2000); Camilla Kronqvist, 'What We Talk About When We Talk About Love' (Unpublished Diss. Åbo Akademi University, 2008); Hannes Nykänen, *The 'I', the 'You' and the Soul*.

15. Cf. Werner G. Jeanrond, *A Theology of Love*, pp. 118–19.

radical difference in the way that the Samaritan acted in comparison with the priest and the Levite. The difference lies in their immediate reactions. In Winch's interpretation the Samaritan immediately perceived a fellow human being, a 'neighbour', in need of help, while the other two reacted with rational deliberation.[16] The emphasis in Winch's discussion lies on the three people coming across an injured man on the road to Jericho.

Building on Nygren's concepts, it is possible to say that the priest and the Levite could be seen as representing an *eros* perspective, whereas the Samaritan expresses an *agape* perspective. From an *agape* perspective, the emphasis in Løgstrup's basic picture lies entirely on that person who encounters another person, who, in his turn, represents a supposed demand (according to the picture). The noticing of the trust and perception of the tacit demand are both characteristics of the subject whose moral action is called upon. When it comes to relating to others, a person whose frame of reference is determined by the basic motif of *agape* will simply perceive of the other as representing trustfulness and, at the same time, a tacit demand. This is part of the characteristic of spontaneity which Nygren attaches to *agape*.

Agape *in a Post-Secular Age*

Due to a long development, the societies in most European countries (at least those outside the formerly communist East), have become more and more secular. As part of this development, religions have become an increasingly private affair outside the public sphere. Contemporary public language has lacked religious connotations.[17] However, in the aftermath of '9/11', a variety of religions have slowly begun to return to the public sphere.

Løgstrup published *Den etiske fordring* in 1956. By that time, public language had become increasingly secular. Because of this, both his examples of trust, and a sensibility concerning moral demands, could be more or less taken for granted by all those who read his book. 'The other' was easy to understand and the moral demand easy to perceive. However, in a multicultural and post-secular situation such an assumption cannot be taken for granted anymore.

Are Nygren's concepts of love applicable to a post-secular situation? In *A Common Humanity*, Gaita has tried to express something that all humans, according to him, have in common despite their socio-cultural differences. For him, the communality is exemplified by a story from his own life. His main point is that we will recognize goodness when we come across it. He tells about a nun

---

16. Cf. Peter Winch, 'Who is my Neighbor', in idem, *Trying to Make Sense* (Oxford: Blackwell, 1987), pp. 154-66 (157); also cf. Hannes Nykänen, *The 'I' the 'You' and the Soul*, pp. 65-6.
17. Nigel Biggar, 'Not Translation, but Conversation: Theology in Public Debate about Euthanasia', in Nigel Biggar and Linda Hogan, eds, *Religious Voices in Public Places* (Oxford: Oxford University Press, 2009), pp. 161-93 (161).

he met in a psychiatric hospital where he worked as a young man. Through the way that nun took care of those truly miserable human beings that were her patients, Gaita thinks he came to witness the most genuine expression of love and goodness. His point is that he has an ability to perceive this although he does not necessarily share the Christian faith of the nun.[18] The question is: can we presuppose a universal human recognition of goodness and of the value of every human being? In order to find the answer to the question, Nygren's concepts of love are instructive.

In an *eros* perspective, the value of the object – of the other – is crucial. It is through establishing the value of the other that we get a reason to treat her or him decently. Such a relation depends on a pre-evaluation of the other. Hence, an *eros* perspective opens up for a discussion of whether each and every person really should be treated in a decent way. Perhaps there are people with qualities that make them less worthy of good treatment. This is the kind of argument we meet in the example of Breivik, but also in much of the rhetoric of the xenophobic political parties. The basic motif of *agape* can be seen as presupposing another way of understanding. A view of life coloured by *eros* is deconstructed when we perceive the world from an *agape* perspective. Would it be possible to save the world this way? Do we here find a universal theory (on theological grounds) that could contribute to the shaping of a common world where 'love is all you need'? The ongoing discussion of post-secularity demonstrates that religious arguments are returning to the public discourse. This return, however, goes hand in hand with a questioning of the universality of secularism. With this loss of the hegemony of the Western secular world-view, we also lose the ability to build upon a common understanding of human worth, like Løgstrup's. Religious and secular arguments exist side by side and do not necessarily lead to the same conclusions.

This is mainly a problem from the perspective of *eros*. In that perspective a common human understanding assumes a joint concept of what may count as a human being, and of how human worth can be established. *Agape*, for its part, is not dependent on the universality of a *theory* of human dignity. To view the world in the perspective of *agape* is to lead a life marked by the experience of being met with love. *Agape*-love is, I think, mostly experienced in the encounter with others who love us unconditionally. In accordance with Nygren's idea, this *is* 'God as love' showing him- or herself to us. At the same time this becomes a moral challenge to anyone who is met with this kind of love: the challenge to spread love through her or his own way of living. Moreover, value in others is created. We cannot know whether such a way of life will impress persons like Breivik. Whoever embraces the perspective of *agape*, Christian or non-Christian, can only hope that this way of living will impress and influence his or her fellow human beings. This is our current predicament, as far as I can see. I trust that Jeanrond would agree with me on such a hope.

---

18. Cf. Raimond Gaita, *A Common Humanity*, pp. 19–20.

9

LOVE OF GOD AND LOVE OF ONE ANOTHER ACCORDING TO PAUL

Jeffrey Bloechl

As has been sometimes noted, the experience of love is immediately also an experience of plurality,[1] since it belongs to loving another person that one welcomes her in her unique being. The Christian tradition – and no doubt others – has long preserved these two dimensions of a single experience at the heart of its conception of a kinship with God the Father. Less than three decades since Jesus had preached love of God and love of neighbour (Mt. 22.35-40; Mk 12.28-31; Lk. 10.25-8), Paul, the first great theologian of the Church, exhorts his community in Rome to a love which will define the service of the Lord (Rom. 12.10). Indeed, this teaching is so prominent in his thought as to function as the centre of gravity in virtually all of his correspondence.

It therefore comes as no small surprise to find some recent interpreters propose a reading of Paul that makes no mention of the central theme of love. The two best known of them are Alain Badiou, in *St. Paul: The Foundation of Universalism*, and Giorgio Agamben, in *The Time that Remains: A Commentary of the Letter to the Romans*.[2] These works are so complex as to deserve separate treatment, yet on the present occasion it is enough to note, first, that Badiou depicts Paul as having had the unique capacity to name the event that is the novelty of Jesus, whereby that event truly interrupts the order of law. Second, Agamben considers Paul to have preached a universal messianic subjectivity only embodied by Jesus, whereby the sum and system of the law may appear to us as an imposition on more original

---

1. Werner G. Jeanrond has reinstated the significance of plurality for the experience of love in Werner G. Jeanrond, *A Theology of Love* (London: Continuum/T&T Clark, 2010). Its contemporary lineage is easily traced to Paul Ricœur. Cf. Paul Ricœur, 'Love and Justice', in Werner G. Jeanrond and Jennifer L. Rike, eds, *Radical Pluralism and Truth: David Tracy and the Hermeneutics of Religion* (New York: Crossroads, 1991), pp. 187–202.

2. Alain Badiou, *St. Paul: The Foundation of Universalism*, trans. R. Brassier (Palo Alto, CA: Stanford University Press, 2003), and Giorgio Agamben, *The Time that Remains: A Commentary on the Letter to the Romans*, trans. P. Daily (Palo Alto, CA: Stanford University Press, 2005).

conditions. Third, whereas the two thus agree in opposing Pauline thought to the finality of law, Badiou's Paul adopts a strictly anti-nomial position while the position of Agamben's Paul is instead anomial.[3] Finally, in both cases, escape from the emprise of the law does not lead to 'the kingdom of the beloved Son' (εἰς τὴν βασιλείαν τοῦ υἱοῦ τῆς ἀγάπης αὐτοῦ; Col. 1.13), but only takes the form of whatever liberation can be achieved according to our capacity for resistance.

A close study of these interpretations of Paul confirms what one immediately suspects: they are delivered from an experience remote from that of Paul himself. Badiou's perspective is strongly informed by a Maoist revolutionary dissatisfaction with the order of modern liberalism (and perhaps particularly that). Agamben writes in the shadow of Auschwitz, in which he sees the consummation of the rationality that has produced modern politics and technology. In both cases, the experience of the law has been an experience of oppression and suffocation. Badiou's notion of the event and Agamben's notion of a messianic subject are meant to reinvigorate a humanity too long depersonalized by a thinking that – frequently against its own stated intentions – addresses each of us as a single instance of a general set. In short, Badiou and Agamben appeal to Paul not in his own spirit of zeal for the message that Christ is the fulfilment of the Mosaic law, but instead in the conviction that his thinking can also be opposed to the view, this time distinctly modern, that for peace between subjects the law will suffice. Of course, to bring Pauline thought to bear specifically on this point, there is no immediate need to emphasize more than his interruption of the previous, prevailing order (Badiou) or else his exemption from worldly order altogether (Agamben). It is this that would appear to validate simple disregard of the call of divine love that Paul's own tradition has always considered essential – and indeed what seems to have made all the difference in his own experience.

In order to prepare for some reflection on the situation of Pauline thought today, we might pause briefly to distinguish three features of the context that has yielded these unexpected readings of his letters. We should begin by acknowledging the unquestioned authority of experiences that have prompted many to profound mistrust of the modern legal and political order. This is a matter of suffering, as recorded unforgettably in atrocities of the camps, but also, though undoubtedly in a different way, the despair of modern urban life. The authority of suffering is assured both morally and phenomenologically. What suffering must *not* do is blind us to the difference between the original richness of texts that can help us see clearly into its causes, and the somewhat impoverished form assigned to them by the history of impatient readings. The history of thought, of great ideas, is more than the history of their popular reception. Neither the Paul who is read only partially by contemporary philosophers nor the modern political thinkers who are their likely targets are quite responsible for everything

3. These positions resemble the antinomianism of, for example, the sixteenth-century reformer Johannes Agricola, for whom grace rendered the law obsolete. Both Badiou and Agamben suggest that the law is even an impediment to freedom.

that has been assigned to them, for better and for worse. And so while it is true that a contemporary reaction to modern political thought has considerable force at the level of experience, where many have been made to suffer by those who align themselves with John Locke or Adam Smith or Karl Marx, it is less evident that that force is compelling at the level of theory, where for example those same thinkers might be expected to speak against the depersonalizing effects of order and law. So likewise with Paul's texts, which an entire tradition has long mined for resources toward developing a vision of community in which each person would be valued as unique before and beyond the mediation of laws. Why should Paul be received as if the interest of his work lies above all in its contribution to a new theory of law, and almost not at all in the fact that he thinks constantly in view of a relation with God by which 'we are discharged from the law' (κατηργήθημεν ἀπὸ τοῦ νόμου; Rom. 7.6)?

Before attempting to answer this question, we might also briefly consider some developments within the theological tradition that seem actively to diminish interest in the experience of God by which Paul was led to reconceive his relation to the law. This is a matter specifically of Paul's mysticism. Without pursuing Paul's mysticism in any detail, let us simply note the most unmistakable instances recorded in the canonical texts. Most dramatically, there is the rapture detailed in 2 Cor. 12: 'I know a man in Christ who fourteen years ago was caught up to the third heaven – whether in the body or out of the body I do not know, God knows ... and he heard many things that cannot be told, which man may not utter'. There are also occasional references to other marks of one who has had intimate contact with God. Paul seems to claim the power to heal (2 Cor. 12.12) and may have spoken in tongues (1 Cor. 13.1 and 14.18). However, before all of these things was the *encounter with Jesus* on the road to Damascus. According to Paul – and the author of Acts – Paul both heard and saw Jesus (Acts 9.3-19, 22.6-11; 1 Cor. 9.1; 15.7-8), in order that Paul 'might preach him among the Gentiles' (Gal. 1.16). There can be no mistake that, as far as he is concerned, his preaching, which did not cease to develop from letter to letter, took root precisely then and there. A few lines after tracing that connection, he underlines its lasting significance: 'I have been crucified with Christ; it is no longer I who live, but Christ who lives in me; and the life I now live in the flesh I live by faith in the Son of God, who loved me and gave himself for me' (Gal. 2.20). For the moment, let us only note the importance of the notion of 'Christ living in me' and remind ourselves of its strict correlate, the notion that my life is properly in Christ (ἐν Χριστῷ). Occurrences of one or another form of these expressions are found throughout the Pauline corpus. In them, we have the unmistakable expression of Paul's understanding of what it means that the Jesus who called to him so unexpectedly had loved him. And the matter could hardly be of greater importance, for he does not hesitate to draw from his own experience implications for us all: it is not only that Christ lives in Paul and Paul in Christ, but indeed that Christ is in all of us as all of us are in him (Rom. 8.1 and 8.5).

What is at issue is the manner in which the community of believers is to negotiate the relationship between their commitments to Jesus and to the law.

Yet we are prevented from understanding this matter clearly by some uncertainty about quite what it can mean for Christ to live in Paul and for Paul to live in Christ. The thought that these formulations express union between God's love and the love of the one who believes in the loving God – and that this would be the key to Paul's sense of having been 'discharged from the law' – has always been alive in the Eastern tradition. In the Western tradition, however, the idea has laboured under strong opposition from those who, like Karl Barth, suspect in any emphasis on Paul's mysticism the latent atheism of those who presume for themselves the capacity to reach the divine.[4] This results in noticeable embarrassment over Paul's own claim to have been 'caught up to the third heaven' (2 Cor. 12.1-5). With such passages suspended from serious consideration, the Jesus who called to him in the desert and the Christ who lives in him must appear to us essentially as the revelation and the content of a new law that discharges us from all other laws. Of course, Paul does on occasion refer in this way to Jesus. In Gal. 6.2 he asks us to 'bear one another's burdens and so fulfill the law of Christ' and in 1 Cor. 9.21, he identifies his adherence to the law of Christ as a distinguishing mark of his vocation to those who have lived outside the Jewish law. But emphasis on all of this risks projecting Christianity, too, overtly as a religion of law, rather than one of a way open to believers by divine grace. Not that grace is opposed to the law; it is rather the means by which one might follow and fulfill it. Needless to say, this means is given in boundless love (Eph. 3.17-19). Such a love is the key to Jesus as Christ, and it is also the key to Paul's conversion to him. To the degree that this inflection has been downplayed in modern Western theology, it stands to reason that the resultant image of Paul as above all concerned with a new law that would raise us up against all other laws has seemed amenable to the incomplete readings developed in the studies by Badiou and Agamben – let us not forget it: in the search for a less totalizing and less suffocating notion of community.

None of this is to suggest that Badiou and Agamben have taken any particular care to read Barth, and still less that the Barthian approach to Paul is in some way opposed to the idea that Pauline thought is guided by an experience of Jesus Christ as love. Yet it does highlight the fact that under certain important influences within modern theology, Paul has been read in a manner that de-emphasizes the same theme that contemporary philosophical readings have subsequently felt no need to address at all. Without supposing any causal link between the two, we can nonetheless propose to read in their contiguity an interesting sign of the times: whereas the modern theological approach to Paul has often wished to address the experience of perfect love properly through an

---

4. See, Karl Barth, *Church Dogmatics*, vol. IV, 3/2, trans. G. W. Bromiley (Edinburgh: T&T Clark, 2010), pp. 538–9. The reading of Paul as mystic attracted some attention following the publication of Albert Schweitzer, *Die Mystik des Apostels Paulus* (Tübingen: Mohr Siebeck, 1930), but soon faded. For reasons that deserve separate exploration, some scholarship has returned to the topic. For an excellent review, see Jeffrey Keiser, 'Crucifying Adam: the Mysticism and Mystagogy of Paul', *Arc* 35 (2007), pp. 189–210.

expanded account of law, contemporary philosophy has begun to address the law without any interest in love.[5] Nothing prevents us from taking a somewhat expanded lesson from these short reflections on some interpretations of Paul: if perhaps in the theological approach we recognize some prudent hesitation about the precise form of God's presence to humanity, in the philosophical approach we detect a sense that the thought of God, especially as perfect love, has become unintelligible. Without pretending to understand the conditions under which this latter thought might assert itself, and without either confirming it or contesting it, we might nonetheless ask what it may cost. And we can do so without leaving the question of community – of love of God and love of another – in the Pauline corpus.

We do not know precisely when Paul's experience of the love of Jesus yielded his conception of the community of believers united in their love of Jesus, but there can be little doubt that the two are thought together throughout his correspondence. To the Corinthians, for example, he writes that, 'the love of Christ constrains us [συνέχει ἡμᾶς], because we are convinced that he died for all' (2 Cor. 5.14); and that according to this constraint whatever we do, if we have not love in doing it, nothing is gained (1 Cor. 13.1-3). Here is the spiritual root of the Christian community whose lineaments are worked out in a more corporeal language: the community that is the body of Christ is inspired by a love that opens its members to be loving in all things, especially in their relations with one another. Hence does Paul later enjoin the Romans to 'owe no one anything, except to love one another; for he who loves his neighbour has fulfilled the law' (Rom. 13.8). This love defines an entire *mode of being* that is no longer contained exclusively by our mortality. 'If we live, we live to the Lord, and if we die, we die to the Lord; so then whether we live or whether we die, we are the Lord's' (Rom. 14.8). As for what this means in ordinary lives, it is the guiding principle by which to understand some dramatic revisions proposed for our earthly attitude in Ephesians (5.21: 'be subject to one another out of love for Christ'). Even in 1 Cor. 7 this principle is apparent; Paul's difficult statements concerning sexual and conjugal life are not moral exhortations so much as a call to the eschatological horizon of commitment to faith in the love of Jesus.

In Paul's preaching, what evidently sustains this vision is the close relationship between his own identification with Jesus and his call that all believers in Jesus follow his example. We have already taken note of the mystical dimension of that identification: Paul responds to the sacrificial love of Jesus that swept over him unexpectedly on the road to Damascus with an act of loving surrender of his own. We have also taken note of the centrality of his notion of Christ living in us and us living in Christ for a proper understanding of who we are. At this point, we are fully prepared to recognize in the translation of that personal experience of

---

5. But not only the *modern* theological approach. One should not forget that Thomas Aquinas was willing to think of a law that is inscribed onto our hearts before it is committed to any writing, and to associate this inscribed law properly with Christ. Thomas Aquinas, *Summa Theologica* I-II, q. 106, art. 3.

Jesus as love into a general theory of the soul called to love Jesus as the true origin of what is sometimes called Paul's 'universalism' – that is, before any question of a radical politics.⁶ Or better, we can assert, against any number of philosophical readings, that the true radicality of the Pauline theory of community evidently flows from a source that is, for him, essentially religious.⁷

What might be some features of this community of love? Everything depends on the personal dimension of the defining *experience*. Jesus Christ calls in love to me, as me, and I respond in love. This love enjoins me to love others, as my sisters and brothers before God the Father. It makes little difference whether the privileged model is the family or the body. Each of us is loved by the Father, and loved by her sisters and brothers, specifically as herself. Each of us is indispensible. Each of us is valued without possibility of substitution by someone else. To be a member of a family is to still be oneself and yet more than oneself, as a member of a community that needs one to be precisely oneself. My brother takes things for himself, and it is precisely as such, with that power, that he has his own importance for the whole family. Each brother is thus more than a single child who possesses and even consumes things for himself insofar as he is called to the spirit that is offered in Jesus as Christ. How does this offer move us from self-assertion and self-gratification to willing commitment to the family? Once again, not by the enforcement of some higher law, stipulated by a force that commands only a new form of submission, but also not by withdrawal from any and every law. Love is offered to each of us, in him- and herself, whereupon each of us either rejects that offer in freedom or else recognizes that offer in freedom. Paul's christological definition of the offer and the way of life urged by the offer is well known. In the first instance, as a matter of the call, we encounter the self-emptying Christ, whose love went so far as to accept death on the cross. In the second instance, as a matter of our response, we commit ourselves to imitate that selfless love in the cultivation of a tender readiness for compassion.

This, finally, puts us in the position to take the measure of a reading of Paul – and more generally a political theory as such – that would unfold as if without positive reference to the transcendent love of Jesus as Christ. The community of faith proposes a plurality that is, if anything, greater than that of the modern and anti-modern conceptions advanced in recent centuries. The Christian community that Paul opens to anyone of good intention admits and attends to a uniqueness in each person that is ensured by a relation with the God who cannot be contained in any worldly horizon, even if that God is nonetheless present there. Yet this is also a politics that attends to the whole, not least because each of the members

---

6. Here I rejoin a central though unstated theme of Stanislas Breton, *Saint Paul* (Paris: PUF, 1988). For Breton, Paul's pertinence for politics lies essentially in the inspiration of his thinking by an extra-political source.

7. One could say still more. Perhaps such a theory of community is possible because the religious experience, even as mystical experience, already contains a *communitarian* seed. This would mean attributing to the genius of Paul a capacity to find in mysticism, as a private and personal experience, the possibility of its own sublation.

has a vital relation to all of the others. At the same time, it is eminently concrete, since it is upheld by an attitude of love that is to permeate everything we do. So likewise would the ethics accompanying it promote a relation among kindred, of one person to the other person, that cannot be reduced either to any will to totalization or any wish to interrupt totalities. In Pauline thought – and, I am inclined to say, in all Christian thought – the key to plurality and care for others is the love of Jesus as Christ. If the faith that this requires is no longer possible for some of us today, then we find ourselves ready to address a recent sign of the times through the lens of a somewhat older concept. It is not impossible that the most lasting effect of the so-called 'death of God' will prove to be a diminished capacity to care for one another, unnoticed as we attempt to exorcize our sense of desolation by giving ourselves up to the politics of revolt.

10

PAUL RICOEUR AS OTHER

Bengt Kristensson Uggla

Paul Ricoeur – A Puzzle for Philosophy

For more than half a century, Paul Ricoeur (1913–2005) was omnipresent at the forefront of philosophical developments. However, despite his profound and provocative influence, his position in philosophy remains somewhat enigmatic.[1] What may be recognized as the major reason for why Ricoeur appears to be a puzzle for philosophers is mainly associated with his many connections to theology. Many philosophers have been so puzzled by this, that they have sometimes even recognized him as the other, terming him a theologian – in opposition to his rejection of the label 'theologian'.

If we consider the fact that the general history of hostility between theology and philosophy stretches back to the 'origins' of our civilization, we may understand why theology, in modern times, has tended to be regarded as a ghost of a repressed memory constantly chasing the identity of philosophers. Today, the controversies around secularity and post-secularity have become urgent matters. Effectively, this means that the challenges associated with Ricoeur can be said to be equivalent to coping with the most crucial issues of our time. Thus, the enigmas associated with dealing with Ricoeur are expressions of dilemmas of extraordinary importance from a post-secular perspective.

Undeniably, religion is present throughout Ricoeur's comprehensive publication list. The occurrence of this is most obvious in his many articles. Yet, we find a recurrent discussion in his major monographs, even though two clear periods characterized by different publishing strategies may be delineated. In his early works on Karl Jaspers and Gabriel Marcel we are confronted with a great number of religious themes.[2] For readers who are trained as theologians, it is not difficult to detect the profound influences of Martin Luther's theology particularly in the

---

1. Cf. Bengt Kristensson Uggla, *Kommunikation på bristningsgränsen: En studie i Paul Ricoeurs project* (Stockholm: Östlings Bokförlag Symposion, 1994); idem, *Ricoeur, Hermeneutics, and Globalization* (London: Bloomsbury, 2010).

2. Cf. Paul Ricoeur with Mikel Dufrenne, *Karl Jaspers et la philosophie de l'existence*

philosophical anthropology of Ricoeur's philosophy of the will.[3] The internal structure of his interpretation of Luther's concept of *self-arbitre* can even be recognized as a predecessor of Ricoeur's concept of the *cogito blessé*. Explicit religious issues are also dealt with in his major studies from the 1960s.[4]

Paradoxically, it was only after Ricoeur received a professorship at the Divinity School of the University of Chicago that a new logic was introduced into his publishing strategy, resulting in a separation of religious topics.[5] The dilemmas associated with this separation became a critical issue in the preparation of *Oneself as Another* where the author not only added three chapters on ethics, but also decided to eliminate two chapters from the final publication.[6] These chapters consisted of the studies on natural theology which were part of the original Gifford Lectures.

Personally, Ricoeur had strong affinities with what he called 'the biblical faith'. He identified himself with Christianity (without claiming any exclusivism). Those who prefer a clear-cut dichotomy between philosophy and theology have been puzzled by a philosopher who explicitly declared that he is one of those who 'identify themselves with the book that itself stems from the metaphorical identification between the Word of God and the person of Christ' in terms of a 'second-degree identification'.[7] A member of the French Reformed Church, Ricoeur donated his library to the Faculté de théologie protestante de Paris. Throughout his career, he was invited to speak to audiences in churches and congregations. Unsurprisingly, he has been a very common reference for theologians.

If we consider that all these circumstances refer to a thinker who strongly refused to identify himself as a theologian, we may recognize why his presence

(Paris: Seuil, 1947); Paul Ricoeur, *Gabriel Marcel et Karl Jaspers: philosophie de mystère et philosophie du paradoxe* (Paris: Éditions du Temps Present, 1948).

3. Cf. Paul Ricoeur, *Fallible Man*, trans. C. A. Kelbley (New York: Fordham University Press, 1986); idem, *The Symbolism of Evil*, trans. E. Buchanan (New York: Harper and Row, 1967).

4. Cf. Paul Ricoeur, *Freud and Philosophy: An Essay on Interpretation*, trans. D. Savage (New Haven: Yale University Press, 1970); idem, *The Conflict of Interpretations: Essays on Hermeneutics*, ed. Don Idhe (Evanston, IL: Northwestern University Press, 1974); and idem, *History and Truth*, trans. C. A. Kelbley (Evanston, IL: Northwestern University Press, 1965).

5. Paul Ricoeur, *Essays on Biblical Interpretation*, ed. Lewis S. Mudge (Philadelphia: Fortress, 1980); idem, *Figuring the Sacred: Religion, Narrative, and Imagination*, ed. Mark I. Wallace (Minneapolis: Augsburg, 1995); idem with André LaCocque, *Penser la Bible* (Paris: Seuil, 1998).

6. Cf. Paul Ricoeur, *Oneself As Another*, trans. K. Blamey (Chicago: University of Chicago Press, 1992).

7. Paul Ricoeur, 'The Self in the Mirror of the Scriptures', in John McCarthy, ed., *The Whole and the Divided Self: The Bible and Theological Anthropology* (New York: Crossroads, 1997), p. 219.

tends to challenge the self-understanding of both philosophy and theology. The attempts to evaluate his particular philosophy have generally resulted in diverse judgements. According to some, Ricoeur is distinguished as one of the major philosophers, while others ignore his philosophy.[8] The already polarized reception has even been aggravated by the uncertainties concerning the relationship between philosophical and theological discourses in his work which also generated complications within the theological reception of his thought. What further complicates the attempts to establish a clear distinction between philosophy and theology in Ricoeur's project is the fact that he claimed that the most important sources for critical thinking have religious origins, because they emanate from religious traditions:

> Critique is also a tradition. I would even say that it plunges into the most impressive tradition, that of liberating acts, of the Exodus and the Resurrection. Perhaps there would be no more interest in emancipation, no more anticipation of freedom, if the Exodus and the Resurrection were erased from the memory of mankind.[9]

The fact that Ricoeur did not identify religious faith with (blind) convictions, but deduced critical thinking as a tradition from religious sources, undermines any attempt to operate according to a simple dichotomy. It is true that Ricoeur believed in the necessity of convictions, but it is equally true that he stressed that all convictions need to be developed by critical distanciations. Hence, not only the internal structure of hermeneutical experience, but also Ricoeur's understanding of the religious experience harbours a remarkably high degree of alienation, due to the omnipresence of different forms of critical distanciations. Ricoeur found it a necessity to ask critically how it is possible to introduce a critical instance into the consciousness of belonging. The dialectic between the experience of belonging, on the one hand, and alienation and distanciation, on the other hand, is 'the key to the inner life of hermeneutics'.[10] This idea of the hermeneutical function of distanciation in all communication has relevance for the strong linkage between Ricoeur's reflection on the *cogito blessé* and his contemplations on the silence of God. These reflections were initially influenced by Dietrich Bonhoeffer, although Ricoeur finally found his most important

---

8. Within the French context, we are confronted with the contrast between François Dosse, *History of Structuralism*, 2 vols, trans. D. Glassman (Minneapolis: University of Minnesota Press, 1997) for whom Ricoeur is the hero in the drama of the development of the humanities, and Vincent Descombes, *Modern French Philosophy*, trans. L. Scott-Fox and J. M. Harding (Cambridge: Cambridge University Press, 1979) who completely ignores Ricoeur when describing the philosophical scene in France.

9. Paul Ricoeur, 'Hermeneutics and the Critique of Ideology', in idem, *Hermeneutics & the Human Sciences*, ed. J. B. Thompson (Cambridge: Cambridge University Press, 1981), pp. 63–100 (99–100).

10. Ibid., p. 91.

interlocutor in Eberhard Jüngel. If we consider Jüngel's profound inspiration on the two Gifford Lectures that were excluded from Ricoeur's study on identity, it is not by coincidence that there is a strong resemblance between Ricoeur's considerations on the ontological commitment of attestation in the last chapter of *Oneself as Another* and Jüngel's plea for the abandonment of God as the guarantor of absolute knowledge as outlined in *God as the Mystery of the World*.[11] When Ricoeur's project reaches beyond René Descartes' cogito as well as Friedrich Nietzsche's anti-cogito, joining Jüngel's project to go beyond both theism and atheism, he opens the perspectives of an affirmation of a trust without any security, undermining all prospects of establishing a simple dichotomy between philosophy and theology.

Theology and (its Obstacles against) Philosophy

Arguably, there are two major contexts of particular interest for Ricoeur's work: the French context (with its epicentre in Paris) and the North American context (with its epicentre in Chicago). Similarly, without ignoring French-speaking scholars, such as Claude Geffré and Jean Greisch,[12] together with Werner G. Jeanrond[13] within the German theological reception, Richard Kearney[14] from Ireland and Peter Kemp[15] from Denmark, arguably the most extensive theological reception has taken place in North America. There are several reasons for this, among which the most important one may be the fact that Ricoeur frequently co-taught together with the theologian David Tracy. Thus, we approach a particularly 'theological' Ricoeur in the United States. This is in stark contrast to the more 'philosophical' Ricoeur in France. A contextualization of these 'two Ricoeurs' is also of interest due to the two different approaches they represent when coping with the relationship between philosophy and theology.

Ricoeur's life among theologians in North America has itself been strongly polarized. 'Two theologians, David Tracy and Hans Frei, have dominated the reception of Ricoeur in North American theology, and characterized the initial

---

11. Cf. Eberhard Jüngel, *God as the Mystery of the World: On the Foundation of the Theology of the Crucified One in the Dispute between Theism and Atheism,* trans. D. N. Guder (Grand Rapids, MI: Eerdmans, 1983).

12. Cf. Claude Geffré, *Le christianisme au risqué de l'interprétation* (Paris: Édition du Cerf, 1983) and Jean Greisch, *L'âge herméneutique de la raison* (Paris: Édition du Cerf, 1985).

13. Cf. Werner G. Jeanrond, *Text und Interpretation als Kategorien theologischen Denkens* (Tübingen: Mohr Siebeck, 1986). Also cf. the English translation *Text and Interpretation as Categories of Theological Thinking,* trans. T. J. Wilson (New York: Crossroad, 1988).

14. Cf. Richard Kearney, *Anatheism: Returning to God after God* (New York: Columbia University Press, 2010).

15. Cf. Peter Kemp, *Théorie de l'engagement,* 3 vols (Paris: Seuil, 1973).

positive and negative responses to Ricoeur's hermeneutics'.[16] Hence, there seem to be two answers to the question of whether philosophical hermeneutics can or cannot be appropriated into theology: a positive one and a negative one.[17] However, Boyd Blundell recognizes the post-liberal critiques by George Lindbeck and Hans Frei as critiques of Tracy's appropriation of philosophical hermeneutics – very little of these critiques actually reaches Ricoeur. By distancing Ricoeur from Tracy, Blundell intended to display that Ricoeur is compatible with Frei's position (even if he has not realized it himself). Finally, Blundell put Ricoeur in the service of Karl Barth's theology. According to Blundell, the French philosopher shares not only a reformed background with Barth, but also that his methodology and respect for the integrity of theology are said to have the same origin. This profound influence from Barth is used as an explanation for what Blundell calls 'Ricoeur's double life': Ricoeur never mixed philosophical and theological reflections; nonetheless, there seems to be an affinity between Ricoeur's hermeneutic philosophy and Barth's christocentric theology.[18]

However, Blundell's conclusion raises a number of critical questions: Did Ricoeur really practice a 'double life'? Is Ricoeur's interpretation of the Christian faith really in accord with Barth's christocentric theology where 'a study of the *real* human can be done only by taking the man Jesus as its starting point'?[19] Here, Blundell's argumentation does not only appear simplistic, but he also ignores fundamental elements in Ricoeur's ontological, anthropological and hermeneutical considerations. Even if Ricoeur's contributions to biblical studies were never published in the same volume as his philosophical work, it is an inevitable fact that his general discussions of theological themes were interwoven into his philosophical works. However, it is even more important to disclose the weak points of Blundell's arguments for structural connections between Ricoeur and Barth.

Here, it is clarifying to turn to the extraordinary critical investigation of Ricoeur's work presented by Kevin Vanhoozer. Even though I find his theological conclusions imprecise and incorrect, his interpretation of Ricoeur's work offers an important contribution due to his identification of structures which were overlooked by Blundell. What becomes clear in Vanhoozer's critical reading is that Ricoeur 'prefers to define the religious dimension in terms of creation rather than Salvation', that 'Ricoeur's mediation of religion and atheism results in a faith in and love of creation', and that for Ricoeur the '"Yes" of Jesus towards creation is stronger than his "No". Meaning is more fundamental than absurdity'.[20] However,

---

16. Boyd Blundell, *Paul Ricoeur between Theology and Philosophy: Detour and Return* (Indianapolis: Indiana University Press, 2010), p. 40. For a similar account cf. Mark I. Wallace, *The Second Naiveté: Barth, Ricoeur and the New Yale Theology* (Macon, GA: Mercer University Press, 1990).

17. Boyd Blundell, *Paul Ricoeur between Theology and Philosophy*, p. 32.

18. Cf. ibid., pp. 51–3; 131.

19. Ibid., p. 154.

20. Kevin Vanhoozer, *Biblical Narrative in the Philosophy of Paul Ricoeur: A Study in*

these observations cause Vanhoozer to reject Ricoeur. The rejection is reinforced by the fact that Vanhoozer insists on describing Ricoeur as a theologian – in order to critique his theological shortcomings. However, what is more obvious is Vanhoozer's lack of theological resources to cope with Ricoeur's philosophy of creation. His inability to identify any positive connections between salvation and creation makes Christ appear in a world that is totally alien to him. Vanhoozer may be right in criticizing Tracy for ignoring Ricoeur's anthropology and ontology due to his negligence of Ricoeur's earlier philosophy. Nevertheless, he is incorrect not only when he labels Ricoeur a theologian, but also in his inability to mobilize any theological interpretation of Ricoeur's preference for creation when speaking about God's presence. His post-liberal christocentric theology, characterized by a profound anti-liberalism, has no theological resources to identify a positive link between creation and christology; consequently, it has no ability to cope with a philosophical anthropology linked to a perspective of creation. Hence, neither the theologians who embrace, nor those who reject him, seem to have access to the necessary theological resources to cope with Ricoeur.

In Ricoeur's work we approach a polyphonic concept of revelation, involving a multitude of genres. This concept of revelation is open to creation; it is linked to an ontological surplus of meaning. It manifests itself as an original 'Yes' – stronger than the 'No' of negative ontologies. We may also add Ricoeur's *indirect* approach which makes mediation a necessity; as well as the Lutheran inspiration that God remains veiled after his revelation. The one who reveals himself is also the one who conceals himself: 'God is like… God is not…'.[21] According to Ricoeur's concept of revelation, the New Testament *continues* to speak about God; Christ is subsumed into an economy of gift where salvation is acknowledged as a recapitulation and restoration of the original creation.

Philosophy of Creation – Theology of Creation?

Although Ricoeur was expressly a Christian philosopher, he was expressly critical of any 'Christian philosophy'. As mentioned above, the relationship between philosophy and theology became prominent when he explained why the two studies, which were originally part of his Gifford Lectures, were finally excluded from *Oneself as Another*. He emphasized the importance of 'an autonomous philosophical discourse' and declared his commitment to keep to the 'asceticism of the argument' in order to avoid both crypto-philosophy and crypto-theology. No 'ontotheological amalgamations' were acceptable to him.[22] His strategy to avoid both assimilation and separation was flanked by a faith that knew itself to

---

Hermeneutics and Theology (Cambridge: Cambridge University Press, 1990), pp. 130; 132; 209.

21. Paul Ricoeur, 'The Self in the Mirror of the Scriptures', p. 218.
22. Paul Ricoeur, *Oneself as Another*, p. 24.

be without guarantee, a cogito that is protected from all self-foundational claims because it appears as a 'wounded cogito'.

The dilemmas associated with the lack of a relevant theological discourse able to transcend the dichotomy of philosophy and theology is further reinforced by the fact that Ricoeur himself seemed to labour with a christocentric understanding of theology. Thus, the result is a philosophy of creation without any theological connections – a philosophy of creation that seems to be theologically unacceptable.

As an ontological prerequisite for Ricoeur's philosophy and anthropology, we may identify what he called a surplus of meaning, associated with the epistemological 'seeing as' and the ontological 'being as'. Against the negativism of existentialism, Ricoeur stressed the 'Yes' of creation, the abundance of the incarnated mystery. Although it may be true that Ricoeur first learned that the subject is not a centralizing master but rather a disciple of a language larger than itself from Karl Barth, the positive understanding of this de-centring of the subject was the recognition of gift. Moreover, it is beyond all doubt that Ricoeur's philosophical and ontological considerations were not derived from a Barthian christological theology.[23] According to Ricoeur, the most fundamental motivations behind the recognition of the limitations of the subject are connected to the perspective of creation. To be de-centred means to be a *recipient* of life from outside, but this de-centring is simultaneously a part of an economy of gift where it is correlated to a centring. The dialectical relationship between the centring and the de-centring of the subject, the productive and the receptive elements of the appropriation of a text, the reorientation generated by the extreme possibilities for self-distanciation in the world in front of the text are all parts of Ricoeur's understanding of the *homo capax*, a dialectical anthropology which aims to reach beyond both anthropocentrism and anthropoclasm. The reason why Vanhoozer finds every kind of philosophical anthropology to be illegitimate[24] is that he fails to recognize the de-centring moves within Ricoeur's dialectical anthropology – as well as the positive implications of the fragility of the subject. Contrary to Vanhoozer's characterization of Ricoeur's anthropological prerequisites as expressions of narcissism, the *homo capax* is never, according to Ricoeur, equivalent to anthropocentrism. The *homo capax* is the human being who both acts and is acted upon – and text interpretation is defined as an extreme experience of self-distanciation.[25]

In order to find an appropriate theological articulation of these fundamental anthropological dynamics, where an initial de-centring move is counterbalanced by a centring move – in line with what could be called Ricoeur's double

---

23. Ricoeur recounts that his early years were formed by a conflict between the influence from Barth's anti-philosophical theology and Bergson's theological philosophy. Cf. Paul Ricoeur, *La critique et la conviction* (Paris: Calmann-Lévy, 1995), pp. 16–17.

24. Kevin Vanhoozer, *Biblical Narrative in the Philosophy of Paul Ricoeur*, p. 119.

25. Cf. Paul Ricoeur, *Oneself As Another*; idem, *The Course of Recognition*, trans. D. Pellauer (Cambridge, MA: Harvard University Press, 2005).

Copernican turn – we may turn to the contribution from the Scandinavian tradition of creation theology – a theology that has been elaborated by theologians such as Gustaf Wingren and Knud E. Løgstrup.[26] Here, we find an alternative model, inspired by Irenaeus, Martin Luther and Nikolaj F. S. Grundtvig, in which God's presence in creation is approached as a prerequisite for an understanding of salvation as a recapitulation and a restoration of creation, in contrast to the predominant post-liberal theological paradigm and its stereotypical articulation of God's exclusive revelation in Christ.

Paul Ricoeur – Anti-Theologian?

Given that Ricoeur was frequently involved in religious issues, it is surprising to recognize his own neglect of dogmatics. Considering Ricoeur's interest, it is remarkable how seldom the philosopher entered into dialogues with systematic theologians (Jüngel being the most significant exception). Far from the almost schizophrenic figure profiled by Blundell, I prefer to emphasize the anti-theological traits in Ricoeur's philosophy. Ricoeur, despite his great interest in the field, tended to ignore theology and theologians – with one major exception: biblical scholars.

Ricoeur had a life-long love affair with the Bible. He published numerous articles on the interpretation of biblical texts. However, it was not the Bible as a container of messages, but 'the world of the text', the Bible as a polyphonic world of discourses, which caught his interest – the Bible as a configuration functioning as a mirror (held by an invisible hand) for the reconfiguration of the self in the world in front of these texts. Ricoeur saw no limitations to the implementation of a critical analysis of either the world in front of these texts or the world of these texts.

When noting that, for Ricoeur, biblical exegesis appeared as the royal road to theology, it is important to add that his main interest was directed towards what he called 'biblical faith' and 'biblical thinking'. The concept of biblical thinking was integral to his hermeneutical ambition to rehabilitate a poetic discourse. This project was developed in *The Symbolism of Evil*.[27] In order to travel beyond the 'desert of criticism', Ricoeur used a methodological approach inspired by Immanuel Kant's aesthetics: '*le symbole donne à penser*'.[28] This means that the symbol *gives* and that this gift invites *thought*. However, before the symbols may speak to us, they need to 'speak to each other' in terms of a circular movement. *The Symbolism of Evil* is a staged circular movement of symbols, where the

---

26. Cf. Gustaf Wingren, *Credo: The Christian View of Faith and Life*, trans. E. M. Carlson (Minneapolis: Augsburg, 1981); and Knud E. Løgstrup, *The Ethical Demand*, trans. T. I. Jensen (Notre Dame, IN: University of Notre Dame Press, 1997).

27. Cf. Paul Ricoeur, *The Symbolism of Evil*, trans. E. Buchanan (Boston: Beacon Press, 1969).

28. In *The Symbolism of Evil*, Ricoeur uses the phrase '*le symbole donne à penser*' repeatedly.

biblical myth is subsumed in a wider economy of symbols. Ricoeur's recognition of the symbolic dimension as the most fundamental in language is the centre of his impressive investigations of metaphor and narrative in the 1970s and 1980s. Also in his later work he returned to the idea of the birth of philosophy in non-philosophy. The insight that poetic language teaches us what we otherwise could not have recognized was an important theme in the 'Interlude' on tragic action, dedicated to the memory of his son, Olivier (who committed suicide), in *Oneself as Another*.[29] Ricoeur's *The Course of Recognition* reiterates that philosophy must learn from tragedy, even though it does not proceed conceptually. The pre-philosophical discourses carry a surplus of meaning. They are richer than philosophy because they can say more – not as allegories, but as symbols giving rise to thought – if we are capable of *interpretation*.[30]

What may appear as Ricoeur's ignorance of systematic theology can be traced back to the strong influence of Immanuel Kant's *Religion within the Limits of Reason Alone*, where the focus is turned from God towards religion as representation.[31] Instead of metaphysical speculation, Ricoeur focused on limit-expressions and limit-experiences. Religious language 'uses limit-expressions only to open up our very experience, to make it explode in the direction of experiences that themselves are limit-experiences'.[32] His 'biblical thinking' radicalizes the experience of discordance and distanciation. There is a strong anti-speculative dimension in Ricoeur's religious considerations that prevents him from being or becoming too involved in doctrinal discussions. Hence, we may identify an anti-theological approach in Ricoeur's preference to talk about 'biblical faith' and 'biblical thinking' instead of 'theology'. It is a matter of fact that Ricoeur gave priority to pre-theological expressions of religious faith (which included the linguistic mediations of this faith) and the circulation of meaning within the framework of a greater polyphony. A confrontation with Ricoeur as the other may remind theological dogmatics and systematics of the fullness of language.

---

29. Paul Ricoeur, *Oneself as Another*, pp. 241–9.

30. The use of a three-level model in Ricoeur's *Symbolism of Evil* is repeated by Ricoeur in *Lectures on Ideology and Utopia*, ed. G. H. Taylor (New York: Columbia University Press, 1986); and *Memory, History, Forgetting*, trans. K. Blamey and D. Pellauer (Chicago: Chicago University Press, 2004).

31. Cf. Immanuel Kant, *Religion within the Limits of Reason Alone,* trans. T. M. Greene and H. H. Hudson (New York: Harper & Row, 1960).

32. Paul Ricoeur, *Figuring the Sacred*, p. 61.

11

THE OTHER OF DIALECTIC AND DIALOGUE
David Tracy

Two contemporary Western theorists, Mikhail Bakhtin and Hans-Georg Gadamer, have focused attention across the disciplines on dialogues. The words 'dialogue' (Gadamer) and 'dialogic' (Bakhtin) have related but quite different meanings in these two influential contemporary theorists on dialogue. Their clash on the meanings of dialogue can, I suggest, clarify certain elements in the discussion of dialogue across the disciplines. Gadamer's concept of dialogue has, in the traditions of hermeneutics and critical theory, been both expanded (Paul Ricoeur) and criticized and corrected (both Paul Ricoeur and Jürgen Habermas) while still maintaining Gadamer's basic philosophical theory of dialogue.

In this essay I shall argue that Bakhtin's literary theoretical notion of the dialogic needs, at some point, the philosophical theory of Gadamer to prove more useful as a philosophical theory on dialogue across the disciplines. At the same time, I shall argue that Gadamer's philosophical theory of dialogue, although philosophically both original and important, has led other dialogical thinkers to recognize a need for a serious rethinking of some of the Gadamerian over-claims on the purity and sufficiency of strictly philosophical dialogue. Bakhtin's notion of the 'dialogic' can help to foreground and even fragment those Gadamerian over-claims.

Mikhail Bakhtin on Dialogic

First Bakhtin: the Russian literary theorist, linguist and social analyst has been deeply influential for a unique understanding of what he named the dialogic imagination. Bakhtin principally focused his attention on the modern novel, especially such multi-voiced, polyphonic novels as François Rabelais' *Gargantua and Pantagruel* and Fyodor Dostoevsky's *The Brothers Karamazov*.[1] Unlike most

---

1. Inter alia, see Mikhail M. Bakhtin, *The Dialogic Imagination: Four Essays*, trans. C. Emerson and M. Holquist (Austin: University of Texas Press, 1981); idem, *Problems of Dostoevsky's Poetics*, trans. C. Emerson (Minneapolis: University of Minnesota Press, 1984);

critics of *The Brothers Karamazov*, Bakhtin does not focus his critical attention on the peculiar temperaments in the characters of each brother but on their ideas in dialectical, often conflictual dialogue with one another. In that peculiarly Bakhtinian sense, *The Brothers Karamazov* is indeed dialogic: open, multi-voiced, intellectually plural. In principle, the philosophical and theological conversations of the *Brothers* could go on indefinitely. Bakhtin privileges polyphonic novels as well as similarly open ancient dialogues, especially those open ancient dialogues held at a symposium-feast. A symposium, after all, encourages many speakers and rarely presents final conclusions on the issue at stake.[2]

With his valuable literary-theoretical model of the 'dialogic', Bakhtin criticizes even the great Leo Tolstoy (in my judgement, unfairly) as monologic largely because of the famous authorial (and, therefore, monologic) essays interpreting the narrative of *War and Peace*. In a Bakhtinian sense, *The Brothers Karamazov* remains open like a sympotic dialogue; *War and Peace*, however, can be read as a narrative-treatise where a single view prevails (as in Aristotle's treatises). There is, of course, nothing wrong with the literary form 'treatise' on its own terms for Bakhtin, but a novel should be dialogic not treatise-like monologic. Treatises are valuable to argue for and to clarify one's position; Bakhtin himself, after all, writes treatises, not novels. However, the dialogic encourages a multi-vocal, even heteroglossic radically open text where no one viewpoint is allowed to prevail.

The power of Bakhtin's analyses of 'the dialogic' is clear: Bakhtin's dialogic is more a literary genre than a philosophical category, although, as in the *Brothers*, the dialogic novel clearly includes philosophical and theological discussion. The dialogic – especially the modern novel as distinct from the classical epic – subverts any monolithic claim to *the* exclusive truth: dialogue rejects any authoritarian closure of dissenting voices. The dialogic encourages the playful, the disorienting, the ludic, the aporetic, even, in its postmodern forms (Italo Calvino or Thomas Pynchon), the aleatory. For Bakhtin, dialogue demands an open, multi-vocal text subversive of any closed, authoritarian or totalitarian society. Bakhtin's own totalitarian Stalinist society, in fact, exiled this crypto-Russian Orthodox thinker far away from the centres of Soviet political and cultural power. Moreover, the affinities of Bakhtin's position on the dialogic bears real affinities to many postmodern underscorings of the aleatory novel of 'pure difference'.

Bakhtin's dialogic model deconstructs, fragments, subverts any claims to univocal meaning. As a social theory allied to a literary and linguistic theory, moreover, Bakhtin's formalist analyses of literature and philosophy are joined to his anti-purely formalist analyses of the social-historical-economic realities embedded in language itself as every word always bears within itself multiple traces of its social history. For Bakhtin, the study of particular literary forms

---

idem, *Rabelais and His World*, trans. H. Iswolsky (Bloomington, IN: Indiana University Press, 1984).

2. For the importance of dialogue in a symposium, see the intriguing if erroneously entitled collection of essays, Simon Goldhill, ed., *The End of Dialogue in Antiquity* (Cambridge: Cambridge University Press, 2008).

(dialogue, novel, lyric, treatise, or epic) can never remain merely formalist but must always examine the complex and plural philosophical content rendered present through the dialogic form (again, as in the dialogues in *The Brothers Karamazov*). Moreover, in Bakhtin's analysis, the specific social, political, cultural reality of the period can also be unearthed by a close study of literary forms. For example, Bakhtin analyses specific economic systems, particular historical authoritarian, oligarchic at times and partially democratic regimes like the medieval and early modern hierarchies of sixteenth-century France; these regimes are subverted through parody, caricature, and festive laughter in Rabelais' great carnivalesque sixteenth-century novel, *Gargantua and Pantagruel*.

Bakhtin's model of the dialogic method is opposed to his contemporary Russian literary theorists and linguists. Like other critical theorists (Walter Benjamin), Bakhtin analyses the literary forms exposing the social realities at play in different literary forms (here like Theodor W. Adorno's analyses of the social realities embedded in different musical forms). Bakhtin always understood his work to expose not just literary genres but the social realities disclosed by genres, especially through intensified, nuanced ludic uses of formally literary language. Moreover, for Bakhtin, not only dialogic literary language but all language in principle contains the social uses of language. Every text implicitly contains in it the whole history of its uses in ever shifting historical, political, social, economic, cultural settings.

Bakhtin's notion of the 'dialogic' can, therefore, fragment certain over-claims by ancient (Plato and Cicero) and contemporary (Gadamer) philosophers on dialogue as the principal route to discovering truth. To my knowledge, Bakhtin never analysed any specific philosophical dialogue. I have elsewhere argued that the ludic, ironic, subversive *Dialogues on Natural Religion* of David Hume is a multi-vocal dialogue *avant la lettre*: a modern radicalized revision of Cicero's already multi-voiced dialogue-treatise *De natura deorum*. Indeed, so pervasive is Hume's irony in the dialogue that a careful reader soon realizes that Hume uses what later became known as an unreliable narrator: one who makes an untrustworthy announcement on who won the argument: The young narrator informs us that Cleanthes, not the more obvious Humean stand-in, Philo, is declared victor.[3]

It is also worth noting that even though Bakhtin himself did not analyse, as distinct from praise, the ancient dialogue form, a Bakhtinian analysis of ancient dialogue-forms would, in my judgement, best fit the sympotic dialogues: the symposiums of Plato, Plutarch, even the less festive but still sympotic Christian dialogue of Methodius.

The sympotic dialogue is a dialogue set at a symposium where several speakers (all male) speak on a chosen topic, such as *eros* in Plato's *Symposium*.[4] Clearly sympotic dialogue, a favoured form among the ancients, is the most natural

---

3. David Hume, *Dialogues Concerning Natural Religion*, ed. Nelson Pike (New York: Bobbs-Merril, 1970), p. 123.

4. See especially Walter Benjamin, *The Origin of German Tragic Drama*, trans. J. Osborne (London: NLB, 1977).

ancient dialogue-form for a Bakhtinian analysis: a festive setting with food, music, sexual playfulness, though it includes several speakers representing very different views. A symposium-dialogue is open, playful, polyvocal and often comic (the arrival of Alcibiades in Plato's *Symposium* or Aristophanes' comic image of an original male/female human body). Best of all, in a scene allowing both Bakhtinian and Gadamerian readings, the *Symposium* famously ends with both the tragedian Agathon and the comic writer Aristophanes asleep at dawn as the still wide-awake and tragic-comic philosopher, Socrates, arises to leave only in order to continue his insistent questionings of all who will listen to him in the *agora*.

Dialogues are natural to any partial democracy like ancient Athens. But has a genuinely public realm for rational dialogue and debate survived in our period? As Habermas argues, the economic-technical realms of purely instrumental reason have effectively colonized the self-correcting dialectical and dialogical forms of classical reason.[5] How democratic – how dialogical – are modern democracies? Democratic ideals do philosophically imply public (John Dewey and Franklin I. Gamwell),[6] reasonable argumentative (Habermas) and dialogical (Gadamer) ideals. But the political and economic relationships in our media-driven technocratic societies so becloud any attempt at public dialogue on the values of democratic life that they effectively render only technocratic discussions of the best instrumental means for economic-political efficiency as the almost last surviving vestiges of possible candidates for public discussion. Efficient technic-economic means can still be publicly debated in our information-saturated and market-driven increasingly globalized world; however, a discussion of shared human ends for common justice and the common good much less what the ancients, medievals, and early moderns called 'the good life' seems increasingly remote.

This clash between an ideal of dialogue and actual power-relationships in a given situation should influence any non-Romantic analysis of the use of ancient dialogue forms in antiquity itself. Recall Thucydides' devastating exposure of the power-backed, lying pretence at dialogue at play in the Athenian ambassadors' claim to genuine dialogue with the Melians.[7] By the presence of their overwhelming forces in view in the sea surrounding the island of Melos, the Athenians, as the overwhelmingly stronger power, make it clear in their so-called dialogue with the Melians that they will completely destroy the Melians if they do not agree to become an Athenian anti-Spartan 'ally'. The actuality of power in the Melian dialogues, as Thucydides exposes, makes any Athenian claim to dialogue in the Melian setting ludicrous, indeed revolting in its lying arrogance.

---

5. Inter alia, see Jürgen Habermas, *Theory and Practice*, trans. J. Viertel (Boston, MA: Beacon Press, 1973).

6. Franklin I. Gamwell, *Democracy on Purpose: Justice and the Reality of God* (Washington, DC: Georgetown University Press, 2000).

7. Robert B. Strassler, ed., *The Landmark Thucydides: A Comprehensive Guide to the Peloponnesian War* (New York: Simon & Schuster, 2008), pp. 350–7.

The standard, self-serving lies of ages-old imperialism and colonialism – offering 'dialogue' only to save its imperialist face – is exposed for all to see as the lie it is in Thucydides' incomparable analysis of the power-forces underlying all imperialist claims to dialogical respect for colonized others. The colonialized other is never a genuine other but always, as the great Roger Casement demonstrated in his studies of Leopold II's Belgian Congo, the Brazilian and Peruvian Amazon rubber plantations and his own native Ireland, still a colonized other.

In sum, Bakhtin's dialogic ideal emphasizes *di* of dialogue – two or more voices must be at play. Bakhtin's dialogue is always polyphonic, multi-vocal, open, often festive. Gadamer's dialogical (not dialogic) thinking, however, emphasizes not *di* but *dia* of dialogue – through; only through dialogue, inquiry as dialogue including argument and dialectic, can discursive reason discover the truth. The back and forth question and answer form of a dialogue is for Gadamer, as for his mentor Plato, the most reasonable way to reach truth.

Hans-Georg Gadamer on Dialogue

In modern Western philosophy, the most persuasive philosophical model for dialogue remains the Gadamerian hermeneutical model of conversation. This model is basic even though, as I shall suggest later, Gadamer's model of dialogue needs criticism of its over-claims to purity and sufficiency.

First, however, Gadamer's model itself:[8] the event of understanding happens through dialogue; we are taken over by the question of the dialogue through the logic of questioning. *Logos* comes or happens through (*dia*) the to and fro movement of questioning to which dialogue partners commit themselves. The logic of dialogue is the logic of question and answer between dialogue-partners – whether two or more conversation partners or a reader in dialogue with a text, symbol, ritual or historic event.

On this Gadamerian model, the logic of question and answer constituting a dialogue is more an ontological than merely an epistemological reality. Ontologically, dialogue is a particular kind of game. As in any game, the conversation is destroyed if controlled by the self-consciousness of the players. A self-conscious actor, like any self-important player in any game destroys the game by refusing or being unable to enter any game with others since he or she is trapped in the only game he or she knows – his or her own ego drama. Anyone who wishes to play must abandon self-consciousness to the logic of the to and fro movement of the particular game. In the game of conversation, the game is the to and fro movement of the logic of question and answer in shared questioning. In giving oneself to the question at issue, the player experiences the ontological reality of being-played – as in sports when a player announces that at a certain moment the players felt out of themselves and 'in the zone'.

---

8. Hans-Georg Gadamer, *Truth and Method*, trans. J. Weinsheimer and D. G. Marshall (New York: Crossroad, 1989), pp. 362–79.

Since the key to dialogue for Gadamer is the logic of question and answer, neither self-consciousness nor Friedrich Schleiermacher's self-conscious empathy, the emphasis of dialogue must shift from the self to the other – the person, the text, the symbol or the event – that is driving all the questioning in the dialogue. All contemporary dialogical philosophies are part of the contemporary turn to the other. On Gadamer's model, in dialogue the self is not in control; the other – the subject matter, the question, the person, the event as other, the to and fro movement of questioning – must be in control. For Gadamer, the dialogue, or for Bakhtin, the dialogic self remains an infinite, never completed task. The self-in-dialogue also finds its self-reflective understanding exceeded by the event of dialogical understanding of the other. The self experiences understanding (*logos*) only through (*dia*) the dialogical event of understanding the other, whether that 'other' or that 'different' be person, text, symbol, or event. Each of us is always other to those we trustingly, not condescendingly, name the 'other' or the 'different'. Dialogue is not principally about dialectical oppositions, but more often about polarity of contrast (Alfred N. Whitehead) or even sheer difference (Gilles Deleuze and, differently, Jacques Derrida). Dialogical understanding is an event that happens only through the dialogue itself.

In sum, Gadamer is the major modern philosopher of dialogue as the route to understanding. He argues philosophically for the following four shared characteristics of modern Western hermeneutics on dialogue:

1. One must acknowledge the finitude and historicality of all human understanding, hence Gadamer historicizes ancient rhetoric.
2. The *focus* of hermeneutical philosophy must be on the other as a genuine alterity to the self, not as a projected other by the self. Here Gadamer joins the contemporary or postmodern turn to the other over against the modern turn to the subject.
3. The dialogical self experiences an excess to its ordinary self-understanding which it cannot control through conscious intentionality or through any ego-driven desire for more of the same. Therefore each self must 'let go' to the dialogue itself. This move is Gadamer's most Bakhtinian move although he does not spell out its infinite openness with the radicality that Bakhtin does. Gadamer's description of dialogue is far less festive or playful than Bakhtin's but his model is also modelled on a game. For Bakhtin, the dialogical game is a multi-vocal, even heteroglossic, subversive, never closed game. For Gadamer, dialogue is more a game-like sports or drama which is modelled on the to and fro movement of all games. In the game of dialogue, the back and forth movement of question and answer rules the game. Gadamer's model of dialogue also remains open since each dialogical response gives rise to ever new questions in the infinitely self-correcting role of reason.
4. The dialogue works as a dialogue only insofar as the other – whether any text, person, symbol or event – is empowered through the very dynamic of the to and fro movement of dialogical questioning. A non-dialogical other is no

genuine other but projected other – a false other projected by the ego upon and therefore concealing some real other by the ego's needs and desires.

To risk oneself in dialogue, for example, in contemporary interreligious dialogue, does not mean to enter with a lack of either self-respect or of respect for one's own traditions. Gadamer's philosophical model for genuine dialogue may, in my judgement, inform the dialogical elements partially present in inter-institutional religious dialogues more than Bakhtin's festive dialogic model does. In these very important contemporary interreligious dialogues in our fragile global situation, religious institutions and authorities, as well as the individuals representing them in these dialogues, rarely involve themselves in the risk of a full-fledged dialogue in Gadamer's radical sense. In Gadamerian dialogue (which in my judgement, is dialogue philosophically construed correctly), one *must* risk one's present self-understanding and commitments if one is to dialogue with any genuine other. As a dialogue partner, one should, as noted above, of course, possess self-respect, but, as a necessary part of that self-respect, one must also be ready to expose oneself as oneself to a genuine other as other. In principle a dialogue partner must risk conversion to the other's position if one becomes thus convinced of the truth of the alternative through (*dia*) the dialogue itself.

Full-fledged dialogue demands that kind of risk of radical change through dialogue. However, inter-institutional, interreligious and inter-cultural dialogues do not ordinarily carry that risk. Rather they usually serve more as honest attempts to clarify borders, as well as to search for some possible common – often ethical – values that can be jointly acted upon to alleviate suffering and fight injustice. Compared to the demands of genuine philosophical dialogue as described above, these institutional conversations are not in truth fully dialogues. Nevertheless there exist genuinely dialogical elements in all such official interreligious dialogues. Otherwise religious institutional participants would not be involved at all in any conversation. For example, the medieval historian Lucy Pick[9] has shown how, in medieval Spain, what can seem to later eyes as merely polemical exchanges between minority Jews and majority Christians in twelfth-century Toledo did include important dialogical elements. In fact, for once the exchanges were not principally polemical. These Toledan twelfth-century Jewish-Christian discussions sponsored but not controlled by the local bishop were rare attempts at some mutual clarification, unlike the more usual medieval polemical Christian-controlled power-saturated debates. The Toledan discussions with partial but real dialogical elements were designed principally to clarify the limits and boundaries of the different religious communities. Peace between communities is partly dependent on a shared clarity of the nature and of the significant differences of each community's people, practices and beliefs. Inter-cultural and interreligious dialogues (even the partial ones of institutional authorities) are more often exercises in clarifying cultural identities rather than full-fledged dialogues. At the

---

9. Lucy Pick, *Conflict and Coexistence: Archbishop Rodrigo and the Muslims and Jews of Thirteenth-Century Spain* (Ann Arbor, MI: University of Michigan Press, 2004).

same time, they remain valuable moments in what may eventually prove a more full-fledged dialogue as a dialogue where the risk of conversion to the other's position is a necessary element to assure an authentically dialogical reality.

There is no reason why Gadamer's philosophical model of dialogue cannot be corrected from its too optimistic traditional humanistic reading of the Western tradition on dialogue by means of Bakhtin's festive plurivocal dialogic reality. Gadamer can also be corrected by Walter Benjamin's more suspicious and subversive sense of dialogue with the traditions: 'Every great work of civilization is at the same time a work of barbarism'.[10]

Fragmenting Traditional Dialogue Through Suspicion of Its Lack of Radical Openness

A fragmenting of Gadamer's model of dialogue, indeed a temporary rupture of that model, is what Ricoeur famously named a hermeneutics of suspicion[11] as distinct from Gadamer's hermeneutics of trust. Most hermeneutics of suspicion are allied to some form of critical theory, that is any theory which, unlike traditional theory, attempts to spot and partly heal often unconscious or at least unacknowledged problems (power-relations) fragmenting and disrupting the conversation. In a hermeneutics of suspicion, one does not focus on conscious errors but on unconscious but systemically functioning distortions in the dialogue.

Classical Freudian psychoanalysis is not strictly speaking a dialogue. Rather psychoanalytic theory is an interruption of our ordinary, everyday and even our philosophical dialogues. Psychoanalysis is undertaken to expose a repressed unconscious feeling. Classical Freudian psychoanalysis, as Jacques Lacan has rightly insisted against modern ego-psychology, is a non-dialogical interaction where one party (the analyst) employs a critical theory used to spot the other party's unconscious illusions, self-delusions and repressed feelings. Once put into practice by the analyst, psychoanalytic theory precisely as a critical theory, uncovers and thereby gives some limited emancipation from formerly repressed feelings. Repressed unconscious feelings systemically function to disrupt and fragment one's conscious rational life including, in principle, one's attempts at dialogue – whether the ludic dialogues of Bakhtin or the philosophical dialogues of Gadamer. Only rationalists think that they can argue away unconscious distorted feelings that can keep erupting to divert the to and fro movement of dialogue. Sexism, racism, antisemitism, elitism, classism, homophobia, Eurocentrism, *ressentiment*, Islamophobia, or colonialism and other fatal 'isms' exposed by critical theories are more likely to be unconscious but systemically functioning distortions, not simply conscious errors that further dialogue however well-intentioned will correct.

10. Walter Benjamin, 'Theses on the Philosophy of History', in idem, *Illuminations*, ed. Hannah Arendt, trans. H. Zohn (New York: Schocken Books, 1969), pp. 245–55.

11. Inter alia, Paul Ricœur, *Freud and Philosophy: An Essay on Interpretation*, trans. D. Savage (New Haven, CT: Yale University Press, 1970).

Since Augustine, Western Christian theology has used not only a basic theological hermeneutics of trust (nature-grace) but also a powerful hermeneutics of suspicion (sin-grace) to expose in the ego a largely unconscious distorted systemic disorientation named 'sin', as distinct from those conscious moral errors often named 'sins'. Pervasive in individuals, in communities, in all history, 'sin' demands not only enlightenment but redemption. Only the Other Power of God's grace for the Christian, not the self-power of Pelagius' moral reform, can uncover and liberate one from sin. On its own, the self, even Gadamer's humanistic dialogical self, cannot ultimately face either God as Infinite Other or neighbour as finite other to be loved. In Martin Luther's chosen language, the self remains '*curvatus in se*' with no exit save through God's grace.

There is no innocent tradition; there is no innocent text; there is no innocent reading (including this one). All our religious and secular traditions are pluralistic, fragmentary and ambiguous (true and false, good and evil, holy and unholy) traditions. Before modern feminism, what cultural or religious tradition had faced every historical tradition's unconscious, systemically functioning sexism? What cultural or religious tradition can now ignore this? Once one is no longer innocent about one's own pluralistic and ambiguous traditions, one's ability to dialogue with other social, political, cultural, philosophical and religious traditions is enhanced, not diminished. Dialogue becomes more aware, more open to both retrieval and suspicion, more attentive through modern critical theories as well as ancient and modern theological critical theories like Augustine on sin-grace or like ancient tragedy. If one is trying to dialogue in a violent hurricane, it serves no good to pretend (as in some too blissful readings of the joys of 'dialogue') that we are all dialogically experiencing together a welcome summer breeze. Dialogue is always serious, demanding, difficult but possible for those willing to risk it. The alternative to dialogue – increasing conflict, violence, polemics, fundamentalisms, exclusivity – is literally hope-less. All attempts to clarify what dialogue is now seem a necessary intellectual exercise.

Therefore, dialogue – the real thing I have described above first in Bakhtinian and then Gadamerian terms – is a tough-minded option. Dialogue demands the risk of exposure to an other whose very existence challenges me to acknowledge my responsibility to the other. Emmanuel Levinas' insistence on using the expression 'exposure to the other' rather than Martin Buber's more gentle expression 'encounter with the other' is a plausible word-change. In fact, dialogue with the other (person or text or event or symbol) demands the willingness to risk one's present self-understanding.

In all situations, at all times, the question of dialogue ultimately remains Socrates' question to Protagoras, 'What shall be our mode of conversing?' – precisely, Werner G. Jeanrond's[12] life-long dialogical work and inter-cultural practice culminating in his brilliant development of a 'hermeneutics of love'.

---

12. Werner G. Jeanrond, *Text and Interpretation as Categories of Theological Thinking*, trans. T. J. Wilson (New York: Crossroad, 1988); idem, 'Toward an Interreligious Hermeneutics of Love', in Catherine Cornille and Christopher Conway, eds, *Interreligious Hermeneutics* (Eugene, OR: Wipf and Stock, 2010), pp. 44-60.

12

ENCOUNTERING THE OTHER: THE CONCEPT OF ENCOUNTER IN PHILOSOPHY AND THEOLOGY

Matthias Petzoldt[1]

Encounters are more practical than theoretical. The reality which is evoked in the encounter with the other seems to differ from what is academically accessible. Martin Buber and Emmanuel Levinas are academics who devoted their attention to the practice of encounters. Since it is striking that their studies revolve around the role and relevance of language, I combine their conceptualizations of encounter with the philosophy of language, utilizing John L. Austin's theory of speech acts. I argue that the encounter of 'other with other' can create a reality of trust *in-between* the two others – a reality which has implications of philosophical and theological importance. Since the reality of trust is fundamental for Christianity, the practice of encounters is crucial for fundamental theology.[2]

Martin Buber

In the aftermath of World War I, dialogical personalism became increasingly important. The designation of dialogical personalism captures a wide range of philosophical and theological approaches which – despite their differences – were united in criticizing the separation of subject and object in Western thought. Martin Buber's (1878-1965) contributions were crucial. His *I and Thou* (1923) begins with the distinction between the two 'primary words' which can be spoken by a human being: '*I-Thou*' and '*I-It*'.[3]

---

1. Translated by Ulrich Schmiedel.
2. For the concept of fundamental theology cf. Werner G. Jeanrond and Matthias Petzoldt, 'Fundamental Theology', in *Religion: Past and Present*, vol. 5 (Boston: Brill, 2009), pp. 277–87.
3. Martin Buber, *I and Thou*, trans. R. G. Smith (Edinburgh: T&T Clark, 1937), p. 3. [The English translation of Buber's *Ich und Du* is still stirring controversy. I follow Ronald

The reality of encounter is allocated to I-Thou: 'When *Thou* is spoken, the speaker has no thing. He has indeed nothing. But he takes his stand in relation'.[4] Hence, in contrast to I-It which evokes the reality of an experience, I-Thou evokes the reality of an encounter. When Buber writes that 'The *Thou* meets me through grace – it is not found by seeking. But my speaking of the primary word to it is an act of my being, is indeed *the* act of my being', he is not only criticizing the separation of subject and object; he is stressing the significance of language for I-Thou.[5] It is the pragmatics as opposed to the semantics of language which is crucial here: when the other speaks to me, she or he creates me through her or his speaking. Yet, is I-Thou limited to human beings who can communicate through language? Buber responds to this question: structuring I-Thou into spheres, he elaborates on the ontology of encounter. In encounters with both somebody and something, I-Thou might be evoked. For Buber, the something is exemplified by a tree: 'It can, however, also come about … that in considering the tree I become bound up in relation to it. The tree is now no longer *It*'.[6] Buber continues: 'Let no attempt be made to sap the strength from the meaning of the relation: relation is mutual'.[7]

Buber's ontology of encounter appears to idealize the encounter. 'The relation to the *Thou* is direct', he explains in order to emphasize the distinction between I-Thou and I-It.[8] 'No aim … no anticipation intervenes between *I* and *Thou*. … Every means is an obstacle. Only when every means has collapsed does the meeting come about'.[9] To be sure, it would be a reduction to simplistically charge Buber with a devaluation of I-It for the sake of I-Thou. Both are appropriate for him. Buber is concerned with distinguishing the rationalities of these two distinct primary words. Obviously, the rationality of the encounter might be degraded into the obsession to control the other – my Thou – thus turning it into It. Nonetheless, one has to ask whether the 'real' reality of encounters between I and Thou might differ from Buber's ideal(ized) characterization by immediacy.

Interestingly, Buber, the unmatched translator of the Hebrew Bible,[10] reserves immediacy – strictly speaking, complete immediacy – for the relationship to the

---

G. Smith's translation from 1937 since it is usually used in the translation of Emmanuel Levinas' works. However, Walter Kaufmann's translation – which renders 'Du' with 'You' as opposed to 'Thou' – comes closer to the intimacy and immediacy of Buber's concept of dialogue. Kaufmann has argued for his translation in Walter Kaufman, 'Buber's Religious Significance', in Paul Schilpp and Maurice Friedman, eds, *The Philosophy of Martin Buber* (LaSalle, IL: Open Court, 1967), pp. 665–86. (U.S.)]

4. Martin Buber, *I and Thou*, p. 4.
5. Ibid., p. 11.
6. Ibid., p. 7.
7. Ibid., p. 8.
8. Ibid., p. 11.
9. Ibid., pp. 11–12.
10. Together with Franz Rosenzweig, Buber translated the Hebrew Bible. Cf. *Die Schrift: Aus dem Hebräischen verdeutscht von Martin Buber gemeinsam mit Franz Rosenzweig* (Stuttgart: Deutsche Bibelgesellschaft, 1994).

'eternal *Thou*' who, according to him, might be encountered in everybody and everything: 'Every particular *Thou* is a glimpse through to the eternal *Thou*; by means of every particular *Thou* the primary word addresses the eternal *Thou*'.[11] For 'the extended lines of relation meet in the eternal *Thou*… Through this mediation of the *Thou* of all beings fulfilment, and non-fulfilment, of relations comes to them: the inborn *Thou* is realized in each relation… It is consummated only in the direct relation with the *Thou* that by its nature cannot become *It*'.[12]

Buber's thinking continues to inspire Christian and non-Christian theologians.[13] By mapping the reality of encounter, he discovered philosophically and theologically uncharted terrain in what could be called a philosophy as poetry. He has been criticized for the utilization of this language as it pushes language beyond language, so to speak. Indeed, his poetic philosophy (or philosophical poetry) poses problems which it cannot solve, let alone solve with precision. But before one criticizes the language of his philosophy, following Buber, it might be germane to ask his critics exactly what precision they demand of him. If precision means the precision of the kind of knowledge that is gained through a detached analysis of reality which is controlled by a subject, then it is the non-personal precision which Buber would subsume under I-It as opposed to I-Thou. According to Buber, the attempt of the subject to gain knowledge about her- or himself by following the logic of subject-theory is doomed to failure. The knowledge a person would gain would not be the knowledge of the encounter of 'other with other'.

Emmanuel Levinas

In critical conversation with Buber, Emmanuel Levinas (1906–95) approached the reality of encounter through the lens of Edmund Husserl's phenomenology and Martin Heidegger's ontology. Levinas appreciated how Buber switched from the relation between subject and object to the relation between I and Thou. 'Truth, therefore, is not grasped by a dispassionate subject who is a spectator of reality, but by a commitment in which the other remains in his otherness'.[14] However, for Levinas, Buber's conceptualization of the encounter is not precise enough – a

11. Martin Buber, *I and Thou*, p. 75.
12. Ibid.
13. In Germany, theologians such as Friedrich Gogarten and Emil Brunner were influenced by Buber. Cf. Martin Leiner, *Gottes Gegenwart: Martin Bubers Philosophie des Dialogs und der Ansatz ihrer theologischen Rezeption bei Friedrich Gogarten und Emil Brunner* (Gütersloh: Gütersloher Verlagshaus, 2000). For a contemporary application and adaptation of Buber's philosophy to theology cf. Christina Aus der Au, *Im Horizont der Anrede: Das theologische Menschenbild und seine Herausforderung durch die Neurowissenschaften* (Göttingen: Vandenhoeck & Rupprecht, 2011).
14. Emmanuel Levinas, 'Martin Buber and the Theory of Knowledge', in idem, *The Levinas Reader*, ed. Sean Hand (Oxford: Blackwell, 1989), pp. 59–74 (67).

limitation 'in a work which is otherwise rich in insight'.[15] Hence, Levinas attempts to conceptualize the encounter more precisely.

Whereas Buber stretched the encounter of I and Thou beyond inter-personal relationships, Levinas exclusively elaborates on the encounter of personal others. This encounter can be explained ethically. Sceptically, Levinas asks: 'Is dialogue possible without *Fürsorge*? If we criticize Buber for extending the I-Thou relation to things, then, it is not because he is an animist with respect to our relations with the physical world, but because he is too much the artist in his relations with man'.[16] Only faintly does Levinas criticize the inclusion of God into the I-Thou relation, offered by a theology which, following Buber, is 'somewhat too well-informed on the nature of God'.[17] Elsewhere, the critique is transformed into Levinas' engaged talk of 'illeity'.[18] In his autobiographical sketch entitled 'Signature', Levinas concludes that it 'has been possible to present ... this relation with the Infinite as irreducible to "thematization". The Infinite always remains a "third person"'.[19]

What runs through Levinas' thought is the asymmetry in the encounter of 'other with other' – the central critique of the 'reciprocity of the I-Thou relation'. As he explains:

> [I]t is questionable whether the relation with the otherness of the Other which appears as a dialogue ... can be described without emphasizing paradoxically a difference of level between the I and the Thou. The originality of the relation lies in the fact that it is not known from the outside but only by the I which realizes the relation. The position of the I, therefore, is interchangeable with that of the Thou. ... For if the self becomes an I in saying Thou, as Buber asserts, my position as a self depends on that of my correlate and the relation is no longer any different from other relations: it is tantamount to a spectator speaking of the I and Thou in the third person. ... But in the case of ethical relations, where the Other is ... higher than I ..., the I is distinguished from the Thou not by the presence of specific attributes, but by the dimension of height, thus implying a break with Buber's formalism. The primacy of the other does not qualify what is a purely formal relation to the other, *posterior* to the act of relating, but directly qualifies otherness itself.[20]

---

15. Ibid., p. 72.
16. Ibid., p. 73.
17. Ibid., p. 71.
18. Cf. Emmanuel Levinas, 'Meaning and Sense', in idem, *Basic Philosophical Writings*, ed. Adriaan T. Peperzak, Simon Critchley and Robert Bernasconi (Bloomington, IN: Indiana University Press, 1996), pp. 33–64.
19. Emmanuel Levinas, 'Signature', in idem, *Difficult Freedom: Essays on Judaism*, trans. S. Hand (Baltimore: John Hopkins University Press, 1990), pp. 291–5 (295).
20. Emmanuel Levinas, 'Martin Buber and the Theory of Knowledge', p. 72.

After *Totality and Infinity* (1961), Levinas concentrates on language.[21] Again, the medium of language is important and instructive for the conceptualization of the encounter of 'other with other'. Crucially, in 'Language and Proximity', Levinas attempts 'to conceive together language and contact'.[22] As he stresses in the conclusion of the study, the attempt was accomplished 'in analysing language independently of the ... truth of the information transmitted, in grasping in them the event of *proximity*'.[23] Proximity is ethically explained as an obsession with the face of the other.

In *Otherwise than Being* (1974), Levinas clarifies that he is concerned with the 'pre-original saying'.[24] 'But this pre-original saying does not move into a language, in which saying and said are correlative of one another'.[25] Since it is the presupposition for the saying of the said, it cannot be exhausted by the apophantic. Accordingly, 'the signification of saying goes beyond the said. It is not ontology that raises up the speaking subject; it is the signifyingness of saying going beyond essence that can justify the exposedness of being, ontology'.[26] Here, transcendence comes in for Levinas – beyond being. 'The first word says only the saying itself before being... But if the first saying says this very saying, here the saying and the said cannot equal one another. For the saying in being said ... breaks the definition of what it says ... The first saying is to be sure but a word. But the word is God'.[27]

The Reality of Encounter

In contrast to the philosophies of Martin Buber and Emmanuel Levinas, the theory of speech acts of the Oxford philosopher John L. Austin (1911–60) explores language with analytical methods. Austin stresses the significance of performative utterances which create reality – instead of describing or defining it – in order to criticize how both empiricism and positivism misunderstood language due to the '"descriptive" fallacy'.[28] Initially, Austin conducted his fieldwork on the assumption that performatives plainly and simply 'do not constate anything at

---

21. Emmanuel Levinas, *Totality and Infinity: An Essay on Exteriority*, trans. A. Lingis (Pittsburgh, PA: Duquesne University Press, 2001).

22. Emmanuel Levinas, 'Language and Proximity', in idem, *Collected Philosophical Papers*, trans. A. Lingis (Boston: Nijhoff, 1987), pp. 109–26 (125).

23. Ibid.

24. Emmanuel Levinas, *Otherwise than Being or Beyond Essence*, trans. A. Lingis (Pittsburgh, PA: Duquesne University Press, 2000), p. 5.

25. Ibid., p. 6.

26. Ibid., pp. 37–8.

27. Emmanuel Levinas, 'Language and Proximity', p. 126.

28. John L. Austin, *How To Do Things With Words*, ed. James O. Urmson and Marina Sbisáa (Oxford: Clarendon, 1975), p. 3.

all'.[29] Soon, however, he realized that there is indeed information in performative utterances. What followed from this realization was his differentiation of utterances according to their locutionary, illocutionary and perlocutionary content.[30] Yet this differentiation does not falsify Austin's discovery that performative utterances create as opposed to constate (describe and define) reality. John R. Searle's (born in 1932) distinction between the language of information and the language of relation echoes Austin's discovery. Searle adopted and adapted the theory of speech acts in order to distinguish between institutional and natural facts. Such a distinction is crucial for understanding institutions like marriage, which are based on performatives as opposed to constatives.[31]

Whether inside or outside institutions, performative utterances are indispensable for the encounter with the other. Utterances like 'I trust you' or 'I mistrust you' are constitutive of interpersonal relationships. Arguably, it is such performative as opposed to constative language which runs through the philosophies of Martin Buber and Emmanuel Levinas. Hence, it is promising to engage in a conversation between these philosophies and Austin's speech-act theory.[32]

First and foremost, it has to be noted that although the medium of language is central to these philosophies, one must not overlook that there is performativity in nonverbal acts such as gestures. However, non-verbal acts create reality (as opposed to describing and defining it) only through their verbal interpretation. One has to understand the conventional codes in which the acts are embedded and embodied in order to decode these actions, nonverbal or verbal. Hence, language – particularly, face-to-face communication through language – is the essential means of encounter in both the past and the present.[33]

Does the conceptualization of encounter through the analysis of speech *ipso facto* objectify the encounter? Against such objectifications, one could take recourse to Buber's distinction of I-Thou and I-It. Yet, as appropriate as such a cautionary recourse is, it runs the risk of misunderstanding the significance of the conceptualization of the encounter. The analysis of speech does not objectify the other, turning Thou into It, but it objectifies the reality of the I-Thou. Objectification is necessary. The *in-between* of I and Thou can be perceived by a third person. In this way it can be reflected in a third person perspective: from the outside as opposed to the inside. Especially those who experience the encounter need to gain distance from the encounter in order to perceive it. Indeed, it is

---

29. Ibid., p. 5.
30. Cf. ibid., pp. 121–32.
31. Cf. John R. Searle, *Speech Acts: An Essay in the Philosophy of Language* (Cambridge: Cambridge University Press, 1969).
32. For a short summary of the reception of the theory of speech acts in theology, cf. Matthias Petzoldt, 'Sprechakt/Sprechakttheorie', in Oda Wischmeyer, ed., *Lexikon der Bibelhermeneutik* (Berlin: De Gruyter, 2009), pp. 565–6.
33. Matthias Petzoldt, 'Die Theologie des Wortes im Zeitalter der neuen Medien', in Ulrich H. J. Körtner, ed., *Hermeneutik und Ästhetik: Die Theologie des Wortes im mutimedialen Zeitalter* (Neukirchen-Vluyn: Neukirchener Verlag, 2001), pp. 57–97 (82–4).

an outside-perspective as opposed to an inside-perspective which is adopted in Buber's philosophy (although Buber seems to brace himself against it through his poetry). Hence, the theory of speech acts is useful for the analysis of encounters provided that one bears in mind that the reality which is analysed is the reality of interpersonal encounters, I-Thou as opposed to I-It. The method of analysis – outside-perspective as opposed to inside-perspective – would be misunderstood, if one imposed it on the ontology of encounter; it would result in falling prey to what Austin criticized as 'descriptive fallacy'.

Apparently, it is the descriptive fallacy which Levinas bears in mind when he stresses that the first word does not identify anyone or anything. Indeed, it appears as if Levinas affirmed Austin's assumption that performative utterances do not convey any content – an assumption which Austin modified through his distinction of the locutionary, the illocutionary and the perlocutionary act. However, the appearance might be deceptive. Levinas is concerned with the distinction (not the separation) between the act of speech on the one hand and the content of the act of speech on the other. Accordingly, Levinas' interpretation of language comes close to the theory of speech acts: when one is addressed by the other – one person speaking to another – proximity is manifested, irrespective of the propositional content of the address. However, is it useful to characterize the language in which the saying and the said are not necessarily identical as 'pre-original'? The theory of speech acts paints a plainer picture of the language of the encounter. Everybody is born into conventions of language. Through these conventions, one learns how to understand the encounter with the other through language: to veil or to unveil oneself, to trust or to mistrust one's other. Hence, although Levinas – following Husserl's phenomenology – distances philosophy from questions of the transcendental subject, these questions haunt his philosophy when he attempts to locate the power of the saying before the said. Locating the power of the saying *in* the said, Austin's theory of speech acts is both more pragmatic and more promising.

Importantly, according to Levinas, pre-original language is marked by the responsibility of the one for the other. He points out that 'proximity is a responsibility that does not refer to my freedom. ... It is the state of being a hostage'.[34] The ethics which fuels Levinas' philosophy emerges and re-emerges: communication – the encounter of other and other in which proximity is manifested – is *the* 'ethical event' for Levinas.[35] Yet, although Levinas' conceptualization of encounter in a concrete event is convincing, one must ask whether 'ethics' is an accurate and appropriate characterization of such an event. Is it not the elementary experience of the healing or the un-healing, the salvific or the un-salvific, which manifests itself in the in-between: to be accepted or not to be accepted, to be healed or not to be healed, to be trusted or not to be trusted, to be loved or not to be loved? Of course, these experiences imply ethics. Yet, the event is what makes the encounter the encounter; ethics is a *consequence* of the event which transcends and

34. Emmanuel Levinas, 'Language and Proximity', p. 123.
35. Ibid., p. 124.

transforms the persons involved in it – neither person can control the in-between of the encounter. With these ethical implications in mind, it is necessary to criticize Buber's idealized account. Encounters happen differently under different circumstances, expected or unexpected. Encounters can be salvific or non-salvific, healing or non-healing, authentic or in-authentic.[36] Encounters can fail. Against Buber's claim that 'real living is meeting' one therefore has to bear in mind that encounters might either invigorate or interrupt life.[37]

Moreover, since language is central to the conceptualization of the practice of encounters, encounters seem to be a reality exclusive to human beings. For Buber, however, the concept of encounter captures the relationship of the I to somebody or to something. In addition to the example of the tree mentioned above, he reflects on encounters with 'intelligible forms. There the relation is clouded, yet it discloses itself; it does not use speech, yet begets it'.[38] In these encounters, we 'perceive no *Thou*, but none the less we feel we are addressed and we answer … We speak the primary word with our being, though we cannot utter *Thou* with our lips'.[39] Indeed, we refer to the encounter with other civilizations and other cultures. Within pedagogy, it is discussed whether education could and should be conceived of as formation through intentional encounters with foreign worlds.[40] Arguably, what runs through this discussion is again the significance of performative as opposed to constative language. However, encounter means first and foremost the encounter with persons. Encounters with artefacts – textual or musical, for instance – are deduced from interpersonal encounters. It is a person which addresses me when I am addressed by an artefact. The metaphor of address/addressing is appropriate here because there are always persons 'behind' these textual or musical artefacts. Yet, what leads to the limits of the concept of encounter is the familiarity one might have with a pet animal. For in referring to encounters with nature, it has to be shown that one is not plainly and simply imposing one's obsessions or apprehensions onto the encountered.

Finally, Levinas' critique of the extension of the concept of encounter to God through the notion of 'illeity' is intriguing for Christianity. However, if Christian theology is the reflection upon faith in Christ, Levinas' critique misses the point. Faith in Christ means trust – a trust which was established through Jesus of Nazareth's address to and acceptance of his contemporaries. These contemporaries were touched by him: they were forgiven by him; they were blessed by him;

---

36. Matthias Petzoldt, 'Wahrheit als Begegnung: Dialogisches Wahrheitsverständnis im Licht der Analyse performativer Sprache', in idem, *Christsein angefragt: Fundamentaltheologsiche Beiträge* (Leipzig: Evangelische Verlagsanstalt, 1998), pp. 25–40.

37. Martin Buber, *I and Thou*, p. 11.

38. Ibid., p. 6.

39. Ibid.

40. Romano Guardini and Otto F. Bollnow, *Begegnung und Bildung* (Würzburg: Werkbund Verlag, 1969); Berthold Gerner, ed., *Begegnung: Ein anthropologisch-pädagogisches Grundereignis* (Darmstadt: Wissenschaftliche Buchgesellschaft, 1969); and Robert Schneider, *Begegnen als pädagogisches Handeln* (Marburg: Tectum, 2011).

they experienced hopefulness, happiness and health in community with him. Jesus' address and acceptance – his implicit and explicit performatives – created the reality of salvation through faith in him. Essentially, such faith *is* trust. In Jesus' name, the contemporaries who trusted in him transmitted his implicit and explicit performatives to generation after generation. Thus, trust was created again and again: the reality of salvation through faith in Christ. Accordingly, the faith of Christians is the transmission of Jesus' performatives: *Sprachgeschehen*. In such a *Sprachgeschehen*, the in-between which involves both Christ and Christians is continually constituted and reconstituted. It is the reality of encounter which is the foundation of faith, the faith which is critically and self-critically reflected in beliefs.

In sum, conceptualizations of the practice of encounter are crucial for philosophy and theology. The combination of Martin Buber's and Emmanuel Levinas' philosophies with John L. Austin's theory of speech acts allows for a conceptualization which clarifies how the reality of encounter – *in-between* 'other and other' – is created through language: performatives as opposed to constatives. Whereas the persons involved in the encounter of other and other cannot be objectified without reducing their otherness, the event of encounter can become the object of study. Nonetheless, encounters are more practical than theoretical.

13

IN-BETWEEN SUBJECTIVITY AND ALTERITY: PHILOSOPHY OF DIALOGUE AND THEOLOGY OF LOVE

Claudia Welz

It was during his research stay at the University of Copenhagen that I got the chance to get to know Werner G. Jeanrond. He was working on his *Theology of Love*. In a discussion, he remarked that instead of understanding love as being based on subjectivity, love should rather be taken as the 'framework' in which subjectivity can be understood properly.

This remark seems quite natural if ensuing from a relational conceptualization of selfhood, but it has a revolutionary ring if heard against the backdrop of a theory that prioritizes the perspective of the first person and equates it with the perspective of a transcendental 'I'. If this 'I-pole' is seen as the 'agent of manifestation' to and by which otherness can appear, even highly complex phenomena that encompass more than one person can only be described in the way they appear to 'the' experiencing subject. Accordingly, love appears as an emotional or intentional act of feeling-valuing, through which the beloved is presented to me: as *my* experience of the alterity of 'another I'.[1] But if it is correct that the second- and third-person perspectives are irreducible to the first-person perspective, how do we account for what cannot be reduced to it?

In this contribution, I will examine that which lies 'in-between' subjectivity and alterity – first, by drawing on the philosophy of dialogue; second, by exploring the theology of love; and finally, by discussing the above-mentioned remark.

Philosophy of Dialogue

In the Postscript to *Der Andere* (1965), Michael Theunissen calls attention to the incompatibility of the philosophy of dialogue on the one hand and the

---

1. Cf. James G. Hart, *Who One Is*, Book 1: *Meontology of the 'I': A Transcendental Phenomenology* (Dordrecht: Springer, 2009), pp. 208–14.

transcendental theory of intersubjectivity on the other hand.² He tries to mediate between these positions and acknowledges that the other is *both* the one who is constituted by the subject *and* the one who transcends subjective constitution; *both* the one who alienates me from myself *and* the one who leads me back to myself.³ If the event of the encounter precedes the individual partners of dialogue in the sense that they originate in this event 'between' them, this *Zwischen* – the sphere of actuality *between* selfhood and alterity – has priority over the sphere of subjectivity. Yet, how is it possible to convincingly delineate the genesis of different perspectives out of the non-perspectival sphere 'in-between' us? Theunissen argues that in this sphere, the 'I' is no longer the centre. Rather, one is decentred, and the appropriation of the other's otherness turns into the becoming-other of one's own self.⁴

According to Theunissen, Martin Buber's *I and Thou* (1923) documents the discovery of a relation based on the sphere 'in-between', which can neither be attributed to an 'I' nor a 'Thou', nor a third factor comprising both of them. The sphere between the partners of dialogue prevents their melting together by at once separating and connecting them. Mutually influencing each other, they are constituted by that which happens between them: their encounter. Theunissen infers that selfhood and alterity are equiprimordial.⁵ In this line, Buber writes, 'I require a You to become; becoming I, I say You'.⁶ Modifying Jn 1.1 where 'the Word' is the very first, he states: 'In the beginning is the relation' – which is ontologically significant as a 'category of being, as a form that reaches out to be filled'.⁷ Buber even speaks of 'the *a priori* of relation' that is prior to the relationships in which 'the innate You is realized in the You we encounter'.⁸ Self and other are radically interdependent. One needs to be addressed by others before being able to speak to them; in soliciting another, one's own words and deeds react on oneself. For Buber, '[r]elation is reciprocity'.⁹

How does he characterize the 'in-between' through which the 'I' and the 'Thou' communicate with each other? Buber describes the I-Thou-relation as being 'immediate' in the sense that the encounter cannot be anticipated by any preconception. How, then, can two persons understand each other? The key notion that

---

2. Cf. Michael Theunissen, *Der Andere: Studien zur Sozialontologie der Gegenwart* (Berlin: De Gruyter, 1977), p. 491.

3. Cf. ibid., p. 502.

4. Cf. ibid., pp. 487–90.

5. Cf. ibid., pp. 259; 264–6; 273–4. For the relation between dialogue, dialectics, and recognition, cf. Arne Grøn, 'Dialektik og dialogik', *Fønix* 7/4 (1983), pp. 252–77; idem, 'Anerkendelsens dialektik og begreb', in Peter Thyssen and Anders M. Rasmussen, eds, *Teologi og modernitet* (Århus: Aarhus Universitetsforlag, 1997), pp. 50–65.

6. Martin Buber, *I and Thou*, trans. W. Kaufmann (New York: Touchstone, 1996), p. 62.

7. Ibid., p. 78.

8. Ibid.

9. Ibid., p. 67.

allows us to understand how understanding between human beings comes about is 'spirit'. Buber defines it as follows:

> Spirit in its human manifestation is man's response to his You. ... [I]n truth language does not reside in man but man stands in language and speaks out of it – so it is with all words, all spirit. Spirit is not in the I but between I and You. It is not like the blood that circulates in you but like the air in which you breathe. Man lives in the spirit when he is able to respond to his You.[10]

The ability to respond to one another is here taken as the presupposition of communication. The response-ability in question is not located in a subject having such a capacity. Rather, it is attributed to a power that is not at the disposal of any individual, but discloses its presence in the event of speech. Just as language does not reside in us, while we are immersed in the language that is spoken around us, 'love does not cling to an I, as if the You were merely its "content" or object; it is between I and You'.[11] As 'responsibility of an I for a You' love cannot consist in any feeling, but is accompanied by feelings: 'Feelings dwell in man, but man dwells in his love'.[12]

It is striking that love corresponds to language in being beyond any powers of a person. Buber calls it a 'metaphysical and metapsychical fact'[13] – which implies that love, too, is a 'spiritual' relation to the extent that its 'structure' resembles the immaterial 'fabric' of the spirit between 'I' and 'You'. The spirit is a gift we cannot ascribe to ourselves. Now, if the spirit arising between us and becoming present among us is not man-made, where does it come from? This brings us to the theological aspects of Buber's philosophy of dialogue. The 'dialogical principle' stems from an experience of faith (*Glaubenserfahrung*), and therefore it had first to be translated into philosophical terminology.[14]

The Third Part of *I and Thou* is about God, 'the eternal You' in whom the lines of all other relationships intersect: 'Every single You is a glimpse of that'.[15] In relating to visible human beings and worldly life, we also relate to the invisible God. Nonetheless, God is neither identical with human beings nor the world in which they live. That or those differing from God can instead become the place of a theophany. 'But as surely as God embraces us and dwells in us, we never have him within'.[16] Buber is not a pantheist. Rather, following the Chassidic tales, he sees the world as a locus of encounter between God and man. His most essential concern is 'the close association of the relation to God with the relation to one's

---

10. Ibid., p. 89.
11. Ibid., p. 66.
12. Ibid.
13. Ibid.
14. Cf. Michael Theunissen, *Der Andere*, p. 258.
15. Cf. Martin Buber, *I and Thou*, p. 123.
16. Ibid., p. 152.

fellow-men'[17] – the underlying assumption being that the divine can be differentiated from the human. Buber designates God as 'the absolute person' who carries his absoluteness into his relationship with us so that we need not turn our back to any other I-You relationship.[18] On the contrary, if we can encounter God in encountering another human being, the God-relationship is not external to interhuman relations, but remains their perennial middle.

As Theunissen interprets it, this 'middle' is the same as the sphere 'in-between' all beings, and consequently, God is 'die Wirklichkeit des Zwischen': the existing actuality of the 'in-between' that links up all relationships.[19] Buber conceives of God as eternal presence, which is revealed and concealed in the encounter with a mortal 'You' – but is Theunissen right in calling Buber's theological approach 'ontotheology', and in criticizing that Buber's philosophy of dialogue cannot account for the human being as created by God?[20] Alternatively, Theunissen suggests speaking not of God, but only of 'the kingdom of God' to designate the spiritual community where the 'I' reveals itself to a 'Thou' in language and love. For, on his view, philosophy cannot become theology, which speaks of God himself.[21]

If one accepts this definition of the difference between philosophy and theology, one must also accept that philosophy cannot account for the genesis of subjectivity – at least not inasmuch as it has its origin in the *Zwischen*. In this point, one might then feel compelled to assume, philosophy must be supplemented by a theology of creation and of love. Let us follow this lead in order to test it, and have a look at Jeanrond's theology of creative love.

Theology of Love

In the Christian tradition, God is often identified with love. This tradition has its roots in the New Testament, especially in 1 Jn 4.16, according to which 'God is love, and those who abide in love abide in God, and God abides in them' – a triple that is quoted repeatedly in *A Theology of Love* (2010). What does it mean to abide in love or in God? Provided that God is omnipresent, it cannot mean that one has to move to a certain place. Rather, it means that one lives in a certain way, namely lovingly. What is special is not the locality of events happening between persons, but rather the modality of their relations. We have already learned from Buber that love cannot be traced to human subjectivity if it is a gift that one cannot give to oneself. Yet, if this gift is present only in being passed on, we nonetheless cannot dispense with the loving subject. If love is not from the start inherent in the subject, the question is how one comes to love in the first place.

17. Ibid., p. 169.
18. Cf. ibid., p. 181.
19. Michael Theunissen, *Der Andere*, p. 336.
20. Ibid., pp. 338; 506.
21. Cf. ibid, pp. 506–7.

This question is taken up in Chapter 4, 'Rediscovering the Loving Subject', where Jeanrond observes that medieval authors – as distinct from Augustine – 'reflect more on the God-given *human* capacity to love'.[22] The chapter deals with Bernard of Clairvaux, Thomas Aquinas, and women mystics. 'For many theological voices of the twelfth and thirteenth century, the human being was capable of love after all, thanks to her likeness to God. ... All human beings carry this *imago Dei* within themselves'.[23] Love is seen as equivalent to the image of God in human beings. Is love, then, divine or human? If we answer that it is both, we also need to explain how God and man work together in love, particularly in situations in which love is counter-intuitive and does not correspond to any desire for the other. How to love those whom one does not love naturally?

In Chapter 5, 'Love as Agape', the section about Søren Kierkegaard's theology of universal neighbourly love touches upon this problem. Jeanrond refers to Kierkegaard's *Works of Love* (1847), where God is described as 'middle term' (*Mellembestemmelse*) in the love of neighbour, and sets forth that for Kierkegaard, 'human beings can be genuine agents of love, but only in so far as their love is related to divine love'.[24] He unfolds that human persons can actively relate to God and their neighbour in love, with God being the 'centre of love' – an understanding of Christian love that is 'deeply inspired by the Johannine theology of love'.[25] Accordingly, Kierkegaard is quoted for the belief that 'God is Love, and therefore we can be like God only in loving, just as we also, according to the words of the apostle, can only be *God's co-workers – in love*. [...] But when you love the neighbour, then you are like God'.[26]

The love of neighbour also reveals specific characteristics of the *Zwischen*: Kierkegaard believes in God being 'between' the human lovers in such a way that God is not what keeps them away from each other, but rather that which binds them to each other, for God himself is the love *through* which they love each other. That God is in their midst means also that they are equal before God, that they have to deal with God in *everything*, and that *everyone* is to be seen as someone to be loved as one's neighbour.[27] Against this backdrop, the following three points of criticism against Kierkegaard's position do not seem self-evident to me:

22. Werner G. Jeanrond, *A Theology of Love* (London: Continuum/T&T Clark, 2010), p. 67.

23. Ibid., p. 68.

24. Ibid., p. 108 with reference to Søren Kierkegaard, *Works of Love,* trans. H. V. Hong and E. H. Hong (Princeton, NJ: Princeton University Press, 1995).

25. Ibid.

26. Ibid., p. 109.

27. Cf. Søren Kierkegaard, *Works of Love*, p. 140. Also cf. Claudia Welz, 'Keeping the Secret of Subjectivity: Kierkegaard and Levinas on Conscience, Love, and the Limits of Self-Understanding', in Claudia Welz and Karl Verstrynge, eds, *Despite Oneself: Subjectivity and its Secret in Kierkegaard and Levinas* (London: Turnshare, 2008), pp. 153–225; and eadem, 'How to Comprehend Incomprehensible Love? Kierkegaard Research and Philosophy of Emotion', *Kierkegaardiana* 24 (2007), pp. 261–86.

First, while Kierkegaard without doubt stresses the difference between Christianity and Judaism, I do not think that he presents 'Christian love as clearly separated from its Jewish roots'.[28] There is a certain ambiguity in his way of bringing Christian love of enemies into prominence while grounding his argument in a tradition that is common to Jews and Christians. In reply to the question of why it is our duty to love the neighbour, Kierkegaard recurs to the motif of the human being created 'as' or 'in the image of God' (Gen. 1.26). Emphasizing that every human being counts as one's neighbour, Kierkegaard finds 'a common watermark' (*et fælles Mærke*) on everyone, which 'eternity's light' makes visible despite our dissimilarity in other respects.[29] Hence, non-preferential love of neighbour becomes possible through the focus on God's imprint on *all* of our fellow human beings.

Second, based on the statement in *Works of Love* that through self-denial 'a human being gains the ability to be an instrument by inwardly making himself into nothing before God', Jeanrond accuses Kierkegaard for asking from the self 'to get rid of all self in the act of loving' and claims that human love therefore 'has no dignity on its own. Human beings seem not to be lovable in terms of being creatures bearing God's image'.[30] However, we should not forget that self-denial requires a strong self. *Making* oneself into 'nothing,' into an 'unworthy servant' through unselfish action is not the same as *being* nothing – otherwise one could neither give nor sacrifice oneself in love.[31] The problem Kierkegaard addresses is that human beings often want to be loved for some trait or accomplishment that excludes others from being lovable alike.

Third, what is Kierkegaard's 'antidote' against such selfishness? Kierkegaard views the love of neighbour as a God-given power which no one 'deserves' but which everyone can practice in praise of God. He calls it the Spirit's love or *Aands-Kjerligheden*.[32] Since Jeanrond and I agree about the insight that, for Kierkegaard, the origin and effect of love lie beyond human ability, I cannot follow him when he writes that Kierkegaard 'just cannot imagine that any form of human love might already be inspired by the Holy Spirit'.[33] If Kierkegaard is right in assuming that God is the 'middle term' in human love of neighbour, human love of neighbour is impossible without God's help.

Shall we follow Kierkegaard in determining God as *Mellembestemmelse* in inter-human love relations? If we do so, we are forced to the conclusion that the sphere between us is not merely human, all too human, but open for divine inspiration. In understanding God as perennial middle of human love relations,

---

28. Werner G. Jeanrond, *A Theology of Love*, p. 111.
29. Søren Kierkegaard, *Works of Love*, p. 89.
30. Werner G. Jeanrond, *A Theology of Love*, p. 112 with reference to Søren Kierkegaard, *Works of Love*, p. 365.
31. Cf. Claudia Welz, 'Love as Gift and Self-Sacrifice', *Neue Zeitschrift für Systematische Theologie und Religionsphilosophie* 50 (2008), pp. 238–66.
32. Cf. Søren Kierkegaard, *Works of Love*, p. 146.
33. Werner G. Jeanrond, *A Theology of Love*, p. 113.

Buber comes overly close to Kierkegaard's model of the God-relationship. It is the strength of this model to see God *both* as immanent in human life (to the extent that this life is filled with love) *and* as the one who transcends all human affairs. Kierkegaard's and Buber's conceptualizations of the relation between the love of God and the love of neighbour underline that nobody can love God without loving the neighbour. Conversely, God's invisibility or alleged 'absence' cannot serve as an excuse for not loving the people one sees.[34]

The strength of this model is lost when God is not viewed as the power through which we love others, but only as one *relatum* among others. In his chapter on 'Love' in *The Oxford Handbook of Theology and Modern European Thought* (2013), Jeanrond mentions that Christian theology must never cease to explore 'approaches to the dynamic and transformative network of loving relationships, i.e. my relationship to other human beings, to God, to the created universe, and to my own emerging self'.[35] If the God-relationship is just one item added to a variety of loving relationships, one might get the impression that it is of the same kind as other relationships. In this case, one loses sight of the idea that the God-relationship is the fundamental relationship that bears and preserves all others. Wishing to respect God's incommensurability and unconditionality, we should avoid common parlance relativizing his absoluteness. However, how can God remain 'beyond being' *and* be accessible and addressable? Buber tried to solve this dilemma by inventing the paradoxical notion of God as 'absolute person' capable of creating and re-creating mortal life. A Christian theology of creative love can resort to the doctrine of God's Trinitarian self-differentiation.

By now, we have become acquainted with a Jewish and a Christian version of what may be called 'relational ontology'. They converge on one point: whenever the sphere 'in-between' us is enriched with love, human agency and divine activity concur. Yet, it is nearly impossible to specify how exactly this happens. Theunissen's description of the sphere between subjectivity and alterity indicates that this might be due to the non-perspectival nature of this sphere. Therefore, we need to reflect upon love's perspectivity in order to discuss the implications of Jeanrond's promising remark that, instead of understanding love as being based on subjectivity, love should be taken as the 'framework' in which subjectivity can be understood properly.

Love's Perspectivity

What is it that love can tell us about subjectivity? It is uncontroversial to claim that love is a power that transforms those who form a relationship. However, what

---

34. Cf. Arne Grøn, 'Liebe und Anerkennung', *Kerygma und Dogma* 40/2 (1994), pp. 101–14.

35. Werner G. Jeanrond, 'Love', in Nichoals Adams, George Pattison and Graham Ward, eds, *The Oxford Handbook of Theology and Modern European Thought* (Oxford: Oxford University Press, 2013), pp. 233–52 (250).

is at stake in the discussion between transcendental phenomenology, philosophy of dialogue and theology of love is the question of whether a relational ontology, which does not prioritize the first-person perspective over the second- or third-person perspectives, can also provide us with a theory of subject-constitution.

If those participating in a relationship are to emerge from their relation, their individual presence as well as their co-presence is already presupposed. But how come that we find ourselves involved in the dynamics of difference between subjectivity and alterity without being able to account for these dynamics and our own emergence from them?

Perspectivity would get lost if love were fusion making two into one. Love includes perspective-taking; yet experience tells us that the difference between perspectives does not disappear in love. How are we to understand love's perspectivity if love indeed is spirit, that is, not a possession that could be 'owned' by the lover, but rather a power of creation that cannot become effective *without* a loving subject, yet takes effect *with* it only in such a way that love at the same time surpasses this subject's possibilities? Given that a subject cannot account for how its own subjectivity emerges, who would be qualified for this job? Consulting a neutral observer would not help, for the third-person perspective is not suitable as an insider-perspective. By contrast, the second-person perspective seems to be eligible, at least if it is the perspective of a 'You' that has itself been involved in the interactive process, which has formed and transformed the subject in question.

Along these lines, the philosopher James G. Hart has in *Who One Is* (2009) portrayed 'Love as the Fulfillment of the Second-Person Perspective'. Although announced programmatically in the heading to Chapter IV in Book 1, Hart does not say explicitly how this is to be understood. The readers have to reconstruct what he has in mind, and this is what I try to do in this section. Quoting Edmund Husserl, Hart holds that '[l]ove is the I's turning of itself to that which draws this I in a totally individual way and which, when it would be attained, would count as its fulfillment'.[36] This sentence is formulated in the subjunctive mood. It is not granted that the intentional object actually is attained. Hart argues that in love, my life is thoroughly with the other, for the other, and in opposition to the other, and that love creates a unity, which is sustained incessantly 'from below'. The 'You' persists, but is taken up in a 'We'. Love is establishing a co-subjectivity, a common life for a 'We'.[37] However, when the 'You' is included in a 'We', this does not dissolve the dynamics between 'I' and 'You'. As the other is uniquely self-experiencing, too, he or she can also incorporate the perspective of others into his or her own agency and perception.[38]

If this is correct, love is the fulfilment of the second-person perspective because the other is not just seeing the beloved from 'outside', but comes to participate in his or her perspective through the reflected glance. The second-person perspective is fulfilled by that which exceeds what one person alone can see. For Hart, love is

36. James G. Hart, *Who One Is*, Book 1, pp. 206–7.
37. Cf. ibid., pp. 224–35.
38. Cf. ibid., p. 198.

the appropriate epistemic act for presencing another because it intends the other *through* but as *beyond* his or her distinguishing attributes. The 'You' is taken up into a 'We', but the 'We' never replaces or obliterates the other 'I'.[39]

As love can neither be 'owned' by the lover nor the beloved or a third person observing the two, it is in my view most adequate to describe it as an event happening in the sphere 'in-between' persons, which cannot be reduced to a first-personal experience. Attempts of exchanging the first-person singular with the first-person plural are not helpful here because the 'We' is itself constituted on the basis of individuals meeting one another face to face. Hence, Hart's description of the 'We' as co-subjectivity needs to be developed further. If the two – the 'I' and the 'You' – cannot be treated as if they were only one, occupying one perspective in love, the spirit of love may instead be formally described as the interrelation of different perspectives. This conclusion seems unspectacular. However, it offers an alternative to Theunissen's thesis of the non-perspectival nature of the sphere 'in-between'. Accordingly, I would like to describe the 'in-between' as a multi-perspectival event of loving vision.

Conclusion

What does this imply for the interpretation of Jeanrond's remark about subjectivity that is, on his view, to be conceived within the context of love? For human lovers, this implies that each one learns to see him- or herself in unexpected ways through the gracious glance of another who sees 'more' in me than I myself can see. We cannot dispense with the plurality of perspectives. In love, in devotion to the other, one's attention is deviated from oneself. Yet, even though the self is decentred, it does not 'lose' itself; it receives itself from the other in the sense that the other can see what the 'blind spot' of the first-person perspective covers up. After all, the line of vision is two-way. To love means to communicate – not only about that which we have in common. As a creative sphere of actuality, the 'in-between' is also the stage for the not-yet, for an unforeseeable future.

According to a theology of love which identifies God with love, God is in play *in* or *as* the 'in-between' human beings to the extent that this sphere is characterized by love. While the theologian who believes in creative love can ascribe subject-constitution and the genesis of different perspectives to God, the philosopher who wishes to account for this process without speaking of God does not have this option. Does this mean that philosophy just leaves a 'blank space' where theology speaks of God? Far from it! There is a huge difference between describing the phenomenon of love with or without reference to God – a difference influencing the way love is experienced. Further, this difference has an impact on human self-understanding, especially in regard to how one defines the conditions of human agency.

39. Cf. ibid., pp. 214–26; 244.

The difference may be summarized in one word: *grace*. Someone who experiences grace experiences the charm of something happening to one's amazement. The experience of grace cannot be led back to one's own efforts. One cannot thank oneself for that which happened graciously. And one can neither point to anyone else thanks to whom it might have happened, in particular when enmeshed in a conflict that seems insurmountable.

We cannot take it for granted that there is love between human beings. How come when it happens to be there? Its attribution to human subjects alone would be just as under-theorized as its attribution to God alone. But in what manner can we then account for the good happening 'in-between' us? In fact, we cannot. That's why love is one of the greatest mysteries of our life.[40]

---

40. I wish to thank Ulrich Schmiedel and James M. Matarazzo, Jr. for their careful and insightful help in pruning this (originally overlong) contribution.

Part III

THEOLOGICAL OTHERS AND OTHER THEOLOGIES

14

THE OTHER LANGUAGE: RELIGION IN MODERNITY

Knut Wenzel

Poetry, like art in general, is by principle more than it is. A piece of art, a poem, establishes its shape by way of distanciation from reality, by isolating itself from the nexus of *Lebenswelt*. This formative process of self-distanciation does not precede the final work, a poem being its result, but is the very structure of any work of art. It is, at the same time, a process that transforms a longing for reality, or 'the real', into a meaningful 'thing of beauty'.[1] A poem receives its meaningfulness through its artful structure, but not *from* it. A love song sings the language of love, and the more artfully it does so, the better it might be. But it would not bear any meaning whatsoever, if it did not do so for the sake of love. The desire for reality, the longing for love, being transformed into beauty – or at least into something readable, meaningful – is the poem's still-beating heart. The poem, as any work of art, does not simply emerge out of a process of sublimation. Instead, it is a process that never comes to a definite end. Art is sublimation of a desire for 'the real' into beauty – permanently endangered by taking back the validity of that desire. In the entirety of this foundational dialectic, a poem is (or can be) meaningful. It 'is' more than it is: it 'means' (and does not know, define, or rule) 'the real'. To put it in the poetological line of Christopher Middleton: A love poem is 'a song that drinks the scent of a space unborn'.[2]

When these reflections hold true in the case of art, and poetry in particular – and it is but an abbreviation of reflections central to Theodor W. Adorno's aesthetics[3] – how much more is it the case regarding religion! It might intuitively be plausible to conceive of religion as language: a basic, possibly even universal, *structure*, a register of historically, culturally, and socially shaped *semantics*, a set of *imaginations* and *conceptualizations* (likewise laden with historical

---

1. In the sense the Hothouse Flowers put it: 'A thing of Beauty is not to be ignored', 'Thing Of Beauty' on *Songs From the Rain*, 1993.

2. Christopher Middleton, 'The China Virgins', in idem, *Collected Poems* (Manchester: The Carcanet Press, 2008), pp. 380–1 (381).

3. Cf. Theodor W. Adorno, *Ästhetik (1958/59)* (Frankfurt/M.: Suhrkamp, 2009), pp. 54–71.

impregnations), community-building *institutions*, and communal *pragmatics* – to conceive of religion as language means to speak of a structure, of semantics, conceptualizations, institutions, pragmatics – *liturgies* – of meaning. It could not be more evident that the meaning of religion is not its language – as the truth of a dogma is not identical with the dogmatic formulation – because religion is the language that deals with reality in its absoluteness, with God as the 'real Absolute'. If the assertion that it is the nature of poetry to be more than it is might be subject to discussion, then the same assertion is undeniably essential to any self-concept of religion – it is then a definite assertion that is binding for theology, though not necessarily for any external view on religion, be it that of a sociology or of a philosophy of religion.[4]

Stressing the claim that religion is 'more' than it is – just by being what it is – clearly includes the issue of reference, or referentialization. A symbolizing structure only really means something when it means something real. Religions cannot become completely 'post-modernized', just as poems about love cannot either, I presume. Perhaps we are witnessing the dawn of a new realism in philosophy;[5] however, there is an old, if not archaic, realism conveyed by religion throughout the centuries. But the coverage of the notion of 'being more' is wider than this. In deciphering the 'Biblical Code'[6] aided by various philosophies – from Platonism to Analyticism, from Aristotelianism to Idealism, from Stoicism to Existentialism, from Thomism to Marxism, from the Art of Commentary to the Philosophy of Hermeneutics – the Christian tradition has developed a variety of notions – or metaphors – of this 'being more', thus lifting up the discursive structure of religion – a symbolizing system open to the 'real Absolute' – onto the surface of its thematic productivity. Not just 'being more', but thematically reflecting this 'being more' as the foundational dimension beyond its control, religion is thus a precarious discourse, a discourse broken up. To illustrate the brokenness, I will now only mention a few of such metaphors.

There is the biblical כָּבוֹד *(kabod),* naming a divine attribute and a gift of a divine attribute: God accords what is exclusively his to his creature. This gracious gift is nothing the creature would be in vital need of, but without this gift his and her life would be impossible. *Kabod*, God's surplus (and yet necessary) gift, his *gloria*, his *doxa*, or as some have translated it – his elegance. Imagine the effect of the translation on the understanding of one of the most frequently quoted sentences by the Church Fathers, Irenaeus' *vivens homo gloria dei*: 'living man is the elegance of God'!'[7]

---

4. The implied continuity between poetry and religion could be made explicit with reference to Paul Ricœur's philosophy of revelation; cf. Paul Ricoeur, 'Toward a Hermeneutic of the Idea of Revelation', *Harvard Theological Review* 70 (1977), pp. 1–37.

5. Paul Boghossian, *Fear of Knowledge: Against Relativism and Constructivism* (Oxford: Clarendon Press, 2006).

6. Northrop Frye, *The Great Code: The Bible and Literature* (New York: Harcourt, 1982).

7. Irenaeus, *Adversus haeresis*, IV, 20.7.

The entire theology of grace (to address another concept of a precarious religious discourse) operates under the signature of exuberance. It is the superfluous grace that constitutes, redeems, and accomplishes creation. From the perspective of grace, reality is shaped by superfluity. Grace is not the answer to need. It rather is the expression of an unconditioned free will.

But there is not only a line of fullness, being marked by the notions of *kabod* and grace. There is also a line of void. There is an experience of the absence of the absolute, of its unrepairable loss, of its unattainability; and subsequently there is a discourse of mourning, of grief, and sorrow.[8] Michel de Certeau identified the Christian mystic tradition as a discourse of missing the absolute. Mysticism reacts to the absolute's unattainability by enacting a hysterical discourse. Addressing the real Absolute, religion goes to extremes. And it generates strategies of coordinating its extremism. One of these strategies can be found in the fascinating metaphor central to the mystic experience of Marguerite Porète: *Loin-Près*. She experiences the presence of the Lord, and addresses him, as remote-intimate. Jesus, the subject of her love, is at the same time intimate to this love and absolutely out of its reach. This is what it means to love the Absolute – absolute love: to love, and to not have, the beloved.

Another coordinative concept is that of negative theology. The characterization 'negative theology' is misleading. The dynamics of the naming of God not only run through affirmation, negation, and finally an unrestrained overabundance, but the enactment of negative theology's liturgy exposes within the act of faithful affirmation the two impossible dimensions of this act. Religion is a hysterical discourse, negative and positive at once, a discourse without a centre, a de-centred discourse, its centre being outside, out of sight, beyond in every sense. God is out of everything – *superior summo meo* – even when he is *interior intimo meo* (more intimate than my inner self).[9] To speak of God is to say that to everything – to 'the everything' – there is an 'out-there'. Religion is a discourse not simply about God as 'the Other' in addition to the world as 'the Identical'. Religion does not insinuate an additive relation between world and God, the identical and the other. Speaking of God religiously (there are many other ways to do so) means to identify otherness as a dimension of each and everything, not in the sense of black being the other with respect to white, or the addressee to the addresser, but in the sense that there is otherness to the world in its entirety, to reality as such. This is a difficult thing to say. Can there be reality as such, in addition to which there is otherness? Religion does not think reality – the world – as totality. Rather it conceives of reality as being open by principle, of being incomplete in itself. Is there a positive definition of incompleteness? The best at hand is still morphologically constructed as negation: *infinity*. Reality in its wholeness is infinite. Bearing in mind Emmanuel Levinas' distinction between

---

8. Michel de Certeau, *The Mystic Fable: The Sixteenth and Seventeenth Century*, trans. M. B. Smith (Chicago: The University of Chicago Press, 1992).

9. Augustine, *Confessiones*, III, 6.11.

totality and infinity,[10] we can say: Religion thinks God is the positive definition of the infinity of reality.

To say that there is infinite openness to reality is not tantamount to saying that it leaks. Infinity, although taking away every boundary, is not a weakening qualification. Rather, it assigns a perfection other than totality. Totalitarian perfection is a horizontal, an additive business, it is deadly dull. The infinity proposition maintains that reality's *potentia perfectionis* reaches out beyond the imaginable, expectable, calculable. The infinity dimension is not the simple prolongation of what has always already been seen and known. It rather is an openness towards a realization of the other that cannot be derived from what is. Otherness becoming real is like filling the infinite openness without ever consummating it. Even a state of fulfilment would not replace infinity, but would be the fulfilment of reality in its infinity. Does otherness, by becoming real, transform into sameness? The quality of the other does not depend on a state of 'unrealized reality' but on reality's infinity. As this will not be engulfed even in a state of fulfilment, there will be otherness to a fully 'realized reality', in contradiction to simplistic concepts of identity that tend to let all elements of otherness integrate into 'the identical'. The Christian tradition speaks of perfection as the eschatological integration of 'the same' into 'the other', of all things into God.[11] Yet this idea suffers from the same simplicity as the previously mentioned identity concepts, it lacks a dialectical relation of sameness and otherness being more appropriate to reality. One way to escape from this binary, non-dialectical relation of the same and the other might be found in avoiding to think of fulfilment as 'realized reality', as complete realization of that which is not yet realized in the 'here and now', and to think fulfilment instead as absolute communication which has become real.[12] Communication, being an interaction rather than a process, connects subjects (and not modes of being). Subjects are irreducible to each other or to an abstract principle. By connecting them, communication indicates their reciprocal irreducibility. Communication – liturgy of otherness. Liturgy addresses worldly communication in its wholeness to God. Being symbolized – being symbolically represented – by way of the sacred liturgy, the worldly communication receives a dignifying recognition *coram Deo*.

Bringing it all before God means to obtain recognition for the dignity of worldly communication (for the world as it carries out itself in communication) through an act of communication that transcends the mere immanence of this world. The constellation of *coram Deo* sheds an enlightening light on the alterity-structure

---

10. Cf. Emmanuel Levinas, *Totality and Infinity: An Essay on Exteriority*, trans. A. Lingis (Pittsburgh, PA: Duquesne University Press, 1969).

11. 'When all things are subjected to him, then the Son himself will also be subjected to the one who put all things in subjection under him, so that God may be all in all' (1 Cor. 15.28).

12. I am working on a theological concept of absolute communication. A study on the *Grundlegung der Fundamentaltheologie als Poetik des Glaubens* (*The Foundation of Fundamental Theology as Poetics of Faith*) will hopefully be published in 2015.

of this world-as-(inter-subjective)-communication: as God is not an immanent aspect of the worldly communication that is brought before him and is being recognized by him through the intermediation of the sacred liturgy, the (human) subject is not absorbed in the immanence of communication. Religion, being constitutively hysterical about the intimate absence, the absent intimacy of the 'real Absolute' – 'other language' – is a proper advocate of the internal otherness, but not immanent, to this worldly reality.[13]

Modernity emerges out of the spirit of subjectivity, out of the emancipatory history of discovery and advocacy of human subject-autonomy. One of the foundational texts of modernity, Pico della Mirandola's *Oratio de hominis dignitate* (1496), cross-connects myth and modernity.

In pre-modern ages, when the fields of social, political, cultural discourses had more or less been shaped by religion, the latter hardly was identifiable as 'other language'. Extreme versions of it filtered out, giving alterity a sometimes shrill voice: mysticism, asceticism, millennialism. Entering modern times, religion did best in its radical versions: *devotio moderna*, Reformation, Spanish mysticism, Pietism… modes of subjectivity were their radicalism. There is a subliminal stream of subject-articulation in biblical, Jewish, and Christian traditions. It emerges, when God addresses Adam, speaking out his name; it runs through the psalms; it gains a paradigmatic shape in Mary's reaction to what the angel announced to her; it receives a definite realization in the life, preaching, and practice of Jesus of Nazareth, the corpo-realization of God's salvific presence; it finds its voice in the authorities of the Rabbinic tradition; it crosses through Augustine's *Confessiones*; it inspires the Franciscan reform movement of the thirteenth century. Coming up the ages on this way, the subliminal stream of subject-articulation awaits its historic, secular explication. Does religion await – modernity? Modernity plays this part anyhow, intentionally taking over the religious heritage. Modernity inheriting religion becomes explicit in Ludwig Feuerbach's epochal programme of translation: the essence of religion is – anthropology.[14]

To re-integrate projective heteronomy into self-confident autonomy: is this not a programme worth of being called modernization? However, such a concept

---

13. In the very last text published in his lifetime, Karl Rahner reminds us of the crucial centrality of analogy in theology, offering a 'hysterical' definition of the concept: 'We talk about God, about God's existence, characteristics, about three persons in God; we speak of God's freedom, of God's binding will, and so forth. Of course, we need to proceed in this manner; we cannot simply keep silent about God. Indeed, it is only after we have first spoken that it is possible – really possible – to be silent. But in such discourse we usually forget that any statement made about God is legitimate only to the extent that it is always simultaneously negated. It is a question here of enduring the uncanny suspension between affirmation and negation as the true and only fixed term of our knowledge'. Karl Rahner, 'Experiences of a Catholic Theologian', *Theological Studies* 61 (2000), pp. 3–15 (5).

14. '[T]he secret of theology is nothing else than anthropology – the knowledge of God nothing else than a knowledge of man!' Ludwig Feuerbach, *The Essence of Christianity*, trans. M. Evens (London: John Chapman, 1854), p. 206.

of modernization turned out to be inconsistent. The principle of autonomy would not find a satisfying representation in the attitude of self-confidence as is made visible in the character of the office-employee Bartleby, displaying a deeply melancholic kind of autonomy.[15] Moreover, self-confidence would turn out to be an attitude not of trust but of anxiety; fuelled by an urge for survival it would produce alienation, consumption, annihilation. It is this equation of survival and destruction that reveals what has been analysed as the dialectic of enlightenment.[16] However, religion became visible as not being completely identical with heteronomy. Instead, to practice religion unrestrictedly appeared to be a genuine expression of self-realization under the conditions of modernity. The process of modernization, having picked up high speed during the last decades, did not produce a disappearance of religion as the classical theory of secularization had predicted. That classical theory has failed.[17]

Undoubtedly, religion undergoes significant transformations under the influence, if not pressure, of a globalized modernity. Religion pluralizes and individualizes; religious corporations – churches, communities, parishes – are rapidly losing their binding-power, wherever educated urban middle-class-based societies gain a politically and economically stable level of realization; religious identity becomes diffuse, fluid, *bricolage*-like – in one word: it becomes subjective – and this to an extent that it seems appropriate to address this very subjective spirituality, or piety, as faith rather than as religion. There is faith uncovered by religion. Only when this religion-reduced-to-faith is ignored, contemporary European societies might be falsely judged as being 'secularized' (in the sense of 'de-religionized').

What is it that keeps religion alive – attractive to people living in complete concordance with modernity? It is not the promise of a pre-modern, cosy home; offers of that type are legion. It is the feeling that the description systems and practices which modernity offers as devices for the handling of reality, in their totality, fail to exhaust reality. Their shortcoming is twofold as they fail to describe reality in its inexhaustibility although they are designed to usurp it both theoretically and practically. Religion in modernity appears to be not another description system or practice of accomplishment, but a discourse that keeps present the inexhaustibility of reality, its alterity dimension. Far from being a strategy to cope with contingency,[18] religion strengthens the evidence of the experience of reality's contingency; the latter understood as reality's infinite openness rather than limitedness.

Religion comes under the pressure of modernization not only in the sense that it appears 'atavistic' in relation to modern standards of rational reasoning,

---

15. Herman Melville, *Bartleby The Scrivener*, originally published in: *Putnam's Monthly Magazine*, 1853.

16. Max Horkheimer and Theodor W. Adorno, *Dialectic of Enlightenment*, trans. E. Jephcott (Stanford, CA: Stanford University Press, 2002).

17. Cf. Charles Taylor, *A Secular Age* (Cambridge, MA: Harvard University Press, 2007).

18. Hermann Lübbe, *Religion nach der Aufklärung* (Köln: Styria, 1986), pp. 160–78.

democratic governance and inclusive civil society; religion comes under the pressure of a dynamics of modernization that targets the total submission of reality under the sovereignty of purpose-rationality.[19] The more it is exposed to this pressure, the more religion incorporates the inexhaustible otherness of reality, the more it becomes modernity's other language. Religion reacts to the totalizing dynamics of a reifying modernization by self-radicalization. Modernity answers by the allocating of programmes to pacify religion – Jürgen Habermas' proposal of taming religion by translating its semantic potential into secular language being the most discussed one in recent times.[20] But religion will not surrender otherness to sameness.

Religion witnessed the upcoming of modernity as emancipation of the subject, a process familiar to its own mission of empowerment: encouraging man to live. But the emancipatory narrative of modernity, at the same time, challenges the essentially religious concept of grace. Religion then witnessed the transformation of a history of emancipation – which has closely been related to the history of progress *as* breaking nature's superiority – into a pursuit of total dominance over nature, over reality. When the breaking of nature's overwhelming power reverts into subduing reality in the modes of analysis, technique, eloquence ..., religion answers with an ever more radical, disturbing or even objective, articulation of the other. There is an interdependence between modern totalitarianism and religious extremism. The history of emancipation, inscribed in the heart of modernity, bears a traumatized memory of violence that has accumulated the complete complex of survival from the beginning of humanity. The impetus to survive already bears in its core a will to total command: total knowledge, total control, total power, total productivity, total consumption. The history of humankind's survival – which in fact is a dialectical history of loss and survival – recalls the human subject as vulnerable rather than vital. The human subject is the one that could get lost, and knows it.

A resilient religion pushes the dialectic of enlightenment even further: the process of liberation from heteronomous powers – whether they be of a natural or of a socio-historico-political kind – reverted into strategies of total subjugation of reality, a process which has been sold as modernization. What is more is that the enduring existence of religion under the condition of modernity falsifies the totalitarian pretensions of this kind of a reified modernity. The totalizing grasp will never reach the absolute; in terms of discourse, the absolute is ungraspable.

---

19. Cf. Hans Albert, 'The Myth of Total Reason: Dialectical Claims in the Light of Undialectical Criticism', in idem, *The Positivist Dispute in German Sociology*, trans. G. Ady and D. Frisby (London: Heinemann, 1976), pp. 163–97.

20. Jürgen Habermas, 'Faith and Knowledge', in idem, *The Future of Human Nature*, trans. H. Beister and W. Rehg (Cambridge: Polity Press, 2003), pp. 101–15; Jürgen Habermas et al., *An Awareness of What is Missing: Faith and Reason in a Post-Secular Age*, trans. C. Cronin (Cambridge: Polity Press, 2010); cf. Knut Wenzel and Thomas M. Schmidt, eds, *Moderne Religion? Theologische und religionsphilosophische Reaktionen auf Jürgen Habermas* (Freiburg: Herder, 2009).

The absolute will always be the other to any gesture of identification. The enduring presence of religion discloses an access for modernity to conceive of itself as a non-totalizing discourse. In the light of a non-totalizing modernity, to be religious appears as a testimony for autonomous freedom; to be religious means to be modern.

Facing religion still present, modernity might find an attitude of revising its totalizing tendencies, an attitude of rediscovering its primary history of man as a fragile subject of emancipation. A discourse which dares to be incomplete bears witness to the vulnerability of its very subject. By displaying figures and features of sacred shelter – like the *Schutzmantelmadonna*, the Virgin of Mercy, in the Catholic tradition – religions do not insinuate a supernatural security sphere. Rather, they indicate the indigence and dignity of protection of the bare human subject.

If religion cannot fully be integrated within modernity without being simply anti-modern or atavistic, but instead reflects on issues genuine to modernity,[21] it can be identified as the other language of modernity. Two discourses, languages, cultures, attitudes, desires, that can neither absorb each other nor take over the other's part; two discourses that are caught in an interdependency of otherness, unable to merge one into another, therefore, desperately needing each other; two discourses that appreciate the concerns of the respective other as if they were their own; two discourses that might re-identify themselves in the eye of the other: these discourses constitute a constellation of concern and fallibility, of meaning and incompleteness, of consciousness and desire – a constellation of love. To speak in (terms of) love is to speak low but intensely, to mean and not know, to doubt and be enchanted, to be up to date and vintage, to hold and to lose, to experience and to imagine: to love does not mean to integrate all this into an identical oneness, but to communicate in the thickness of it, to create a new reality out of the incomprehensible. Religion does not treat this creative love as mere discourse effect. Like a poem of love, it regards the language of love as language of ultimate meaning. Religion addresses the reality of love itself: addressing it as the love of God, God as love.[22]

---

21. In particular, a human being discovering her- and himself in its absolute dignity, which instantaneously relates them to reality as such, to a reality that in its wholeness and inconsumability both confronts the self as its other and appears as a condition of the possibility of the subject's self-determination.

22. A topic Werner G. Jeanrond has elaborated on comprehensively: Werner G. Jeanrond, *A Theology of Love* (London: Continuum/T&T Clark, 2010).

15

LAUGHING AT THE OTHER

Ola Sigurdson

What, if anything, does humour have to do with the other? A first impression is, most likely, that humour is something good. Humour is a perfectly innocent and simple pleasure. We – those of us living today in Western societies after modernity – would probably regard anyone who was critical of humour as dour, dry and cheerless. How can anyone object to having a good time? It surprises us to read about ancient philosophers or theologians having anything to say against laughter and cheerfulness. But this is actually the case. Consider, for instance, St. John Chrysostom who has the following to say about laughter in a homily:

> to laugh, to speak jocosely, does not seem an acknowledged sin, but it leads to acknowledged sin. Thus laughter often gives birth to foul discourse, and foul discourse to actions still more foul. Often from words and laughter proceed railing and insult; and from railing and insult, blows and wounds; and from blows and wounds, slaughter and murder.[1]

Chrysostom is quoting Paul, first by assembling Eph. 4.29 and 5.4, to say: 'Let no foolish talking nor jesting proceed out of thy mouth', and then 1 Tim. 5.6: 'she who liveth in pleasure is dead while she liveth'. The kind of pleasure Chrysostom warns against is not only the pleasure that comes from humour, but also luxuriousness that might lead to drunkenness, violence, extortion and rape. Against the objection that going to the horse-races or the theatre, or playing dice, could hardly be considered a crime, Chrysostom counters that this might well lead to graver sins, so it is best to avoid such pleasure-seeking altogether.

Undoubtedly, to a contemporary reader the warning against laughter (and other things too) seems to be a prime example of cheerlessness, leading to the suspicion that it might characterize the Christian tradition as such. However,

---

1. St John Chrysostom, 'Homily XV', in idem, *On the Priesthood; Ascetic Treatises; Select Homilies and Letters; Homilies on the Statues, A Select Library of the Nicene and Post-Nicene Fathers of the Christian Church*, vol. 9, ed. Philip Schaff (Peabody, MA: Hendricksons, 1995), p. 442.

when it comes to humour it is possible to come up with counter-examples, such as – for instance – Desiderius Erasmus' *Praise of Folly*.[2] Erasmus' book is written in a witty style to amuse his friend Thomas More and is actually (as it seems on the surface at least) endorsing some of the pleasures strongly disapproved by Chrysostom, while still claiming to be a work of piety. In the words of Erasmus, Folly complains of the ingratitude that has been shown to her: 'throughout all the ages nobody has ever come forward to deliver a speech of thanks in praise of Folly'.[3] Folly was nursed at the breast of 'two charming nymphs', Drunkenness and Ignorance, but has been raised in a household together with such figures as Self-love, Flattery, Forgetfulness, Idleness, Pleasure, Madness, Sensuality, Revelry and Sound Sleep.[4] In other words, quite a company, and none that Chrysostom would have approved of. Furthermore, Folly boasts about her presence in all manners of life, and claims, 'no party is any fun unless seasoned with folly'; indeed, 'no association of alliance can be happy or stable without me'.[5] The fool is happier than the wise man, according to Erasmus.

No doubt Erasmus is acerbic as well as ironic in some of his comments about wisdom, philosophy and theology, given that he himself surely led a life in pursuit of knowledge and wisdom. But there is in fact a version of folly that could be said to characterize the piety that Erasmus is endorsing in *Praise of Folly*. When he suggests that 'the Christian religion has a kind of kinship with folly in some form', I take it that he is not being ironic.[6] Since Christianity often takes a position that is contrary to the wisdom of the world, there is no other alternative than to imagine that in the eyes of the world, it is a kind of folly. So even if Erasmus has much to say against theology in his own time, such criticism does not affect the life of simple piety. The learning of theologians as well as philosophers is indeed a folly in comparison to the simple life of the pious person, expressed in good deeds rather than learned dispute. There is a great deal of scepticism in *Praise of Folly*, but on the whole it is actually endorsing folly, at least what would count as folly in the eyes of some of the contemporary learned in Erasmus' time. My question, however, is not what kind of folly Erasmus wants, but why Erasmus and Chrysostom are so different in their assessment of humour. The answer, I would suggest, has to do with ambiguity and history. Let me look at these in turn.

The Ambiguity of Humour

There is ambiguity in laughter and humour, and this was perceived early on in the Christian tradition. In the narratives about the crucifixion, the crowd was mocking the suffering Christ: 'He saved others; he cannot save Himself. He is the King of

2. Desiderius Erasmus, *Praise of Folly*, trans. B. Radice (London: Penguin, 1993).
3. Ibid., p. 12.
4. Ibid., pp. 17–8.
5. Ibid., pp. 32; 35.
6. Ibid., p. 128.

Israel; let him come down from the cross now, and we will believe in him. He trusts in God; let God deliver him now, if he wants to' (Mt. 27.42-3). This mocking of Christ at the cross is an exemplary illustration of what is probably one of the most common usages of laughter, namely to establish one's superiority over the person one is laughing at. In humour theory, this is what usually goes under the name of the 'classical' or even the 'superiority theory'. According to John Morreall, one of the foremost theorists on humour, this is '[t]he oldest, and probably still most widespread theory of laughter' and in essence its point is that 'laughter is an expression of a person's feelings of superiority over other people'.[7] This is a theory that could be found in most of what Plato, Aristotle, Quintilian and other thinkers from antiquity have to say on the matter. But it is also expressed in an illustrative fashion by the early modern philosopher Thomas Hobbes, who observed that the 'passion of laughter is nothing else but a sudden glory arising from sudden conception of some eminency in ourselves, by comparison with the infirmities of others, or with our own formerly'.[8] Laughter as an instrument of superiority might even have an evolutionary basis, as the neuroscientist and psychologist Robert R. Provine suggests in *Laughter: A Scientific Investigation*. The evolutionary point of laughter is to establish a bond between human beings, to build community and to make friends; this bonding also implies that its function is to establish a distinction between friend and foe or insider and outsider. 'Laughter scorns the victims and feeds the wrath of the aggressors'.[9] If this is correct (and I have really no doubt that it is), then it is no wonder that the 'superiority theory' also may be the 'classical' theory that we would expect to find in anyone reflecting on the nature of humour, be they ancient or modern.

If laughter was understood according to this classical tradition, both in its philosophical and in its rhetorical aspects, then it is no wonder that a Christian theology, which had meditated upon the passion narratives in the Gospels, regarded laughter with suspicion. As an instrument of mocking the crucified Lord, in no way could laughter and humour be understood as a simple and innocent pleasure; quite the contrary, the central narratives seem to suggest that it was a tool of power. I have no intention of trying to defend Chrysostom here, nevertheless, his suspicion of the vicious effects of laughter might not entirely miss the mark, even if there is more to say about laughter than he has done.

The History of Humour

What, then, is the difference between Chrysostom and Erasmus with regard to laughter? About eleven centuries. I would argue that the understanding of

---

7. John Morreall, *Taking Laughter Seriously* (Albany: State University of New York, 1983), p. 4.
8. Thomas Hobbes, *Human Nature and De Corpore Politico* (Oxford: Oxford University Press, 1999), pp. 54–5.
9. Robert R. Provine, *Laughter: A Scientific Investigation* (New York: Penguin, 2000), p. 47.

laughter changed through the centuries, and that Christianity was instrumental in this change. It is a well-established fact that the Renaissance signified a re-evaluation of laughter in Christianity. As Michael A. Screech writes: 'In the Renaissance, Christian laughter swept into prominence, aided by the conviction that Man is a laughing animal. It is right for him to laugh'.[10] The wording of 'Man as a laughing animal' suggests an influence from Aristotle, who in *Parts of Animals*, suggested that a human being is 'the only animal that laughs', thus implying that this is one of the characteristic traits of human existence.[11] Since Aristotle had risen to prominence in Christian theology and philosophy during the twelfth and thirteenth centuries, mainly through Thomas Aquinas, his anthropology was incorporated into Christian theology. Jacques Le Goff suggests the following outline of the historical development in the Middle Ages: first a period of 'repressed' and 'stifled' laughter from the fourth to the tenth century, then a period of both liberation and control and the scholastic assessment of laughter and finally a period of more 'unbridled' laughter.[12] Le Goff, then, does not agree with the thesis of Mikhail Bakhtin that the Middle Ages were, on the whole, a period of sadness, whereas the Renaissance liberated laughter. Even if Bakhtin's *Rabelais and His World* is a brilliant book that has been immensely important to the historical study of laughter, his contrast between the Middle Ages and the Renaissance is overblown.[13]

If there might be more of a continuity on laughter between the Middle Ages and the Renaissance than Bakhtin allows for, this does not mean that the Renaissance has no special significance in the history of laughter. Another book by a renowned philosopher – one that Bakhtin perhaps was influenced by – is Ernst Cassirer's *The Platonic Renaissance in England* from 1932.[14] In this book, Cassirer traces a genealogy of ideas from the Italian Humanists through the Cambridge Platonists and their influence on thinkers such as Gotthold Ephraim Lessing, Johann Gottfried Herder, Johann Wolfgang von Goethe, Friedrich Schiller, and Immanuel Kant. Among these ideas was the importance of humour: 'the Renaissance ... endowed the comic with new force and new meaning'.[15] Cassirer recognizes the critical power of humour, but most of all highlights it as a force of 'balance and reconciliation'.[16] Humour came to take on a new form or

---

10. Michael A. Screech, *Laughter at the Foot of the Cross* (London: Penguin, 1999), p. 4.

11. Aristotle, *Parts of Animals*, 673b.

12. Jacques Le Goff, 'Laughter in the Middle Ages', in Jan Bremmer and Herman Roodenburg, eds, *A Cultural History of Humour* (Cambridge: Polity Press, 2005), pp. 50–1.

13. Mikhail Bakhtin, *Rabelais and His World*, trans. H. Iswolsky (Bloomington, IN: Indiana University Press, 1984).

14. On the relation between Ernst Cassirer and Mikhail Bakhtin, see Brian Poole, 'Bakhtin and Cassirer: The Philosophical Origins of Bakhtin's Carnival Messianism', *South Atlantic Quarterly*, 97:3/4 (1998), pp. 537–78.

15. Ernst Cassirer, *The Platonic Renaissance in England*, trans. J. P. Pettegrove (Austin: University of Texas Press, 1953), p. 170.

16. Ibid., p. 171.

quality in the Renaissance through such writers as Thomas More, Erasmus and William Shakespeare as a medium of reconciliation. In Lord Shaftesbury's apology for humour, Cassirer detects a sense of humour that is something else than an attempt to establish one's superiority through 'intellectual sarcasm' or 'intellectual irony', namely a 'liberating, life-giving, and life-forming power of the soul'.[17] Through his reading of the Renaissance, humour came to take a part of Cassirer's own philosophy, and it is in a later work, *An Essay on Man*, that he most succinctly formulates this special quality of humour, namely sympathy: 'Comic art possesses in the highest degree that faculty shared by all art, sympathetic vision'.[18] This kind of humour and the kind of laughter it provokes is distinct from the kind that the superiority theory depicts; neither is it an attempt to escape the miseries of life through an optimistic cheerfulness because it does not see comedy and tragedy as opposites.

This does not mean, of course, that at one time laughter was *only* understood according to the superiority theory, but then everybody changed his or her mind. According to Erasmus himself, St Jerome, famous for his translation of the Bible into Latin, 'amused himself' with 'freedom and sarcasm', so there is actually at least one precedent for Erasmus' book during the lifetime of Chrysostom.[19] Neither did everyone in the Renaissance give up the superiority theory, as the example from Thomas Hobbes shows. But I would suggest that there was a general change of perception of laughter, reaching some kind of prominence in the Renaissance as well as in Romanticism and Idealism. Shaftesbury was important to Kant, especially to his aesthetics, as Kant develops his account of the *Witz*. Irony and humour play important parts in the aesthetics of German Romanticism on the whole, especially for Jean Paul, but are also put to a more fundamental philosophical or theological use in Georg Wilhelm Friedrich Hegel and Søren Kierkegaard. But I have to leave this interesting discussion for now, to return to my thesis that Christianity – or perhaps even Christian theology – might have been instrumental in the changing perception of the role of humour in human existence.

A Comic Revolution

One reason for the widespread scepticism with regard to humour among many of the theologians of the first centuries, among them Chrysostom, might be precisely a scepticism of its use as an instrument of domination. Reading the passion narratives about the mocking of the crucified Christ, it must have been clear how laughter was used to establish superiority over the other human being. If Christ in Christian theology was understood as a stand-in for every fellow human being,

17. Ibid., p. 183.
18. Ernst Cassirer, *An Essay on Man: An Introduction to a Philosophy of Human Culture* (New Haven: Yale University Press, 1944), p. 150.
19. Desiderius Erasmus, *Praise of Folly*, p. 7.

then laughter could be taken in general as a means of harming the other. Those Christian theologians who were well read in the classical literature would have had an understanding of laughter congruent with such behaviour, and consequently they were prone to reject laughter. If one were to object that some of the Christian authors were not precisely innocent of a certain priggishness, but also were using irony and sarcasm as a weapon of their own, I would not dispute such a claim. My claim is merely that the classical understanding of humour was not one that, for good reasons, some of the early theologians would be very keen to endorse.

But there is also another, let me call it 'poetical', reason why the early theologians were hardly interested in taking up the classical view on humour, a reason that also had to do with the gospels. I presume that to most readers of the gospels, if their eyes or ears have not been dulled by habit, there are moments in the gospel that could strike them as 'funny' in the humorous sense. Take, for instance, the narrative about Jesus' triumphal entry in Jerusalem, riding on a donkey, in Mt. 21. The crowd greets Jesus as a king, but he must be a strange kind of king, at least compared to such royalty of our time, who chooses a donkey for a triumphal entry – the donkey being an animal for work (also in biblical times) rather than a magnificent animal adding to the pomp of a king entering his kingdom. If this is not a political satire, I don't know what a political satire is. Aside from what actual forms of satire scripture may contain, there is another, more profound aspect of humour that it conveys; one which, I suspect, was instrumental in changing the understanding of humour.

The German philologist Erich Auerbach might be the one who has put forward this thesis most clearly in *Mimesis: The Representation of Reality in Western Literature*. It was a stylistic convention for classical authors that tragedy narrated elevated themes in a high style whereas comedy recounted the ordinary in a low style. Compare, for instance, Aristotle who in his *Poetics* differentiates between comedy and tragedy by what kind of people they describe: 'the one would make its personages worse, and the other better, than the men of the present day'.[20] But there is also a difference in the manner that they speak about their subject, according to Aristotle, and this difference is discussed throughout the entire *Poetics*. There is, in Aristotle's choice of words, a sense of what is here called the superiority theory, since he calls what is comic 'the ridiculous' and what is ridiculous 'the ugly': 'As for comedy, it is (as has been observed) an imitation of men worse than the average; worse, however, not as regards any and every sort of fault, but only as regards one particular kind, the ridiculous, which is a species of the ugly'.[21] Aristotle's statement exemplifies what Auerbach calls the 'antique stylistic rule', which does not allow any mixing of genres.[22]

The gospels, however, violate this convention, and speaking of the scene of Peter's denial found in all four gospels, Auerbach writes: 'It is too serious for

---

20. Aristotle, *Poetics*, 1448a.
21. Ibid., 1449a.
22. Erich Auerbach, *Mimesis: The Representation of Reality in Western Literature* (Princeton: Princeton University Press, 2003), p. 44.

comedy, too contemporary and everyday for tragedy, politically too insignificant for history – and the form which was given it is one of such immediacy that its like does not exist in the literature of antiquity'.[23] In other words, the gospels, whatever else they are, stood for a rhetorical revolution in antiquity that gradually and slowly undermined the stylistic conventions of its age as the Christian movement grew. This difference in style between the classical authors and the gospels was, moreover, no random feature, but firmly established in some of the core features of Christian theology, the incarnation and the passion. With regard to the latter, Auerbach writes:

> That the King of Kings was treated as a low criminal, that he was mocked, spat upon, whipped, and nailed to the cross – that story no sooner comes to dominate the consciousness of the people than it completely destroys the aesthetics of the separation of styles; it engenders a new elevated style, which does not scorn everyday life and which is ready to absorb the sensorily realistic, even the ugly, the undignified, the physically base.[24]

Or one may have it the other way around, namely as a new form of comedy which, despite its everyday form, is able to speak of the highest themes. As Auerbach points out, this rhetorical and poetical revolution did not change everything overnight. Actually it took quite a while until this revolution had settled. Augustine as well as Dante were important landmarks in the working out of this revolution. Nevertheless, as Auerbach puts it, '[t]he age of separate realms of style is over'.[25]

The gospels did not speak in an elevated style, from a position looking down on the events that they were relating. The implicit and explicit dismissal of the antique style convention that separated the low from the high came to confer a new dignity on the everyday matters of life. I would suggest that they gave birth (or at least contributed) to a new form of comedy that could not rest contentedly with the old form, especially when it was understood as a way of establishing one's superiority with regard to one's fellow men and women. There is no need to suggest that Chrysostom was a closet stand-up comedian to say that there is some reason for his suspicion of laughter; laughter could be used as an instrument of power, and as such it deserved to be criticized. However, such a suspicion did not mean the end of humour in the Christian tradition. On the contrary, it was instrumental in giving birth to comedy in another form. As Auerbach suggests, this new form of humour has its theological base in the doctrine of the incarnation. Let me thus, by way of conclusion, say a few words about comedy and the incarnation.

23. Ibid., p. 45.
24. Ibid., p. 72.
25. Ibid.

The Comedy of the Incarnation

A theologically legitimate form of comedy could not be one that advocates superiority over the other; neither could it stand for escapism, since this would challenge both the doctrine of creation and the doctrine of redemption. After all, it is *this* world that is supposedly to be redeemed through the work of Christ. The doctrine of the incarnation, that God is present in the human life of Jesus Christ, is, if I may put it in Auerbach's terms, a way of holding together the everyday and the eternal without confusing the two. The trajectory of God's salvation is not to look down upon the follies of human beings from above, but to identify oneself with the fallen conditions of creation in solidarity. What is referred to in theology as the fall is, then, not a fall 'downwards' but rather the opposite, 'upwards'. The fall is a flight from the embodied, material and finite conditions of human existence, a fall that is comic in the discrepancy between the actual conditions of our existence and what we wish these conditions to be.

One kind of comedy can be found in the over-spiritualized person that refuses to see how he or she is dependent upon other human beings for his or her sustenance, as in Kierkegaard's example of the professor who is so absent-minded that he must ask his wife if it is he who is talking now or someone else. But another kind of comedy could be found in the person who so identifies with her or his material conditions that he or she refuses to see how his or her life is lived in relation to a divine Other (whatever form the transcendent might take for the person) that questions what is taken for granted. This theory of humour has a lot in common with what is usually referred to as the 'incongruity theory', except that it might not be a theory at all, at least if Kierkegaard is right in assuming that humour is a movement that is impossible to conceptualize due to its dynamic as opposed to static character.[26] As the proverbial slip on the banana peel illustrates, comedy is about movement, about a movement that ultimately takes place in relation to an o/Other that never could be reduced to something too well known. As in all good humour, there is an element of surprise in our relation to the other without which the other would not be other and humour would not be hilarious. If humour is something more than laughing at the jokes one already knows, then comedy is the realization that the other may surprise us. This is, ultimately, why incarnation calls for comedy and *vice versa*.

---

26. On the incongruity theory, see Morreall, *Laughter*, pp. 15–19; on Søren Kierkegaard's view on humour, see his *Concluding Unscientific Postscript to Philosophical Fragments*, trans. H. V. Hong and E. H. Hong (Princeton: Princeton University Press, 1992).

16

FOREIGNNESS AS FOCAL POINT OF OTHERNESS

Pierre Bühler

'J'arrive où je suis étranger'.[1] The French poet Louis Aragon evokes the precarious character of human life, experienced as the reality of getting older, losing one's strengths, and realizing the approach of death. It is expressed as the growing of a dissimilarity with oneself that culminates in the feeling of foreignness: 'I arrive where I am foreigner'.

In what follows, I would like to take a close look at a special form of alterity: the alterity of the foreigner. Foreignness can be considered as focal point of otherness. If meeting the other can be a quite normal experience in human life, meeting the foreigner has its own hurdles. In foreignness there seems to be a sharper and stronger form of otherness. Foreigners come from another culture, they speak another language, they have different rules of living, different ethical values, and perhaps a different religion. Therefore, they often undergo measures of exclusion, generated by feelings of fear, insecurity and danger. More than the other who, even in her or his otherness, may be close to us, belonging to the same community of life, the foreigner is experienced as a threat, and that makes the meeting with her or him much harder. Using Greek roots, we speak of 'xenophobia', and that means precisely the 'fear of the foreigner', and this fear can easily be radicalized into hostility against foreigners. In the extreme case, it can become hatred of foreigners. In this sense, there is a special challenge for Christianity in this topic, and many ethical and political implications are connected to it in today's world. Facing foreigners, today's world is a world of exclusion rather than a world of inclusion. Implicitly, our topic might evoke crucial geopolitical areas such as the Island of Lampedusa where foreigners drown, the frontier between the United States of America and Mexico where foreigners are killed, and the absurd wall which tears apart Palestine.

---

1. Louis Aragon, *Le voyage de Hollande et autres poèmes* (Paris: Seghers, 2005), p. 93.

A Short Etymological Note

Let us begin with etymological observations. In American English, it is quite common to use the word 'alien' in order to designate a foreigner. It comes from the Latin *alienus* which refers to the 'other'. If we would focus our attention exclusively on the concept of alien, our topic could be easily drawn back to the main topic of this *Festschrift*. Foreignness would be reduced to one form of alterity.

However, with regard to their etymology, the words 'foreigner' and 'stranger' insist on a more specific accent: they have their roots in the late Latin adjectives *foranus* and *extraneus*, both of which mean 'coming from outside'. They refer to the Latin prepositions *foras* and *foris* as well as *extra*, which signify the outside or what is outside. Hence, the crucial and central association for our reflection on foreignness is not otherness (as in 'alien'), but *exteriority*. The concept of exteriority implies a vital radicalization of the topic: meeting the one who comes from outside.

Understanding the Foreigner: A Hermeneutical Task

Theo Sundermeier, a German theologian born in 1935, who specialized in inter-cultural and interreligious understanding, has written a small study which is interesting for our reflection: *Den Fremden verstehen*.[2] The study on how to understand the foreigner is construed not as a theoretical, but as a practical hermeneutics, which is to be applied in conflict situations. One precisely qualified question runs throughout the study: how shall I meet the foreign lady who lives in the apartment upstairs? Sundermeier's challenge is to reach 'a successful coexistence in which everyone stays who they are, nobody is assimilated, and nevertheless an exchange happens in which the dignity of the other is respected and reinforced'.[3]

Sundermeier's study in the practical hermeneutics of the foreigner is inspired by many experiences he gained during a longer stay in Brazil. Consequently, we can detect the influence of the Latin American theology of liberation. Sundermeier chooses an interdisciplinary approach: contributions from anthropology, philosophy, communication theory, the history of arts and the history of religion help him to conceive of a dynamic perspective on foreignness. These different disciplines propose various tools for coping with the task of understanding the foreigner. However, this task is not easy, because by understanding the foreigner I could rob her of her foreignness. Here, Sundermeier would refer to a 'hermeneutics of assimilation' (*Vereinnahmungshermeneutik*). He sees such

---

2. Cf. Theo Sundermeier, *Den Fremden verstehen: Eine praktische Hermeneutik* (Göttingen: Vandenhoeck and Ruprecht, 1996). For a more precise presentation of Sundermeier's study, cf. Pierre Bühler, 'L'étranger et ses enjeux d'herméneutique théologique', *Variations herméneutiques* 12 (2000), pp. 11–31.

3. Theo Sundermeier, *Den Fremden verstehen*, p. 183 (my translation).

a hermeneutics in Hans-Georg Gadamer, where distance is considered to be problematic. If distance is surmounted, the foreigner ceases to be foreign: she or he has been assimilated. However, is it possible to conceive of a concept of understanding which lets the foreigner keep her foreignness? To designate such a concept, Sundermeier refers to a 'xenological hermeneutics' (*xenologische Hermeneutik*).[4]

In order to clarify what he means by xenological hermeneutics, he elaborates on different models of encounter. The first is the model of equality: it negates foreignness, because it presupposes that all are similar and equal which is why difference is impossible. The second model – the model of radical alterity – has the opposite problem: the foreigner is so different that there is no possibility of recognition. This radical other can provoke fear or fascination, but she or he cannot prompt mutual respect. In the third model, which is referred to as the model of complementarity, the foreigner is understood as *alter ego*: she or he is recognized and respected as a complement to the self, in so far as she or he is giving to the self what it lacks. Finally, Sundermeier turns to a fourth model which is inspired by systems theory. He calls it the model of homeostasis. Here, what makes the difference between two beings is understood as what is connecting them to each other. Hence, everyone can keep her or his identity while a bond between the different identities is created – a bond which establishes mutual recognition.

Building on the fourth model, Sundermeier develops and defines a method of understanding the foreign as a *Gegenüber*, a term which could be rendered as a *vis-à-vis*. The model progresses by describing and deepening the encounter on four successive levels. There is no direct access to the *vis-à-vis*. On a first level, I can only perceive her or him through manifestations that allow me to realize her or his presence. Such a distant descriptive analysis is placed under the phenomenological *epoché*, the suspension of judgement. On a second level, the foreigner shows some significant signs, specific markers of her or his identity (such as her or his rules of life, clothes or cuisine). I am getting more involved: my observation becomes participative; I begin to contextualize what I perceive in participation, so that sympathy is generated. On a third level, my *vis-à-vis* may communicate symbols, which is to say: she or he shows me symbolized expressions of her or his deep convictions about life, about her or his ultimate values, about her or his sense of existence or about her or his religion. Through partial identification with her or him, I can begin to feel empathy, developing an interpretation of her or his deep beliefs by comparison with my deep beliefs. However, the deepest understanding is reached only on the fourth level, the level of relevance: it happens as conviviality, in which a real and relevant coexistence can be learned. Recognition

---

4. In a certain way, we could say that Paul Ricœur's conception of distanciation comes close to Sundermeier's xenological hermeneutics, because it attributes a positive meaning to distance within the process of understanding; cf. Pierre Bühler, 'Ricœur's Concept of Distanciation as a Challenge for Theological Hermeneutics', in Joseph Verheyden, Theo L. Hettema, and Peter Vandecasteele, eds, *Paul Ricœur: Poetics and Religion* (Leuven: Peeters, 2011), pp. 151–65.

and respect can take place, expressed in a mutual translation or transfer from the one to the other. It is a living community, established in three main forms: helping each other in solving problems, learning with each other by sharing abilities, and celebrating with each other.

The Levels of Encounter

The Foreign vis-à-vis	Subjective Attitude	Objective Recording	Level of Action
Level of Phenomena	Epoché	Description	Distant Perception
Level of Signs	Sympathy	Contextualization	Participative Observation
Level of Symbols	Empathy	Interpretation by Comparison	(Partial) Identification
Level of Relevance	Respect	Translation and Transfer	Conviviality

Theo Sundermeier, *Den Fremden verstehen*, p. 155 (my translation)

The xenological hermeneutics which Sundermeier developed has one crucial and central presupposition – distance. Distance is a moment in the process of understanding the foreigner; therefore, it is vital for both my relation to the foreigner and my relation to myself – the subject of my understanding of the foreigner. I have to cope with the fact that I also am a *vis-à-vis*, I am my own foreigner. Hence, if I am ready to deal adequately with the foreignness in myself, I am ready to deal adequately with the foreignness of the foreigner.[5]

Here, the challenge of foreignness becomes a theological challenge. It is interesting to note that Sundermeier considers theology as a vital resource for his reflection – together with the disciplines mentioned above. His conviction is that the confrontation with one's own foreignness has to be inspired and instigated by a foreignness which is not one's own – the foreignness of God. To explore the foreignness of God – beyond Sundermeier – is our next step.

Biblical Perspectives on Foreignness

If the concepts of 'foreigner' and 'stranger' evoke the exteriority of 'the one who comes from outside', we could say that Christianity stresses the exteriority of God: God is *extraneus* and *foranus*. We cannot curtail him through our categories, we cannot confine him in our caprices, we cannot possess him for our purposes. He comes from outside, challenging us, calling us and calling us in question, taking us along in stories, he wants to live with us. In Exodus and Leviticus, the exteriority of God is marked by a variety of occurrences of the expression 'outside the camp'. The

---

5. Paul Ricoeur thematized the otherness of oneself in *Oneself as Another*, trans. K. Blamey (Chicago: University of Chicago Press, 1992), pp. 297–356.

outside is the privileged place for the encounter with God, as the topic of the 'tent of meeting' demonstrates: 'Now Moses used to take a tent and pitch it outside the camp some distance away, and calling it the "tent of meeting". Anyone enquiring of the Lord would go to the tent of meeting outside the camp' (Exod. 33.7).

Playing with these associations, the Epistle to the Hebrews expresses God's exteriority in its theology of the cross: Christ died not inside, but 'outside the city gate'. 'And so Jesus also suffered outside the city gate to make the people holy through his own blood' (Heb. 13.12). In the following verse, the christological statement is immediately followed by the imperative to leave the camp, to go outside the city gate together with the crucified: 'Let us, then, go to him outside the camp, bearing the disgrace he bore' (Heb. 13.13). Thus, the exteriority of the cross becomes the exteriority of the lives of the believers. The believers are always already on the way; their 'being on the way' is eschatological. 'For here we do not have an enduring city, but we are looking for the city that is to come' (Heb. 13.14). Speaking of Abraham's descendants, the Epistle also points out: 'And they admitted that they were aliens and strangers on earth' (Heb. 11.13). Obviously, being aliens and strangers should motivate us to welcome aliens and strangers. Therefore, the Epistle exhorts believers to practice hospitality, evoking implicitly how Abraham welcomed the three strangers who eventually appear to be God's messengers: 'Do not forget to entertain strangers, for by so doing some people have entertained angels without knowing it' (Heb. 13.2; cf. Gen. 18.1-15).

It is interesting to note that the welcoming of foreigners and strangers can be described as conviviality in love. The command to 'Love your neighbour as yourself' can be turned into the command to 'Love the alien as yourself', as Lev. 19.33-34 argues: 'When an alien lives with you in your land, do not ill-treat him. The alien living with you must be treated as one of your native-born. Love him as yourself, for you were aliens in Egypt. I am the Lord your God'. In the same way as the Epistle to the Hebrews, Leviticus appeals to the foreignness of his addressees to justify the divine command to love the foreigner – 'for you were aliens in Egypt'.

A Literary Parable: Babette's Feast

Karen Blixen, a Danish author (1885–1962), published her works, partly in Danish and partly in English, under different pseudonymous identities. The short story *Babette's Feast* was first published in 1950 in an American magazine, and then reedited in the collection *Anecdotes of Destiny*, published in 1958 under the pseudonym of Isak Dinesen.[6]

---

6. Isak Dinesen (Karen Blixen), *Babette's Feast and Other Stories* (London: Penguin Books, 2013), pp. 21–68. Gabriel Axel (1918-2014) made a very beautiful movie out of Blixen's story: *Babette's Feast*, Denmark, 1987. For a more complete analysis of the story, cf. Pierre Bühler, 'Le repas, parabole du Royaume? Lecture théologique du *Festin de Babette* de Karen BLIXEN', in G. Bertrand, ed., *Le goût : Actes du Troisième Colloque Transfrontalier de Dijon, 12-13 septembre 1996* (Dijon: Dicolor, 1998), pp. 231-7.

The short story takes place in Berlevåg, a town in Norway, at the end of the nineteenth century. Two old sisters, Martine and Philippa, are leading a small Lutheran congregation which was founded by their dead father, called 'the Dean'. Living a very ascetic life, they are devoted to the members of the community, caring for the needy people in the city. The Dean's disciples have grown older, they not only get 'whiter or balder and harder of hearing', but also 'somewhat querulous and quarrelsome'[7] so that conflicts arise within the congregation.

In the two sisters' household lives a French woman called Babette. She once arrived as a refugee, 'haggard and wild-eyed like a hunted animal',[8] with a recommendation letter by an old friend of the family. She had to flee the civil war in Paris. The two sisters adopted her, even if they were trembling at the idea 'of receiving a Papist under their roof'.[9] 'Babette can cook',[10] said the recommendation letter and it quickly appeared to be true: she became a trusted and devoted servant, preparing meals for the poor and helping the two sisters in all their social work. 'Her quiet countenance and her steady, deep glance had magnetic qualities; under her eyes things moved, noiselessly, into their proper places'.[11] Thus, even if the old brothers and sisters of the congregation 'had first looked askance at the foreign woman in their midst',[12] she was progressively accepted into the community.

Before leaving Paris, Babette had bought a lottery ticket. One day, a letter arrives at Berlevåg, announcing that she had won a huge amount of money. As the congregation is planning the celebration of the Dean's hundredth birthday, Babette asks a great favour: the permission to prepare for the congregation a French celebratory dinner for which she would pay with the money she gained. After much hesitation, the two sisters accept, even if they are afraid of French luxury.

Babette orders the required ingredients from Paris, and they arrive, sent by boat to Norway. The more stuff arrives, the more the anxiety grows. For the two sisters, it looks more and more like 'a witches' sabbath',[13] and during the night, they dream nightmares of poisoning. The congregation's members gather to discuss the problem. They promise one another that they would just accept the trial of this meal in silence, that 'they would, on the great day, be silent upon all matters of food and drink. Nothing that might be set before them, be it even frogs or snails, should wring a word from their lips'.[14]

The great day arrives. The congregation gathers. They begin to eat in silence and submission. Yet, while they are eating, a miracle happens. The excellent plates and the best wines follow each other through the evening; more and more, the old

---

7. Isak Dinesen (Karen Blixen), *Babette's Feast*, p. 23.
8. Ibid., p. 35
9. Ibid.
10. Ibid., p. 34.
11. Ibid.
12. Ibid., p. 37.
13. Ibid, p. 46.
14. Ibid., pp. 46-7.

brothers and sisters begin to speak, to tell stories, to joke. They enjoy the evening. Suddenly, there are no more conflicts. The meal creates a spirit of reconciliation, making things light. 'The convives grew lighter in weight and lighter of heart the more they ate and drank. They no longer needed to remind themselves of their vow'.[15] A special guest of the evening, General Loewenhielm, a man of the world, being able to recognize the high gastronomical quality of this meal, speaks about the infinity of grace which takes everybody and everything to its bosom. As if this grace would become reality around the table, peace and mercy take place in the happy conviviality of the old people: 'Taciturn old people received the gift of tongues; ears that for years had been almost deaf were opened to it. Time itself had merged into eternity'.[16] During the meal, snow has fallen over the city. So when the company breaks up, it has become difficult to walk. The guests waver on their feet, stagger, fall in the snow, and so the author comments: 'as if they had indeed had their sins washed white as wool, and in this regained innocent attire were gamboling like little lambs'.[17] She adds: '"Bless you, bless you, bless you", like an echo of the harmony of the spheres rang on all sides'.[18]

'I was once cook at the Café Anglais', reveals Babette, telling the two sisters that she had used the whole money for their dinner. After their astonishment passed, one of the sisters says to Babette: 'In Paradise you will be the great artist that God meant you to be ... Ah, how you will enchant the angels!'[19]

Conclusion

Karen Blixen's short story is a profound illustration for the exhortation in Heb. 13.2 not to forget to entertain strangers 'for by so doing some people have entertained angels without knowing it'. Karen Blixen goes even further, by giving Babette the dimension of a christological character. Playing implicitly with biblical references, she writes: 'The stone which the builders had almost refused had become the headstone of the corner'.[20] However, at the same time, for the two old sisters, this cornerstone keeps its 'mysterious and alarmed feature', 'as if it was somehow related to the Black Stone of Mecca, the Kaaba itself'.[21] The foreignness has not disappeared. Here, it is underlined through an Islamic contextualization of the headstone. It has still to be accepted as foreignness, and not to be domesticated: only then the cornerstone can be a real cornerstone. Hence, we may say that Blixen's short story is an adequate expression of Sundermeier's xenological hermeneutics – or, as Louis Aragon put it: 'J'arrive où je suis étranger'.

15. Ibid., pp. 57–8.
16. Ibid., p. 61.
17. Ibid., p. 63.
18. Ibid.
19. Ibid., p. 68.
20. Ibid., p. 37; cf. Ps. 118.22; Mt. 21.42; Mk 12.10; Lk. 20.17; Acts 4.11; 1 Pet. 2.7.
21. Isak Dinesen (Karen Blixen), *Babette's Feast*, p. 37.

17

SEXUAL DIFFERENCE IN CHRISTIAN DOCTRINE AND SYMBOLISM: HISTORICAL IMPACT AND FEMINIST CRITIQUE

Kari Elisabeth Børresen

The Epistemological Revolution of Feminism

It is essential to observe that modern feminism, which claims the bio-sociocultural equivalence of women and men, results from the greatest epistemological revolution in human history. This recent collapse of global androcentrism represents a more fundamental challenge to all age-old world religions than the previous upheavals of geocentrism and anthropocentrism. No actualization of gender equivalence is documented in any civilization before the twentieth-century European welfare states. Because religion is a fundamental factor in all societies, it is essential to clarify how religious gender models shape sociological gender roles.[1] This interaction is a global phenomenon, but my brief outline is focused on the influence of Christianity in European culture. Modern religious accommodation to women's socio-political equality with men started in the so-called Protestant countries of Northern Europe, whereas asymmetrical gender disparity remains important in the so-called Catholic and Orthodox countries of Mediterranean, Central and Eastern Europe.[2]

Therefore, women have obtained cultic capability in Protestant denominations, where they can receive priestly and episcopal ordination. Women's cultic incapability is still imposed in the Catholic and Orthodox Churches, where only men can be ordained.

---

1. The term sex refers to biologically programmed male or female sex, the term gender refers to culturally shaped functions and roles of women or men.
2. Cf. Kari E. Børresen and Sara Cabibbo, eds, *Religion, Gender, Human Rights in Europe* (Rome: Herder Editrice, 2006).

Global Androcentrism

In order to understand the revolutionary impact of modern feminism, it is necessary to emphasize that all global religions are fundamentally androcentric. According to Asian Hinduism and Buddhism, women are not defined as proper human beings, but placed between men and animals by the universal wheel of reincarnation and rebirth, which is determined by the ethical performance in previous lives. This ontological gender hierarchy reappears in the creation myth of Plato's *Timaeus*, a central text in the European history of ideas.[3] According to the variants of Near Eastern monotheism, namely Judaism, Christianity and Islam, each human being has only one terrestrial existence. Given the fundamental paradigm of *one* God who creates *two* different sexes, with non-interchangeable roles, women are included as subordinate members of humankind. Consequently, the axiomatic precedence of male humanity is not defined in ontological, but in functional terms. This means that female humanity is created to serve men's procreation of offspring.[4]

The Reason for Women's Existence

A basic question in all global religions is to explain the reason for women's existence. According to both ontological and functional gender hierarchy, the universal answer is that women are indispensable instruments to counteract death by giving birth. In pre-modern societies, this female sex role is perceived as receptive *vis-à-vis* the active male seed. Although necessary for human survival, female corporeality is despised in all world religions, precisely because of this link between death and fertility. In consequence, we find a pervading dualism between soul and body and a conflict between God-love and sexual love. Such antagonisms are often based on a cosmic strife between good and evil powers, for example in the so-called Gnostic variants, which competed with mainstream doctrine in ancient Christianity. The rise of Christian monasticism results from moderate *enkrateia*, where sexual asceticism is practised to achieve spiritual union with God. In opposition to Gnostic variants of radical *enkrateia*, Patristic writers allow sexual activity for ordinary believers, when limited to procreation in marriage.[5]

---

3. Plato, *Timaeus*, 41d–42d, 90e–91.

4. Cf. Kari E. Børresen, ed., *Christian and Islamic Gender Models in Formative Traditions* (Rome: Herder Editrice, 2004).

5. Cf. Giulia Sfameni Gasparro, *Enkrateia e Antropologia* (Roma: Instititum Patristicum 'Augustinianum', 1984); Aline Rousselle, *Porneia: On Desire and the Body in Antiquity* (New York: Basil Blackwell, 1988); Giulia Sfameni Gasparro, *Agostino: Tra Etica e Religione* (Brescia: Morcelliana, 1999); Emanuela Prinzivalli, 'Early Christian Anthropology: Gender Models in Creation and Resurrection', in Kari E. Børresen, ed., *Christian and Islamic Gender Models*, pp. 43–65.

Double Creation

Since ancient Christianity was inculturated in a Greco-Roman context of Platonic dualism, traditional Christian anthropology defines the human being as a mixture of a sexed, mortal body and an incorporeal, immortal soul.[6] The Latin Church Father Ambrose stated that the rational soul has no sex. The leading Greek Church Father Gregory of Nyssa defined the human being as a hybrid with an immortal, angelic mind and an animal, mortal body. This Patristic anthropology relates to an idea of God's so-called double creation, introduced by the Jewish exegete Philo of Alexandria. In order to combine the two different stories in Gen. 1 and 2, Philo interprets Gen. 1.26-7a as the first creation in God's image of a purely spiritual human prototype, whereas the sexual differentiation described in Gen. 1.27b-28 and in Gen. 2.7, 18, 22-3 refers to God's second creation of human corporeality.[7] Accordingly, the sexual difference of male and female bodies is often explained as a cause of or a consequence of the initial sin in paradise. Hence, the perfect human prototype is either pre-sexual or male, whereas Eve is instrumental for Adam's fall.

Unique Creation

The Patristic paradigm of double creation was gradually overcome by the leading Latin Church Father Augustine. In his work *De Genesi ad litteram*, he managed to affirm the unicity of God's creation, by combining the instantaneous *informatio* described in Gen. 1 and the subsequent *conformatio* described in Gen. 2. The first creation story shows that the souls of Adam and Eve are made in definitive form, whereas all other human beings are created in germ form, as *rationes seminales*. The second creation story concerns God's formation of the first couple's bodies and the continuous deployment of all living creatures throughout the ages. This exegetical device permits Augustine to connect the sexual difference with the preceding image-text, so that the corporeal formation of Adam and his female helpmate is linked to the creation of Godlike humanity. Nevertheless, this inclusive exegesis does not affect the gender hierarchy established by God in creation. On the contrary, Augustine underlines that the purpose for creating Adam's woman is strictly physiological: 'I do not see in what sense woman was made a helper for man, if not for the sake of bearing children'.[8] Hence, the God-willed subordination of female humanity remains

---

6. Cf. Kari. E. Børresen and Emanuela Prinzivalli, eds, *Le Donne nello Sguardo degli Antichi Autori Cristiani* (Trapani: Il pozzo di Giacobbe, 2013), *Las Mujeres en la Mirada de los Antiguos Escritos Cristianos, Siglos I–VIII* (Estella: Verbo Divino, 2014).

7. Cf. Richard A. Baer, Jr., *Philo's Use of the Categories Male and Female* (Leiden: Brill, 1970); Dorothy Sly, *Philo's Perception of Women* (Atlanta, GA: Scholars Press, 1990).

8. Augustine, *De Genesi ad litteram*, 9.5.

normative in this world, only to be overcome by eschatological equivalence in heaven.⁹

Human Godlikeness

Christian gender models are structured by axiomatic interaction between theocentrism and androcentrism, with a correlated exclusion of femaleness from the Godhead. In Christian anthropology, fully human status is defined as being created in God's image. Based on interacting concepts of God and Godlike humanity, this privilege is explicitly attributed even to subordinate women through historically shifting, inculturated exegesis of core biblical texts (Gen. 1.26-27; 2.7; 1 Cor. 11.7; Gal. 3.28). In feminist perspective, it is essential to recognize how the doctrinal process of including female humanity in creational Godlikeness is realized from Late Antiquity to the twentieth century. This achievement is summarily outlined in three stages, from manlike Godhead and Godlike maleness, via metasexual Godhead and asexual *imago Dei*, to holistic, male or female Godlikeness, correlated to an inclusive description of God with both female and male metaphors.[10]

Godlike Maleness

The stage of Godlike maleness corresponds to an andromorphic concept of God, where the human prototype is male, so that Adam is created in God's image. Nevertheless, women can achieve this prerogative by 'becoming male' through redemptive incorporation into Christ (Rom. 8.29; Col. 3.10-11; Eph. 4.13; Ev. Thom. 114). This first doctrinal stage was valid into the fifth century and persisted in medieval Canon Law. Here, women's lack of creational *imago Dei* was invoked in order to justify the bio-social inferiority and the cultic incapability of human femaleness, precisely termed *impedimentum sexus*.[11]

---

9. Cf. Kari E. Børresen, *Subordination and Equivalence: A Reprint of a Pioneering Classic* (Kampen: Kok Pharos Press, 1995). Eadem, 'Patristics', in Øyvind Norderval and Katrine Lund Ore, eds, *From Patristics to Matristics: Selected Articles on Christian Gender Models by Kari Elisabeth Børresen* (Rome: Herder Editrice, 2002), pp. 15–89. Eadem, 'Gender Models in the Christian Tradition', in Irmtraud Fischer and Christoph Heil, eds, *Geschlechterverhältnisse und Macht: Lebensformen in der Zeit des frühen Christentums* (Münster: LIT, 2010), pp. 13–32. Eadem, 'Challenging Augustine in Feminist Theology and Gender Studies', in Karla Pollmann and Willemien Otten, eds, *The Oxford Guide to the Historical Reception of Augustine* (Oxford: Oxford University Press, 2013), pp. 135–41.

10. This doctrinal process, from Genesis to the twentieth century, is analysed in Kari E. Børresen, ed., *The Image of God: Gender Models in Judaeo-Christian Tradition* (Minneapolis, MN: Fortress Press, 1995).

11. Cf. Alastair J. Minnis, 'De impedimento sexus: Women's Bodies and Medieval Impediments to Female Ordination', in Peter Biller and Alastair J. Minnis, eds, *Medieval Theology and the Natural Body* (York: Medieval Press, 1997), pp. 109–39. John Hilary

Asexual Godlikeness

The stage of asexual Godlikeness corresponds to a metasexual concept of God, structured from the third to the fifth century by Greek and Latin Church Fathers. Based on Platonic anthropology, they redefined human *imago Dei* in terms of sexless privilege, linked to the incorporeal and immortal soul. Referring to Stoic ethics, where even females (and slaves) have reason and virtue, these 'feminist' Church Fathers could *backdate* women's spiritual Godlikeness to creation, despite the axiom of non-Godlike femaleness. In consequence, the monotheistic paradigm of one God, creating two different sexes with asymmetrical, gender-specific functions and roles, remained normative. Women could only actualize their sexless equivalence in this world by escaping their bio-social subordination through ascetic *defeminization*.[12] This strategy led to female monasticism, which expanded in the Middle Ages, mainly recruiting daughters of the nobility. It is essential to observe that the Patristic concept of sexless *imago Dei* became dominant in medieval theology and remained standard in Catholic doctrine until the early twentieth century, whereas asexual Godlikeness is still preserved in Orthodox doctrine.

Holistic Godlikeness

The stage of inclusive Godlikeness is initiated by Northern-European Church Mothers, from the twelfth to the fifteenth century.[13] These Matristic writers had

---

Martin, 'The Ordination of Women and the Theologians in the Middle Ages', in Bernard Cooke and Gary Macy, eds, *A History of Women and Ordination*, vol. 1 (Lanham, MD: Scarecrow Press, 2002), pp. 31–175; Ida Raming, 'The Priestly Office of Women: God's Gift to a Renewed Church', in Bernard Cooke and Gary Macy, eds, *A History of Women and Ordination*, vol. 2, (Lanham, MD: Scarecrow Press, 2004), pp. 3–305; Kari E. Børresen, 'The Ordination of Women: To Nurture Tradition by Continuing Inculturation', in Øyvind Norderval and Katrine Lund Ore, eds, *From Patristics to Matristics*, pp. 275–87.

12. This 'ascetic feminism' is well researched, see for example Elizabeth A. Clark, *Ascetic Piety and Women's Faith: Essays on Late Ancient Christianity* (Lewiston, NY: Edwin Mellen Press, 1986); Kari Vogt, 'Section II, Matristics: Late Antique, Early Christian and Islamic Foremothers', in Kari E. Børresen and Kari Vogt, *Women's Studies of the Christian and Islamic Traditions, Ancient, Medieval and Renaissance Foremothers* (Dordrecht: Kluwer Academic Publishers, 1993), pp. 153–242.

13. Cf. Kari Elisabeth Børresen, 'Section III, Matristics: Mothers of the Church', in Kari E. Børresen and Kari Vogt, *Women's Studies of the Christian and Islamic Traditions*, pp. 243–314; Kari E. Børresen and Adriana Valerio, eds, *Donne e Bibbia nel Medioevo (secoli XII-XV). Tra Ricezione e Interpretazione* (Trapani: Il Pozzo di Giacobbe, 2011); *La Biblia y las Mujeres: Medioevo II (siglos XII–XV). Entre recepción e interpretación* (Estella: Verbo Divino, 2012); *Frauen und Bibel im Mittelalter: Rezeption und Interpretation* (Stuttgart: Kohlhammer, 2013). Also cf. Kari E. Børresen, 'Matristics', in Angelo Di Bernardino, ed., *Encyclopedia of Ancient Christianity*, vol. 2 (Downers Grove, IL: InterVarsity Press, 2014), pp. 730–5.

internalized that all human beings are created in God's image, but they did not invoke the correlated ideas of women's 'becoming male' in Christ. Nevertheless, they understood the interaction between concepts of God and human Godlikeness. The German abbess Hildegard von Bingen and the English anchoress Julian of Norwich use female metaphors to describe God's revelatory Wisdom and God's pre-existent, incarnate Son. In Hildegard's *Scivias*, God's *sapientia* appears as a female figure.[14] In Julian's *Showings*, 'Christ our Mother' refers not only to Christ's incarnate human nature, but extends to God's Son as Second Person of the Trinity.[15] With this new God-language, they manage to provide a divine model of female *imago Dei* by describing God as gynaecomorphic.

Feminist Strategies from Renaissance to Enlightenment

When higher learning was moved from medieval monasteries to the new universities, which were reserved for men, women's monastic culture gradually declined.[16] From the sixteenth century onwards, Protestant suppression of Catholic monasteries and the canonical enclosure of nuns decreed by the Council of Trent finally arrested Matristic theology.

Already in the fifteenth century, the secular feminist writer Christine de Pizan opposed clerical misogyny by invoking doctrinal models of women's intellect and virtue. Nevertheless, it is important to observe that seventeenth-century 'femmes savantes', like Marie Le Jars de Gournay and Anna Maria van Schurmann, represent a regression to the Patristic stage, when they invoke women's sexless *imago Dei* in order to claim women's right to education. Likewise, French salon-feminism affirms the Cartesian adage: 'l'esprit n'a point de sexe'. When Mary Wollstonecraft argues against Jean-Jacque Rousseau's gender-specific education of Sophie as Émile's subservient future wife, she also repeats the Patristic attribution of asexual *imago Dei* to human females. Invoking women's Godlike rationality in order to obtain women's right to receive the *same* education as men, Wollstonecraft insists that such equal training is necessary to ensure the socio-political equality of both sexes.[17]

---

14. Cf. Hildegard of Bingen, *Hildegardis Bingensis Scivias, Corpus Christianorum Continuatio Mediaevalis*, vol. 43–43A, ed. Adelgundis Führkötter and Angela Carlevaris (Turnhout: Brepols, 1978).

15. Cf. Julian of Norwich, *A Book of Showings to the Anchoress Julian of Norwich*, 2 vols, ed. Edmund Colledge and James T. Walsh (Toronto: Pontifical Institute of Mediaeval Studies, 1978).

16. The classical study of this decline is Eileen Power, *Medieval English Nunneries: c. 1275 to 1535* (Cambridge: Cambridge University Press, 1922).

17. Cf. Mary Wollstonecraft, *A Vindication of the Rights of Women* (Cambridge: Cambridge University Press, 1995), originally published in 1792.

The Matristic Revival

In order to realize this radically new goal of equal civil rights, nineteenth-century feminists rediscover the Matristic interaction between womanlike Godhead and Godlike women. Pioneers like Aasta Hansteen and Elizabeth Cady Stanton use female metaphors to describe God as a model of women's Godlikeness. Precisely because all Christian institutions invoked God's creational gender hierarchy to oppose women's socio-political rights, these secular activists responded with theological arguments. Nevertheless, the holistic concept of *imago Dei*, where both male and female human beings are created in God's image, was first accepted in early twentieth-century Protestant theology, less from feminist motifs than by Modernist critique of traditional Platonized anthropology. Apparently unaware that this new inculturation is alien to Catholic androcentric typology, inclusive human Godlikeness was endorsed in Catholic theology after the Second Vatican Council.

An Updated Imago Dei *and an Outdated Typology*

It is essential to recall that both Catholic and Orthodox doctrine preserve the typology of Adam-Christ and Eve-Church (Rom. 5.14; Eph. 5.32). The resulting incoherence between an updated holistic *imago Dei* and an outdated androcentric typology is manifest in John Paul II's Apostolic Letter *Mulieris dignitatem* (1988). Referring to women's 'genio femminile' and Mariotypic 'dignity', he upholds the traditional categories of motherhood or virginity as exemplary for female existence.[18] Euphemistically concealed by so-called 'complementarity', this apologetic discourse repeats the eighteenth-century ideal of sexual polarity against feminist claims of women's sexless equality with men. The papal scope is to bolster traditional division of gender roles in church and society, with special focus on women's cultic incapability.

Likewise, Cardinal Joseph Ratzinger's letter to all Catholic bishops on 'The collaboration of men and women in the Church and in society' (2004) seeks to protect the pre-modern paradigm of functional gender division against modern feminism. His apologetic term *collaboratio* is quite misleading, since this document does not describe functional collaboration of the sexes in all fields of human existence. The letter argues against a so-called 'gender ideology', misinterpreted as sexual antagonism, where women fight to obtain traditional male roles. This paternalistic discourse repeats previous exegesis and theological anthropology, with focus on motherhood and so-called family values. Apparently accommodating women's modern activity outside the domestic sphere, the letter allows them to pursue this 'mothering' also in society. In order to favour gender-specific 'complementarity', the Vatican is eager to construct a so-called New Catholic

---

18. Cf. Kari E. Børresen and Kari Voigt, 'Section IV: Feminologie Institutionelle', in Kari E. Børresen and Kari Vogt, *Women's Studies of the Christian and Islamic Traditions*, pp. 341-65.

Feminism, where the pre-modern paradigm of functional gender division is transposed from the order of creation and redefined in terms of ontological sexology, to be anchored in the order of salvation.[19] This inverted version of the Church Fathers' 'feminist' attribution of a sexless *imago Dei* to women already from creation, is recently invoked in terms of ontological typology, to defend male priesthood as a Christlike and gender-specific sex role.

The Cultic Incapability of Female Humanity

In medieval Canon Law the cultic impediment of female corporeality was based on the literal exegesis of 1 Cor. 11.7: 'for man is the image and glory of God, but woman is the glory of man'. Interpreted as women's God-given lack of creational *imago Dei*, this Pauline exegesis of the creation stories was codified in the *Corpus Iuris Canonici* of 1582, which was used until 1917. Abandoning these traditional premises after the Second Vatican Council, the Roman Catholic Church can no longer use logical arguments to ban women's ordination. Nevertheless, exclusively male priesthood is upheld in the *Codex Iuris Canonici* of 1983, canon 1024. This means that Godlike women cannot be ordained to function as Christlike priests, *in persona Christi*. Catholic feminist theologians invoke women's holistic Godlikeness in order to claim women's cultic capability. In the Orthodox Churches, the traditional exclusion of women from priestly ordination is mainly based on Mariocentric interpretations of early Christian typology, so that Orthodox feminist theologians continue to invoke women's sexless equality with men.

The growing Catholic debate on women's ordination started soon after the Second Vatican Council and was tolerated as an open question until John Paul II's firm prohibition in *Ordinatio sacerdotalis* (1994). He proclaimed that the Church is not permitted by Christ to ordain women, because the Lord is against female priests. Therefore, Christ did not ordain his mother, Mary! When this perfectly anachronistic argumentation fell to the ground, Cardinal Joseph Ratzinger found it necessary to certify the pope's magisterial teaching as a part of the Church's binding faith in *Responsio* (1995). The current ban on female priests serves as an indispensable test of doctrinal obedience in Vatican nominations of bishops and approval of professors in theology. Nevertheless, the claims for women priests are steadily increasing in the Roman Catholic Church, although feminist professors employed in institutions controlled by the Vatican have to be 'prudent' in order to keep their *missio canonica*.[20] An especially grave example of canonical discipline is the *Normae de Gravioribus Delictis*, issued by the Congregation for the Doctrine

---

19. Cf. Tina Beattie, *New Catholic Feminism: Theology and Theory* (London: Routledge, 2006).

20. Cf. Walter Gross, ed., *Frauenenordination: Stand der Diskussion in der katholischen Kirche* (München: Wewel Verlag, 1996); Sabine Demel, *Frauen und kirchliches Amt: Vom Ende eines Tabus in der katolischen Kirche* (Freiburg i. Br.: Herder, 2004).

of the Faith (2010). Here, attempted ordination of women is not only condemned together with clerical child abuse, but deemed a more grave offense against the sacrament of Ordination, to be punished by automatic excommunication. This means that human femaleness does not only constitute a cultic impediment, but is rejected as a cultic perversity.

The New Bishop of Rome

Francis I, in his Apostolic Exhortation *Evangelii Gaudium* (2013), repeats John Paul II's discourse on women's maternal genius, but with more focus on their indispensable contribution to society:

> I think, for example, of the special concern which women show to others, which finds a particular, even if not exclusive, expression in motherhood. I readily acknowledge that many women share pastoral responsibilities with priests… But we need to create still broader opportunities for a more incisive female presence in the Church.[21]

Unfortunately, the new bishop of Rome also repeats women's exclusion from sacramental priesthood and accentuates the typological argument of Christ's incarnate maleness: 'The reservation of priesthood to males, as a sign of Christ the Spouse who gives himself in the Eucharist, is not a question open to discussion, but it can prove especially divisive if sacramental power is too closely identified with power in general'.[22] From a feminist perspective, the basic challenge of women's *impedimentum sexus* is aggravated when Christ's perfect maleness is enhanced by typological ontology. This makes the functional power of male priests irrelevant. The core question is the axiomatic androcentrism of traditional christology, which upholds the gender asymmetry of Catholic and Orthodox doctrine and symbolism.

Premodern Sexology and Universal Human Rights

In a global perspective it is necessary to emphasize that the ontological or functional gender hierarchy is incompatible with the modern secular principle of equal human rights for both sexes. In the European context, this conflict is mainly focused on Islam, but it is equally pertinent to traditional Christianity. From a doctrinal point of view, Christian gender models are even more problematic.

It is important to observe that the basic antagonism between the fundamental human drives of religion and sexuality, which structured Christian asceticism and shaped Augustine's fateful original sin, is alien to Islamic anthropology. Here,

---

21. Apostolic Exhortation *Evangelii Gaudium*, Chapter Two, II, n. 103, p. 82.
22. Ibid., n. 104, p. 83.

Adam's fall is not catastrophic, death is a natural phenomenon, and women's axiomatic subordination is not divinely ordained, but defined as a socio-economic fact. The early Christian parallel between monotheism and monogenism is absent, since all living beings are created in pairs, but in both systems female humanity is destined to serve male procreation. Given God's absolute transcendence, the Christian concept of human Godlikeness is alien to Islam.[23]

In traditional Christianity and Islam, God is the supreme Law-Giver. Consequently, Vatican documents from Paul VI, John Paul II and Benedict XVI affirm that the papal *magisterium* can only endorse secular human rights if deemed compatible with God-given natural law. In consequence, the Holy See has not acceded to the *Charter of Fundamental Rights of the European Union* nor to the *European Convention of Human Rights*. Likewise, Islamic accommodation to secular human rights is only possible if deemed compatible with the *Sharia*. This means that secular *Droits de l'homme* can be endorsed in terms of God-given *male* rights, whereas *Universal Human Rights* for both sexes are irreconcilable with God-given *female* rights. This clash of religious and secular norms became manifest by the concordant Vatican and Islamist refusal to accept The United Nations' *Convention on the Elimination of All Forms of Discrimination Against Women* (CEDAW). The reason is that, for the first time in international law, reproductive autonomy is here defined as a human right. In fact, women's access to autonomous fertility control is perfectly alien to the monotheistic *raison d'être* of female humanity. This anti-feminist impact of pre-modern sexology is further demonstrated by the concordant Vatican and Islamist opposition to women's reproductive rights at the United Nations Conferences on Population in 1994 and on Women in 1995 with continued obstruction at subsequent meetings.[24] In the European Union, where all countries have ratified CEDAW, many member states have established national concordats with the Holy See. In consequence, despite the CEDAW's obligation 'to eliminate discrimination against women', several states support traditional gender models by granting the Vatican control of religious teaching in public schools, appointment of theology professors in state universities and influence of Canon Law on civil legislation.[25]

23. Cf. Barbara Freyer Stowasser, *Women in the Qur'an: Traditions and Interpretation* (Oxford: Oxford University Press, 1994); Biancamaria Scarcia Amoretti, 'La création de l'humanité dans le Coran', in Kari E. Børresen, ed., *Christian and Islamic Gender Models*, pp. 85–99; Ziba Mir-Hosseini, 'Justice, Equality and Muslim Family Laws', in Ziba Mir-Hosseini, Kari Vogt, Lena Larsen and Christian Moe, eds, *Gender and Equality in Muslim Family Law* (London: Tauris, 2013), pp. 7–34.

24. Cf. Kari E. Børresen, 'Religion Confronting Women's Human Rights: the Case of Roman Catholicism', in Øyvind Norderval and Katrine Lund Ore, eds, *From Patristics to Matristics*, pp. 289–308. Kari E. Børresen, 'Sexologie religieuse et droit humains des femmes', *Yearbook of the European Society of Women in Theological Research* 14 (2006), pp. 119–31.

25. Cf. Kari E. Børresen, 'Gender, Religion, Human Rights in Europe', in Lene Sjørup and Hilda Rømer Christensen, eds, *Pieties and Gender* (Leiden: Brill, 2009), pp. 55–64.

Religious Freedom and Women's Human Rights

This policy demonstrates the collision between collective freedom for pre-modern religions and individual human rights in modern secular societies. It is essential to observe that when freedom of religion was defined as a human right in the United Nations' *Universal Declaration of Human Rights*, the scope was to protect individual citizens against political coercion from the state, but did not consider the ideological incoherence between pre-modern religious systems and modern democratic societies. This defect resulted from a false understanding of religion as a private matter and not as a collective socio-cultural factor. It is significant that when religious freedom (*for* the Church, but not *in* the Church) was finally accepted by the Second Vatican Council by the Declaration *Dignitatis humanae*, this complete reversal of previous teaching, as expressed in Pius IX's anti-modernist *Syllabus*, was primarily intended to protect the Catholic Church in Communist states.

Conclusion

This brief survey of gender models in Christian doctrine and symbolism demonstrates that the most urgent challenges faced by our *Mater Ecclesia* are linked to human corporeality, especially femaleness. Clerical celibacy, women priests, female reproductive autonomy, marriage and divorce are the burning topics raised by Catholic Reform movements, like the international *Wir sind Kirche*.

The fundamental difficulty is that traditional christology, ecclesiology and mariology are structured in terms of male-centred and dualistic anthropology, which was self-evident in Christian antiquity. After the modern collapse of androcentrism, this synthesis of doctrine and symbolism is no longer applicable, and must be replaced by a renovated God-language. In this grave situation, our *Mater Ecclesia* can imitate the previous main inculturations in Church history, as acted out by Ancient Church Fathers and Medieval Church Mothers. It is essential to understand that God communicates with human beings in incarnate and therefore conjectural ways. Thomas Aquinas expressed this divine pedagogy as God's action *creaturarum respectu*, and Nicolas Cusa used the expression *humano modo*. When the Vatican Magisterium is imposed as immovable guardian of the Church's *depositum fidei*, which is defined to be transcultural and transhistorical, this stratagem is both false and theologically counterproductive. Renovation of Catholic doctrine and symbolism is indispensable in order to obtain the necessary pastoral reforms in the Church.

18

THE OTHER ON THE CROSS

Anne-Louise Eriksson

The notion of 'the cross' as a central concept within Christian theology has long caused major problems, especially within feminist theological discourse. Jesus' suffering on the cross has been theologically misused in ways that have led women to silently take upon themselves the burden of violent and abusive relationships. However, along with others, both men and women, feminist theology today shares a resistance to the seemingly contradictory idea of a loving God who sacrifices his son. If that is what it takes for humanity to be saved, the decent human response – and most in line with a Christian ethos – would perhaps be: thanks, God, but no thanks.

Crux probat omnia

Nonetheless, the central position of the cross is inevitable in all Christian theology. The theology of Martin Luther has – more than any other theology – been referred to, and understood, as *a theology of the cross*. The cross not only reveals what God is doing in order to save humanity – thereby providing an answer to Luther's horror-struck question concerning his salvation – but the cross also reveals who God is. The cross proclaims a God in pain and passion: a suffering God. For Luther, knowledge of God is knowledge of the cross, where God is simultaneously hidden and revealed, and beyond the grasp of human control. The scholastic tradition, within which Luther himself was trained as a theologian, was forcefully repudiated by Luther's theology. Theologians who attempted to systematically control and confine the knowledge of God were accused of working within a framework which Luther called a theology of glory, while authentic knowledge of God could only be gained through a theology of the cross.[1]

One might wonder whether Luther would label the attempts of today's theologians to make sense of God's sacrifice and Jesus' suffering in the same way. He probably would. However, it is a fact that the late twentieth and early twenty-first

---

1. Alister E. McGrath, *Luther's Theology of the Cross* (Oxford: Blackwell, 2004), p. 149.

century have seen many efforts to construe christology, and more particularly atonement theology, less androcentric, bloody and brutal than the atonement theories of medieval times: christologies that do not legitimate male dominance by seeing the maleness of Jesus as an ontological statement about the gender of God specifically, and the greater value of the male gender generally; and atonement theologies that do not glorify suffering, or present a God whose 'love' demands a bloody sacrifice, or turn the question of salvation into an all-male affair.[2]

One early feminist example of christological struggles that deserves to be mentioned is that of Rosemary Radford Ruether, who poses the question as to whether it is possible to liberate christology from patriarchy. In order to do so, women must, according to Radford Reuther, be allowed to represent Christ. Creation is by its nature equal, and denying women christological representation is an abuse. She goes on to claim that the paradigmatic meaning of Jesus has nothing to do with his maleness, but everything to do with his message, and the path that Jesus shows us is not only *his* path but a calling for every Christian. Moreover, Christ is not the only way for God to be present in the world. Accepting the limitations of the Christ symbol enables us to see that it is possible for God to meet us in many different ways.[3]

Another example is Rita Nakashima Brock, who calls the cross event 'cosmic child abuse' and points out how the death of Jesus has been misused by patriarchal theology in ways that legitimize obedient subordination. Nakashima Brock claims that humans from birth are neither good nor evil. If our basic needs for love and care are met, we will be able to give love and care ourselves. However, the justice of love is not possible within an individualist paradigm. Nobody can represent love by her or himself – not even Jesus. Jesus dying alone on a cross is, therefore, not a sign of God's love, but the consequence of the fact that Jesus was prepared to die for what he believed. What saves us is the 'resurrection community', those who refused to give up after Jesus' death, but returned to his grave to take care of the body. Today, *we* are this community. When we refuse to give up we are bringing about divine power that maintains and sustains life, says Nakashima Brock.[4]

Finally, there is Eleanor McLaughlin, who sees the christological challenge as a problem of identification. What is needed is an image of God incarnate that can be experienced both as female and as male. In the same way as the Chalcedonian theologians struggled with how to express the two natures of Christ, we must

---

2. Sofia Camnerin, 'Försoningens mellanrum: en analys av Daphne Hampsons och Rita Nakashima Brocks teologiska tolkningar' (Unpublished Diss. Uppsala: Uppsala universitet, 2008); Anne-Louise Eriksson, *Kvinnor talar om Jesus: en bok om feministisk kristologisk praxis* (Nora: Nya Doxa, 1999).

3. Rosemary Radford Ruether, *Sexism and God-talk: Toward a Feminist Theology* (Boston, MA: Beacon Press, 1993).

4. Rita Nakashima Brock, *Journeys by Heart: a Christology of Erotic Power* (New York: Crossroad Press, 1988).

struggle today to find images that express two genders in Christ. The transvestite – *the cross-dresser* – offers such an image.[5]

Challenging and inspiring as these models once were, they seem nevertheless to evade the *scandalon* of the cross: God, hidden and revealed in a unique way in the pain, the abandonment and the dying and death of the man Jesus. No wonder, then, that many Lutheran feminist theologians – trained, like me, in the shadow of a 'theology of the cross' – have felt the need to further explore the cross from a feminist perspective. Examples of more specific Lutheran feminist elaborations of 'cross theology' are Mary M. Solberg, who proposes the cross as an epistemological point of departure for compelling knowledge about ethical accountability;[6] Deanna A. Thompson, who accentuates the need to call victims and oppressors what they are. Yet at the same time she claims that Luther's theology of the cross offers useful perspectives for feminist theology. According to Thompson, Christ is 'the only victim who never also occupied the status of oppressor. … Christ becomes *our* victim whenever we don the role of oppressor'. We are therefore judged by the cross as much as we are reached by the gospel, in that 'our participation in sin and suffering does not have to define us'.[7] A third Lutheran feminist example is the Icelandic theologian Arnfríður Guðmundsdóttir. Like Thompson and Solberg, she stresses that (women's) suffering must be taken seriously. In *Meeting God on the Cross* she emphasizes both the need to remember that it is God who is hanging on the cross and the resurrection of the one who is hanging on the cross. She writes that 'the cross becomes a testimony to God's true identification with the human condition … while the resurrection shows us that there is more to the cross than God's solidarity with the suffering and the oppressed'.[8]

These brief presentations do not do justice to the theological struggle with the cross that has been going on from the perspective of women and other oppressed groups.[9] It nevertheless forms a background for my exploration. Although not a Lutheran scholar in the sense that I have been researching Luther or Lutheran theology specifically, I was raised, and later trained as a theologian, within a Lutheran framework. Luther's elaboration of the cross and his emphasis on justification by grace alone has been fundamental for my perception of myself before God. It has, however, not always been a theology that I have found healthy for me as a person. I have not been able to make sense of a God demanding sacrifices

---

5. Eleanor McLaughlin, 'Feminist Christologies: Re-Dressing the Tradition', in Maryanne Stevens, ed., *Reconstructing the Christ Symbol: Essays in Feminist Christology* (New York: Paulist Press, 1993), pp. 118-49.

6. Mary M. Solberg, *Compelling Knowledge: A Feminist Proposal for an Epistemology of the Cross* (Albany, NY: State University of New York Press, 1997).

7. Deanna A. Thompson, *Crossing the Divide: Luther, Feminism, and the Cross* (Minneapolis: Fortress Press, 2004), p. 149.

8. Arnfríður Guðmundsdóttir, *Meeting God on the Cross: Christ, the Cross, and the Feminist Critique* (Oxford: Oxford University Press, 2010), p. 142.

9. Another important work deserving mention is Marit Trelstad, ed., *Cross Examinations: Reading the Meaning of the Cross Today* (Minneapolis: Fortress Press, 2006).

in order to save me, and although I have shared the feminist theological critique of traditional christologies, I have not been comforted by the constructive work done thus far. The solutions presented seem to me either to evade the claim of the Christian tradition that Jesus in a unique way is God incarnate and that his death on the cross is essential to human salvation, or they stay captured within a theological framework that promotes suffering and sacrifices, grounded in male activity.

What follows is a personal attempt to escape the problems of 'the Father who sacrifices his Son' including the legitimization of male supremacy. Simultaneously, I attempt to remain rooted in a Lutheran understanding of justification by grace, and of the cross as the only way to authentic knowledge of God. Without the explicit use of such 'Lutheran language', it is nevertheless my hope that the Lutheran theological tradition within which I was raised will resonate throughout my contribution.

Submission or Dependence

A few years ago, responding to Sarah Coakley's *Powers and Submissions*[10] at a theological symposium in Lund, I asked, when discussing Coakley's take on *kenōsis*, how the term 'dependence' would work instead of 'submission' for the development of a *kenōtic* theology that takes the cross seriously. Must *kenōsis* necessarily be understood as a relinquishing of power that leads to submission? Could it not be seen instead as an acceptance of dependence? For me, this is not just a matter of semantics. The vulnerability associated with dependence differs from that which follows from submission. Accepting dependence entails acknowledging my need for 'the other', be it God, other humans or the whole of creation. Whereas, in my mind, submission implies surrender, passivity as opposed to activity, dependence means *needing* something or someone and thus leaves room for me to take an active part in how the fulfilment of my needs is to be played out. Saying, 'I depend on you' is not necessarily to surrender, but to acknowledge mutuality and responsibility. It admits to vulnerability without denying the possibility of taking part in determining the conditions of the relationship.

What if the cross conveys a message that does not primarily emphasize submission, but rather mutual dependence between God and his or her creation? To me, that would pose different questions from those we usually ask concerning omnipotence and omnipresence, perhaps even omniscience. It also – or so I argue – lessens the negative impact that theologies dealing with the meaning of the cross have had on women throughout history.

---

10. Cf. Sarah Coakley, *Powers and Submissions: Spirituality, Philosophy and Gender* (Oxford: Blackwell Publishing, 2002).

'I and You' and Radical Otherness

There is something in 'dependence language' that resembles Martin Buber's 'I and You', and Emmanuel Levinas' notion of the 'radical other'. I admit to being rather unwilling to hear this resemblance. Reading Simone de Beauvoir's *Le Deuxième Sexe* in my early twenties made it quite clear to me that 'the other' was the second, a realization that perhaps was strengthened by the fact that 'the other' and 'the second' translates into the same words in Swedish.[11] From such a perspective, talking about God as 'the other' therefore seems to be the ultimate hubris. It means turning God into an object.

But the concept of 'the other', with or without a capital 'o', has undergone much rethinking and reassessment during the last century. Levinas has left the Hegelian 'master-servant'-inspired point of departure that was Beauvoir's, where the master/man/subject becomes an 'I' in relation to the slave/woman/object, and developed an understanding of the other as an 'other' whose otherness is radically different, not the opposite of the 'I'. A radical 'other' calls for a response; an 'other' that in a way seems to come first, not second, thereby transforming an isolated 'I' into a responsible subject.

In Buber's thinking, the relationship between 'I' and 'You' reveals a mutual holistic existence of two beings.[12] 'I' and 'You' meet without any qualification or objectification of one another. It is a relationship that transcends all forms of human control, closure and systematization. It happens in everyday life in relation to other humans, animals and nature. Though in a way mundane, it is at the same time, according to Buber, nonetheless the only way in which it is possible to interact with God. All 'I-You' relationships do in some way connect to the eternal relationship with God. But being a relationship where 'You' cannot be controlled, means that it is a relationship that cannot be prescribed. When actively pursued, the relationship turns into an 'I-It' relationship where the 'I' masters the other. Only when 'I' stays open to the possibility of an 'I-You' relationship is it possible for God to become a 'You' different from me as a response to my reception.

Levinas draws on Buber's philosophy when he puts 'the face of the other' at the centre of his ethical philosophy. He emphasizes the radical alterity of the other, which resists all categorization. Such lack of control is of course complicated for the human mind to handle. How can we experience that of which there are no concepts as means of understanding? Hence, we tend to reduce and, in Levinas words, 'totalize' the other's otherness by naming, thereby reducing the face to an object which ultimately means to perpetrate violence on it.[13] However, bearing in mind Buber's distinction between 'I-You' relationships and 'I-It' relationships, we are reminded of the fact that when such reduction happens, the face of the other escapes us. The face turns into an 'It', in Buber's language, or into 'someone like

---

11. Both 'the second sex' and 'the other sex' translate into '*det andra könet*'.
12. Martin Buber, *I and Thou*, trans. R. G. Smith (London: Continuum, 2004).
13. Emmanuel Levinas, *Totality and Infinity: An Essay on Exteriority*, trans. A. Lingis (Pittsburgh, PA: Duquesne University Press, 1969).

me', in the language of Levinas. The face of the other is present only when it is out of our control.

The Other and the Cross

Experiencing and elaborating 'the cross' as an encounter with a radical other indicates that, when we are looking at Jesus on the cross, we are facing neither the opposite of us nor someone like us, but someone different. The notion of incarnation tends to lure us into forgetting that. The fact that incarnational theology tells us that God knows what it is to be human does not mean that humans know what it is to be God. The attempt of androcentric theology to place 'the image of man' in the centre of theology has been a pivotal point in feminist critique of traditional theology from the very beginning.[14] But God on the cross is still hidden from us and cannot be controlled by the subject. In Levinas' language, the otherness is not a negation of the subject/me, it is not the opposite of me – which women are taught to believe when looking at Jesus on the cross – nor (or even less) is it someone like me – which men are taught to believe when looking at Jesus on the cross. God's otherness transcends the 'I' and cannot be defined by me.

When we stay open to this presence of a radical otherness we are also reminded that the person who was crucified is God, not someone like me. That, in turn, offers a way of experiencing the cross not as an image of a father sacrificing his son, but of a vulnerable God facing us. In this sense we can, with Luther, speak of a hidden God on the cross, but also of a God who is revealed. And God reveals God's self as a 'You' with a face.

While the idea of *kenōsis* speaks of submission and the relinquishing of power, assuming that there is power to relinquish, the radical other on the cross tells another story. Domination cannot be part of the relationship between an 'I' and a radical other. 'I am who I am', says God to Moses (Exod. 3.14). You do not know me. My otherness hides me from you. Jesus, about to receive his sentence from Pontius Pilate, says: 'You have no power over me' (Jn 19.11). This is so because God can be faced on the cross only when I accept God's otherness, when I accept that 'I' have no power over 'You'. However – and this is equally important – neither does the otherness of the radical other control the 'I'. God cannot prevent the subject (me) from killing Jesus or all others that we dominate and subjugate. Hence, finally: what is revealed is what I would call *mutual dependence*.

Traditional theologies need a powerful God in order to maintain order: a God made in the image of man, legitimizing the power of men. But the story of the incarnate God does not speak of power at all. On the contrary, the Jesus of the gospel keeps refuting power. Still, that does not mean that he presents himself as – or encourages anyone else to be – subordinate or submissive. The word that perhaps best describes the quality of the encounters between Jesus

---

14. Valerie Saiving Goldstein, 'The Human Situation: A Feminine View', *The Journal of Religion* 40/2 (1960), pp. 100–12.

and others is freedom: freedom for me to be who I am, and for you to be who you are. In other words, it seems that Jesus accepts the radical otherness of everyone around him, and what he asks of them is to do the same. He asks us not to perpetrate violence on him, not to kill him by making him into our image, by using and abusing him, by controlling him. In a way, such freedom is the opposite of dependence. But freedom that emanates from independence is always just freedom *from*. It is freedom saying: I do not need you – which is actually not true. I *do* need you because there is no 'I' without a 'You' or an 'It'. But 'I-It' relationships are limiting; they force me to exercise 'power over', thereby restricting the 'I' to being either the opposite of, or the same as. Thus, independence is not the same as freedom.

By Grace Alone: Scary Trust or Barren Control

Freedom emanating out of dependence is scary. It is made up of grace and trust alone, and cannot be earned or brought about by the 'I' itself. It is a freedom crying out: 'I' depend on 'You'. I need you to be a radical other that allows me to be who I am, in the same way as you are who you are. It is freedom that can be lived only by accepting the gift from a 'You' that chooses not to kill me by mastering me.

Women and other subjugated people need independence from a Hegelian otherness where we are mastered, objectified and turned into something 'second-class'. We need to be free from male mastery of who we are, but that kind of freedom depends on the acknowledgement of a radical otherness. Such dependence, be it dependence on God or on the world, points not only towards vulnerability, but also towards mutuality, responsibility, and the possibility of taking part in determining the conditions of the relationship. Whereas submission implies surrender and passivity, dependence leaves room for taking an active part in how the fulfilment of one's needs is to be played out.

At the cross I look into the face of someone different from me, someone who tells me: I am who I am, and you have no power over me; someone who cannot be reduced to fitting into human categories like gender and race, or perceived through human hierarchal structures like fathers and sons. Utilizing such categories is to exercise control and perpetrate violence, turning the face of the other into someone like me or the opposite of me, thereby transforming the 'I-You' relationship into an 'I-It' relationship where God cannot be found. Remaining in the face of the radical other, however, sets me free to be who I am: someone who is capable of killing the other and someone who is, at the same time, in the hands of the other she or he could kill. Thus, the face of the other on the cross turns me into a human being who cannot avoid the choice between scary trust and barren control.

The history of Christian churches is marked by barren control: powerful structures, buildings and hierarchies, where submission has been praised as a virtue for the oppressed and where men of power have preached a God in their image. Yet, throughout this history there have always been voices opting for scary trust, whispering what humans seem to prefer not to hear: I need you, and I need you to be different from me. I need you to meet me through the face of a radical other.

19

THE OTHER WITHIN AND THE OTHER WITHOUT

George Newlands

Backwards, Christian soldiers! What comes most naturally to mind when European citizens think about the churches? That great servant of the Christian church, Cardinal Martini of Milan, in his last public statement suggested – and it was not simply what Karl Barth would have described as '*beiläufig*' – that the Catholic Church was about '200 years out of date'.[1] From the public statements of many of the churches within the UK in the last decade, it would be hard not to think that they are deeply stuck in the mindset of the early 1950s. As for the Orthodox churches, one is reminded, perhaps appropriately, of what Donald MacKinnon described as 'aphasia'. If we now turn to Dietrich Bonhoeffer's famous question of how the next generation shall live, it would seem that generation XYZ has already practically vanished from the radar.[2]

Werner G. Jeanrond privileges the seminal importance of what he terms 'irreplaceable otherness'.[3] 'Love respects the otherness of the other including the radical otherness of God while desiring a union with the other'.[4] We see at once that for Jeanrond respect for otherness is not merely a requirement of ethics or dogmatics, but a *praxis* firmly anchored within our relationship to God. Otherness is of course a notoriously complex concept. In our relationships we may fluctuate between notions of alterity and notions of identity, between recognition and rejection. I shall explore otherness in relation to the work of the Holy Spirit, focussing upon two issues which have also been central to Jeanrond's concern – relations with other faiths, and relations within the Christian faith concerning differences of gender and sexuality.

---

1. The interview in which he made the statement was printed in the Italian newspaper *Corriere della Sera*, 31 August 2012.
2. Dietrich Bonhoeffer, *Letters and Papers from Prison: The Enlarged Edition*, ed. Eberhard Bethge (New York: Macmillan, 1972), pp. 3–4.
3. Werner G. Jeanrond, *A Theology of Love* (London: Continuum/T&T Clark, 2010), p. 148.
4. Ibid., p. 230.

What is the Spirit saying to the churches? Different Christian traditions bring different insights. In Germany, Michael Welker emphasizes the variety of the actions of the Spirit in the Bible, and the need for understanding the Spirit within the spheres of politics and economics.[5] In the US, Peter C. Hodgson associates the Spirit with emancipatory theologies.[6] Amos Yong stresses the fallibility of appeals to the Spirit to construct what he calls 'a pneumatological theology of hospitality', mindful of the role of the Spirit in movements for liberation.[7] Anselm K. Min, a Korean American, offers the most specific integration of the work of the Spirit with the building of solidarity, especially with the most economically impoverished.[8] Roger Haight sees the Spirit provoking interreligious engagement from within the Christian tradition.[9] John B. Cobb understands the Spirit as a guard against assaults on human dignity.[10] In the UK, John Polkinghorne opens the question of the relation of notions of the Spirit to cosmology.[11]

With these insights in mind, I would like to say something like this: Spirit, Son and Father are simultaneously active in the economy of creation and reconciliation. As the Spirit gives the gift of divine love to the Son, the Son to the Father and the Father to the Spirit, the three give simultaneously to the church and to the world alike. The Spirit is dynamically active in the interstices of world and church at every level, a gracious presence recognized by faith. The form of Christ in the world is also the form of Spirit in the world. The church is church when it listens for the real world and the world is the real world when it listens for the true church.

Martin Luther, ever suspicious of 'enthusiasm', maintained that everything said about the Spirit apart from Word and Sacrament is of the devil. (When church committees produce implausible reports based on weak arguments, they usually end with the assurance that the Holy Spirit is guiding the church to take some undesirable action.) But like all famous dicta, Luther's formula is not infallible.

---

5. Michael Welker, *God the Spirit*, trans. J. F. Hoffmeyer (Minneapolis: Augsburg Fortress, 1994); idem, ed., *The Work of the Spirit: Pneumatology and Pentecostalism* (Grand Rapids: Eerdmans, 2006).

6. Peter C. Hodgson, *Winds of the Spirit: A Constructive Christian Theology* (Louisville: Westminster John Knox Press, 1994).

7. Amos Yong, *Who is the Holy Spirit? A Walk with the Apostles* (Brewster, MA: Paraclete Press, 2011).

8. Anselm K. Min, *The Solidarity of Others in a Divided World* (London: Continuum/T&T Clark, 2004).

9. Roger Haight, 'The Holy Spirit and the Religions', in David Jensen, ed., *The Lord and Giver of Life: Perspectives on Constructive Pneumatology* (Louisville: Westminster John Knox Press, 2008), pp. 55-70.

10. John B. Cobb, 'The Holy Spirit and the Present Age', in David Jensen, ed., *The Lord and Giver of Life*, pp. 147-62.

11. John C. Polkinghorne, 'The Hidden Spirit and the Cosmos', in Michael Welker, ed., *The Work of the Spirit*, pp. 169-82.

Faith understands the work of the Spirit as concrete, bringing into focus the presence of God in the world. Faith is sustained by the sense of the promise of this presence, whether it is experienced directly or indirectly. The light of the Spirit of the risen Christ shines in the darkness, and the fruit of the Spirit is love, often in the teeth of suffering. The Spirit's presence is not always signalled by euphoria, it may be experienced as a presence through pain. However, it is not always signalled by suffering for the concentration on such signals could induce unnecessary preoccupation with suffering. Yet it has been experienced as a calming presence in the midst of the most chaotic circumstances. There is here something of the hiddenness of grace, given to be given away.

The church is the church of the Spirit. Faith believes that all the fragments of humanity will be gathered up into the divine presence in eternity. When theologians think of theological anthropology, they tend to be swiftly reminded of Luther's striking phrase, *simul iustus et peccator*. The church is a church of people aware of their shortcomings in the face of the divine unconditional hospitality.[12] Being human involves incommensurable paradoxes, a tension that is both creative and destructive.

The religious are called to maximize the reconciling dynamic of religion. The secular are called to bring humane insight to bear on the continuing inequalities in society. There is a long way to go. Merciful justice is foundational to the Creator Spirit, and uniquely instantiated by God. Christ engaged with improbable conversation partners and people at the edges of the city – *outsiders*. Christ was crucified *outside* the city, an event not unrelated to the marginalized others of every city. Hence, an exclusive spirit is not the Spirit of Christ-likeness.

The Spirit is not confined to Christian community. Can we relate Christian notions of the Spirit to the lives of the countless people who profess no Christian faith or no faith whatsoever? In medieval times the locus of the Spirit was the church and the church's tradition. The Reformation related the Spirit centrally to the Bible. Pietism appealed to the fruits of the Spirit in the heart. The Enlightenment construed this appeal as a guide to ethics. Friedrich Schleiermacher linked the Spirit firmly to the experience of the presence of Christ. Orthodox Protestantism and Catholicism brought back the traditional theological qualifiers. Barth modified these qualifiers christologically. In Pentecostalism, the qualifiers exploded into charismatic reception of the gifts as inspirational.

Where everything and anything becomes possible, one needs safeguards, but within a radically changed and changing context. The mainline churches referred to biblical and traditional reservoirs of authoritative Christian experience. However, the presence of multiple readings rendered the notion of *one* canonical construal less tenable: we can neither reduce Spirit to Word, nor Word to Spirit. Eventually, it becomes possible to speak of different orthodoxies with a commonality within difference – *a Hospitable Spirit, a Hospitable Spirit of Charity*. Word is the Word incarnate, committed to difference and diversity among often struggling people. The letter kills, the Spirit gives life.

---

12. George Newlands and Allen Smith, *Hospitable God - The Transformative Dream* (London: Ashgate, 2010).

Obviously, it would be entirely possible to continue with a discussion of such deep theological mysteries as 'semelfactive quiddities' in order to emerge with a modestly respectable conclusion. Instead I try to respect the intellectual courage of our recipient by continuing with two less easily finessed topics, the Other Within and the Other Without. What do I mean by these Others?

The Other Within

The Other Within refers to difference in terms of gender and sexuality. At most acts of Christian worship there are more women present than men. Why think of men or women as the Other? Men do this because that is the tradition of the church, or – to be precise – it has appeared to be. We have frequently created an entirely artificial image of women as other. Of course men are men and women are women, and a diminishing of diversity is no solution. But in church there has been an *unequal* otherness, which can make the otherness of women a male construct which is disregarding the otherness of women – otherness to be recognized and respected.

Selecting randomly from a huge raft of theological reflection by women, Elisabeth Schüssler Fiorenza's *In Memory of Her*, stressing a Discipleship of Equals, is a magisterial blueprint for the proper acknowledgement of women at every level of Christian community.[13] Yet decades after the appearance of this groundbreaking study there has been only limited progress, not only within the Catholic community in which she stands. Even in churches where equality is enshrined in legislation we still have a long way to go. We need to recognize the cumulative effect of a culture of intentional suppression and instinctive subordination. This also applies to our perception of the roles of women in wider society.

The weight of a tradition of distortion of the otherness of the other bears perhaps even more heavily on homosexual Christians, gays and lesbians. Few issues have as strongly exercised the churches in this millennium. It almost seems that a special circle of Dante's inferno has been created for people, above all *Christian* people, who are attracted to the same sex. To be fair, this voice has been heard elsewhere, not least in the 2013 House of Commons debates on homosexual marriage. This tradition will be a disaster for the effectiveness of the Church in the next generation. We are concerned here not simply with the plausibility criteria for church, we are concerned here with the truth of the Gospel. How could the traditional guardians of the faith be so wrong? The corrosive effect of a cumulative culture of inducing guilt seems easily to outweigh the intellectual dimension. Perhaps I may conclude with one paragraph from a statement from *Affirmation Scotland* which I had the privilege of helping to draft some years ago.[14]

---

13. Elisabeth Schüssler Fiorenza, *In Memory of Her: A Feminist Theological Reconstruction of Christian Origins* (New York: Crossroad, 1983).

14. Cf. www.affirmationscotland.org.uk, accessed 26 September 2014.

We affirm that in God's self-giving to humanity in the incarnation in Jesus Christ we find the ultimate expression of divine hospitality. God's greatest gift to us, the source of all our giving, is the Gospel. Central to the Gospel are generosity and hospitality. Christian hospitality is hospitality to the stranger. 'I was a stranger and you welcomed me.' Jesus was with the lepers. Jesus made himself an outcast and died for the outcast – this was courageous hospitality. We affirm that this is the essence of the Gospel and we pledge ourselves to support those who are at risk, wherever and however we are able. We are called to tell the world that there are no outsiders.

Clearly, the respect for differences in gender and sexuality are not the largest challenges to the mission of the churches in the present. These concerns are particularly acute in the Western World. However, they provide a public and publicly visible litmus test of the churches' internal response to the Gospel. To seek to enforce conformity is not the Christian way, and to neglect advocacy and affirmation of what we believe to be true is equally unhelpful.

What is the Spirit saying to the churches internally? It is crucial to balance the need to critique the negative with the need to celebrate the positive. Where tradition leads to a preoccupation with the ultimately inconsequential, encouragement may be found within the interpretation of tradition in contemporary communities – which is to say, within tradition. The winds of the Spirit have never been confined to a pipeline of tradition. Christian faith always looks forward to a promised future of fulfilment, based on the hope of love which is at the heart of the Gospel.

The Other Without[15]

When we ask what the Spirit is saying to church internally and externally, we cannot presume or pretend to know the answer with certainty. Yet wherever the Spirit is active in creation, we believe that it is active as the Spirit of Christ.

The activity of the Spirit is fortunately not confined to Christian contexts. In recent years theology has concentrated on dialogue in the Abrahamic tradition, especially with Islam. Instead of a concentration which often focuses on the contrast of these cultures, it may be helpful to see the contrast against the background of world cultures. I am a little concerned about a possible drift towards a tyranny of the text. To counter this drift, I focus on the Spirit in relation to East Asian religion, notably in China. There are 1.6 billion people in China. The great majority of whom (approximately 85 per cent) would claim to have no religion, while a minority have commitments to Buddhism (7 per cent), to Daoism, to Confucianism and to Christianity (approximately 2 per cent each). To be sure, even minorities add up to considerable numbers. A full-scale discussion

15. An extended version was delivered as the Presidential Address to the Society for the Study of Theology at the University of Nottingham in April 2013.

of this subject is beyond my competence. What follows is a suggestion that Christian theology has potential to be a conversation partner, in ways which only Chinese people themselves can determine, in an area where comparatively little engagement currently takes place.[16]

It is often noted that large numbers of modern Chinese people appear to have no sense of transcendence, and there is uncertainty about the status of values. (This is not confined to China!) Simultaneously, there has arisen awareness of a need for values, and a desire to link the contemporary quest with the tradition of reflection on spirituality in Chinese culture.

Dialogue between West and East has been developed in various ways, as in the 'Boston Confucianism' of Robert Neville,[17] and between John Cobb and process philosophers with Chinese philosophy. It may be that aspects of the Christian understanding of God as Holy Spirit could facilitate such a dialogue. Somewhat as diverse approaches to the theology of the Holy Spirit in Christian tradition may lead to unforced consensus on the character of the Spirit as Holy Spirit, we may consider whether a similar pattern might lead to a deeper engagement with Chinese religion. The Spirit of the Third Church of the Vertical City, as in areas of modern China, could be a potential growth point of such dialogue.

I underline some paradoxes. Appeal to the Spirit is a call to relationality in love. Yet claims to be commanded by the Spirit have been an excuse for violation of human dignity on a minor or a massive scale throughout history. Although Christianity is one dimension of the Abrahamic tradition which has contributed enormously to human flourishing, we know that aspects of this tradition have been harmful on a wide range of issues. Reliance on 'certainty' about God's law may provoke and perpetuate injustice.

We must look beyond a pooling of traditional resources. One important source has been the European Enlightenment. The development of Human Rights, despite its flaws, has been a great achievement.[18] We may look to dialogue with Eastern culture as a way to make all our contributions to the future of humanity more effective. This is not an issue of the non-religious modifying the religious, but of a wider equilibrium of a *non-competitive* nature. A Christian understanding of humanity has to reiterate the priorities of love.[19]

The obstacles are obvious. Evidently, there is a truth in the familiar saying that we can go global by going local; yet, equally, we need to lift our eyes beyond the local to the global. This is not a call for more and yet more resolutions of the World Council of Churches. It is a suggestion that church and theology reflecting

---

16. See now David F. Ford, 'Flamenco, Tai Chi and Six-Text Scriptural Reasoning: Report on a visit to China', *Cambridge Inter-Faith Programme Papers* 10 (2012).

17. Robert Neville, *Boston Confucianism* (Albany, NY: State University of New York Press, 2000).

18. George Newlands, *Christ and Human Rights: A Transformative Engagement* (Aldershot: Ashgate, 2006). George Newlands and Richard Amesbury, *Faith and Human Rights* (Minneapolis: Fortress Press, 2008).

19. Werner G. Jeanrond, *A Theology of Love*, pp. 173–238.

on the church has a vital part to play in the providence of the transformative God. It is perhaps unlikely that Christianity, even as it grows and grows at an astonishing speed, will become more influential than the cultures of the many ethnic minorities in China. The main growth will probably be of a Christianity which blends traditional and local cultures with a conservative faith.

In the last twenty years there has been a quest in China for a 'socialist spiritual civilization'. This civilization has proved hard to define, given the increasing awareness of difference and diversity among the Chinese peoples. 'One size fits all' slogans are not persuasive. What can be offered to such a complex civilization? We have suffered in the past from authoritarian theologies. Eastern religion respects humility (although it has often been just as authoritarian as Western theologies). Against the taint of cultural imperialism we need *non-competitive* structures. No doubt, such structures are already there – we can only offer to make common cause in their utilization. One obvious practical step is to support the many avenues of 'soft diplomacy' which already exist to promote understanding. There is always the danger that this becomes power politics by another name, but the improper abuse does not take away the proper use. In such ways we may hope to share the fruits of our own difficult learning process, while not prescribing how spirituality and religiosity in China are to be moulded. These are naïve suggestions for a conversation of daunting proportions.

The potential for Christianity in China is great, but there are problems. Consider the parallel of South Korea where there has been huge growth in Christianity, often linked to a perception of Western values as creating material prosperity. This has led to considerable inter-church conflict and to intolerance towards other religions. The result is a decline in Christian profession. Similarly, in China there is a huge appetite for Western values among the young. However, the growth of a strongly conservative Christianity may lead to intra- and inter-religious intolerance, thus becoming a challenge to the government's declared aim of achieving social harmony. There will be times when Christian defence of human dignity may clash with governmental policy. But a Chinese Christianity closely resembling American 'Tea Party' style politics would not be a step forward. Facing this challenge it seems to me that a contribution which stresses the varieties of the forms of the Spirit of Christ in the world could be helpful in promoting engagement over a constantly changing context. Emphasis on areas of convergence between visions of the dynamic action of the Spirit might facilitate that coming together of different ways of living Christianity which is essential to discipleship. A Christian community so related could make a sane contribution to development – locally and globally.

Effective conversation does not take place with eyes wide shut. In China, despite the real changes since the chaos of Maoism, the problems are on-going. Nonetheless, Chinese delegates were involved in the drafting of the United Nations' *Universal Declaration on Human Rights* in 1948, which could be said to be eminently compatible with Confucianism, where there is a long tradition of stressing the importance of human dignity. The insight that human dignity involves identity as relationality and reciprocity could be seen as a particularly Asian contribution.[20]

Within the spiritualties and philosophies of China, we find a long tradition of recognition and respect of difference. Confucianism has been the most pervasive, but it has not usually been as aggressive as Abrahamic religions have been. There has been hugely varied discussion of transcendence and immanence, of ethical codes and ethical conduct. 'It is always better to give than to receive' has been perceived as an ironic comment on much ecumenical discussion. Simply to be self-giving may not be what is needed. We should make an effort to receive, to be receptive to our conversation partners. That is what I have been attempting to do here.

The Spirit and the Other Within and Without: Conclusions?

It seems to me that we should begin from the particularity of our own intellectual and spiritual traditions. *But we cannot stop there.* We should recognize the global dimensions of Christian service to humanity, more than we have often done. For each of us this recognition will involve different insights, trusting in the conversation to sift out better and even better proposals. If charity famously begins at home, we especially have much inclusivity to make up for. We are called to embody a vision with the justice of human dignity at its core, and we can never give up on this call. The churches remain pointers to the transcendent love of God, sometimes despite the churches. Perhaps we can go forward with chastened hope, and without drawing too many premature conclusions.

---

20. Cf. John Berthrong, 'Human rights and responsibilities: a Confucian perspective on the Universal Declaration of Human Rights' and Sumner B. Twiss, 'Confucian values and human rights', in Joseph Runzo, Nancy Martin and Arvind Sharma, eds, *Human Rights and Responsibilities in the World Religions* (Oxford: Oneworld Publications, 2003), pp. 199–205 and pp. 283–99.

20

AUGUSTINIAN LOVE

Rowan Williams

Werner G. Jeanrond's wide-ranging *A Theology of Love* includes a chapter on Augustine's concept of love, divine and human, dealing not only with the Saint's understanding of sexuality and marriage, but with far wider issues around 'subjectivity, agency and community', to borrow the subtitle of one section.[1] Following Hannah Arendt's well-known discussion of Augustine's doctrine of love in her doctoral thesis,[2] Jeanrond concludes that this is a 'theology of love [that] does not help us to form human community'.[3] Augustine's understanding of the optimal form of community, the Church, depends on the idea that ecclesial solidarity is necessary primarily because of the fact of sinful solidarity, not as a form of transfigured mutuality, which is surely what the New Testament requires us to believe. We are primitively linked with each other by original sin, by a shared inheritance; grace binds us together so that we are better able to resist the pull of a world in which human solidarity means only death. And because no human person can be loved in and for himself or herself, as *De Doctrina Christiana* famously says, but only for the sake of God, no real content can be given to the mutual love of believers. Grace *dissolves* the solidarity of sin so as to connect us directly with God; from this point on, our relations with one another are indirect or even abstract, never relations of true interdependence, and what unites believers is faith rather than love. Put more sharply, love ceases to be 'constitutive' for the Church, except in the sense that *God's* love is the sole creative agency at work, drawing individuals out of the toxic community of original sin. Love as something undertaken by human subjects is not ultimately of value here.

---

1. Werner G. Jeanrond, *A Theology of Love* (London: Continuum/T&T Clark, 2010), pp. 57–61.
2. Cf. Hannah Arendt, *Der Liebesbegriff bei Augustin: Versuch einer philosophischen Interpretation* (Berlin: Springer, 1929). The thesis was written in 1927–28 and published in 1929. For the English translation cf. *Love and Saint Augustine*, ed. Joana V. Scott and Judith C. Stark (Chicago: Chicago University Press, 1996).
3. Werner G. Jeanrond, *A Theology of Love*, p. 61.

Now this is, to put it mildly, an odd reading.[4] Jeanrond very properly points out the problematic character of most Augustinian teaching about sex and the body (though even here there is more to be said: as usual, what is interesting about Augustine is not the attitudes he shares with his contemporaries but what is unique to him[5]); but the broader analysis is puzzling. I want to invite him to a re-reading of Augustine without the distorting medium of Arendt's interpretation, which I believe is eccentric to the point of perversity, in the hope of showing that what is most central in Augustine's understanding of love is by no means so alien to Jeanrond's own concerns. To do this in full detail would need a far longer exposition than can be offered in a brief essay; so what I shall do is to take three related aspects of the mature Augustine's theology which unambiguously tell against Arendt's version. But one general observation may be in order at the outset. Arendt's focal argument is that the effect of Augustine's teaching is to withdraw the human subject from the public and political sphere; love as he understands it is 'worldless', to use her terminology,[6] and functions as an alternative to the *agon* of political labour, the construction of actual communities of law and human nurture. She is of course writing in the middle of a cultural crisis about the moral possibility of politics, the Germany of the 1920s, and Augustine has become for her the symbol of a 'beautiful-souled' diversion from the political imperative. But a less constrained reading would be able to show how Augustine is arguing in effect that the very notion of the 'public' and the 'political' depends on a Christian anthropology, in the sense that only a rectified love, delivered from crippling self-referentiality, can prevent us from spinning apart into unmanageable rivalry. Augustine is constantly beginning his analysis not simply from a generalized conviction about 'original sin' but from a highly specific diagnosis of how self-defence, self-deceit and self-aggrandizement combine to poison interrelation in human affairs. Augustine, far from dissolving solidarity in favour of a community held together by the implicitly violent imperative of holding a single faith,[7] is seeking to identify the ways in which sin's solidarity is – paradoxically – what dissolves any *actual* human communality, so that grace becomes the means of releasing the possibility of concrete and truthful social existence. The themes we are going to look at here should all be thought through in the light of this fundamental point.

4. For a thorough critical examination of Arendt's Augustine, cf. Thomas E. Breidenthal's 1991 Oxford D.Phil thesis 'The Concept of Freedom in Hannah Arendt: A Christian Assessment' (Unpublished Diss. University of Oxford, 1991), and idem, 'Arendt, Augustine and the Politics of Incarnation', *Modern Theology* 14/4 (1998), pp. 489–503.

5. Cf. Margaret Miles, *Augustine on the Body* (Missoula, MT: Scholars Press, 1979).

6. Cf. Hannah Arendt, *The Human Condition* (Chicago: University of Chicago Press, 1958), p. 53.

7. Arendt argues this from the first of Augustine's *Homilies on the First Epistle of John*. Her interpretation is cited in Werner G. Jeanrond, *A Theology of Love*, p. 60: a seriously eccentric reading of a text in which faith in the Risen Christ is treated as the doorway to that mutual communion which is the earthly form of our salvation.

The first of these is to do with Augustine's account in the *Confessions* of his own early experience of love – and more particularly of *loss*. In *Confessions* IV. 4–9, Augustine describes what he went through when an intimate friend of his teenage years died (having been baptized in his last illness). This account is the earliest we have in Western literature of the complex processes of bereavement – anger, self-doubt and 'survivor's guilt', the pain of seeing familiar, once shared, sights now organized around an absence, wanting to be dead, fearing death, and so on. A pivotal moment in this account is the poignant and pregnant phrase in IV.7: 'What mindlessness it is not to know how to love human beings humanly [*humaniter*]! And what a foolish human I was then, so impatient in coping with the human condition!' What he portrays is thus in some way an 'inhuman' love: by investing his very identity in the relation with his friend, Augustine has involved himself in a deeply ambiguous mode of subjectivity, in which, in the absence of the loved one, what is 'there' to be loved is the emotion of grief itself. The actual and independent reality of my mortal friend is swallowed up in an absorption with my state of mind and heart, including my memories and images of what I have lost. My love is incapable of letting the loved one be free of my subjectivity, even though death is the most dramatic possible reminder that what I love is not under my control. The logic is that to love 'humanly' would be to love in the awareness that the one I love exists in a context other than my needs or projects. Extreme grief of the kind Augustine describes, with its detachment from the reality of the object of love, implies that I have made the other carry too much in my imagination. Dealing with grief of this sort is learning to return to the fact of shared mortality, to the *humana*, the human affairs or human condition from which Augustine sees himself as shrinking.

This is not an attitude indifferent to the specificity of the object of love, seeing such an object as simply a 'reminder' to love God. There is indeed a sense of solidarity in the mortal condition; and we have to keep a watchful eye on our friendships and loves if we are to avoid using such relationships to assure ourselves that we are not really mortal. In IV.8, Augustine memorably evokes the joys of friendship, including the joys shared in what we would call 'body language', the expressive communication of eyes and faces as well as speech, only to insist that this is *in itself* potentially an escape from a starker reality – so that if interrupted by a death, we feel we have lost ourselves as well as the one we love. Loving humanly, it seems, must be a love that refuses to ignore the mortality and limitedness of what or whom we love. Forget this, and we are left with an intensity of felt intimacy that ultimately and subtly refuses to 'release' the person loved from the bonds of that intimacy.[8] And to love the friend as mortal is to love him or her 'in God': that is to love them as they relate to God. This will sound like a form of Arendt's 'indirect' relatedness unless we recall that for Augustine any attempt to love or indeed to know anything except as related to God is illusory. And this brings us to our second Augustinian theme.

---

8. We might compare this with C. S. Lewis's expressed concern in his celebrated *A Grief Observed* (London: Faber and Faber, 1961), pp. 18–20 that he should not turn his dead wife's memory into a self-serving image under his control.

As has been argued at length by several recent interpreters of Augustine,[9] the discussion in *De Trinitate* of the image of God in humanity turns, *not* on the idea that our inner ecology of memory, intelligence, and will reflects the inner relations of the Trinity, but on the belief that when we look inwards, we see, ultimately, a threefold inner life whose *constitutive object* is God; that is, our remembering, our understanding, and our willing are what they are because they are created so as to have God as their proper object.[10] Being related thus to God is what it is to be a spiritual subject, whether or not we acknowledge this. When under the leading of grace, we consciously align ourselves with this innate God-directedness, the image of God in us comes to light – a remembering which is primitively the remembrance of God, an intelligence which is primitively the understanding of God and a will which is primitively the loving of God. As God in God's own being has God's own self as object, so do we in finite measure. Grace both uncovers and satisfies the 'drawn-ness' towards God that is inbuilt in the structure of mind and sentience. The image of God in human beings is thus the human being turned towards God, having God as object. This implies that if we seek either to know or to love another human subject as if they subsisted independently of this directedness or drawn-ness, we are pursuing a phantom. Just as Augustine's concern in the *Confessions* is to identify and warn against a love that de-realizes its object, so here he is pulling us away from any picture of human actuality that forgets the central and constitutive fact about human subjectivity – that it is oriented towards the endlessness of God.

If that is the case with us as humans, we need to revisit and rethink slightly the difficult language in Augustine's *De Doctrina Christiana* about loving other human beings 'for the sake of God', *propter Deum*.[11] This has an undeniably grudging ring to it: if I say that I love a friend of my spouse 'for the sake of' my spouse, or perhaps that I keep on the shelf a hideous Victorian china dog 'for the sake of' my grandmother who loved it and bequeathed it to me, the implication is clearly that – independently of spouse or grandmother – I would have no particular reason to feel any warmth at all for these objects as such. They have nothing in themselves that is lovable as far as I am concerned, and what makes them appropriate objects of love on my part is their association with another object. But this is not at all the model Augustine is describing. The question which prompts his formulation is whether a human being is appropriately loved in the mode of 'enjoyment', that is, as an end in itself; and his answer, with appropriate qualification, is that this would be to treat another human individual as independently promising final bliss to

---

9. See especially Michael Hanby, *Augustine and Modernity* (London: Routledge, 2003), pp. 27–46; Luigi Gioia, *The Theological Epistemology of Augustine's* De Trinitate (Oxford: Oxford University Press, 2006); Lewis Ayres, *Augustine and the Trinity* (Cambridge: Cambridge University Press, 2010), pp. 273–318. For a thorough overview of the recent debate, see Roland Kany, *Augustins Trinitätsdenken* (Tübingen: Mohr Siebeck, 2007), pp. 393–404.

10. Cf. especially Augustine, *De Trinitate*, XV.

11. Cf. Augustine, *De Doctrina Christiana*, I.xxii.20.

me, signalling nothing beyond itself.[12] This would be to make the other human being something different from – indeed, something *less* than – what it in fact is. Each human subject is both *res* and *signum*, both a true subsistent reality and a sign of its maker. If I refuse to treat it as a sign of its maker, I take something from its actual ontological complexity and dignity, while at the same time effectively inflating that complexity and dignity to a level it cannot sustain. Only God is to be enjoyed without qualification; only God is *a sign of nothing else*.

To say, as Augustine does in *De Doctrina Christiana*, that we therefore 'use' rather than 'enjoy' other human subjects in our love for them is obviously problematic because of the apparent implication that human love is only ever instrumental to something else; and this is clearly what Arendt and, following her, Jeanrond find difficult and unacceptable.[13] The phraseology is indeed rebarbative to anyone who is attuned to the moral problem of 'using' another individual. Immanuel Kant's exhortation to treat others as ends not means is deeply ingrained in the modern reader. But before we completely discard what Augustine argues in *De Doctrina*, we need at least to do justice to the argument, and to recognize that it is an argument which runs through a significant part of his mature work. The fundamental point could be expressed as the concern that *we should not pretend that any human other is God*: that is to say, we should not treat them as if relation with them could secure our eternal bliss, *beata vita*, or as if they could be seen, responded to, known, loved as if they were not images of God – signs of more than they contain or embody. Augustine's terminology of using and enjoying does not do quite what he wants it to do here, and in arguing that God is to be 'preferred to' or, perhaps, 'given priority over' created objects of love, including human others, he comes uncomfortably close to assuming something he is in fact seeking to avoid – the notion that God and human others are in competition for our love.[14] If relation to God as God's image is intrinsic to every human identity, if every human subject knowing and loving himself or herself is in some sense and in some limited measure loving God, whether they are aware of it or not, God *cannot* simply be a rival for our love. It is impossible to love the human other, just as it is impossible for me to love myself, without God being involved as the animating presence to which my subjectivity and the other's subjectivity are always present. And this secures in our love a sense that the other is at some level free of my needs and preoccupations, turned towards God before they are turned towards me and turning back constantly into that light – a theme given definitive expression in Dante Alighieri's parting from Beatrice in the *Commedia*. For Augustine, loving human beings *humaniter* is loving them with regard to what they are signs of – infinite love; and so far from this being a way of rendering others instrumental to my own spiritual advance, contingent occasions for me to learn the love of another (God), this is intended both to liberate the other from my agenda or my fulfilment and to undergird the conviction that the love of the contingent mortal neighbour in her or his contingency and mortality is the

---

12. Ibid., I.iii.3–v.5, xxii.20–xxiii.22.
13. Cf. Werner G. Jeanrond, *A Theology of Love*, pp. 52–8.
14. Augustine, *De Doctrina Christiana*, I.ix.9.

vehicle for loving God, not something which, in straightforwardly instrumental fashion, we discard when the separate and higher purpose is attained.

In keeping with Jeanrond's discussion,[15] my aim is to ask what is to be learned from Augustine, not simply to argue that his account is without flaw or ambiguity; and it seems to me that perhaps the most important insight is precisely this insistence on loving the human neighbour truthfully – as mortal not divine, yet also as irreducibly a sign of God, a subject whose subjectivity means or 'intends' God. The other I encounter is always already engaged with and by God, and any love directed towards them is illusory to the degree it forgets or ignores this. And this is why – to move on to our third theme – the Christian community for Augustine is emphatically not *first* a body united as it were externally, through common expressions or experiences of faith, but a body in which mutual love and service, delight in each other and support for one another in need, do indeed *constitute* the ecclesial identity. A full-scale account of Augustine's ecclesiology would be out of place, but a glance at the *Homilies on the First Epistle of John* will make the point economically enough. In the fifth homily,[16] Augustine speaks about the imperative to be ready to give your life for the sake of a fellow-member of Christ's Body, and goes on to describe our willingness to give up what we do not need in order to meet the material needs of our neighbour as the first step towards 'dying' for the neighbour.[17] It is clear that the love between believers is very much a matter of what is both imperative and possible here and now, in attention to the specific reality of the other. The interplay of love between members of the Body is not some sort of shadow of a more real or fundamental love of God to which the specifics of the human world are irrelevant. In the sixth homily,[18] we have an echo of the argument in Augustine's anti-Donatist polemic about the difference between receiving the outward sign of the Spirit's coming in the sacrament of baptism without receiving the bond of *caritas* in the continuing common life of the community.[19] And in the tenth homily,[20] we find both (again) a clear distinction between faith with and without *caritas* and an argument to establish that the mutual love of Christians is in fact 'the one Christ, loving himself': believers love Christ in loving each other, but it is throughout the act of Christ both loving himself and loving the Father. To imagine that we can love Christ without loving his Body on earth is as much nonsense as to think you can love the Son without loving the Father. Augustine puts it pithily: 'Love can't be divided into parts. Choose for yourself what you'll love and you get the others too'.[21]

15. Cf. Werner G. Jeanrond, *A Theology of Love*, pp. 61–5.
16. Augustine, *Tractatus in Epistolam Ioannis ad Parthos*, V.4.
17. Ibid., V.12.
18. Ibid., VI.10.
19. Ibid., ep. 185.X.43, also cf. Augustine, *De Unitate* IV.7 and *De Baptismo* IV.
20. Augustine, *Tractatus in Epistolam Ioannis ad Parthos*, X.3.
21. The translation is from John Leinenweber, *Love One Another, My Friends: St Augustine's Homilies on the First Letter of John* (San Francisco: Harper and Row, 1989), p. 102. This is a particularly readable version.

The connection of this with the pervasive importance to Augustine of the unity of Head and members, grounded in one of his most frequently cited New Testament texts, Christ's words to Saul, 'Why are you persecuting me?'[22] surely means that whatever is said about *caritas, amor* or *dilectio* in Augustine's work needs to be read in the light of this basic ecclesiological principle. It is not only that, in the most general terms, it is impossible to abstract human individuals from their ontologically given relatedness to God as the natural (even if hidden) direction of their intelligence, memory and will; it is also essential to recognize that loving the human other within the body of Christ entails an even more intimate connectedness between God and the object of love. The other in the Church is a place where Christ's love is active; and the love that is Christ's acting in me moves out to the love acting in the other which simultaneously moves towards me. Whether or not I am actually aware of the full range of human others to whom I am bound in this way (after all, he says, one eye cannot see the other in our own bodies), I am in fact united with them, seeing from the same perspective and moving in the same direction.[23] This is why Arendt's judgement on Augustine's ecclesiology seems perverse: she contrasts the 'interdependence' of natural solidarity with the mutual love at work in the Church, concluding that 'one individual's relationship to another ... ceases to be a matter of course, as it was in interdependence', because the love of the believer is always marked by 'specific indirectness'.[24] Jeanrond summarizes this as implying that 'the community of believers is not built on love, but on a biologically mediated common destiny into which God sends his revelation of grace'.[25] But this is an unsustainable reading of Augustine. Whether Augustine's model is adequate for a contemporary theology of love or not (and I believe it is more adequate than most), it needs to be recognized that it depends radically on the assumption that the human subject is by nature oriented towards God, communicating divine meaning by the bare fact of its intellectual awareness and volitional reaching-out; and by grace embodying the specific act of Christ whose saving work has released this basic intentionality to exercise its proper scope. Our temptation is constantly to project on to the things and persons around us expectations they are unable to fulfil, and so to shrink both them and ourselves.

---

22. Constantly cited in Augustine, *Enarrationes in Psalmos*; cf. idem, *Tractatus in Epistolam Ioannis ad Parthos*, X.3.

23. Ibid., VI.10.

24. Hannah Arendt, *Love and Saint Augustine*, p. 108, quoted in Werner G. Jeanrond, *A Theology of Love*, p. 61. Cf. Elisabeth Young-Bruehl in her excellent biography of Arendt, *Hannah Arendt: For Love of the World* (New Haven: Yale University Press, 1982). See the notes on pp. 74–5 that Arendt's reviewers objected to the fact that she had presented the 'thinker' not the bishop, and that she herself did not see Augustine as essentially a theologian. This is illuminating, but she is not the only reader of Augustine to suffer from the attempt to interpret him as a philosopher in abstraction from the exegetical and theological writings in which we see his concepts actually at work in what he would have thought their proper environment.

25. Werner G. Jeanrond, *A Theology of Love*, p. 61.

We reduce the fathomless meaning of the other (fathomless because of its opening out on to God) to the dimensions of our own need; we enslave ourselves to objects of desire that pretend to a finality and all-embracingness they cannot have. If we try to love human beings independently of loving God, we ignore what they are; we do indeed 'use' them, in the contemporary sense of the word, we make them serve our purposes, and in so doing make ourselves *their* servants in a sense quite opposed to the mutual serving of the members of Christ's Body.

That this is embedded in what is often an uncomfortable vocabulary and argued with a good deal of ambivalence towards the flesh and its emotions is undeniable (though we should not lose sight of the fact that love of one's own body is repeatedly used by Augustine as a paradigm of what proper self-love entails). Yet the question Augustine poses is whether we can shape a viable theology of human love without acknowledging that the dignity of the human object of love is bound up with its character as pointing Godwards. If you begin with an ontology that either sees God as another item in the list of possible objects of love or insists on a radical and near-total discontinuity between the act of God and every finite agency, this 'pointing Godwards' is going to sound uncomfortably like 'pointing *away* from itself'. Augustine challenges us to think again: for him, pointing Godwards is also pointing inwards, pointing to what is most real in the finite object of love – its relation to the infinite act, which is the source of both its being and its meaning. To return to the language of *De Doctrina*, the human subject is indeed a *res*, a subsistent reality, but is equally, like all finite subsistents, a *signum*. It is not exhausted by what it finitely is at any one moment in time. For any finite subsistent, a human or angelic agent above all, to act positively, 'creatively' if you will, is to exercise to the full the capacity to be a sign and thus to prompt and nourish the awareness in other subjects of the infinity of love that is God.[26]

'The human subject is created, recreated and thus ultimately constituted by God's love alone. There can be no talk about any form of co-constituting creativity in human love'.[27] The first sentence is a perfectly accurate summary of not only Augustine's teaching on love and the human subject but, arguably, any serious theological account (any account which assumes the dependence of all things on the free love of the creator). The second suggests that the word 'ultimately' in the first sentence has been tacitly disregarded. Augustine does not maintain that we have no role in shaping one another's human journey in faith and love; the Johannine homilies alone ought to persuade us that he is not advancing some doctrine of the total irrelevance of specific human agency and human relation to the operation of God's action in the Church (a slightly different issue to the question of grace and freedom as Augustine treats it in the anti-Pelagian works[28]).

---

26. See Michael Hanby, *Augustine and Modernity*, pp. 31–41 for an exemplary discussion of the sign's participation in what it signifies, and of how the signified gives form to the concrete singularity which constitutes the sign.

27. Werner G. Jeanrond, *A Theology of Love*, p. 61.

28. The point here is not what grounds or merits divine salvific action but the *form* in which that action is mediated, made intelligible, and embodied in practice.

But he would certainly have argued that the only creativity we could exercise through human love was the mediation of God's love – for the simple reason that the root of love is not in us, any more than the root of our being is in us. It is possible by God's grace for us to be in some measure creative creatures. But unless we remember that we and those we love are alike creatures, we shall cut ourselves off from the only possible source of creativity; we shall be ascribing meanings to the human other that are both more and less than is proper. Augustine is not, I believe, trying to persuade us that loving my neighbour is 'a mere instantiation of my love of God' – the position which Jeanrond rightly sees Karl Rahner as contesting.[29] But the Rahnerian idea that the 'basic human act of attention to the neighbour is always already related to the God of eternal life, even though we may not be aware of this relationship' is, if the reading of Augustine I have been arguing is correct, a version of 'Augustinian love'. Which is why I conclude that Jeanrond's proper and significant concerns for a robustly transformative, politically meaningful, participatory model of what constitutes the Church are served rather than subverted by an Augustinian understanding.[30]

'Acknowledgement of conditionality is the only unconditionality of human love' wrote Gillian Rose.[31] To recognize the boundedness, the difficulty, the failure-haunted character of love, she argues, is essential if we are not to condemn ourselves to the terrors of endless possibility and so endless guilt at our failure to achieve. Augustine would have appreciated this particular version of what it means to love *humaniter.*

---

29. Werner G. Jeanrond, *A Theology of Love*, p. 146.
30. Ibid., p. 247.
31. Gillian Rose, *Love's Work* (London: Chatto and Windus, 1995), p. 98.

21

WHO LOVES? WHO IS LOVED?
THE PROBLEM OF THE COLLECTIVE PERSONALITY

Johannes Zachhuber

In one of the best-known passages in the New Testament, a Pharisee asks Jesus to name the 'first' commandment from God's Law. Christ's celebrated answer, 'You shall love the Lord your God with all your heart, and with all your soul, and with all your strength, and with all your mind, and your neighbour as yourself' (Lk. 10.27) has been variously interpreted. This much however seems clear: Jesus speaks about the love one individual person shows to another. For the addressee is, obviously, an individual who is expected to perform his actions in the spirit of love. When Jesus subsequently illustrates his words by telling the parable of the Good Samaritan, at least in Luke's account, it seemingly becomes unequivocal that the object of love must also be an individual.

Notwithstanding this, we do not only speak of love as a relationship between two individuals. People love their families and their friends not just individually but also collectively. They love (or say they love) their country, their nation or indeed humanity. Is it not also the case that we conversely feel loved by our family or by our friends in a way that cannot evidently be reduced to a relationship between individuals?

Scholars have drawn our attention to the fact that particularly some of our strongest religious affections are directed towards communities. To Émile Durkheim, the experience of collective effervescence is the very foundation of all religion.[1] The object of this experience, the French sociologist argued, is society itself in its concrete physical togetherness; this is then reified into concepts of transcendent reality. While I am not aware that Durkheim or any of his collaborators attempted an interpretation of the double commandment to love in the context of their theory, it would not be difficult, I believe, to picture what such an interpretation would involve. The love of God would in essence be this very collective experience, and the love of neighbour would be its consequence: the

---

1. Émile Durkheim, *The Elementary Forms of Religious Life*, trans. K. E. Fields (London: Free Press, 1995), pp. 226-7.

other becomes our neighbour, our fellow religionist, insofar as she is included in this shared experience as a part of the collective whole.[2]

Historically and empirically, it would be hard to deny that mechanisms of this kind have played their part in the Christian faith. As a religion, Christianity came to inform and form cultures by aligning its concept of love to the community-building tendencies existing among the nations that adopted the faith. This alignment was the basis of the medieval concept of a *corpus Christianorum* and later underwrote ideas of Christian nations. And yet, in spite of its success, its legitimacy never ceased to be controversial. The fervour of this debate is unsurprising given that the question it raises concerns the fundamental identity of the Christian faith: does its concept of love, however much altered, modified and transformed, stand in continuity with traditional human cultural and religious practice? Is therefore, as Albrecht Ritschl argued in the nineteenth century, its realization novel only insofar as its reach extends to the whole of humanity, but otherwise compatible with traditional community types such as the family?[3] In other words, does Christian love merely develop and deepen natural affections attracting and bonding us to our relations, to friends, to members of the same class or to people with the same educational background and similar interests?[4]

Or does it represent a radical antithesis to those forms of tribal loyalty, as Søren Kierkegaard argued in his controversy with the great theologian of Danish nationalism, Nikolai Grundtvig?[5] Is Christian love subversively directed against our deeply internalized sympathies for our near and dear? Is perhaps the love of neighbour more properly the love for the stranger? In this interpretation, Jesus' command to love turns into a radical critique of all existing social and cultural systems, a revelation of 'things hidden since the foundation of the world' (Mt. 13.35). René Girard, characteristically, chose these words from the Gospel as the motto for his own reading of the Christian narrative as being fundamentally opposed to 'mythical' justifications of the violent 'scapegoat' mechanism that has made human civilization possible.[6]

---

2. For an analogous interpretation one may, however, compare Ludwig Feuerbach's view of divine love in *The Essence of Christianity*, trans. M. A. Evans (= G. Eliot) (New York: Calvin Blanchard, 1855), pp. 85-6.

3. Albrecht Ritschl, *The Christian Doctrine of Justification and Reconciliation: The Positive Development of the Doctrine*, trans. H. R. Mackintosh and A. B. Macaulay (Edinburgh: T&T Clark, 1902), pp. 279-82.

4. This is emphatically affirmed by Thomas Aquinas, *Summa Theologiae* II-II, qu. 26, art. 7, *Respondeo*: 'Et sic hoc ipsum quod est diligere aliquem, quia consanguineus vel coniunctus est, vel quia concivis, vel propter quodcumque huiusmodi aliud licitum ordinabile in finem charitatis, potest a charitate imperari'. I owe this reference to Lydia Schumacher whose helpful and incisive comments have improved this essay in many other ways too.

5. Cf. Stephen Backhouse, *Kierkegaard's Critique of Christian Nationalism* (Oxford: Oxford University Press, 2011).

6. Cf. René Girard, *Des choses cachées depuis la fondation du monde: Recherches avec Jean-Michel Oughourlian et Guy Lefort* (Paris: Livre de Poche, 1983).

Such a critical interpretation of the Christian command to love takes its cue from the insight that love based on the experience of community inevitably has an exclusive character: we love our friends and not our enemies; we love our family and not any Tom, Dick or Harry; we love the members of our own people and not the foreigner. We may take this line of argument further by asking whether love that is the result of communal experience is *at all* directed at the other person? Do we really love that individual, or do we not rather love *in* her something else? Rather than loving her as what she is, we appear to love her *as* part of the whole to which she belongs and which she represents for us: our family, our circle of friends, our people or our church. It is this whole; therefore, it is the community to which our love is primarily directed. Our 'love' of the individual person is only a derived phenomenon; it is a mere extension of our attachment to the collective within which the individual disappears as the proverbial drop of water in the ocean.

Such doubts about the legitimacy of a love for collectives seem to lead us straight back to our original intuition that the commandment to love is geared towards individuals who are at least potentially unrelated by any bond of family, nationality or religiosity. The Samaritan in Jesus' parable only *makes* the robbed man his neighbour by turning towards him. Initially, he is, as far as we can see, not at all his 'neighbour'. He does not know him but, on the contrary, recognizes him as a member of another tribe. The sole bond that exists between them appears to be constituted by the loving act itself; an act that originates in one individual and is directed towards another.

Such an interpretation of Christian love has been rather popular with many twentieth-century theologians who sought to distinguish it, as *agape*, from all other varieties of love: love is Christian, according to this interpretation, precisely insofar as it turns to the other *as* other without pre-conditions or provisos. It does not depend on the existence of collective structures into which the acting individuals are integrated; on the contrary, it proves its worth by occurring outside of, and often in opposition to, those structures.[7]

An attempt to interpret love as exclusively an event between two individuals, however, has its own considerable difficulties. They become apparent as soon as we ask ourselves why we turn towards the other. The command to love 'our neighbour' obviously refers to a plurality of people, albeit to one particular individual at a time. If, however, its justification lies exclusively in the individual, it is hard to see how the commandment can, at the same time, have universal validity. Less abstractly, does not 'love' towards another person even if (perhaps especially if) that other person is a stranger to us, always presuppose the identification of that individual with something else? Do we not, in order to love our neighbour, see her as something we know? We might, for example, recognize her as a human being – in this sense Immanuel Kant spoke of the *humanity* we must always respect in

---

7. Cf. Anders Nygren, *Agape and Eros: The Christian Idea of Love*, trans. P. S. Watson (Chicago: University of Chicago Press, 1982). Cf. the critique by Werner G. Jeanrond, *A Theology of Love* (London: Continuum/T&T Clark, 2010), pp. 105–34.

the person of the other.⁸ For him, it is ultimately this *humanity* that guarantees the dignity (not, of course, love) every empirical and individual person is owed.

Yet if this is so, we seem to be faced with just another variant of the theory according to which the ultimate object of love is not the individual. In its place something else, something more universal is loved which, however, in the present case is an abstract idea rather than a concrete community. We perceive in the other a universal property that marks her out as, for example, a 'neighbour' or a human being, and it is this property, not the individual *per se*, that is the object of love strictly speaking.

We thus seem to be faced with a real dilemma. On the one hand, there are good reasons to reconstruct Christian love as an interaction between individuals and be – at least – sceptical towards its application to collective bodies. Yet the reconstruction of love between individuals seems to necessitate, in various forms and under various guises, the introduction of those very entities be it as communities or societies or as abstract cultural or anthropological universals. It appears that love must always be directed at those universals first in order to be applied subsequently to individual persons.

A construct that has often been used to avoid this dilemma is the collective personality. Put simply, the idea is that a collective unit is thought as represented by one individual. One of the most famous and influential examples is the theory of the monarchy which has found a particularly apt illustration in the book cover of Thomas Hobbes' *Leviathan*, 'perhaps the most famous visual image in the history of political philosophy'.⁹ The king is here shown with a body made up of the people: he is therefore both one and many, and the political affections directed at the monarch can consequently be both personal and collective.

Not without a reason, however, did Ernst Kantorowicz give to his classical study of this idea, *The King's Two Bodies*, the subtitle *A Study in Medieval Political Theology*.¹⁰ For behind the political use of the collective personality stands undoubtedly the analogous christological idea according to which Jesus Christ's humanity has a universal dimension that extends beyond his historical individuality. Such a theory is suggested by biblical passages that speak of the church as the body of Christ (1 Cor. 12.12) but also by the mythical identification of Christ as the 'second Adam' (Rom. 5.12-21 and 1 Cor. 15.22). Equally significant, albeit on a subtler level, is the identification found throughout the New Testament, of Jesus with the suffering servant of Isa. 53 who in his turn appears to have been a personification of the people of Israel.¹¹

---

8. Immanuel Kant, *Grounding for the Metaphysics of Morals*, trans. J. W. Ellington (Indianapolis: Hacket, 1993), p. 36.

9. Thomas Hobbes, *Leviathan*, The Clarendon Edition of the Works of Thomas Hobbes, vol. 1, ed. Noel Malcom (Oxford: Oxford University Press, 2012), pp. 128–41 (128).

10. Ernst Kantorowicz, *The King's Two Bodies: A Study in Medieval Political Theology* (Princeton: Princeton University Press, 1957).

11. Charles F. D. Moule, *The Origins of Christology* (Cambridge: Cambridge University

Thomas Hobbes' Leviathan

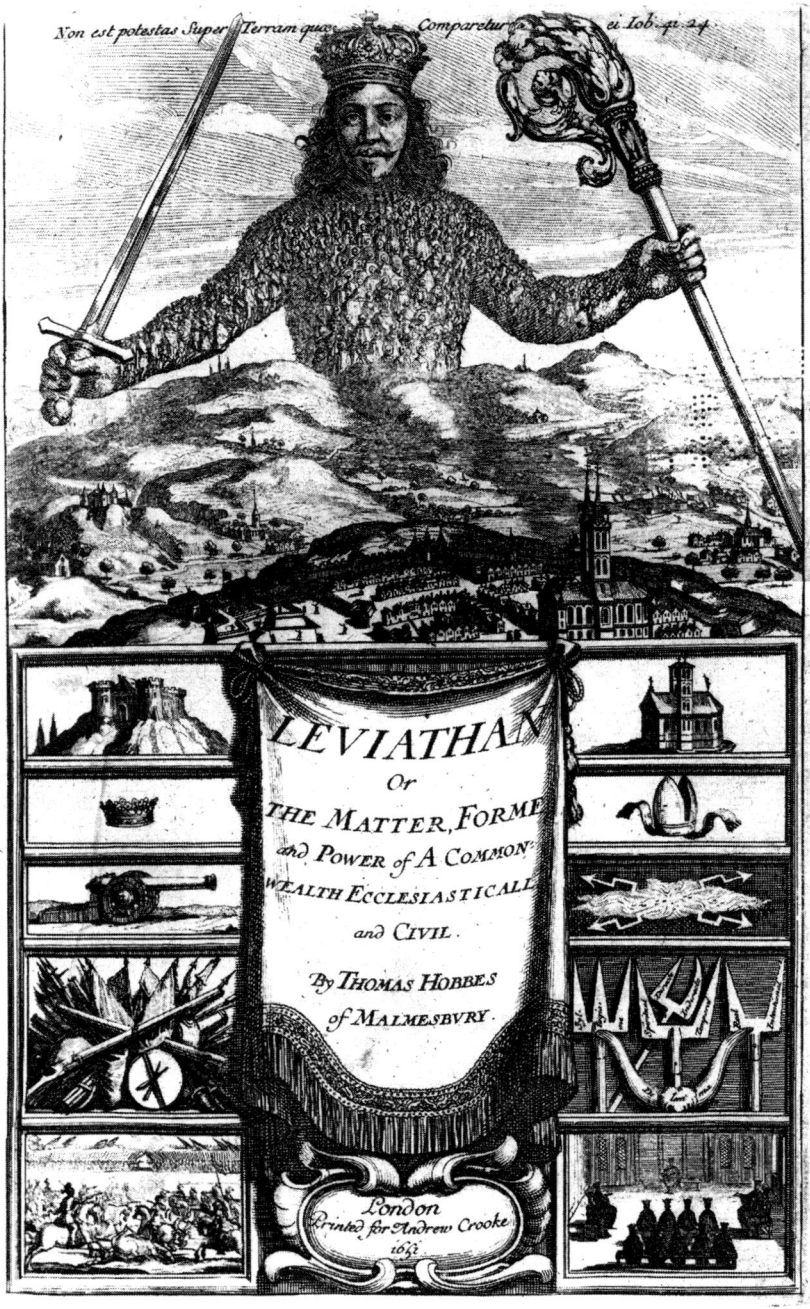

Frontispiece by Abraham Bosse, with creative input from Hobbes, 1651

To gain an impression of the immense historical and systematic significance this corporate interpretation of Christ's humanity has had, it is still advisable to consult August Dorner's comprehensive history of christology, *History of the Development of the Doctrine of the Person of Christ*,[12] whose primary purpose was the reconstruction of the 1800-year long history of this particular element of christological doctrine culminating in his own theory, inspired by Friedrich D. E. Schleiermacher, of Jesus as the 'central individual' (*Zentralindividuum*) which reveals the whole of humanity in one individual.[13]

Dorner was certainly not blind to the ambiguities, dangers even, that lie in a collective interpretation of Christ's humanity. On the contrary, his historical analysis specifically emphasized the many problems and pitfalls this notion had caused for christology in the course of its history. He keenly perceived, in particular, the tendency to lose sight of Jesus' historical individuality in consequence of the affirmation of his human universality. This awareness should not surprise us. Dorner's own work in its immense erudition was ultimately a response to the christology sketched in the final chapter of David Strauss' *The Life of Jesus*, first published in 1835 and one of the most influential theological (and religious) books of the time.[14] Strauss' characteristically bold and radical solution to the age-old problem stipulated an identification of Christ's humanity and the ever-progressing human race in its entirety; its narration in the gospel, he argued, had merely been the mythical expression of a universal truth in a particular history about a single person.[15] It was for this reason that Dorner, in his turn, went out of his way to stress both parts of the word 'central individual': according to him, the universal dimension of Christ's humanity must not on any account lead to annihilation of his concrete historical individuality.

The relationship between the problem of Christ's humanity and the commandment to love comes into view once we recall that, according to the Gospel, it is Christ himself whom we encounter in our neighbour (Mt. 25.40-45). This line of thought – a christological interpretation of neighbourly love – was pursued in twentieth-century theology especially by Dietrich Bonhoeffer. In *Life Together* he formulated that 'a Christian comes to others only through Jesus Christ'.[16] For Bonhoeffer, this mediating position of the redeemer is necessary in order to neutralize the 'natural' forces of social attraction that connect us with people who come from the same or a similar background, who have interests, hold

Press, 1977), pp. 47–54.

12. Isaak A. Dorner, *The History of the Development of the Doctrine of the Person of Christ*, trans. D. W. Simon (Edinburgh: T&T Clark, 1890–2).

13. Cf. Thomas Koppehl, *Der wissenschaftliche Standpunkt der Theologie Isaak August Dorners* (Berlin: De Gruyter, 1997), pp. 21–134.

14. David F. Strauss, *The Life of Jesus Critically Examined*, trans. G. Eliot, 2 vols (New York: Calvin Blanchard, 1860).

15. Ibid., vol. 2, pp. 895–7.

16. Dietrich Bonhoeffer, *Life Together: Prayerbook of the Bible*, trans. D. W. Bloesch and J. H. Burtness (Minneapolis: Fortress Press, 1996), p. 32.

positions or engage in activities similar to our own. Our neighbour, Bonhoeffer urges, is not a 'friend', someone with whom we are inclined to be together, to whom we are attracted or whose company we *prima facie* enjoy. Therefore, only Jesus Christ himself could constitute the bond that connects us with her.

An analogous argument was already proffered by Bonhoeffer in his first published book, *Sanctorum Communio*, which was at the same time his doctoral dissertation. In this writing, he introduced the term 'collective person' (*Kollektivperson*) to describe the character of the community founded by the Holy Spirit: 'Neither unanimity, uniformity, nor congeniality makes it possible, nor is it to be confused with the unity of mood'.[17] On the contrary, Bonhoeffer suggests, the community of the church is characterized by its refusal to abolish or even reduce the multifariousness and the heterogeneity of the individual persons who are its parts: 'the contrasts remain, they even become more acute; in the community all are led to carry their individual viewpoint to the limit, to be really serious about it. ... But – to put it paradoxically – the more powerfully the dissimilarities manifest themselves, the stronger the objective unity'.[18]

While it has to be admitted that in both passages Bonhoeffer's immediate interest concerns the unity of the Christian community, his line of argument nevertheless is of great significance. For it is apparent that Bonhoeffer regarded the collective person that is constituted by Jesus Christ or the Holy Spirit (in this the two writings differ) as an alternative beyond the dilemma we encountered at several stages, between purely individualistic and collective-universal interpretations of Christian love. He sharply rejected the 'idealist tradition' which, he alleged, lacked an adequate concept of the human person and for that reason remained forever trapped in the aporetic duality of individuality and universality.

Applied to our own question, Bonhoeffer's thesis can then be reformulated as follows: the concept of the collective person permits the perception of the individual *as* individual because it is precisely in the affirmation of the unlimited multiplicity and diversity of individual persons that Christ's unifying presence can be perceived.

Bonhoeffer's considerations are of particular importance because of the link he established between the idea of love and christology. The Christian understanding of love cannot be articulated without raising at the same time the question (famously asked by Bonhoeffer himself): Who is Jesus Christ for us today?

This link can, however, only furnish us with the solution to our problem if we can make sure that under the guise of christology the very same problems do not recur that have so far plagued our investigation. This can easily happen if we fail to find a way beyond the alternative between a purely individualistic interpretation of Christ's humanity – in which case his connection with our humanity becomes impossible to explain – and a collective interpretation which, whether conceived

---

17. Dietrich Bonhoeffer, *Sanctorum Communio: A Theological Study of the Sociology of the Church*, trans. J. von Soosten and R. Kraus (Minneapolis: Fortress Press, 2009), pp. 192–208 (192).

18. Ibid.

as an abstract universal or a concrete community, directs our attention away from his unique individuality as a historical person.

At this point, it appears that at least the early Bonhoeffer, whom I have so far used, is not as helpful as we would wish. For his emphatic rejection of the 'abstract' universality championed by the Enlightenment and Idealism together with his adoption of the 'collective person' demonstrates that, in spite of his rhetorical affirmation of the person, he, overall at this stage of his career, tended to prioritize the community over the individual. But if the Church, for example, is a collective person, why then should not one actual person represent it in its entirety? This, obviously, is the role of the Petrine office in Roman Catholicism and, more generally, that of the episcopal office in various historical and contemporary forms of the monarchical episcopacy. If there is any good theological (as opposed to practical or pragmatic) reason for rejecting this ecclesiological model, it surely must be the insight that the kind of unity the presence of Christ provides for the Church is *radically* different from the form that is symbolized by the collective person.

One way of describing this difference may be to point to the ambiguous, indeed nearly precarious, character of Christ's presence since his resurrection which is reflected in the experience of the early church, notably in the biblical Easter stories. His presence can therefore only ever be proclaimed by accepting concurrently that he may encounter us in ways and forms that are unexpected, surprising and often not fully understood.

To this corresponds the observation that the perception of the other as our 'neighbour', which precedes the act of neighbourly love, relies not least on the willingness to see the other as *other* and thus essentially as mysterious and never fully known or reducible to clichés and categories. The other can only encounter us as other if we do not reduce her to that which is familiar and already understood. The demand to see Christ in the other is not, therefore, yet another version of the substitution of the 'neighbour' by something else (in this case Jesus Christ) but the insight that a conscious renunciation of our knowledge and our judgements, which inevitably turn the other into a part of ourselves, is a precondition for the true encounter with, and thus also for the love of, the neighbour.

Considered in this way, the love of neighbour admittedly becomes very nearly something impossible: no wonder, we may think, that Jesus called this the 'greatest' commandment. Yet this realization too is wholesome because it helps us to see that Jesus Christ has his role to play on the side of the loving subject as well. Without wishing to give unqualified endorsement to Augustine's oft-maligned exegesis, according to which the Samaritan in Luke 10 *was* Jesus,[19] it is indeed crucial not to detach the practice of neighbourly love from the continuing presence of Jesus in our own world. In fact, it may well be the case that this practice, where it prevails, provides the strongest grounds for this very belief.

---

19. Augustine, *Quaestiones Evangeliorum*, II 19. Cf. Charles H. Dodd, *The Parables of the Kingdom* (London: Nisbet, 1961), pp. 1–2.

Both subject and object of Christian love, then, are individual persons. Attempts to deny or dilute this insight must be resisted; it is perhaps not out of place to recognize at this point the pivotal contribution Werner G. Jeanrond has made to this important task of contemporary theology.[20] In order to explain the possibility of this kind of agency, however, it is advisable for theology to argue christologically. The major challenge for such a christological reconstruction, for which only some first ideas could be developed in my contribution, consists in the need to hold together the dualities of presence and absence, of individuality and universality, of familiarity and unfamiliarity and to explore their unity as well as their tensions.

---

20. Cf. Werner G. Jeanrond, *A Theology of Love*, p. 166.

22

GEGENÜBER REVISITED: 'THIRDING-AS-OTHERING' IN KARL BARTH'S CONCEPT OF SPACE

Kjetil Hafstad

The spatial turn in philosophy and theology has many faces. One of the important actors of this scene is Edward W. Soja. He introduces his project 'Thirdspace' by questioning familiar ways of thinking of space and spatiality, aiming at 'expanding the scope and ... sensibility of your already established spatial or geographical imaginations'.[1] He assumes that we are always active in the social construction of our embracing spatialities. The knowledge of these processes of construction, however, is lacking. He, therefore, argues for a 'strategic awareness of this collectively created spatiality and its social consequences' in order to make 'both theoretical and practical sense of our contemporary lifeworlds at all scales'.[2] Learning from the profound critical efforts of postmodernity over against 'master narratives', Soja explores what he calls the 'worlds of Thirdspace'.[3]

> Thirdspace itself ... is rooted in ... a recombinational and radically open perspective. In what I will call a critical strategy of 'thirding-as-Othering', I try to open up our spatial imaginaries to ways of thinking and acting politically that responds to all binarisms, to any attempt to confine thought and political action to only two alternatives, by interjecting an-Other set of choices.[4]

Soja is following Henri Lefebvre who insisted on the anti-reductionist phrase: *il y a toujours l'Autre*. However, he continues: 'I have used another term, "trialectics", to describe not just a triple dialectic but also a mode of dialectic reasoning that is more inherently spatial than the traditional temporally-defined dialectics'.[5] I find

---

1. Edward W. Soja, *Thirdspace: Journeys to Los Angeles and Other Real-and-Imagined Places* (Oxford: Blackwell, 1996), p. 1.
2. Ibid.
3. Ibid., p. 3.
4. Ibid., p. 5.
5. Ibid., p. 10.

it fruitful to consider Soja's account of our lifeworlds. Since Peter L. Berger and Thomas Luckmann presented their views on the social construction of reality,[6] including religion, *understanding religion in space* has been an attractive task to investigate. Soja refines the tools to fulfil this task.

In theology, however, space has not been central: we are more familiar with the temporal and the historical. Theology (and Christianity), therefore, stumbled around the concepts of story, history and time.[7] Only recently, scholars have wondered why *space* has played an almost anonymous role in theology. Have theologians not been aware of the fact that we are spatial creatures? Famously, theology has misunderstood space when the natural sciences made their first beginnings, from the violent rejection of Galileo Galilei's heliocentrism by the Inquisition to Martin Luther's contemptuous statement that everyone can see with her or his own eyes that the earth is flat. To date, theology has rarely participated in the evolving understanding of space and spatiality.

I will modestly enter the discussion by exploring the concept of space in Karl Barth's *Church Dogmatics*. There are some features in Barth's theology which invite comparison with Soja's conception of space. The peculiar problems theology meets when Christ is dogmatically understood as simultaneously divine and human, have mostly been 'solved' in the way Thomas Aquinas suggested: by constructing two separate spaces, one world and one 'over-world'. However, we cannot continue with these 'solutions'. If theology cannot make sense in one shared space, it cannot make sense at all. In what follows, I will share a sketch of my reconstruction of Barth's concept of space. The reconstruction is similar to those we find in the spatial turn. Simultaneously, the *Church Dogmatics* contributes to the respect for the otherness of the other. Here we might detect a critical openness in the inquiry which corresponds to the postmodern thinking we find in both Lefebvre's and Soja's work. In *Wort und Geschichte*, I described the multiple relations in which Barth uses the concept of *Gegenüber* (which translates as 'opposite' or – strictly speaking – '*vis-à-vis*') in order to raise the question as to whether this *Gegenüber* can be taken as Barth's concept of space.[8] If space is conceived of as relationally and socially constructed out of what is actually happening, we meet a very dynamic conception of space. I will present some clues to such a concept of space before I explore whether these findings might relate to the discussions opened by thinkers of the spatial turn, such as Soja.[9]

---

6. Cf. Peter L. Berger and Thomas Luckmann, *The Social Construction of Reality: A Treatise in the Sociology of Knowledge* (London: Penguin, 1991).

7. Cf. Aleida Assmann, *Erinnerungsräume: Formen und Wandlungen des kulturellen Gedächtnisses* (München: C. H. Beck, 1999), p. 19.

8. Cf. Kjetil Hafstad, *Wort und Geschichte*, trans. D. Habsmeier (München: Christoph Kaiser Verlag, 1985). In my contribution, I am referring to the unpublished 1985 English translation. I would like to thank David Lewis, the translator, based at the World Council of Churches in Geneva.

9. My attempt is of course a message to my friend Werner G. Jeanrond to express my

According to Barth, the projection of a worldview of Christianity – a cosmology which could be separated from revelation – is impossible. The reason why theology must accept such a limitation is to be found in the fact that the object of theology is the *Word of God*. The Word speaks of God's relation to humanity. Hence, theology is capable of projecting the ontology of humanity but not the ontology of creation in abstraction from the humanity which is defined by the relationship to God.[10]

Barth nevertheless presupposes a theological understanding of space when he speaks of the ontology of a humanity which is living 'under heaven on the earth'. To this extent it could be said that Barth interprets cosmology in the light of anthropology. He explains that 'in practice the doctrine of creation means anthropology'.[11] The explanation must be taken to mean that the doctrine of creation is defined by God's relationship to humanity.

The cosmos is the prerequisite for human life; it surrounds humanity. Yet, how does Barth interpret the non-human creation which forms and informs humanity's environment? In his analysis of Genesis, he asserts that all elements of creation came into being with humanity in view. Creation is a stage for what God has in store for humanity.[12] Consequently, God assigns humanity the lordship over it.[13] Humanity is 'the focal point' in the created world.[14] Accordingly, the environment is *relatively* necessary – unlike humanity which is *absolutely* necessary – to God's project. Barth's point is not that the environment is not absolutely necessary for the life of humanity on earth, but it is to emphasize the difference in significance which exists in relation to God's purpose for creation. Against such a background, humanity's living space has been created in view of God's relationship to humanity.[15] Humanity is positioned in the centre of the cosmos, because humanity is the representative of the mystery of the cosmos. The position of humanity is still further emphasized and enhanced by the fact that humanity knows of this mystery. Barth widens the perspective on individual human life by affirming that this course of events in a life points backwards and forwards – not only in the history of the individual human being but also in the history of the whole creation. Barth thus gives in his doctrine of providence a basis for the assertion that anthropology is the horizon within which the whole cosmos is to be understood. The cosmos was created as counterpart to humanity.[16]

deep respect for his academic work.

10. Cf. Karl Barth, *Kirchliche Dogmatik* (München: Christoph Kaiser Verlag, 1932–67), vol. III/2, pp. 4–5. Also cf. the English translation, *Church Dogmatics*, trans. G. W. Bromiley (Edinburgh: T&T Clark, 1936–77), vol. III/2, p. 6.

11. Ibid., p. 2 (ET, p. 3).

12. Cf. Karl Barth, *Kirchliche Dogmatik*, vol. III/1, p. 234 (ET, pp. 207–8).

13. Cf. ibid., p. 210 (ET, pp. 187–8).

14. Ibid., p. 440 (ET, pp. 383–4).

15. Cf. ibid., pp. 175–6 (ET, pp. 156–7). Cf. Kjetil Hafstad, *Wort und Geschichte*, pp. 230–1.

16. Cf. ibid., p. 231.

The sketch of Barth's doctrine of providence provides a starting point to guide us in our discussion of Barth's view of space. As a formal structure for events in the cosmos, space can only be considered in connection with these events. Space as structure cannot be understood in isolation from the function it has in the history of God's election.[17] The dimension of space has a function which corresponds to the sequences of events outside the history of the covenant. These events, too, are a framework for the covenant history. Hence, it is easy to see why Barth does not offer a separate and special treatment of the dimension of space. He deals most fully with space when he discusses cosmos as consisting of both heaven and earth. But it would be artificial to begin our account of Barth's view of space here. Since space is to be understood as defined by the central event in space, the Christ event, this event is the accurate starting point. Afterwards, we can ask whether the 'space' presupposed in this event is defined in the same way as the 'space' which Barth describes in his treatment of the theme of 'heaven and earth'.

The concept we have selected for our discussion is 'opposite' (*Gegenüber*). Admittedly, it is not obvious that this term reflects Barth's view of space. He himself does not develop and define his concept of space explicitly. The term 'opposite' does nevertheless express the basic structure of the central event which is decisive for all of Barth's conclusions. God is opposite humanity and humanity is opposite God. They confront each other 'face to face' in Jesus Christ. Our choice of 'opposite' is also justified by the frequent use Barth makes of it.[18]

As creator, God himself lives in a *vis-à-vis* relationship. In the created world, this *vis-à-vis* relationship is reflected in God's existence or coexistence with humanity. The creation is the external basis which allows humanity to coexist with God in Jesus Christ. The external basis was formed to make it possible for humanity to be the image of God's own being – for humanity to have the possibility and the reality of living in a *vis-à-vis* relationship. Now we suggest that this relationship is the dimension of space in Barth's conception. The rest of the created world does not automatically constitute the space which allows for such coexistence. Because humanity was created in the image of God *vis-à-vis* the non-human creation, the non-human creation can be defined as humanity's co-creature. These other creatures, however, are *not* the *vis-à-vis* which defines humanity's 'biosphere', the space in which humanity lives. This function is God's alone. When God confronts humanity, when he creates humanity as his *vis-à-vis*, he gives humanity an external form in space. Hence, it is through humanity that the rest of the created world has its image character, its *vis-à-vis* relation to God.[19] That the creature is in harmony with God's being can only become known through humanity. Apart from this relationship, the creature's relationship to God would only be one of difference from God; the creature would not be involved via humanity in a relationship in which God confronts the other who is in correspondence with his own being. There would be no analogy between creator and

---

17. Cf. ibid., p. 232.
18. Cf. ibid., pp. 232–3.
19. Cf. Karl Barth, *Kirchliche Dogmatik*, vol. III/1, p. 206 (ET, pp. 184–5).

creature.[20] Rather, God permits humanity to repeat *vis-à-vis* the fellow human being the covenant which God has established with it. The framework of human life (God and humanity facing one another) cannot be separated from the goal of this *vis-à-vis* relationship (existence in partnership).[21]

If we wish to examine the role of Jesus Christ in the various *vis-à-vis* relationships, it seems reasonable to examine a section of the *Church Dogmatics* in which Barth deals with the activity of Jesus in connection with the dimension of space: 'The Way of the Son of God into the Far Country'.[22] By connecting 'the Son' with 'the far Country', Barth links up not only with Jesus' inner-Trinitarian role, but also with his human activity. In this context, Barth examines the obedience of Jesus to the will of God. Through Jesus' obedience, God takes his way into the far country, into the created world which is distinct from him. But this journey into the far country is the inner basis for God's having fashioned a created world *vis-à-vis* himself.[23]

What about the non-human nature in Barth's concept of space? It starts – as usual with Barth – negatively: the meaning of the fact that the non-human creation acquires its definition *vis-à-vis* God is concealed from humanity. This distinguishes humanity from the rest of the creation. What it means to be human is revealed when, in Jesus Christ, humanity is confronted by God. But we cannot say how the rest of creation is confronted with God in Jesus Christ. Nor can we say, therefore, that the '*vis-à-vis*' relationship revealed in Jesus Christ has an analogy in the relationship between human and non-human animals. There is certainly no question here of an 'I-Thou' relationship.[24] Barth thus builds a sharp boundary around the knowledge accessible to theology. Apart from the sheer fact that the rest of creation has God as its *vis-à-vis*, it is impossible for us to know its real nature.

Barth is able to proceed analogously when he asks whether God speaks directly to animals. His answer is affirmative, but God's speech has different consequences for animals. Here, Barth goes more into detail as to wherein the difference lies. For he says in creation, God spoke directly to the animals. The effect of this was that animals were created. Yet, they are not summoned to make a decision *vis-à-vis* God.[25] Strictly speaking, however, this more detailed description from start to finish derives from Barth's view of the existence of humanity. What he says of the animals is no more than an underlining of the difference between animality and humanity.[26] Barth certainly does not equate this '*vis-à-vis*' with the cosmos, with created space. On the other hand, the word 'cosmos' itself is far too narrow to define the space referred to in Barth's construction. His concern is to identify

20. Cf. ibid.
21. Cf. ibid.
22. Cf. Karl Barth, *Kirchliche Dogmatik*, vol. IV/1.
23. Cf. Kjetil Hafstad, *Wort und Geschichte*, p. 236.
24. Cf. ibid., p. 241.
25. Cf. Karl Barth, *Kirchliche Dogmatik*, vol. III/1, p. 195 (ET, pp. 174–5).
26. Cf. Kjetil Hafstad, *Wort und Geschichte*, p. 241.

the connection and distinction in the existence of God and humanity. To describe it, the cosmos, too, must possess the form of an analogy corresponding to God's existence. The term '*vis-à-vis*', therefore, also acquires significance for Barth's conception of the cosmos. Consequently, we must examine how Barth develops the connection between the cosmos and the '*vis-à-vis*'.[27]

At *one* point in his description of the '*vis-à-vis*', Barth refers explicitly to the concept of space. The reference is made when he describes the created cosmos as consisting of 'heaven and earth'.[28] Heaven and earth were created as an analogy to the dialectic between God and humanity and defined by this analogy. The *vis-à-vis* relationship between God and humanity, which was revealed in the man Jesus, was given a concrete spatial form. It is thought of as a *vis-à-vis*, an opposition in space. And the space is structured, in analogy to the order in the God-humanity dialectic, by an 'above' and a 'below', by heaven and earth.[29]

What is crucial in Barth's account is that he regards space as a parable of the course of events which take place within space. In a definitively established cosmology – from which Barth, as mentioned above, dissociates himself – this 'synopsis' of form and content would be impossible. What Barth says is that created space consists of a *vis-à-vis* relationship whose structural components, heaven and earth, have been defined by the course of events between God and humanity in space.[30] What prevents the two parts from falling apart into separate unrelated spaces is the course of events, the covenant between God and humanity. The covenant made and maintained by God constitutes the cosmos, the unity of space.[31] Barth conceives of space as a *vis-à-vis* relationship. What space really is, however, can only be known when God reveals it by speaking in space – speaking, indeed, to humanity. From the standpoint available to it – which is to say, from earth – humanity is unable to know the structure of space.[32]

In viewing heaven in a dialectical *vis-à-vis* relationship to earth, Barth does not in fact bring two 'spaces' into mutual confrontation. Rather, heaven belongs to the sphere of humanity for Barth. The point of the dialectic does not consist in the division of space but in giving humanity a double determination whereby it lives 'on earth under heaven'. This space then has the function of structuring humanity's relationship to the reality which humanity itself cannot understand – to the reality of God, represented by the 'above' which is heaven. This space orders the existence of humanity *vis-à-vis* everything on earth which lies outside the individual human existence. The *vis-à-vis* dimension explains the characteristic of humanity's conditions of existence. It shows 'from whence' humanity is defined: *vis-à-vis* God. It also shows the way in which humanity's existence is developed:

27. Cf. ibid., p. 242.
28. Cf. Karl Barth, *Kirchliche Dogmatik*, vol. III/3, pp. 486–558 (ET, pp. 418–76).
29. Cf. ibid., p. 486 (ET, p. 417).
30. Cf. ibid., p. 489 (ET, p. 420).
31. Cf. Karl Barth, *Kirchliche Dogmatik*, vol. III/2, p. 11 (ET, p. 11).
32. Cf. Kjetil Hafstad, *Wort und Geschichte*, p. 248.

vis-à-vis fellow human beings, but not in isolation from the non-human creation. The double determination, however, belongs to the same space. [33]

Ultimately, the relationship between the view of space at which we can arrive by natural science and that with which theology must work, according to Barth, can be summarized following Dietrich Bonhoeffer: 'The God who lets us live in the world without the working hypothesis of God is the God before whom we continually stand'.[34] In Bonhoeffer's case, this dictum remained the statement of a programme. Barth's account of the relation of theology to natural science might enable us to give this programme concrete content. It is possible that this content – already discussed above – is not all that far from what Bonhoeffer had in mind.[35]

However, I will expand my reconstruction of Barth's concept of space in order to understand the non-imperialistic way in which Barth describes non-human nature. Creation has its own lights from its creator. Because of his decision to unfold the history of his grace, creation and reconciliation are bound together. Yet if we start from this connection between creation and the goal of creation, it becomes possible to speak of the creation's own distinctive lights – indeed, it becomes possible to refer to such 'dangerous modern expressions' as 'revelation in creation'.[36]

Barth employs the term 'creature' in two senses: it denotes the whole of creation on the one hand, and it denotes a part of the creation on the other – a part which is the object of God's election: humanity. The shifting use of the term 'creature' can suggest that the cosmos has no significance in Barth's theology. It is humanity which has been chosen as God's partner. However, such a choice does not imply any disdain for nature. The humanity chosen as God's partner is chosen *because* it is a part of the natural and animal world.[37] The fact that the natural and animal world is not chosen to be God's partner in the same way confers an inherent value onto the natural and animal world which humanity does not possess. Hence, we might conclude that the natural and animal world is a more direct expression of God's creating Word than the human world. Barth appeals here to John Calvin. Humanity achieves its divine purpose by engaging in the partnership which God has made possible. The animal and the natural world, on the contrary, *act directly* in the way God designed them.[38] Simply by being what they are, they express God's Word. Correspondingly, Barth develops the thought that when humanity fails to fulfil its destiny it does not merely sink to the level of the 'beast' but falls below the 'beast'.[39] Barth stresses the difference between humanity and the natural

---

33. Cf. ibid., p. 251.

34. Cf. *Letters and Papers from Prison*, trans. R. Fuller (New York: Macmillan, 1967), p. 188.

35. Cf. Kjetil Hafstad, *Wort und Geschichte*, p. 257.

36. Karl Barth, *Kirchliche Dogmatik*, vol. IV/3, p. 158 (ET, p. 139). Cf. Kjetil Hafstad, *Wort und Geschichte*, p. 109.

37. Cf. Karl Barth, *Kirchliche Dogmatik*, vol. III/1, p. 175 (ET, p. 156).

38. Cf. Karl Barth, *Kirchliche Dogmatik*, vol. IV/4, p. 189 (ET, p. 116).

39. Cf. Karl Barth, *Kirchliche Dogmatik*, vol. III/2, p. 219 (ET, pp. 183–4).

and animal world, but in such a way that humanity is chosen precisely in the context in which it is placed. Humanity's knowledge of nature is only indirect. It is humanity's lot to view nature with human eyes. Humanity is not entitled, therefore, to disparage nature. For, since humanity is what it is on the basis of God's election, the possibility must remain open that God is pursuing a purpose of which humanity is ignorant. God can have a history of his own with the natural and the animal world, one known to humanity only indirectly, through its own election. Accordingly, in nature there is an air of mystery, because humanity is unable to see the rest of nature with nature's 'eyes'. Consequently, for Barth, reverence is due to nature.[40]

Evidently, Barth was – like any author – confined to the scientific discussion in his own generation. But he was struggling with these confines. It is the struggle which makes it worthwhile to analyse not only the centre of his work, but also the margins. I showed that Barth had a very open attitude to space, contrary to what often is associated with his thinking. I will conclude with three points. First, Barth deconstructs 'space' as something unambiguous. He opens the concept of space beyond what is observable. Second, Barth grapples with the question of space, concentrating on what actually is going on *in* space. Hence, one could refer to him in the analysis of the 'production of space'. He does not distinguish sharply between physical and non-physical (imagined) space – these are not his categories. Rather, he questions the dominant rule of 'physical space' which has been exposed by the thinkers of the spatial turn. Consequently, Barth opens the concept of space for the dimensions of imagination and action. Third, compared to the dogmatic discussion he refers to, Barth conceives of nature as 'outside' of humanity with an uncommon and unprecedented respect. He explores the natural and the animal world with curiosity to pose a theologically vital proposition: God may have direct as opposed to indirect contact with the non-human creation. Hence, human beings should meet non-human beings with respect, with non-assertive statements. In a time when ecological concerns are stirring controversy, such a humble attitude may become more and more fruitful.

Finally, in view of Soja's concept of Thirdspace, Barth's theology might be intriguing and instructive. Soja critiques 'closures and all "permanent constructions"'.[41] He discusses the contributions of bell hooks, underlining how she chose 'marginality as a space of radical openness'.[42] This preoccupation with 'thirding' – trialectis as opposed to dialectics – is in my view confluent with Barth's curious exploration of nature. In addition to God's covenant with humanity, the non-human nature has a third relationship to God. The openness we meet in Barth's interpretation of space can be useful in our discussion of ecology. What we get out of the comparison with Soja's interpretation are not clear-cut answers to the question of how significant concepts like *Gegenüber* or Thirdspace may be. (Both may be very significant indeed.) What makes these authors important

---

40. Cf. ibid., pp. 90–1 (ET, pp. 77–8). Cf. Kjetil Hafstad, *Wort und Geschichte*, pp. 125–6.
41. Edward Soja, *Thirdspace*, p. 61.
42. Ibid., p. 99.

is their unrelenting will to start afresh, not to take any state of the art as the allegedly factual basis of action and reflection. Rather they recognize and respect the otherness of the other which is why they are open to accept their own misunderstandings and misconceptions. Soja summarizes such openness when he describes Michel Foucault's lecture *Des Espaces autres* from 1967.

> Foucault's heterotopologies are frustratingly incomplete, inconsistent, incoherent. They seem narrowly focused on peculiar micrographies, near-sighted and near-sited, deviant and deviously apolitical. Yet they are also the marvellous incunibula of another fruitful journey into Thirdspace, into the spaces that difference makes, into the geohistory of otherness… They are also 'other than' the established ways of thinking spatially.[43]

Barth worked along similar strands, never taking his own results for granted, opening spaces of curiosity, meeting the surprising other.

---

43. Ibid., pp. 162–3.

Part IV

RELIGIOUS OTHERS AND OTHER RELIGIONS

23

EMPATHY AND OTHERNESS IN INTERRELIGIOUS DIALOGUE

Catherine Cornille

Among the many conditions for effective interreligious dialogue, empathy represents the most elusive, but no less essential requirement. In *The Im-Possibility of Interreligious Dialogue*, I discussed the particular function of empathy, its grounds and limits in the process of understanding and learning from other religions.[1] If dialogue is also seen to include the possibility of change and growth through encounter with the religious other, then the possibility of not only grasping intellectually but also resonating experientially with certain teachings and practices becomes particularly important.

However, the term 'empathy' has a chequered history and epistemological status in interreligious hermeneutics. While originally hailed as the means to understand other people's minds, empathy came to be regarded as a particularly unverifiable form of interpersonal and intercultural understanding and therefore left behind as a product of the bygone days of romantic hermeneutics. Of late, empathy has re-emerged as an analytical category in philosophy, grounding its possibility in the existence of so-called 'mirror neurons'.[2] The term empathy has been variously defined as 'the experience of foreign consciousness' (Edith Stein), 'transposition' into the mental lives of others (Wilhelm Dilthey), 'the attempt by one self-aware self to comprehend non-judgementally the positive and negative experiences of another self' (Lauren Wispé), the 'vicariously sharing of an affect' (Nancy Eisenberg and Janet Strayer), as a 'psychological process that makes a person have feelings that are more congruent with another person's situation than with his own situation' (Martin L. Hoffman) or as a form of 'inner or mental imitation for the purpose of gaining knowledge of other minds' (Karsten Stueber). While some definitions focus on the affective dimension of empathy, others emphasize its cognitive nature. The multiplicity of meanings and approaches has

---

1. Catherine Corinille, *The Im-Possibility of Interreligious Dialogue* (New York: Continuum, 2008).

2. See for example the work of Karsten Stueber, *Rediscovering Empathy: Agency, Folk Psychology and the Human Sciences* (Cambridge, MA: MIT Press, 2006).

led to a continuing reticence about using empathy in the process of interreligious understanding.

In his 2010 article 'Towards an Interreligious Hermeneutics of Love', Werner G. Jeanrond, for example, dismisses empathy as a 'mere attitude' of a person toward another person or tradition, suggesting instead a 'critical hermeneutics of love' which involves 'a mutual, though not necessarily symmetrical, relationship with other persons in which some form of union is desired without for that matter diminishing difference'.[3]

One of Jeanrond's concerns is to maintain a sense of difference, without falling into an ideology of radical difference often used in identity politics to exclude or vilify the other and affirm one's own uniqueness. 'When searching for a concept of praxis that would allow both for the disclosure of truth and for a genuine approach to difference,' he states, 'I cannot think of any better concept than love. For in love the emergence of a new body of truth and the recognition of difference go hand in hand'.[4]

A danger of empathy is indeed that it risks projecting one's own inner life onto the other, thereby erasing the challenges and the possibilities of genuine otherness. However, this risk does not diminish the important role empathy plays, either consciously or unconsciously, in interreligious dialogue. Rather than ignore its vital epistemic and religious function, I would like to point to the ways in which otherness comes into play, or rather plays a constitutive role, in the process of interreligious empathy.

The Role of Empathy in Interreligious Dialogue

Interreligious dialogue is here understood as referring to the variety of ways in which individuals from different religions come to learn about and from one another. It involves thus not only an exchange of information, but also an attempt to gauge the meaning and value of the teachings and practices of another religion with an eye to enhancing one's understanding of truth and enriching one's religious life and experience. This involves various steps which each require some degree of empathy. I here understand empathy as the attempt to identify with and to grasp the affective or experiential life of the other. This thus involves both a cognitive and an experiential dimension. I herein follow Max Scheler who distinguishes sympathy as 'fellow-feeling' from empathy as 'all such attitudes as contribute to our apprehending, understanding, and in general, reproducing

---

3. Werner G. Jeanrond, 'Toward an Interreligious Hermeneutics of Love', in Catherine Cornille and Christopher Conway, eds, *Interreligious Hermeneutics* (Eugene, OR: Wipf and Stock, 2010), pp. 44–60 (52).

4. Ibid., p. 54. Jeanrond argues that love is not an exclusively Christian category and may function as a hermeneutical basis for every religion. Cf. also Werner G. Jeanrond, *A Theology of Love* (Continuum/T&T Clark, 2010) pp. 132–4 where he explores the problems of the Christianization of love in dogmatical discourses.

(emotionally) the experiences of others, including their states of feeling'.[5] I prefer to speak of 'resonating with', rather than 'imitating' or 'reproducing' the inner life of the other, so as to distinguish my own empathic understanding from the experience of the other.

The first step in interreligious dialogue involves understanding the other. This requires factual knowledge about the history of the tradition, the contents of its teachings and the practice of rituals. In-depth knowledge of the other tradition also requires study of its languages, philosophical traditions, and different sects or schools. In addition to all this, however, a fuller understanding of the other also requires some sense of, or resonance with, the experiential dimension of the religious life of the other. Experience indeed forms an essential part of religious life, and an understanding of the other thus presupposes the ability to grasp also that dimension of the other's religion. As Simone Weil puts it (using the terms sympathy and empathy interchangeably):

> The comparison of religions is only possible, in some measure, through the miraculous virtue of sympathy. We can know men to a certain extent if at the same time as we observe them from the outside we manage by sympathy to transport our own soul into theirs for a time. In the same way, the study of different religions does not lead to a real knowledge of them unless we transport ourselves for some time by faith to the very center of whichever one we are studying.[6]

Empathy thus broadens and deepens one's understanding of another religion by opening worlds of experience and ways of being religious which are not readily available to purely rational inquiry. Such transposition into the religious life of the other may occur through the imagination and/or through actual participation in the daily actions and the ritual life of the other.

Insofar as interreligious dialogue also includes the possibility of learning from the other, a second step involves reflection on the meaning and value of a particular teaching and practice for one's own religious life. Here, empathy plays an important discerning role. Only those teachings or practices which are experienced as an enrichment of one's own religious life will be more systematically pursued and appropriated. Religious teachings which leave one cold, indifferent, or which elicit aversion or contempt will of course be left alone, or may give rise to critique of the other. The inability to empathize with a particular teaching does not, in itself, form a ground for a negative judgement of the other. Such lack of empathic access may have to do with personal limitations, or with the radical otherness of the other. Whereas empathy thus cannot function as a negative norm, it does operate positively as the impetus for further exploring its compatibility with one's own tradition. It is indeed only when one is deeply touched by

---

5. Max Scheler, *The Nature of Sympathy*, trans. P. Heath (London: Routledge and Kegan Paul, 1954), p. 8.
6. Simone Weil, *Waiting for God*, trans. E. Craufurd (New York: HarperCollins, 2001), pp. 118–19.

the other that one will be inclined to carry over or rediscover that experience in one's own tradition.

The personal empathic response of a single individual will of course rarely be sufficient to generate a broad religious exploration of a particular teaching or practice in another religion. But a more general appeal of certain teachings or practices may point to a certain need or a religious lack which might then be addressed by engaging the insights of another religion. The engagement with other religious traditions moreover forms a fertile soil for new religious insights and experiences, which in some cases may ferment and enrich the tradition as a whole.

Empathy and Otherness

Though empathy thus plays an important role in interreligious dialogue, it has also been subject of considerable critique as a tool of interreligious understanding. Gavin Flood, for example, states that empathy is deeply problematic because it 'does not take account of communication and active understanding ... does not take into account the historicity of the understanding encounter, and ... cannot deal with conflict, or the other's being closed to empathic penetration'.[7] Empathy (as understood in Edmund Husserl's phenomenology) is thus seen as denying the fundamental otherness of the other religion, and the dialogical nature of understanding itself.

The singularity or uniqueness of the religious life and experience of the religious other indeed represents an important obstacle for interreligious empathy. Not only is the experiential life of the other religion constituted by a whole of teachings and practices which are often radically new or alien to the outsider, but every practice and every belief is deeply informed by an attitude of faith which by definition is not shared by a person belonging to a different religion. One may acquire advanced knowledge of the history, teachings, and practices of another religion. And one may enter by way of analogical imagination into some of the experiences of the other. But one is ultimately limited by an inability to share the concrete faith of the other, that which is arguably the most important part of the experience. As Raimon Panikkar put it: 'we cannot understand a person's ultimate convictions unless we somehow share them'.[8] This is precisely not the case for individuals belonging to different religions.

To be sure, individuals from different religious traditions are united by an experience of 'faith' in a reality or principle which transcends the purely finite and material world and which gives meaning to one's life. As such, it is undoubtedly easier for a believer than for a non-believer to empathize with the experience of

---

7. Gavin Flood, *Beyond Phenomenology: Rethinking the Study of Religion* (London: Cassell, 1999), p. 162.

8. Raimon Panikkar, *The Intra-Religious Dialogue* (Mahwah, NJ: Paulist Press, 1998), p. 34.

faith in another religion. However, it is not so much faith in the abstract, but faith in a particular object of devotion which defines the experience of a believer. Here, the faith of an outsider may at times function as an obstacle, since it may overly determine the outsider's conception of faith, or inhibit him or her from imagining any alternate object of faith or content of devotion.

Not only are there fundamental limits placed on interreligious empathy by confessional differences, but every attempt to empathize with even more accessible experiences is always coloured by one's own historical and religious location. As such, interreligious empathy is neither a projection of my experience on the other, nor a duplication of the personal experience of the other, but a dynamic interplay between the two in which a new experience may emerge. In order to emphasize this dialogical nature of understanding, Flood proposes to replace the term empathy with Mikhail Bakhtin's notion of 'live-entering' which involves 'a communicative, immediate experience involving simultaneity but also spatial distinction and the distinction of persons within the dialogical trial of "I", "other" and their relationship'.[9] Rather than abolish or replace the term, empathy may be reconceived as a dynamic and interactive process, rather than as a state, and as a means of approximating, rather than reproducing the experience of the other.

In the process of interreligious dialogue, the goal of empathy lies moreover less in faithfulness to the experience of the other than in expanding one's own religious and spiritual universe, and reflection on its relevance for one's own religious tradition. Here, the alterity of the religious other represents thus not so much an obstacle, but an opportunity. It offers the opportunity to stretch or expand one's religious imagination and attain to subtle nuances or new levels of intensity of familiar experiences, or at times maybe to new experiences. These may then possibly come to enrich one's own religious tradition.

Conditions for Empathy with Otherness

Though otherness plays an important role in the process of interreligious empathy and growth, it is not evident or assured that individuals belonging to one religion may enter empathically into teachings and practices which are different from their own. Empathy proceeds most naturally by way of familiarity. One resonates spontaneously with teachings or practices which are similar to one's own. However, this does not add much that is new and possibly enriching to one's experience and understanding. It is thus the empathic understanding of difference which is both challenging and promising.

In *The Im-Possibility of Interreligious Dialogue* I discussed three conditions or grounds for interreligious empathy: sympathy, experience, and imagination. Each of these poses little difficulty when confronted with familiar teachings and practices. The confrontation with alien views and actions requires more effort, both on the doctrinal and on the practical side. The idea of *sympathy* with beliefs

---

9. Gavin Flood, *Beyond Phenomenology*, p. 163.

which are different, and at times in conflict with one's own, requires great generosity and recognition of the possibility of finding truth well beyond the boundaries of one's own inherited tradition. For many, if not most religions, this combination of humility and generosity presupposes considerable hermeneutical effort. In addition to this institutional or doctrinal permission, sympathy also involves an attitude of personal openness and receptivity toward the potential meaningfulness and the resourcefulness of different worldviews and religious attitudes. This personal sympathy for the religious other may exist without support in religious doctrines or teachings. But for empathy with otherness to make a difference to the religion itself, both would be necessary.

A second condition or facilitating circumstance for interreligious empathy is personal *experience*. The richer and more diverse one's own life of religious experience is, the more likely one will be able to resonate with experiences of the other. The imprint of one's own past experiences indeed functions as what Husserl might regard as the originating norm for understanding others.[10] However, this does not mean that it would be impossible to ever gain empathic understanding of experiences hitherto unknown. Scholars tend to agree that empathy may indeed open a world of new experiences. Scheler, for example, states optimistically that

> we can have a lively and immediate participation in joy or sorrow, can share with others their appreciation of value and can even enter into another's commiseration for a third party, without ever having sampled that particular quality of experience before. A person who has never felt mortal danger can still understand and envisage it, just as he can also share in it.[11]

Though empathy may thus open the door to new experiences, there is little certainty or control over who is able to gain such experiences or how. Scheler believed that the more 'vital' a particular experience, the more chance there was for empathic understanding without prior experience. Referring to the experience of despair of Jesus in Gethsemane, Scheler suggests that it

> can be understood and shared regardless of our historical, racial, and even human limitations. And for every candid heart which steeps itself in that desolation it operates, not as a reminder or revival of personal sufferings, great or small, but as the revelation of a new and greater suffering, hitherto undreamed of.[12]

An important support or stimulus in gaining experiential understanding of the other is participation in their religious life and practice. The sensory immersion in the religious environment of the other often unleashes new feelings and

---

10. Edmund Husserl, *Cartesian Meditations: An Introduction to Phenomenology*, trans. D. Cairns (The Hague: Martinus Nijhoff, 1960), pp. 122–5.
11. Max Scheler, *The Nature of Sympathy*, p. 47.
12. Ibid.

experiences. Thus, individuals who otherwise never experience glossolalia may suddenly start speaking in tongues when the context allows or invites it. And participation in a Japanese tea ceremony may draw one's attention to the present in ways unaccustomed to in prior ritual life.

The most important condition for empathy with otherness is *imagination*. It is the imagination which lifts one beyond one's past repertoire of experience into the world of religious difference. Just as imagination may transport a reader into the life and experience of an author, it may form a bridge to the experiential world evoked by a sacred text of another religion. Insofar as imagination constitutes a highly subjective and volatile faculty, its effects will need to be checked against the reality of the life world of the other. But the combination of sympathy, experience and imagination offers some basis for gaining new experiences or empathizing with forms of religious life different from one's own.

Limits of Interreligious Empathy

Though empathy plays an important role in gaining a deeper understanding of the meaning of teachings and practices of another religion, including unfamiliar ones, it is clear that there are limits to interreligious empathy. First, while one may gain some empathic resonance with the devotional life of the other through analogy with one's own, one misses by definition the attitude of love for the particular object of devotion, which for a believer constitutes the essence of the devotional experience. Second, certain forms of religious life and experience may be impenetrable, either due to personal limitations or institutional restrictions. Individuals simply have varying capacity for empathy in general and interreligious empathy in particular, and what some may experience as a very profound and meaningful datum in another religion may leave others entirely cold. This variability of empathic resonance may lie in one's own religious disposition, devotional personalities resonating more readily with the devotional life in another religion and contemplative persons with contemplative teachings and practices. While it is undoubtedly the case that one's religious experiences and predispositions play an important role in facilitating or inhibiting interreligious empathy, it is still unpredictable which experiences trigger empathic response for whom. The ability of a particular individual to empathize with a certain experience says little about the inherent truth or validity of that experience, just as the lack of empathic access does not necessarily point to its irrelevance. As such, empathy cannot function as a sufficient condition for assessing the validity of a particular teaching or practice for one's own broader religious tradition.

Moreover, empathy will not always yield experiences which will be regarded as a source of enrichment for one's own tradition. The attempt to empathize with the religious other may also lead to disinterest or even contempt for the other. Not all religious experiences are necessarily lofty, enriching or worthy of further cultivation. As such, the capacity for empathy is not sufficient to bring about active interest in or constructive engagement with another religion.

While the possibility of interreligious empathy may be limited by personal religious inclinations and past religious history, it may also be thwarted by a lack of access to the teachings and practices of another religion. In some religions, access to particular teachings and practices requires high levels of initiation, and other traditions reserve certain rituals only for actual members. While this does not *a priori* exclude the possibility of some empathic resonance, it certainly prohibits the practice of ritual participation which is an important conduit for empathy.

In sum, the empathic experience of another tradition should not be focused on making epistemic claims about the experience of the other. Not only is every individual experience essentially inimitable, but the confessional gap precludes full access to the religious life of the other. However, these limits or limitations do not diminish the importance of empathy in interreligious dialogue. Though one's understanding of the other remains that of an outsider, the ultimate goal of such understanding remains the enrichment of one's own tradition, rather than a perfect understanding of the other. As such, even a limited or slanted understanding of the other may elicit important experiences or thoughts which may shed new light on one's own tradition or open up new avenues for religious reflection and growth. Since interreligious empathy remains so unpredictable and subjective, it is evident that it does not in itself constitute a sufficient basis for religious change. Every positive resonance with the religious life of the other will need to be considered in light of a broader appeal as well as religious and doctrinal compatibility. But the process undoubtedly begins with a personally enriching experience of encounter with the religious other.

Whereas the role of empathy in interreligious dialogue is thus limited, it nevertheless offers an important touchstone for both understanding the other and testing the possible relevance of certain ideas or practices for one's own tradition. The widespread appeal of certain teachings or practices of another religion may point to a religious desire which is not met in a particular religion. This might become an indicator of religious elements worth engaging actively in dialogue.

Conclusion

Though rarely thematized, or accessed as a source of reliable information, empathy is both implicitly and explicitly at work in interreligious communication. The suspicions with regard to the use of empathy as a critical category tend to revolve around its subjective nature and a concern to preserve the alterity of the other religion. Empathy is thought to be based on the naïve belief in the possibility of passing over between traditions and understanding the other religion from within, thus erasing the sense of difference. This is partly why scholars like Jeanrond argue for a more hermeneutical approach, in particular a hermeneutics of love. 'Love', Jeanrond writes, 'lives off difference. Difference offers the environment in which love can flourish. Love does not necessarily presuppose that the respective other be liked … Love does not give priority to a kind of understanding that promotes harmony and perhaps even agreement. Nor does it merely seek greater understanding of difference'.[13]

While love may be a foundation for accepting religious difference, constructive dialogue between religions seeks to learn from this difference. And here, empathy continues to play a role, either implicitly or explicitly. Rather than as a means to gain objective understanding of the other, it functions as a tool for gauging the meaning and relevance of a particular teaching or practice for one's own religious life, and ultimately for the life of one's own religious tradition. Here, empathy involves an attempt to broaden one's religious horizon and explore shades of religious experience which might become a source of personal and institutional enrichment. Such exploration of course also involves a significant rational dimension of the study of the texts and teachings of the other religion. But unless one is also moved on a more experiential dimension by certain teachings, one is unlikely to further pursue their relevance for one's own tradition.

The very idea of possibly broadening one's religious horizon presumes the otherness of the other religion. Interreligious empathy may provide some access to a whole array of experiences, some familiar and some new, some elevating and inspiring and some disorienting, dull or even loathsome. It is only insofar as the teachings or practices of other religions yield new and enriching experiences that they are likely to be engaged in further constructive religious effort. And it is only insofar as such positive religious resonance extends beyond a single individual that it may become part of a larger effort of religious growth.

The very possibility of growth in interreligious dialogue thus depends on the recognition of the otherness of the religious other, not as threat or as a source of unbridgeable difference, but as an opportunity to experiment with new forms of religious life and experience. In the process, empathy forms an essential – though by no means sufficient – tool for stretching one's religious imagination and touching the religious life of the other.

---

13. Werner G. Jeanrond, 'Toward an Interreligious Hermeneutics of Love', p. 52.

24

IN THE PRESENCE OF GOD – MAKING ROOM FOR THE OTHER: AN AUTOBIOGRAPHICAL APPROACH

Karl-Josef Kuschel[1]

The (New) Religio-Political Situation

It cannot be denied that there is a fundamental experience of pluralism in contemporary societies. At the beginning of the twenty-first century, many countries in Europe have to cope with the *advances of a religio-political pluralization*. This experience is not a passing phenomenon, but the result of a process of internal differentiation which reaches back for generations. Post-war Germany has gained experience with the phenomenon of religious plurality and pluralism in its recent history: the presence of Judaism which has partially recovered its strength after the *Shoah* (c. 100,000) and the presence of Islam in a size historically unprecedented (c. 3,500,000).

We have to contend with a religio-geographical constellation for which Europe and Europeans have no frame of reference. On the one hand, there is a *bi-lateral constellation* in which secular-humanistic and religious-ecclesiastic ways of life co-exist; on the other hand, there is a *tri-lateral constellation* within religions: the co-existence of Jews, Christians, and Muslims with their internal differentiations. Such a religio-political situation is a novelty for most countries in Europe; it raises tasks of a cultural, political, and theological nature which have not been raised before. The spectrum of reactions to this situation spans from xenophobia to experiences of social and cultural integration, including the experience of dialogue. Dialogue, however, needs dialogical competence – a competence which one does not simply have, but which one has to learn.

I will address this competence before I sketch my personal journey of encounters with others.[2] For it is a fact that in our societies – religious or

---

1. Translated by Ulrich Schmiedel.

2. I could not write these autobiographical sketches to honour Werner G. Jeanrond without remembering my friendship with him – a stable and steady friendship which dates

non-religious – we live with our backs turned to our others, with a tunnel vision only for ourselves, with blinders which prevent us from a shift of perspective in order to positively perceive the presence of the other faith as the presence of the other *faith*. However, to open dialogue with the other can be tedious and toilsome. We have to embark on a journey, a journey with detour after detour.

The Exemplary Inter-Religious Dialogue

For me, there is no more impressive or instructive text about such a journey than that written by the former Chancellor of the Federal Republic of Germany, Helmut Schmidt, published in *Weggefährten* (1996). Schmidt recounts how Israel had been at war with the Egyptians. The last war had ended only four years previously, when the President of Egypt, Anwar El Sadat, a deeply devout Muslim, began his spectacular journey of peace to Israel where he addressed the Knesset, the Israeli parliament. It was 20 November 1977, a significant day in the history of religions – significant to this day. In *Weggefährten*, Schmidt writes about a conversation with Sadat. It took place in the 1970s, on the Nile:

> Once, we were having a conversation about religion which lasted several days. We were travelling by boat on the Nile, upriver, until we reached Aswan. ... The conversation made so deep an impression on me that I took some notes...
> The monotheistic religions, Sadat explained, have common historical roots in the Sinai. ... The origin of the belief in the one God, as testified by the Holy Scriptures, lies with Abraham who seems to have lived in roughly the same age as Akhenaton. Jews, Christians, and Muslims believe that they are the spiritual descendents of Abraham. ... Sadat was hoping for a peaceful encounter of Judaism, Christianity, and Islam. It should symbolically take place at Mount Sinai... There, a synagogue, a church, and a mosque would be built next to one another, a testimony to harmony. Indeed, Sadat laid the foundation for these houses of God in 1979.[3]

However, Sadat's interfaith project was never put into practice. Schmidt continues: 'His assassination on 6 October 1981 put an end to the visions of this utterly unusual man. ... I loved him. ... Our nightly conversations on the Nile are among the happiest memories I have of my political life'.[4] What we read here is exemplary for interreligious learning: initial ignorance – disturbed and destroyed by the encounter with the other. The encounter is crucial. The other outside one's

back many years. I remember our encounters at Lund University in Sweden (I was awarded the honorary doctorate from the Faculty of Theology in 1997) to which I gratefully look back.

3. Helmut Schmidt, *Weggefährten* (Berlin: Siedler-Verlag, 1996), pp. 341-343 (trans. U.S.).

4. Ibid. Cf. Helmut Schmidt, *Religion in der Verantwortung: Gefährdungen des Friedens im Zeitalter der Globalisierung* (Berlin: Propyläen, 2011), pp. 127-8; 129-30; 149-50.

tunnel vision comes into view. What is more, the unique atmosphere alone – a nightly journey on the Nile – is enough to open one's heart. Schmidt describes a life-experience which I can confirm. Usually, what prompts the expansion of horizons is human beings, not books. Suddenly, we are surprised by how little we know about our other, by how much we have in common if we compare traditions, and by how much engagement for peace *could* emerge, if these commonalities were taken seriously. Whenever I read Schmidt's text, I realize what interreligious dialogue could be: to open the other's heart, to make her or him free for the breadth and depth of one's own tradition. My heart has been opened again and again.

Encounters with Jewish Others

Whoever has had experiences like Schmidt will stay on the journey of discovery. In my studies of theology at the University of Tübingen with its cosmopolitan reputation, I was not asked to read the sources of Islamic philosophy or poetry. I was not encouraged to embark on the journey of discovery.

However, in the 1970s Judaism returned to Germany as a lively and a living religion. Impressive and important German-speaking representatives came to debate and discuss with us, such as Schalom Ben-Chorin, Pinchas Lapide, Ruth Lapide, Nathan Peter Levinson, and Pnina Levinson. After the *Shoah*, such encounters could not be taken for granted. As students, we experienced a 'Hebrew Humanism' as it had been lived by Martin Buber. Consequently, we started to take the Jewish roots of Christianity seriously. I cannot forget reading Ben-Chorin's trilogy of portraits of Christianity's protagonists – 'through Jewish eyes'.[5] He wrote from the tradition of the Haskalah, the Jewish Enlightenment, with representatives such as Moses Mendelssohn, Abraham Geiger, Leo Baeck, and Jules Isaac in the eighteenth, nineteenth, and early twentieth centuries. We had profound and pervasive learning experiences: what we – unified and uniformed as we were through our Christian-Catholic socialization – held to be exclusively Christian was Jewish: the double commandment of love, the understanding of God as creator and consummator, as a merciful judge before whom we would have to stand after our deaths.

These encounters changed me. What I learned was twofold: Judaism is not the antecedent of Christianity, the contrast for the self-understanding of the church; Judaism is a distinct and discrete religion with its own claim to truth. Hence, Judaism is a challenge to Christianity. However, the fact that Jesus lived under the historical and cultural circumstances of his time means that he lived

---

5. Schalom Ben-Chorin, *Bruder Jesus: Der Nazarener in jüdischer Sicht* (München: Paul List Verlag, 1967); idem, *Paulus – Der Völkerapostel in Jüdischer Sicht* (München: Paul List Verlag, 1970); and idem, *Mutter Mirjam: Maria in Jüdischer Sicht* (München: Paul List Verlag, 1971). Only one of these studies has been translated into English: Schalom Ben-Chorin, *Brother Jesus: The Nazarene through Jewish Eyes*, trans. J. S. Klein and M. Reinhart (Athens, GA: University of Georgia Press, 2001).

as a Jew: whoever meets Jesus meets Judaism; whoever seeks to understand Jesus seeks to understand Judaism.

In 1978–9, I was able to study at the Hebrew University in Jerusalem. What a world I was able to explore in Jerusalem; what a history, the destiny for peoples and powers which conquered the city, failed, foundered, and forged ahead again. I encountered Orthodox Judaism: lively, it faced me in Mea Shearim, a district of Jerusalem through which I had to walk when I made my daily way to the city centre. My head was filled with stereotypes about Orthodoxy as a life in rigorist isolation. Who would doubt that these might be encountered in Orthodox Judaism? However, I discovered human beings who dedicated themselves to the Torah, God's guidance, in their day-to-day lives, living happily under God, sometimes dancing and singing. Lifelong learning was a commitment for them when they entered into dialogues and discussions with the great rabbis of their tradition. They commanded my respect as I started to compare my life as both a Christian and a Christian theologian with their lives. Was I prepared to adjust and align my life to the scrutiny of God's guidance like the bearded scholars in Mea Shearim with their shtreimels stemming from Eastern Europe of the sixteenth and seventeenth century? Was I prepared to take the scrutiny of my religion as seriously as these Jews?

Certainly, I had no desire to live like them. I embrace the 'freedom in Christ' (Gal. 5.1), yet, I was embarrassed by my clichés, my self-satisfied sentences over 'these Jews'. Challenged by Jewish teachers in the Hebrew University like Ephraim E. Urbach and Shmuel Safrai, I started studying Rabbinic theologies in order to become familiar with Rabbinic thought. In a dusty bookstore, founded by Ludwig Meyer in 1908, close to Jaffa Gate, with books upon books piled up to the ceiling, I got hold of the two volumes of *The Sages* (1979) by Ephraim E. Urbach, something like a systematic theology of Judaism from rabbinic sources.[6] In Tel Aviv, I used my last money to buy a German translation of the Babylonian Talmud, edited by Lazarus Goldschmidt. These are key works; until this day, I have not stopped studying them. The experience of the world of Judaism, decidedly different, with its vast masses of texts, humbled me. I had studied theology, but what did I know about Judaism, about the breadth and depth of its conversation with God? I had to start studying again. The experience of Jewish life in Jerusalem was what motivated me.

I encountered Schalom Ben-Chorin, born in Berlin in 1913 under the name Fritz Rosenthal. He had been living in Palestine since 1935. I do not remember when and where I met him for the first time, yet I do remember his curiosity about me, a young German Catholic theologian who was also a literary scholar. He invited me to his house to celebrate the Sabbath. For the first time, I witnessed the ritual to begin the Sabbath on a Friday: Ben-Chorin, the kippah on his bald head, the tallit over his shoulders, from time to time switching to German to explain the prayers to me. I sensed the commonality with Judaism in the praise of creation.

---

6. Ephraim E. Urbach, *The Sages: Their Concepts and Beliefs*, trans. I. Abrams (Jerusalem: Magnes Press, 1979).

Without Judaism, Christianity would be literally uprooted. It would be uprooted without the character of one of the patriarchs of Israel – Abraham, for it is not a coincidence that the first sentence of the New Testament reads 'An account of the genealogy of Jesus the Messiah, the son of David, the son of Abraham' (Mt. 1.1). I had ignored such signs until I realized that without the depth and breadth of the story of Israel with God, Jesus' message cannot be understood. The connection to Abraham is something unique in the history of religions: God enters into a covenant with Abraham, the sign of which is circumcision (Gen. 17.11-13). To trust in the covenant is a living and lively reality for every Jew considering what the Jewish people have had to experience. Precisely when the covenant is contradicted – deportation and destruction – the trust in the covenant is necessary. I cannot forget what Martin Buber said during a dialogue with theologian Karl Ludwig Schmidt in 1933, only weeks before Adolf Hitler seized power:

> I live a short distance from the city of Worms, to which I am also tied by ancestral tradition; and from time to time I visit there. When I do so, I always go first to the cathedral. It is a visible harmony of members, a whole in which no part deviates from the norm of perfection. I walk around the cathedral, gazing at it in perfect joy. Then I go to the Jewish cemetery. It consists of cracked and crooked stones without shape or direction. I enter the cemetery and look up from this disorder to the marvellous harmony of the cathedral, and it seems to me as if I were looking from Israel up to the Church. Here below there is no suggestion of form, only the stones and the ashes beneath the stones. The ashes are there, no matter how they have been scattered. The corporeality of human beings who have become ashes is there. It is there. It is there for me. It is there for me, not as corporeality within the space of this planet, but as corporeality deep in my own memories, back into the depths of history, back as far as Sinai.
>
> I have stood there; I have been united with the ashes and through them with the patriarchs. That is a remembrance of the divine-human encounter which is granted to all Jews. The perfection of the Christian God-space cannot divert me from this; nothing can divert me from the God-time of Israel.
>
> I have stood there and I have experienced everything myself. I have experienced all the death that was before me; all the ashes, all the desolation, all the noiseless wailings become mine. But the covenant has not been withdrawn for me. I lie on the ground, prostrate like these stones. But it has not been withdrawn for me.[7]

God's covenant with Israel holds – after Christ. Hence, the trust holds that generation after generation will follow. Paul, the Apostle, has not terminated

---

7. Martin Buber, 'Church, State, Nation, Jewry', in David W. McKain, ed., *Christianity: Some None-Christian Appraisals* (New York: McGraw-Hill, 1964), pp. 176–88 (186-7). For the German original, cf. Martin Buber, 'Dom und Friedhof', in idem, *Schriften zum Christentum*, ed. Karl-Josef Kuschel (Gütersloh: Gütersloher Verlagshaus, 2011), p. 175. Also cf. the commentary in ibid., pp. 396–7.

the covenant as can be read in his theological treatise on the future of Israel in Chapters 9–11 of his Epistle to the Romans. Israel has its own way to God, given by God in his own way. Missionary activities by the church would betray these ways. According to Paul, whether the people of Israel will experience a conversion to Christ is not a matter for the church, but a matter for Christ – a Christ who will return at the end of time.

Encounters with Muslim Others

When and where did I encounter Islam? I have to admit that, unlike Judaism, Islam was simply not on the radar, so to speak, of Christian theologians in the 1970s. Islam has existed since the revelation to the Prophet Muhammad was completed in 632. It has grown to about one billion believers. Hence, by its size alone it is a religion comparable to Christianity. Muslims live in the countries of the 'middle belt' of the globe, the so-called 'green belt' from Morocco in the west through Pakistan, the former southern Soviet Republics of Azerbaijan, Kazakhstan, and Uzbekistan to Malaysia and Indonesia in the east. These facts, however, were not taken seriously in the 1970s, politically or theologically. There was no polemic against Islam because Islam was plainly and simply not present, either as a political, cultural or religious challenge.

When Islam became a challenge, we were theologically unprepared. The Oil Crisis in 1973 was a warning. Suddenly, we realized how dependent we were on the Islamic countries. And, suddenly, I realized this dependency, too. I had been living in Jerusalem in 1978/79, yet I had eyes and ears only for Judaism. I could not overlook the Muslims who were living in the city, the pilgrimages to the Al-Aqsa Mosque on the Temple Mount every Friday. I knew that this was not a novelty. Islam had characterized Jerusalem since the seventh century. But I had no antenna for Islam. Today, I am ashamed that, due to my obsession with Judaism, I did not spare a thought for Islam.

However, while I was living in Jerusalem, the unexpected happened. In Iran, the Shah was overthrown. On 1 February 1979, the 'Revolutionary Leader', Ayatollah Khomeini, leaving his exile in Paris, stepped onto Iranian soil. Since then, the Mullahs govern Iran – with all the signs and symptoms of deterioration which appear to accompany any theocracy. A highly symbolic date! Without exaggeration one can say that since 1979 the world has dramatically changed. The outcome of this change is uncertain. What is certain is that Islam reappeared as a factor in world politics, playing the part that it had gradually lost after the end of the seventeenth century with the defeat of the Ottomans at Vienna in 1683. Our economic and political dependency on Islamic countries is not decreasing. We are so connected to the Islamic world that its destiny is also our destiny.

Since the 1990s, I continue to learn through my co-operation with Jewish and Muslim colleagues from all over the world. How can one assess Islam as a Christian? Can I assess it by the criterion used since medieval times: as a mass movement of unbaptized nonbelievers? At some of the conferences which I regularly co-organize in the United States, the name Abraham is heard again and again. I was aware of the fact that he is the 'father' of the belief in the one true God for Jews as narrated in Genesis – but for Muslims? I was surprised when I learned that the Muslims venerate Abraham as a prototype of what 'Islam' literally means: devotion to the will of the one God.

I was drawn to the study of the Qur'an of which I had known as little as Chancellor Schmidt. However, once I embarked on the journey of studying, I discovered what I had not known before. The Qur'an points to the story of Abraham. Islam is called the *millat Ibrahim*, the community of Abraham. A connection to Abraham which is established through Abraham's first born, Ishmael, conceived before Isaac with the Egyptian maid Hagar – or so the Bible tells us in Gen. 16. This Ishmael is already thirteen years old, bearing the circumcision as a sign of the covenant, when Isaac is born. What follows is a drama between brothers, unique in the history of religions: Ishmael, blessed by God, is driven out of his home, literally into the desert. He would have died if it were not for God's intervention. In the desert, the desperate Hagar discovers a water well which gives her and her son, who is crying from thirst, the life-saving water: a sign of God. God wants Abraham's son Ishmael to live, to have a future, a great future – or so the Bible tells us in Gen. 21: 'Lift the boy up and take him by the hand' God says to Hagar 'for I will make him into a great nation' (Gen 21.18). Islam appeals to this very blessing by God. Ishmael is seen in Islam as the progenitor of all Arabs; and according to a post-Qur'anic tradition, the scene at the water well is set in the valley of Mecca where the life-saving water spills from the source *Zamzam*: the origin of the Muslim sanctuary, the *Kaaba*. In every pilgrimage, the drama of the mother and her son is spiritually re-enacted by each and every pilgrim.

Discovering the Abrahamic Root

Theologically, these encounters had considerable consequences for me. I wrote about these consequences in *Streit um Abraham*.[8] One of them is that Muslims do not worship a deity that is alien to Christians, but rather Muslims worship the God of Abraham as testified in the Bible. Only now I understand what the Second Vatican Council said about the faith of the Muslims in *Lumen Gentium*: 'But the plan of salvation also includes those who acknowledge the Creator. In the first place amongst these there are the Mohamedans, who, professing to hold the faith of Abraham, along with us, adore the one and merciful God, who on the last day will judge mankind'.[9] Since my study of Abraham, the reflection on a mutually inter-connected understanding of the relationship between Jews, Christians,

---

8. Karl-Josef Kuschel, *Streit um Abraham: Was Juden, Christen und Muslime trennt – und was sie eint* (Stuttgart: Patmos, 1995). The translation into English was published as *Abraham: A Symbol of Hope for Jews, Christians and Muslims*, trans. J. Bowden (London: SCM, 1995).

9. *Lumen Gentium*, 16.

and Muslims has been a leitmotif in my life, including the practice of what I call 'Abrahamic Ecumenics': Jews, Christians, and Muslims are in need of each other when they are interpreting their Holy Scriptures, when they are interpreting what God intends for them. Thinking in an inter-connected way leads to the understanding of the self *through* the other. Such understanding presupposes that we make room for the other in the presence of God – to listen to the other's witness of God.[10]

Are we far from a *Theology of the Other* under the current circumstances?[11] I conclude with Ben-Chorin. In 1993, he was interviewed by the German magazine *Der Spiegel*. The interview ends with what one could call Ben-Chorin's legacy – a legacy to which I feel indebted in my reflections on a theology which makes room for the other in the presence of God.

> If I had been told fifty years ago how well the relationship between Judaism and Christianity would develop – particularly in Germany – I would not have deemed it possible. I think that the Arab-Muslim side should become increasingly conscious of the fact that both of us, Jews and Arabs, are children of Abraham. Abraham had two sons: Ishmael, the progenitor of the Arabs, and Isaac, the progenitor of the Jews. They were not fond of each other. However, facing the corpse of their father, in the cave of Machpelah, they mourned together, becoming reconciled. It is my hope and my prayer that this reconciliation will repeat itself.[12]

---

10. Werner Jeanrond has made important and instructive contributions to a theology which engages with others and otherness. Cf. Werner G. Jeanrond, 'Thinking about God Today', in Werner G. Jeanrond and Aasulv Lande, eds, *The Concept of God in Global Dialogue* (Maryknoll, NY: Orbis, 2005), pp. 89–97. Also cf. idem, *A Theology of Love* (London: Continuum/T&T Clark 2010), pp. 239–59.

11. Cf. Karl-Josef Kuschel, 'The Open Covenant: The Need for a "Theology of the Other"', in Werner G. Jeanrond and Aasulv Lande, eds, *The Concept of God in Global Dialogue*, pp. 63–87.

12. Schalom Ben-Chorin, in '"Israels Luft macht radikal": Der deutsch-israelische Schriftsteller Schalom Ben-Chorin über Frieden, Juden und Deutsche', *Der Spiegel* 35 (1993), pp. 144–50 (50) (trans. U. S.).

25

RELATED RIVALS:
HOW CHRISTIANS AND MUSLIMS
MIGHT RELATE TO ONE ANOTHER

Susanne Heine

Christianity and Islam are different world religions, though closely affiliated with each other. In their scriptures, Bible and Qur'an, the two religions share many narratives, notions and prominent persons, and – above all – the belief that the one unique God communicates with his creatures. Hence, when Christians first met Muslims they not surprisingly considered Islam a heresy of Christianity. However, the times have changed: today, we look for commonalities, such as the figure of Abraham who seems to provide a common source. But at a closer look, the figure and function of Abraham in Bible and Qur'an differ to a high degree. Jesus plays a prominent part in both religions, too, albeit – again – a different one.

Islam insists on being a distinct religion because of its self-understanding as the restorer of monotheism which, according to the Muslim self-understanding, was corrupted during the course of time. By confessing Jesus Christ as the revealer and the revelation sent from God, Christianity became a religion of its own. Unlike Islam, which reaches back behind both monotheist religions by referring to Abraham (who was neither a Jew nor a Christian, but devoted to the one God), Christianity grew out of Judaism, but remained rooted in it. Consequently, many surahs of the Qur'an display a polemic style. Occasionally, the prophet Muhammad is called on to say 'No', as in Sura 2.135: 'They say, "Become Jews or Christians, and you will be rightly guided." Say, "No, [ours is] the religion of Abraham, the upright, who did not worship any god besides God"'.[1]

Thus, in their belief Christians and Muslims are both related and rivals at the same time. The question of how to deal with this 'difference in relation' or 'relation in difference' has received diverse answers throughout history. In Arabia, Christians and Muslims were in dialogue from the beginning of the Islamic movement. Their interaction left marks in the text of the Qur'an. The following centuries also attest to a great number of religious disputations of a high intellectual

---

1. The translation is taken from *The Qur'an: a New Translation*, trans. M. Abdel-Haleem (Oxford: Oxford University Press, 2004).

and spiritual level on both sides. These disputations were mostly undertaken to carefully prompt a changing of sides. However, we also have witness of both accusing each other of delusion and deceit, in-between polemics and apologetics. Recently, two main approaches have developed: on the one hand, differences are transformed into contrasts according to the disputations of the past; on the other hand, differences are transformed into a 'mishmash' according to the pluralism of the present. These extremes are still on the agenda inside and outside academia. In what follows, however, some alleys – including blind alleys – to a dialogue beyond these extremes shall be examined from a Christian perspective.[2]

Tensions and a New Paradigm

Christianity and Islam are consecutively linked, because Islam followed Christianity. As both religions confess the one unique God as creator of all beings including human beings, Islam relates itself to the antecedent monotheistic religions. It does so by approving the previous prophets, including Jesus, while at the same time distancing itself from the Christian understanding of Jesus as revealer and saviour due to the message of the Qur'an which forms and informs the centre of a new creed, including Muhammad as the ultimate prophet. The resulting tension between continuity and discontinuity is resolved by postulating that the coming of Muhammad was already announced in the Jewish and Christian scriptures. Since Christians cannot share this notion, the tension between continuity and discontinuity persists – and what persists with it is the tension between Christians and Muslims.

Christianity followed the same pattern in order to establish continuity and discontinuity with Judaism by postulating that Jesus was already announced in the Jewish scriptures, a notion Jews cannot accept. Yet for a Christian identity, there is neither need nor necessity to look out for continuity with the subsequent religion of Islam, at least not theologically. Hence, the tension between continuity and discontinuity endures, and on such a basis both religions are not able to come to terms with one another.

Yet a new paradigm can be recognized since the middle of the twentieth century. Religion no longer stands at the centre of communication; rather, religion finds itself within a new social reality. The increasing presence of Muslims in Europe – many are already naturalized citizens – calls both religions to deal with each other in an adequate and acceptable way for the sake of social peace. Christians and Muslims reside as neighbours, attend the same classes at schools, meet in lecture theatres at universities, and at the places at which they work. This situation requires cooperation in order to foster a coherent society for which

2. My contribution honouring the spirit of Werner G. Jeanrond's work is owed to encounters with him. Moreover, the experiences I gained in thirty years of Christian-Muslim dialogue influence my exploration of the alleys and blind alleys of dialogue.

the members of both religious communities are responsible according to their religious obligations.

Hence, religion remains an important issue today, but within a different situation: it is a question of respectfully encountering each other, of becoming more acquainted with each other, of revising mutual misunderstanding while abandoning mutual defamation. However, how can such an encounter be achieved without skipping religious commitments and conducts of life in favour of an allegedly neutral secularized attitude?

Developing Identity

Tensions are the gateway to encounter. Without tensions, there is no need for dealing with each other. Accordingly, for Christians, there is no reason to blame Islam for emphasizing its differences from the Christian creed. Through this emphasis, Islam becomes constituted as 'the other' – yet the other who is related through the common belief in the one unique God. Relations consist of two parties who are facing each other as others: *You are not me, I am not you*. What ties the parties together is that today they live in one societal environment.

Otherness brings about identity, specifying who these others who encounter each other are – be it individual or communal others. The way in which identity develops could be compared with the formation of a canon of scriptures as performed by both religious communities. When individuals or groups of different identities meet, it is important to know: *This is me, that is you*. Such knowledge excludes two dead ends: one is amalgamating the differences by adapting oneself to the other which results in assimilation; the other is demarcating and denigrating the other through a rigid concept of identity. Either way, the other is doomed to vanish. Encounter, however, implies the otherness of the other.

Identity cannot be considered a matter of fixed dimensions, but is able to develop, provided the other offers resistance. The resistance corresponds to the canon of scriptures again, the texts of which resist alienation by the interpreter's personal idea or ideology or by a dogmatic mind-set which asserts that there is only one correct interpretation. By continuous open-minded interaction, identity can be maintained and modified in order to reach a deeper understanding of the text and at the same time of the reader of the text, of the other and of oneself as the other. What the Apostle Paul says in an eschatological prospect also applies to *this* life: knowing means to become and to be known (1 Cor. 13.12).

In philosophical perspective, it is a dialectical issue: there are two reverse moments which relate to each other; while the one refers to the other, the other refers to the one – if these moments are separated, each moment is left one-sided.[3] Hence, in the communication between persons, to realize means to become and

---

3. Cf. Arno Anzenbacher, *Einführung in die Philosophie* (Linz: Verlagsgemeinschaft, 1981), p. 96.

to be realized. Accordingly, identity is able to develop without losing itself. When self-awareness ensues it may open one's eyes to new insights: for having wronged the other, or for not yet having developed one's potentials. If it is successful, such a process encourages mutual understanding – a reason to rejoice about the opportunity to come together in spite of and at the same time because of differences.

Overcoming Aggression

Resistance provokes aggression against the other, be it a textual one which opposes comprehension or a personal one who opposes expectation. It was Sigmund Freud who dealt with this phenomenon in the context of the dynamic of love. For him, all human beings rely on each other. The reliance starts with the little child longing for tender attention and protection, and the attachment figures who want to be appreciated and even admired. However, these desires are frequently frustrated, because it is impossible for any person to supply all the traits which are necessary for fulfilment; therefore, relationships entail aggression.[4]

This ambivalence of love also characterizes the relation between adults. Theodor Reik, Freud's critical colleague, separated Freud's conjunction of sexuality and love, setting personal love apart in its own right. Yet, for Reik, falling in love means encountering a fictional image which asks for assimilation: *I should be like you, and you should be like me*.[5] By skipping the otherness of the other, such a process will result in disappointment and – in the worst case – in rivalry and resentment, in power play, in feeling victimized and in the urge to hurt the other, often accompanied by a destructive sense of guilt and a destructed self-esteem. Evidently, such results are not only possible in love affairs, but also in the affairs between individuals or groups with different religious commitments.

All this may predispose a person to succumb to the temptation of fundamentalism. Doubtlessly, fundamentalism is a modern phenomenon. From a psychological perspective, the adherents of religious fundamentalism display poor self-esteem accompanied by a feeling of humiliation and victimization. The resentment is transformed into a sense of omnipotent grandiosity which supports self-esteem. Psychologist Vamik Volkan employs the metaphor of an imaginary lantern with a transparent side and a non-transparent side. He argues that 'the religious fundamentalist is preoccupied with keeping the opaque side of the lantern turned against the real world that is perceived as threatening and frustrating'.[6] This goes hand in hand with 'submission to or fusing with divinity,

---

4. Sigmund Freud addresses this conflict of ambivalence again and again. Cf. Sigmund Freud, *Totem and Taboo*, trans. J. Strachey (New York: Routledge, 2001) or idem, *Civilization and Its Discontents*, trans. D. McLintock (London: Penguin, 2002).

5. 'Sich zu verlieben heißt, dem erdachten Bild zu begegnen'. Theodor Reik, *Geschlecht und Liebe* (München: Kindler, 1965), p. 100.

6. Vamik D. Volkan and Sagman Kayatekin, 'Extreme Religious Fundamentalism and Violence: Some Psychoanalytic and Psychopolitical Thoughts'. I quote from the manuscript

searching for total perfection yet fearing failure'.[7] The fundamentalists seek each other; they gather in a tent, so to speak, a community which provides a sole and single common identity. Those who are outside the tent are qualified for being combatted.[8]

Eventually, aggression cannot be avoided. However, it is a matter of debate as to whether aggression which turns into fixed resentments can be overcome by recollecting one's own personal qualities, and, in the case of Christians and Muslims encountering each other, their respective traditional qualities.

The Importance of Empathy

Feeling threatened, being biased by resentment on the one side and feelings of grandiosity and superiority on the other side, destroys the ability for empathy, for feeling attached to others with compassion and clemency. Christian and Muslim believers are attached to God as compassionate, a forgiving God who wants his creatures to act according to this attribute. To be sure, a belief which animates a conduct of life does not emerge from sticking to a creed; rather, encountering God's presence makes the creed. By experience and not by learned or logical arguments, a human heart receives assurance in faith as described and depicted in the spiritual and ritual settings of Bible and Qur'an.

What lends credibility to religious individuals and groups is – first and foremost – devotion due to certainty in faith as well as offering help to those who need it due to the conviction that all are created by God. To meet in such a way is promising for the connection of Christians and Muslims since it allows both sides to enact and re-enact the existential importance of a life led by trust in God. As a consequence, empathy can be developed for what human beings desire – what they are afraid of or what they are grateful for – all of which can be brought before the one unique God in worship. Even such worship is done in different ways; yet, it is done with the same hope, a hope which may enable human beings to cope with distress in the light of a grievous *Dasein*.

Within such a practiced spirituality, the other becomes the other in a specific way: *I am near to you, you are near to me*. This must not result in blending the differences, for Christians cannot share the Muslim creed referring to the Qur'an being God's ultimate revelation, and Muslims cannot pray in the name of the triune God. In a religious community, worship requires a distinctive intimate space. However, empathizing with each other may mean helping each other practically, but also praying for each other or sending greeting cards to each other as signs of respect on the occasion of the respective faith's festivals. Common events may be designed by praying as well as reading and reciting from Bible and

which Volkan sent me. A slightly different version of the paper was published in *Psyche en Geloof* 17/2 (2006), pp. 71–91.

7. Ibid.
8. Cf. ibid.

Qur'an in parallel groups, and in doing so, both religions give witness to the one unique God, the Lord of the world.

The Importance of Modesty

Empathizing with each other within a spirituality which allows for trust in each other forms the basis for discussing religious issues. Potentially, such discussions might lead to conflict; actually, this can be restrained by being mindful of the possibility of misunderstandings. Again, it might be helpful to compare dealing with (sacred) texts in attempts to apprehend them to dealing with persons who desire to understand each other.

Christianity and Islam are often reproached for their claim to absoluteness, prompting and provoking intolerance by isolating each other. Yet, the claim is produced by an outside perspective which reduces religions to different creeds and customs. This is not the perspective of a convinced believer who relates to the one unique God to whom alone the concept of absoluteness can be assigned. The possessive rhetoric of *my truth is not your truth, and your truth is not my truth* could be called a denial and disowning of God as the one who is the paragon of all truth.

Consequently, it is appropriate to avoid such rhetoric not only from an outsider's point of view but first of all from an insider's theological point of view. When Christians and Muslims say that God reveals his truth in order to lead his creatures to relate to him so that they can take responsibility for their fellow beings, this does not, on the one hand, mean that God displays all of his truth which transcends that which he has chosen to reveal. On the other hand, there are the recipients of sacred texts who need to comprehend these texts, but their comprehension is limited by contexts such as different familiar descents, different affiliations, different cultural or political traditions. These differences prompt different interpretations.[9]

Regardless of whether the Bible is considered the witness of God's revelation and the Qur'an is considered the revelation of the word of God to Muhammad, in either case the recipients are called to apprehend their texts and they produce a variety of individual and communal interpretations. There will always be a difference between what believers hold to be the truth and the truth God represents in his immeasurability; however, this difference keeps the pursuit of truth on-going which makes new insights possible.

What follows from this is that any interpretation presupposes some ethical and theological standards:[10] the willingness to understand what is not yet part of

9. Cf. Jeanrond's account of 'The Transformative Power of Reading', in Werner G. Jeanrond, *Theological Hermeneutics: Development and Significance* (London: SCM Press, 2002), pp. 93–119.

10. For the ethics of interpretation cf. Werner G. Jeanrond, *Text und Interpretation als Kategorien theologischen Denkens* (Tübingen: Mohr Siebeck, 1986), pp. 119–26.

one's own body of knowledge, the openness to assume that spiritual knowledge is not gained by learning, but by inaccessible insight which is not only a theological, but also an epistemological principle. Moreover, the text must be respected as different from the reader of the text, as an 'other'; interpretation and the object of interpretation must not be short-circuited since the testimony of the text is richer than what interpreters are able to grasp – above all, such richness holds true for sacred texts referring to God. Hence, understanding is connected to the endeavour of coming to terms with something 'other'; it requires the virtues of self-reflection, empathy and modesty. Qualifying one's own interpretation does not mean to relativize it in the sense of 'anything goes'. Rather, it means to relate the understanding of human beings to God's intangible truth. This should form the backdrop for debates about religious issues between Christians and Muslims.

Translating the Other

Interfaith dialogues begin when both partners explicate their self-understanding with regard to their creeds, traditions, and life-orientations. As the Islamic scholar Abdoldjavad Falaturi put it: 'A vital dialogue which leads us further is only possible if each partner represents his own religion responsibly, speaking out of his own conviction'.[11] This excludes looking at both religions from an outside perspective as well as aiming at theological consensus. Rather, if the different genuine self-understandings can be expressed independently, interaction becomes possible.[12] It is unavoidable that another religion can only be understood by means of one's own religious perspective. At a first glance, both partners discover differences – albeit on the basis of similarities, because without any analogies there is no access to understanding: something completely different lies beyond conceiving. Often, Christian-Muslim dialogues end up at that stage and the partners separate without having understood each other. Differences as well as similarities also entail delusions since concepts cannot be nailed down to only one meaning. Hence, the dialogue might progress when the partners recognize that the same concept can carry different meanings, and different concepts may capture the

---

11. 'Ein lebendiger, weiterführender Dialog kann ausschließlich dort stattfinden, wo jeder der Gesprächspartner aus Überzeugung und Verantwortung seine Religion vertritt'. Abdoldjavad Falaturi, *Dialog zwischen Christentum und Islam* (Hamburg: Islamische Akademie, 2002), p. 74 (my translation).

12. The description of the process of interaction is inspired by an interreligious research project in which Christians and Muslims participated. I chaired the project for seven years; the results will be published in 2014. Cf. also Susanne Heine, Rüdiger Lohlker, and Richard Potz, *Muslime in Österreich: Geschichte – Lebenswelt – Religion. Grundlagen für den Dialog* (Innsbruck: Tyrolia, 2012); Evangelische Kirche A. und H. B. in Österreich, eds, *Respektvoll miteinander: Evangelische Christen und Muslime in Österreich: Eine Orientierungshilfe* (Wien: Evangelischer Presseverband, 2012).

same meaning. The vagueness of concepts demands of us to figure out what their purpose is by reflecting on their contexts.

Obviously, what is sketched here is not really a new approach to dialogue, but dialogue becomes more complicated between Christians and Muslims when different languages are involved: Arabic for the Qur'an, Hebrew and Greek for the Bible and the language in which the partners communicate, while using the respective translations of their sacred texts. Moreover, often the Qur'an refers to Christian concepts so that one might speak of notions which travel through texts, through traditions and religions.

Understanding each other is possible within a long-term process by looking for translational analogies in meaning which may be only loosely linked to identifiable concepts. Through such a translation from one tradition into the other, the partners can come closer to each other than they could have imagined before: *I translate you into my religious notions and language, you translate me into your religious notions and language.*

This approach works by mutual questioning, admitting approval or disapproval. If one translates the other into one's own religious language in order to understand her or him, the other is obliged to answer to avoid a false peace: you have understood me or you have not yet understood me. Such a process provokes specifications within one's own tradition; one has to scrutinize what is evident for oneself but not for the other. Such a back-and-forth movement takes time. It comes to a resolution only when the respective other is able to say: 'You understand me and my religious commitment'.

The Benefits of Dialogue

Obviously, one may ask what the benefits of such a process are. The dialogue partners who represent two religions remain others in their otherness. Nonetheless, several benefits can be discovered. For instance, a differentiating dynamic *within* both religions comes to the fore revealing both religions as ways of life. Questions asked by the interfaith partners often turn out to be questions to one's own tradition which is why interreligious dialogue results in intra-religious dialogue.

Above all, when understanding starts with recognizing differences on the basis of analogies, the differences are also signposts to what both religions have in common. Christian-Muslim relations cannot be established by summing up similarities *and* dissimilarities, but by searching for dissimilarities *in relation to* similarities and similarities *in relation to* dissimilarities. To understand each other on such a basis means doing justice to each other. As in any relationship, the otherness of the other cannot be deleted. What can be achieved is this: *understanding and feeling understood.*

26

'WHO PRACTICES HOSPITALITY ENTERTAINS GOD HIMSELF'

Mona Siddiqui

I first met Werner G. Jeanrond when in 2004 he came to the University of Glasgow as a Robertson Fellow. The Robertson Fellowship usually lasted for a period of two weeks and I remember Werner Jeanrond being one of the few visiting lecturers (in my time at Glasgow) who made an effort to meet staff in and outside his field while he was there. I found him interested in people and not just their academic disciplines and this is what drew me to him as a colleague and then in subsequent years as a friend. Later on when Werner Jeanrond joined the University as the Professor of Divinity his office was next door to mine. It seemed to me that we were destined to become close colleagues.

He knew from the beginning that I was engaged in interreligious work, namely the theological relationship between Islam and Christianity. From our many conversations he probably also sensed that I followed no real academic methodology; I was a maverick in some ways. My primary training was in *fiqh*, the science of Islamic jurisprudence and the interface between Islamic law and ethics. My interest in Christian theology grew from my encounter with Christian scholars around the world who in their own ways were engaged in some form of dialogue. Many of these scholars made time and space to hear me at a time when many of my Muslim colleagues remained a little suspicious of my intentions. My whole premise for this scholarly engagement was based on the gradual realization that through these encounters and the mutual study of theology, I had changed as an academic and as a person. I thought more deeply about my own faith when I listened to Christians talk about their faith. Over the years, people who had started out as strangers had blessed my life through their words and their friendships.

Werner Jeanrond and I are both scholars of religion as well as people of religious faith. Yet most of our conversations were not about the complexities of doctrines and differences. Rather it was more the challenges of religious faith often embedded in some global news story which provided the stimulus for many of our conversations. On my part these conversations never felt contrived or heavy; they were serious but good-humoured because we were able to be open and reflect, often critically, on our own religious tradition. Neither our identities nor our religious convictions are fixed in the way we often assume they are; we are all influenced by our daily encounters, our friendships and if we are fortunate by occasionally meeting people whose words and actions inspire us to lead better lives. Calling ourselves Muslims and Christians is one way to say something about who we are but faith in God is not about silent labels; it requires words and expression. We have to reflect on the goodness of God in our own lives, the way we talk to one another, the way we listen to one another, our patience when we hear something we disagree with, and our courage to put things right with grace. Most importantly those of us who value dialogue in a variety of forms know that absolutist views of truth are not conducive to mutual learning and the spirit of self-reflection, both of which are necessary ingredients to the moral life and to a life of learning. We also recognize the limits of language in how we talk of truth and transcendence. This is not some soft liberalism or a call to relativize everything, but actually a call to humility. Whatever our personal convictions, human beings only learn when they engage with others to open up new ways of thinking about the things which really matter in life. This is how we grow and eventually open ourselves to receiving and challenging traditional wisdom. Unfortunately, academics can become so precious about associating disciplines with identities that many would consider their own specialisms as too distant for any dialogical purpose. But here, they often fail to see that what really matters is that all our academic disciplines can have a life beyond books and articles. I strongly believe that the purpose of all learning should be about changing the world for the better in some small way. The academy can be an end in itself but we also have a moral imperative to engage with others if we feel that the interaction can make even the smallest contribution to human and societal moral progress.

I suspect Werner Jeanrond always knew that these were the main reasons why I was engaged in public life right from the beginning of my academic journey and he showed interest in this aspect of my work. I have always argued that academics need to be engaged with global events and in our current climate especially, scholars of religion should speak out about the tensions in various religions and the contested place of religion in public life. Thus, Werner Jeanrond would often pop his head round the door to comment on a recent BBC *Thought for the Day* or some other broadcast or inquire about a recent other public engagement. I for my part, weary of working at my desk for hours, would often go next door to say hello and enter a friend's world for a few minutes.

Both of us have some appreciation of the significance of dialogue between religions. Dialogue remains a contested term, a rather undefined discipline of which many remain suspicious. But rather than trying to confine dialogue to a discipline, I regard it as a journey left open and untamed in which we are all given the chance for self-transformation. Meaningful religious dialogue is not easy; rather, I would argue it demands a particular kind of intellectual devotion. There is nothing which stirs the soul more than listening to someone speak of how God is a presence in their lives. In my own experience I have found the best dialogue partners to be those who also show and practice hospitality. By hospitality here

I mean generosity of spirit, people who are willing to surrender something of themselves and show an intellectual vulnerability in this dialogical engagement.

Our capacity to be both strong and vulnerable is not a weakness but a rich paradox. Dialogue demands the confidence to be strong in your faith yet to be humble when listening to others. It demands the willingness to be open to the supreme possibility of learning from another in the hope that one is left feeling a little unsettled and searching. This kind of faith is not about theological jingoism but a thoughtful gentleness in the presence of someone with whom we are willing to take a risk in our journey towards God. It is this process of mutual learning which perfects one's own God consciousness. An intellectual artful dialogue is a worthy exercise but a dialogue which touches peoples' hearts is the product of a generous and hospitable character. It contains a soulful quality which is palpable while remaining impossible to measure.

Hospitality and generosity of spirit may not be the same thing but they are part of the same virtue ethics. Yet it is precisely because hospitality is regarded as a virtue and not as a natural instinct that it needs to be cultivated. If the ancient Greeks practised hospitality often from fear of the gods, it soon becomes apparent that in monotheism hospitality is also commanded as a divine duty with etiquettes addressed to both the one who gives it and the one who receives it.

Hospitality traditions run through Christianity and Islam very often depicted in scripture within the wider context of God's continuing test of his prophets. It is these tales which reflect God's power and presence in the course of human history. In Islam, prophecy is the ultimate accolade bestowed by God and it is through prophecy and tales about the prophets that God conveys his divine messages in the course of human history. There is no real philosophy or theory of prophethood in the Qur'an except that God's prophets and messengers are a sign of his mercy (*rahma*)[1] and the stories of previous prophets are mentioned as part of God's revelatory scheme:

To every people was sent a messenger. (Q 10.47)
We have sent you inspiration as we sent it to Noah and the messengers after him. We sent inspiration to Abraham, Isma'il, Isaac, Jacob and the tribes, to Jesus, Job, Jonah, Aaron, and Solomon and to David we gave the Psalms. (Q 4.163)

The concept of hospitality always involves the concept of a stranger. But as Franz Rosenthal points out, although there were strangers everywhere in Muslim societies, 'within the community of believers and wherever Muslims were in political control, there was in theory, no such distinct category as a "stranger".'[2] Thus, the ideal was that every Muslim was always at home with other Muslims and thus could not be seen as a separate category. This contrasts with the concept of the stranger in Classical Antiquity where the stranger was often seen as a

---

1. For ease of reading, I have omitted all diacritics from the Arabic transliterations.
2. Franz Rosenthal, 'The Stranger in Medieval Islam', *Arabica* 44 (1997), pp. 35–75 (36).

problem.³ Rosenthal also elaborates upon another strong theme in the Islamic tradition which is that the ancient use of travel as a metaphor to describe man's sojourn on earth had the obvious implication in Islam 'that human beings are strangers always and everywhere'. The Muslim Sufis appropriated this metaphor to reflect an inner religiosity whereby being a stranger turned into a lifestyle:

> If life on earth was a journey, this fact had to be made apparent by constant travel, and if, further, this meant being a stranger, its outwards manifestation was for Sufis to present themselves as strangers. They should not stay in one place.⁴

The themes around 'strangeness' in this world also led many devotees to claim that the soul too is a stranger in this world. Nevertheless for the purpose of this essay and to draw the distinction between religious teaching and lived reality, the term stranger applies to anyone who is simply unfamiliar and to whom hospitality is owed as a religious, social and moral duty. Recent comparative studies on hospitality often use the stories of Abraham to depict the necessity of hospitality in desert life where it always involves an element of risk taking. The first story is that of Abraham and the approach of three strangers to his house. The three men are actually angels in disguise and the story of Abraham's hospitality towards them is to be found in both Gen. 18 and Q 51.25, albeit with variations. Despite the differences between the biblical and Qur'anic stories, both versions speak of an Abraham compelled to show hospitality to the 'honoured guests' whom the Qur'an calls 'unusual people' (*munkar*). Hospitality is not a choice here but a religious duty and therefore should not be confused with contemporary understandings of charity. The second story is that of Hagar, the mother of Ismail, whom Abraham has to leave in the desert, according to some sources because of Sarah's jealousy and also because God commands Abraham to take Hagar and Ismail away. God has another purpose for their lives, an esteemed Arab genealogy and a prophetic line which ends with Muhammad himself. Unaware of this future, as Abraham leaves Hagar he prays to God 'To fill the hearts of some among men with love towards them, and feed them with fruits so that they may give thanks' (Q 14.37). The concept of hospitality exists therefore between human beings and between man and God. As human beings, we do not know how God reflects this hospitality but we can try to articulate it in the same way that we recognize hospitality between human beings. Abraham is worried as to who will feed Hagar and Ismail and asks God for nourishment and protection and indeed Hagar is welcomed by a local Bedouin tribe and settles among them.

For the Arabs in particular hospitality is an ancient concept, a humanizing element involving both guest and host. Miriam Shulman and Amal Barkouki-Wlnter explain the important role that hospitality plays in the harsh environment of the Middle-East: 'The virtue seems an ineluctable product of the landscape …

---

3. Ibid., p. 54.
4. Ibid.

to refuse a man refreshment in such a place is to let him die, to threaten the open-handedness nomadic peoples must depend on to survive'.[5]

Thus hospitality is not just a social act, it is a moral imperative. The offering of food and shelter, the very basics to survival appear to be part of the virtue ethics of Semitic civilizations and as Snjezana Akpinar writes of the Arabs, 'Linked closely with honor and chivalry, hospitality was considered an act of unconditional surrender to the needs of others. Islam accepted this heritage at its very inception'.[6] Akpinar continues with the observation that throughout much of Islamic literature and poetry in particular, 'God is portrayed as a guest for whose visit one must be always prepared'. This is because a visit by a stranger offers the opportunity 'to transform rancor and anger'.[7] In showing hospitality, humankind is given an opportunity to give and to receive for the stranger is not a friend and may be sent to test our faith in God. God does not reveal himself in Islam but God is present in our encounter with one another. While the traditions of hospitality focus mainly on providing material hospitality, this very act has an emotional and psychological effect on the giver and the recipient and can thus transform the relationship between two people. In demanding hospitality from God we act with hope in God's plan for us. The true nature of God's hospitality may be yet to come but our lives provide opportunities to find traces of God in the reciprocity of our relationships. One could argue that the recipient of our hospitality is standing in the place of God. Nowhere is the divine human relationship captured more poignantly than in the following *hadith*:

> Abu Hurayra said, 'The Messenger of Allah, may Allah bless him and grant him peace, said, Allah, the Mighty and Exalted, will say on the Day of Rising, "Son of Adam, I was ill and you did not visit Me." The man will say, "O Lord, how could I visit You when You are the Lord of the worlds?" He will say, "Do you not know that My slave so-and-so was ill and you did not visit him? Do you not know that if you had visited him, you would have found Me with him? O son of Adam, I asked you for food and you did not feed Me?" He will say, "O Lord, how could I feed You when You are the Lord of the worlds?" He will say, "Do you not know that My slave so-and-so asked you for food and you did not feed him? Do you not know that if you had fed him, you would have found that with Me. O son of Adam, I asked you for water and you did not give it to Me." He will say, "O Lord, how could I give You water when You are the Lord of the worlds?" He will say, "My slave so-and-so asked you for water and you did not give it to

---

5. Miriam Schulman and Amal Barkouki-Winter, 'The Extra Mile: Hospitality in Judaism, Christianity and Islam', *Issues in Ethics* 2/1 (2000). For a broader discussion of the theme, see Silas Webster Allard, 'In the Shade of the Oaks of Mamre: Hospitality as a Framework for Political Engagement between Christians and Muslims', *Political Theology* 13/4 (2012), pp. 414–24.

6. Snjezana Akpinar, 'Two Responses to "Interreligious Dialogue and Spiritual Hospitality": Hospitality in Islam', *Religion East and West* 7 (2007), pp. 23–7.

7. Ibid., p. 24.

him. Do you not know that if you had given him water, you would have found that with Me?' '⁸

Our hospitality towards one another generates a positive response from the angels themselves. Many traditions speak of angels not visiting the home of those who do not receive guests. The linking of hospitality with this kind of supernatural imagery makes well the theological point that being hospitable to others is essential to a good and virtuous character and synonymous with faith itself:

> The Emissary of God (may God bless him and grant him peace) was asked 'What is faith?' He said, 'The giving of food and the exchange of greetings.' 'In expiation and grades [of good deeds]', he said, 'the giving of food and the praying by night while people are asleep [is best].' He was asked about the pilgrimage acceptable to God and he said, 'It is the giving of food and of goodly words.' Anas said, 'A house which is not entered by a guest is not entered by angels'.[9]

Muslim theological discussions on hospitality invariably include food and drink for feeding others whether stranger or guests. This reflects the essence of a common humanity. In Ghazali's *Ihya Ulum al-din*, many of the *hadiths* place hospitality by way of giving food and water in the same category as worship; providing hospitality is seen as worship of the highest kind:

> The Emissary of God (may God bless him and grant him peace) said, 'If a visitor comes to you, be generous in your hospitality to him'. He said, 'In paradise there are rooms from inside which the exterior can be viewed, and from outside which the interior can be viewed; they are for the soft spoken who have provided food for people and prayed at night when people are asleep'.[10]

As Valerie Hoffman writes, Ghazali 'devotes far more space to the virtue of offering food, and the manner to offer and receive it than he does to the virtue of fasting'.[11] Food is so essential to hospitality that it is said we are accountable to God for all that we spend except the food we serve our guests for God himself would be embarrassed to ask about that.[12] Typical among the many *hadiths*

---

8. A *hadith* is a saying attributed to the Prophet Muhammad. This is *hadith* no. 896 from Imam al-Nawawi's *Riyad as-Salihin, The Meadows of the Righteous*, http://www.sunnipath.com/library/Hadith/H0004P0144.aspx, accessed 26 September 2014.

9. Al-Ghazali, *On the Manners relating to Eating, Kitab adab al-akl*, Book XI of *The Revival of the Religious Sciences. Ihya Ulum al-din*, trans. D. Johnson-Davies (Cambridge: The Islamic Texts Society, 2012), p. 30.

10. Ibid., p. 20.

11. Valerie J. Hoffman, 'Eating and Fasting for God in Sufi Tradition', *Journal of the American Academy of Religion* 63/3 (1995), pp. 465–85 (474).

12. Al-Ghazali, *On the Manners*, p. 19.

Ghazali cites is, 'There is no good in one who does not offer hospitality'. However, Ghazali's discussion of hospitality focuses on hosts and guests who know each other rather than the stranger who is a person unknown to us and may simply be passing through. It seems that one has a moral duty to provide hospitality to the stranger for all the reasons outlined above, but between the invited guest and host there are rights and obligations on both sides and a number of manners to be observed. Many of the *hadiths* speak of the unlawfulness of going to someone's house at mealtimes in the hope of being fed. Other sources speak of the kinds of food which should be presented to the guests so that one should be generous without displaying any affectation or ostentation. Then there are the *hadiths* which caution the guest not to overstay their welcome thus causing undue burden on the host. However, it is always recommended that one does not decline an invitation. Ghazali again makes the point by saying:

> A man ought not to decline [an invitation] because of distance or because of the host's poverty or lack of social standing. A distance that can normally be endured should not cause one to abstain. That is why it is said in the Torah or one of the sacred books, 'Walk a mile to visit a sick person, two miles to take part in a funeral, three miles to accept an invitation and four miles to visit a brother in God.' Precedence was given to accepting an invitation and paying a visit because through these one fulfils the right of the living who are more deserving than the dead.[13]

The duty to meet and engage with others is a religious duty, fundamental to fostering companionship and community, but hospitality is not easy and nor can we always foresee the consequences of giving and receiving. I chose the theme of hospitality for this short essay because hospitality across most religious traditions is seen as an ennobling feature and remains one of the most universal human social activities. We are relational beings and wanting connection with others is essential to being human even though the offer of hospitality always involves a risk. The rewards of hospitality are that when shared and nurtured, hospitality can often lead to friendships and friendships take us one step further towards a more intimate bond. Friendships are both a gift and a task and rely on shared lives, conversations and mutual experiences. They are shaped by the personal, the social and the political and give value and meaning to our lives. The classical philosophers considered the value of friendship in creating the moral framework of a good society and concluded that friendships are what make life worth living.

Categories of friendship are implicit in many of the central sociological and ethical questions of today and have a stake in defining who we are as individuals and also who we are as communities in a multi-racial, multi-faith and multi-cultural environment. The modern age is defined by the processes of migration and renewed interest in identity formation. Friendships have assumed a new significance in our globalized world where different cultures, races and religions

---

13. Ibid., p. 33.

engage in private and public spaces. So, who we choose to entertain, trust and have as friends matters and says something about our cultural attitudes and individual desires. Even if there are risks involved in the cultivation of new friendships, we should still ask ourselves a fundamental question which is that in fragmented and divided communities who do we trust and who are our friends? The answer to this question will tell us more about ourselves than we realize.

I left Glasgow University in 2011 and Werner Jeanrond himself is now working in Oxford. Time and distance mean we don't see much of each other now but in thinking about this essay I have to some extent reflected on the movement of our relationship – the arrival of the stranger, a shared hospitality and finally a generous and cherished friendship. For my part I know that God has been present throughout this journey.

27

BEYOND INDIFFERENCE: RELIGIOUS TRADITIONS AS RESOURCES FOR INTERRELIGIOUS TOLERATION

Christoph Schwöbel

The Provocations of Intolerance and the Risks of Indifference

Tolerance, the 'impossible virtue',[1] is very much in demand in the situation of religious and ideological pluralism in a globalizing world. In every sphere of life we seem to be confronted with the otherness of the other as an alluring attraction and as a threatening alternative to who we are and what we are. This is experienced in a radical way in religious pluralism where the very presence of practitioners of other religions with their places of worship and their ways of structuring their lives calls our own religious beliefs into question, simply by making us aware that they require justification, if not for others than for ourselves. If we look a little closer, we see that we are always on both sides of the requirement of toleration. We are at the same time the ones who are called to tolerate, and the ones who depend on the toleration of others. Developing personal virtues and social strategies of mutual toleration seems to be a necessary condition for the being of pluralist societies, and even more so for their well-being.

However, we have to recognize that religiously pluralist situations also provide rich opportunities for the growth of intolerance where the otherness of the other is not endured but is seen as something that needs to be overcome. Religious intolerance is a dangerous fire accelerant in all situations of conflict between different cultures and religions in multi-cultural and multi-religious societies, which threatens the unstable coexistence of diverse groups in one society, because it undermines the modes of social interaction and cooperation on which societies depend. It is not difficult to identify the motivational background of intolerance. One can easily enumerate the following factors: the involuntary exclusion from the opportunities of participating in social goods, whether they are material or

---

1. Cf. Bernard Williams, 'Toleration: An Impossible Virtue', in David Heydt, ed., *Toleration: Elusive Virtue* (Princeton: Princeton University Press, 1996), pp. 18–28.

symbolic goods; the inclusion in groups, forms of interaction or systems of rules which one rejects; the dialectic of anxieties of inferiorities and desires of achieving superiority; attacks on symbols which function as identity markers; and the experienced threat to one's identity as the denial of recognition.

Confronted with forms of intolerance, the tradition of establishing strategies of toleration on the basis of universalist principles of morality, rooted in the tradition of the Enlightenment, seem largely ineffective in providing an antidote to intolerance, especially in religious contexts. Demanding assent to formal moral principles seems to neglect the particularities of religious beliefs; enforcing a principle of abstract equality risks denying the real differences between people of different religious convictions. The common denominator of such approaches seems to be a denial of difference that resists abstract strategies of universalization. Treating religion as a purely personal and private matter confronts religious believers with the demand: 'If you are less religious … then you can be more tolerant'. It is not surprising that this is perceived by religious believers either as an attitude of indifference, of not taking the differences between religious forms of life seriously, or as a form of relativism, denying the truth claims and moral obligations of religious traditions. Indifference has many faces: from abstract egalitarianism to formal universalism, which is characteristic of modernism, to the aesthetic relativizing of differences, often found in post-modern views. These attitudes all have one point: as the negation of difference, indifference is the negation of the identity of the other. As such indifference is not a strategy of promoting tolerance, but reveals an attitude of intolerance.

Religious Traditions as Resources for the Formation of Tolerance

The common failure of strategies of moral universalism consists in their failure to connect the virtue of tolerance to the religious beliefs and convictions of believers. For religious believers, acting *as if* their religious beliefs were true, is not enough to support such a difficult virtue as tolerance. An alternative would be to seek the roots of tolerance in the religious traditions, from what believers believe to be true and obligatory for their way of relating towards others. The *'if… then…'- structure*, connected with demands to be less religious in order to be more tolerant, is in this way replaced by the *'because… therefore…'-structure* which attempts to discover the grounds for the virtue of tolerance in the specific religious convictions of believers. In order to be tolerant, believers would not be confronted with the demand to be less religious, but with the invitation to be more religious – to deepen their commitment to their particular religious roots.[2]

The formal structure of tolerance can be described in the following way: 'A' *(the subject of tolerance) endures* 'B' *(the object of tolerance) on the basis of*

---

2. For a full account of this approach cf. Christoph Schwöbel, *Gott im Gespräch: Studien zur religiösen Gegenwartsdeutung* (Tübingen: Mohr Siebeck, 2011), pp. 1–178.

'C' *(the particular reasons for tolerance) with the aim 'D'.* We can quickly see the wide variety of notions of tolerance we can generate when we substitute the formal placeholders with concrete descriptions. (A) can be understood as individuals or groups; (B) can cover a wide variety of persons, beliefs, attitudes and practices. This immediately makes us aware that the primary objects of toleration are persons and groups of persons whom we respect although we object to their beliefs and practices. We may not introduce too sharp a distinction between persons and their beliefs, because the identity of religious persons is, in their own understanding, shaped by their beliefs and behaviours, and tolerating them without these would introduce a highly problematic understanding of otherness: I can tolerate you as something other than what you yourself believe to be. Here 'otherness' is an ill-disguised excuse for indifference. Everything, however, seems to revolve around the reasons for tolerance (C). If we try to find the roots of tolerance in the religious beliefs of believers, then (C) qualifies all the other material substitutions for the components of the formula. To give a rather obvious Christian example: if I believe myself to be created in the image of God together with all other human beings, then the 'object' of my toleration also falls into that category and every possible aim I envisage for toleration is necessarily painted as a possible future for God's images. In the case of religious beliefs, the reasons for tolerance (C) connect my understanding of my religious identity (A) with my understanding of the others I try to tolerate (B) and so envisage a common future (D). Whether I can see the others with their differences as part of my future is the endurance test for tolerance.

We have reached a preliminary result. If we attempt to offer grounds for the toleration of other believers, drawn from the resources of our own religious tradition, then the grounds on the basis of which we describe our identities and the grounds for tolerance of other religious believers have the same roots. The cultivation of my religious identity and developing a culture of toleration cannot be understood as opposites, but have the same ground. This has two obvious implications. First of all, if religious believers are prone to be intolerant of other religions and their believers, as a common prejudice has it, it would make sense to develop reasons for toleration which could convince those we want to motivate for toleration. Reasons rooted in religious traditions could offer strong motivations or grounds for tolerance for religious believers. Secondly, I cannot tolerate what I do not know. Toleration can only be directed towards specific contents of specific beliefs and towards particular aspects of particular practices. Hence, interreligious tolerance must be placed in the context of interreligious dialogue. This offers the chance for the others to present their own views so that I can respond to them and their views. Furthermore, it allows us to reflect on our interconnection as it is perceived and as it is practised in interreligious dialogue. Public debates on interreligious tolerance very often lack both knowledge of the others' religion, based on what they say about themselves, and a concrete view of the interdependence of religious traditions, challenged to be tolerant.

Reasons for Tolerance in Three Traditions

Theologically, religions cannot be understood from a standpoint above concrete religions. We can only understand other religions from the standpoint of our own religion, trying to relate to the religion of others by means of dialogical exchange and translation and by the analogical extension of what we know from our own religious traditions. The religious reasons for toleration are always tradition-specific. It would, therefore, make sense to reflect on the possibilities for tolerance as they can be developed within the Christian traditions. For my own tradition of Lutheran Christianity this would mean to develop a conception of tolerance on the basis of faith.[3] In an important article, Gerhard Ebeling has tried to contrast the tolerance of God and the tolerance of reason.[4] With the expression 'the tolerance of God' (*tolerantia Dei*) he refers to an element of Martin Luther's theology which employs the notion of tolerance to explain God enduring our sin before we were justified and tolerating us as justified sinners. One paradigmatic scriptural passage where this is developed is Paul's exploration of the logic of reconciliation in Romans. Paul asserts that 'God proves his love for us in that while we were sinners Christ died for us' (Rom. 5.8). God tolerates our sinfulness in order to justify us so that reconciliation begins by God relating in his love to us 'while we were enemies' (Rom. 5.10). It is not easy to move from God's tolerance to our tolerance of the believers of other faiths – Luther, at least, never does that. However, rooting our tolerance of others in God's relationship to us as believers seems to point to a crucial element of the Christian understanding of tolerance on the basis of faith. This can be further developed by referring to the exclusive particles of Protestant self-understanding that we are saved by faith alone, through grace alone, because of Christ alone, as Scripture alone reliably proclaims it to us.

In a Lutheran interpretation, the emphasis that we are justified by faith alone refers to the constitution of faith by vindicating the Gospel of Christ through the Holy Spirit for us. Thus, we are enabled to trust in God. Faith is, therefore, not a human possibility but made possible and actual by God's work in us. Faith is constituted for us and not constituted by us. In encountering other faiths, Christians have to recognize that those believers also claim that their faith is not the result of human effort but something they experience as a gift. Is the recognition that the faith of others is also passively constituted for them not a sufficient reason for an attitude of tolerance based on the insight of the constitution of one's own faith? Furthermore, in claiming that we are saved by grace alone the Reformation wanted to exclude any other conditions for salvation apart from God's grace in Christ. This excludes not only good works, a favourite topic in the polemic of the Reformers against the remaining Catholics, but also the right beliefs. We are not

---

3. Cf. Christoph Schwöbel, 'Toleranz aus Glauben', in idem, *Christlicher Glaube im Pluralismus* (Tübingen: Mohr Siebeck, 2003), pp. 217–43.

4. Cf. Gerhard Ebeling, 'Die Toleranz Gottes und die Toleranz der Vernunft', in Trutz Rendtorff, ed., *Das theologische Erbe der Aufklärung* (Gütersloh: Gütersloher Verlagshaus, 1982), pp. 54–73.

saved because we believe the right things about God. This would also support an attitude of toleration on the basis of faith towards those who believe other things about God than we ourselves do. The unconditional character of God's grace is expressed in Reformation theology by insisting that Christ alone is the saviour. God's work in Christ alone is sufficient for salvation. What about the so-called 'Scripture Principle' that all doctrine has to be based on scripture alone? Is this a claim to exclusivity, which turns all other theological traditions into interpretations of scripture, not detrimental to tolerant interreligious relations? The so-called Scripture Principle underlines the external constitution of our relationship to God. We must be addressed by the word of scripture, witnessing to the word of God, and cannot find God in the depth of our religious interiority. This is, at least, an element which Protestant Christianity has in common with the other monotheistic religions. One could point to many experiences where interreligious dialogue was carried to another level by interpreting one's own scriptures in the presence of the other and by trying to understand the scriptures of the other, interpreted in their words, on the basis of one's own faith and one's own scriptural reasoning. In addition, the biblical scriptures offer ample material for the discussion of issues of intolerance and tolerance, perhaps most provocatively so in Jesus' hospitality to those who by all religious and moral standards of their times were hard to tolerate, and by practising this hospitality as an effective sign of God's creative justice.

Interpreted in this way, what we understand as being constitutive for our faith also becomes the ground for the toleration of the faith of others. What the four exclusive particles have in common is the consistent self-relativizing of the Christian 'religion' over against its ground and subject matter. This self-relativizing is, however, completely different from a relativistic principle, because it points to the constitution of faith by God as the ground of faith outside and beyond ourselves. This creates the space and time for tolerating others and their religion. By grounding faith and tolerance in the *otherness* of God, who is not identical with our religion and only becomes the ground and subject-matter of our religion by God's free and gracious self-manifestation, space for tolerating others is opened up. Claiming that only God is absolute implies the non-absoluteness of Christianity as a religion along with all other religions. Furthermore, since the otherness of God is understood in Christianity as having its concrete form in God's creative, reconciling and perfecting love, it receives another emphasis.[5] The otherness of God's love is not just that God's love is creative whereas our love is attracted to what we find lovable. The otherness of God's love has its concrete form in bringing justice to the unjust, in justifying sinners, in disclosing truth to those trapped in the net of deception and falsehood and including those into communion who have excluded themselves from it. The otherness of the creator

---

5. Werner G. Jeanrond, *A Theology of Love* (London: Continuum/T&T Clark, 2010), p. 230: 'This careful attention to otherness ... provides also the model for the emergence of loving relationships between Christians and non-Christian others. From such a perspective, no interreligious dialogue or encounter is of any real interest if it is not carried out in a spirit of love'.

finds its concrete expression in the otherness of the reconciler, offering peace to God's enemies (Rom. 5.1 and 8) and so including them into the perfected communion of God with God's reconciled creation.

Engaging with the religious tradition of Christianity to explore the resources for interreligious toleration, carries us beyond Christianity as a religion and draws us into reflection of the otherness of God. The religious engagement with the question of tolerating other religions becomes a theological engagement with God and God's otherness. Another way of expressing the difference between God and everything that is not God is by referring to the divine attributes. Can Christians claim that God is omnipresent and at the same time regard the other religions as a quasi godless zone where God is definitely not present? Can Christians claim that God is omnipotent and at the same time assume that the other religions do not contribute to the way God is working God's purpose out? Can Christians claim that God is love and at the same time define the boundaries of God's love by the limits of our intolerance? However, God's otherness also implies that while we would certainly have to affirm God's presence for and in other religions and their believers, and so approach other religions with the expectation to find the presence of God in them, we can only do so on the basis of what God has disclosed to us in God's self-disclosure in Christ through the Spirit. We remain bound to what we can know by the light of grace, illuminating the light of nature, while we still expect to be surprised and our anxious questions answered in the light of God's glory in the Kingdom of God.[6] What we already know of God's grace from God's self-disclosure – amazed by the grace 'that saved a wretch like me' – creates more space for toleration than could ever be envisaged by the demands of religious self-preservation and identity politics. The theological self-relativizing of the Christian religion in exploring the roots of interreligious toleration turns out to be an experience of being relativized by the otherness of God. It is, nevertheless, worthwhile to raise a self-critical question: Can the theological self-relativizing of the Christian religion be prevented from turning into a general relativism which would again lose the emphasis on otherness that seems crucial for exploring the religious roots of tolerance?

When we turn now to other religious traditions we do so by looking for analogical structures, which combine similarity and dissimilarity. In the case of Islam[7] we find that modern theological interpreters of the Qur'an try to establish the notion of tolerance in revelation itself. Revelation is understood to have a fundamental unity because it has one author. This unity, however, is internally differentiated according to the respective occasions for the sending down of revelation. Does this unity in diversity of the divine revelation provide a basis from which reasons for toleration could be deduced? The discussion revolves around one central Qur'anic passage in which the correlation between unity and diversity is explained as being rooted in God's will.

---

6. Cf. Martin Luther, *On the Bondage of the Will*, Luther's Works, vol. 33, ed. Philip S. Watson (Philadelphia: Fortress, 1972), p. 292.

7. Cf. the discussion of some significant aspects in Joshua Cohen and Ian Lague, eds, *The Place of Tolerance in Islam: Khaled Abou El Fadl* (Boston, MA: Beacon, 2002).

For each of them we have established a law,
and a revealed way.
And if God wished,
God would have made you a single nation;
but the intent is to test you
in what God has given you.
So let your goals be everything good.
Your destiny, everyone, is to God,
Who will tell you about
That wherein you differed. (Q 5.48)

The otherness of the other is here described as being rooted in the unity of the will of the one God. Since God in his unity must be seen as the ground for difference, difference is to be tolerated in submission to the will of God. This is also extended to the question of believing: whether or not humans believe is ultimately rooted in the will of God. Hence, the use of coercion and violence in questions of religion is explicitly denied. Moreover, the otherness of the other is undergirded by the unity of the human race. Humans are created from one man and one woman but they are made into nations and tribes so that they can know one another. The measure of their recognition is righteousness before God, the omniscient one (Q 49.13). A special role is given to the people of the Book, 'Jews, Christians, and Sabeans', because they believe in God, the last judgement, and the obligation to perform deeds of virtue. To them a just reward is promised. 'Truly those who believe [in this Revelation], and the Jews and the Christians and the Sabeans – whoever believes in God and the Last Day and performs virtuous deeds – their reward is with their Lord, neither fear nor grief shall befall them' (Q 2.62; and similarly Q 5.69).

Viewed from a Christian perspective we find here a very similar self-relativizing of the beliefs and practises of religion over against their source, the one God. If toleration is to have a secure grounding in tradition then it must be rooted, primarily, in the will of God and, secondarily, in the virtuous deeds which humans are to perform. A central question, and one that is well known from the history of Christianity, is whether this form of grounding tolerance in submission to God and in righteous deeds also provides the basis for toleration within one's own religion. Hence, the question is how the theological grounds for respecting the otherness of the other can be translated into a practice of toleration, which can be exercised in different political settings. Does a practice of tolerance, which is consistently grounded in submission to God, include the possibility of a distinction between religion and political order?

When we turn from the conversation between two related monotheistic religions to Buddhism and its understanding of toleration we turn to a religious way of life which receives its distinctive features not from the otherness of God but from the interconnectedness of all aspects of 'reality'.[8] According to the

---

8. For a comprehensive overview cf. Perry Schmidt-Leukel, ed., *Buddhism and Christianity in Dialogue* (Norwich: SCM, 2005); idem, ed., *Buddhist Attitudes to other*

teachings of Gautama Buddha in the Dharmacakra Pravartana Sūtra everything is causally connected through dependent origination (*pratītyasamutpāda*). This universal causal interrelatedness underlies the teaching of the four noble truths, the understanding of *karma*, the doctrine of the not-self (*anātman*), the teaching of emptiness (*śūnyatā*). The difference that is introduced into this flux of interconnectedness is caused by the self-centredness of the human, which finds its expression in craving and ignorance. The teaching of the Buddha offers a way out of this fateful and painful self-dislocation of the human in the flux of everything. In Japan, tolerance as a Western concept was introduced, like the concept of religion (*shūkyō*), into Buddhist thought during the late nineteenth century. In the process of the assimilation of this notion in Japan during the Meiji Era, tolerance (*kanyo*) was associated with the third of the six virtues, patience (*ninniku*, or in Sanskrit *kśanti*). It expresses the awareness of the plight of one's own self, when it is confronted with the deviating opinions of others. On this view, the otherness of others makes one painfully aware of the otherness of one's own self. Liberation can only be found by the enlightenment with the truth that there is no difference: 'emptiness is fullness, fullness is emptiness'. Here we encounter a completely different notion of difference compared to the monotheistic religions which has very different implications for understanding tolerance. Tolerance is no longer respect for the otherness of others but compassion for those who through the otherness of others are made aware of their own otherness, a painful difference that needs to be overcome in *nirvāna*. This leads to the question: Can the difference of the other be an occasion for tolerance, or must tolerance be replaced with compassion when the liberating insight suggests that there is no difference, only indifference?

Tolerance Among the Virtues of Hospitality

These theological reflections on the religious roots of interreligious toleration have tried to indicate that there are possibilities for providing reasons for tolerance from within the different religious traditions. Such considerations have their significance and their limitation in offering an entrance into the practice of tolerance. In the context of interreligious relations, tolerance is only one of the virtues of hospitality.[9] It is important because it shows that a welcoming space for the other can be found within one's own tradition. It is, however, no more than an invitation. How that space is to be filled with fruitful conversations, promising interactions, and hopeful cooperation for the common good of the society, where the respective others receive and give more than toleration, is another matter.

Religions (St. Ottilien: EOS, 2008). From a Buddhist perspective cf. R. P. Jain, *Buddhism and Its Christian Critics* (Delhi: MPS, 2011).

9. Cf. Catherine Cornille, *The Im-Possibility of Interreligious Dialogue* (New York: Crossroads, 2008), pp. 177–210.

Part V

GOD AS OTHER AND THE OTHERNESS OF GOD

28

LOVED BY THE OTHER:
CREATIO EX NIHILO AS AN ACT OF DIVINE LOVE

David Fergusson

All love includes the experience of otherness.[1]

The doctrine of creation out of nothing has often been understood as an enunciation of divine sovereignty. The *ex nihilo* concept deliberately excludes any competing or countervailing reality other than God to explain the origin as well as the preservation and the purpose of the cosmos. While the doctrine has held sway in the history of the church, it has been challenged for its morally dubious construction of God in terms of a controlling power. As a consequence of this critique of the *ex nihilo* tradition, recent attempts to articulate the love of God have reverted to the notion of creation out of chaos with its roots in the Hebrew Bible. The image of wrestling with recalcitrant material has been judged more adequate to the vulnerable action of God upon the cosmos. By contrast, creation out of nothing with its associations of caprice and control appears to resonate with hierarchical models of the relationship of God to God's creation. In her formidable attack on the tradition, Catherine Keller castigates its masculinist *Tendenz* as it emerged in the early church. 'The Father needs nothing but his own logos to create. This is a rhetoric of sheer power'.[2] In what follows, however, I shall track the conception and reception of the *ex nihilo* doctrine in the history of Christian thought to suggest that it is more patient of the love of God than is suggested by critics. My claim is that it is a necessary condition for understanding God in terms of the personal other.

---

1. Werner G. Jeanrond, *A Theology of Love* (London: Continuum/T&T Clark, 2010), p. 254.

2. Catherine Keller, *The Face of the Deep: a Theology of Becoming* (London: Routledge, 2003), p. 53.

The Articulation of Creatio ex nihilo

By the end of the second century, the doctrine of creation out of nothing had emerged as the standard teaching of the church. The subsequent unanimity of support for this doctrine is one of the most intriguing episodes in the history of dogma. Once defended, it was perceived as the only adequate Christian alternative against Greek accounts of matter and Gnostic myths of emanation. Although the doctrine is not formulated in Gen. 1, it is claimed to adequately articulate the relationship of God to God's creation as it is understood throughout the Bible. Hence, creation out of nothing was conceived as a concept for the articulation and interpretation of biblical themes and topics, even if it was not explicitly taught in scripture.

The philosophical traditions of ancient Greece regarded the eternity of matter as an axiomatic assumption. We can detect the idea in a succession of thinkers including Parmenides, Plato, and Plutarch.[3] Their argument against creation out of nothing was simply that nothing could come out of nothing. If once there had been nothing, there would still be nothing. However, since we know that there is now something, we must assume that there had never been nothing, but something. The eternity of matter was therefore an assumption that seemed intuitively correct.

The classical philosophical statement of creation is presented in Plato's *Timaeus*, a dialogue that exercised much influence over Christian cosmology. According to Plato, the creator's work is to impose order upon disorderly matter. Some early Christian theologians appear to have held that Plato's myth of creation was consistent with the teaching of Gen. 1 as it resonates with the commitment to creation out of formless matter in Wis. 11.17. Hence, Justin Martyr could claim a dependence of Greek philosophy upon the writings of Moses.[4] Yet as Gerhard May claims, by the end of the second century the doctrine of creation out of nothing had become a settled teaching with arguments systematically advanced in its favour.[5] Theophilus of Antioch argues that the eternity of matter compromises the sovereignty of God. Nothing can be co-eternal with the one God without itself being considered divine. The splendour of God is attested by the creation of everything *ex nihilo*. 'But the power of God is revealed by his making whatever he

---

3. The standard work on the emergence of the *ex nihilo* doctrine is Gerhard May, *Creatio Ex Nihilo: The Doctrine of Creation out of Nothing in Early Christian Thought* (Edinburgh: T&T Clark, 1994). Also cf. the symposium edited by Janet Martin Soskice, 'Creation "*Ex Nihilo*" and Modern Theology', *Modern Theology* 29 (2013). The *ex nihilo* arguments tend to be grounded initially in a Hebraic account of creation rather than on distinctively christological grounds. This is confirmed by Markus Bockmuehl's evidence for precursors to this tradition in earlier Palestinian Judaism: 'Creatio ex nihilo in Palestinian Judaism and Early Christianity', *Scottish Journal of Theology* 65/3 (2012), pp. 253–70.

4. Justin Martyr, 'First Apology', in *The Ante-Nicene Fathers*, vol. 1, ed. Alexander Roberts and James Donaldson (Edinburgh: T&T Clark, 1873), p. 182.

5. Cf. Gerhard May, *Creatio Ex Nihilo*, pp. 118–78.

wishes out of the non-existent'.[6] Here we begin to detect something like a set of standard arguments for the *ex nihilo* doctrine. Each of these arguments is directed against claims for the eternity of matter. If matter is unoriginate, then God cannot be reckoned the creator of everything. God's nature as the source of everything is thus compromised. Moreover, if the unoriginate matter is co-existent with God, then matter appears to be divine. Such a divinity of matter would disrupt the priority of God in relation to created reality. Finally, the grandeur of God is better represented by a creation out of nothing than by a creation out of something.

In their polemics against Gnosticism, both Irenaeus and Tertullian extend the doctrine of creation out of nothing. It is required not only to contest the assumption about the eternity of matter, but also to maintain the strict ontological distinction between God and God's creation. The cosmos does not represent a series of ontological gradations emanating from the divine outwards; there is one God, and everything else exists through the power of the Word. Since this Word of God is to be regarded as of the divine essence, it cannot be an intermediate deity that links God with God's creation. On both sides, therefore, the distinction of creator and creation requires the doctrine of creation out of nothing. Hence, we must think of the cosmos as the creation of the one God from out of nothing. Here, 'nothing' plainly and simply means 'not something'. It is not a shadowy substance suspended between being and non-being. Instead, we should regard it merely as a way of saying what is not – neither matter nor emanation.

Crucially, there is no necessity in the creation of the world. God does not need to make the world. As a free act, creation is a gratuitous act of divine grace. This notion is not without its difficulties and there are ways in which it was qualified throughout the history of the church. Here, however, we can note that the emphasis upon the *ex nihilo* doctrine from the end of the second century entailed a stress upon creation as a free act of God.

The distinction between God's two hands and the world which is created out of nothing is already stressed by writers such as Irenaeus. It adumbrates the claim that *logos* and *pneuma* must finally be viewed as of the essence of God, rather than pre-eminent creatures. Accordingly, the notion of a creation out of nothing is further consolidated by the outcome of the Nicene controversy in the fourth century. There is one triune God, three persons each in relation to the other fully expressing the divine being; and there is also God's creation which does not proceed from out of the divine being. Nevertheless, it was important to stress that the creation is related to the creator: creation is the locus for continual divine action. Hence the ontological difference between God and God's creation does not entail a lack of divine involvement or absence of love. Instead, it is better to think of the difference between creator and creature as the difference which enables the relationship between them. The ontological size-gap does not make the one remote from the other: it is a distance that allows for a close and constant interaction of a particular form. Hence, we might see the *ex nihilo*

---

6. Theophilus of Antioch, *Ad Autolycum*, trans. R. M. Grant (Oxford: Clarendon, 1970), p. 27 (2.4).

doctrine as providing the necessary conditions for the divine action which can be characterized in more personal categories than is otherwise possible. The conceptual space that is mapped out by the differentiation of God and creation as two separate realities facilitates forms of interaction which are more appropriately articulated in personal rather than impersonal language.[7] This inflection of the *ex nihilo* concept can be illustrated by the historical examples of Augustine, Thomas Aquinas, and Martin Luther.

Augustine

In Augustine's theology, the doctrine of creation out of nothing is fundamental. It informs the ways in which he construes creation in its relationship to God. The tendency of the world to fall into disorder, the threat of non-being, and the radical dependence of beings are shaped by the *ex nihilo* tradition. Carol Harrison argues that this tradition is constitutive for Augustine's theology after his conversion in 386.[8] It enables him to eschew dualism, to borrow from while significantly modifying Neo-Platonism, and to provide the conceptual framework for the articulation of central concepts of his theology.

Manichaeism offers a sophisticated cosmology and anthropology not dissimilar to earlier forms of Gnosticism. The cosmos is the site of warfare between the forces of good and evil. Human beings with their mixed moral record are a microcosm of this. Augustine rejects Manichaeism with help from the Neo-Platonist account of emanation. Although Augustine rejects the emanationist scheme *per se*, the ontological difference between the creator and the creation is adopted and adapted from Neo-Platonism: the creator is transcendent, independent, incorporeal and incorruptible and the creation is immanent, dependent, corporeal and corruptible. Hence, there is a categorical difference between creator and creation.

His account of creation out of nothing, adopting but adjusting Neo-Platonist categories, enables Augustine to articulate the convictions to which he adhered after his conversion and then with increasing insistence during the intense Pelagian controversy. The initial goodness of the world can be affirmed. It proceeds from the will of the one who is pre-eminent in goodness. The world comes from God; it is destined to return to God. Yet, because it is created, the world has the ontological instability that causes it to be threatened by evil. Evil is not a positive cosmic force (as in Manichaeism), but is the privation of good; it is an absence that causes the defect. So Augustine can explain evil without recourse to dualism.

Augustine insists upon the need for a constant giving of divine grace to sustain the human creature. The gift is not a one-off endowment of created capacities. The

---

7. Here I am largely in agreement with Kathryn Tanner who points out that transcendence does not denote distance in the *ex nihilo* tradition, but a modality of personal divine action. Cf. Kathryn Tanner, 'Creatio ex Nihilo as a Mixed Metaphor', *Modern Theology* 29/2 (2013), pp. 138–55.

8. Cf. Carol Harrison, *Rethinking Augustine's Early Theology* (Oxford: Oxford University Press, 2005), pp. 75–114.

fragility of the human will entails a continual dependence upon God's grace for succour and strength to resist temptation. Hence, Augustine's use of the doctrine of creation out of nothing is closely intertwined with a radical theology of grace. It abolished the substantial dualism of Manichaeism and the ethical dualism of Pelagianism by emphasizing the dependence of the contingent creation upon its creator. God does not need to create the world; God's decision to create is unconstrained. 'And the statement "God saw that it was good" makes it quite plain that God did not create under the stress of any compulsion, or because he lacked something for his own needs; his only motive was goodness; he created because his creation was good'.[9]

In this respect, Augustine's doctrine of creation differs from later deist constructions of the relationship between creator and creation. The spiritual and moral relation of the world to God is maintained by the manner in which the world derivatively possesses the form of the divine likeness. Creatures can participate, albeit in a manner appropriate to their created status, in the divine life. So even while affirming the doctrine of a free creation out of nothing, notions of emanation, participation and gradation of being are never far away in Augustine's theology. These ensure that the love of God is central to the exposition of the *ex nihilo* doctrine.

Thomas Aquinas

But why does God create at all? Creation is to be explained neither by internal nor external constraint. According to medieval scholasticism, it is the nature of the good to express itself, to pour its love into what it is not. Here Neo-Platonist themes continue to resurface in Christian theology.[10] This divine self-expression is manifested primarily in the Trinitarian persons and secondarily in the creation of the world. The image of the artist is deployed, although it is stressed that this is only a creaturely image: an artistic production expresses something of the character of its author. This notion is adopted by Aquinas in his discussion of creation.

The manifestations of divine love in creation are varied. For example, it appears in the diversity of creatures that form part of the rich tapestry of creation, each reflecting something of the mystery of God the creator.[11] The world is teeming with different life forms; this spatio-temporal diversity is a mark of the creativity of divine love. The commitment here to a kaleidoscopic creation of profuse beauty may explain why Catholicism was better placed than Protestantism to appropriate later evolutionary notions after Charles Darwin. Aquinas develops a theology of diversity with the claim that God desires that there should be a multitude of creatures – an array of animate and inanimate forms of existence. God produced manifold things so that what was wanting in one expression of divine goodness

---

9. Augustine, *City of God*, trans. D. Knowles (Harmondsworth: Penguin, 1972), p. 457.
10. Cf. Zachary Hayes, *The Gift of Being: A Theology of Creation* (Collegeville, MN: Michael Glazier, 2001).
11. Ibid., p. 48.

might be supplied by another; for goodness, which in God is single and uniform, in creatures is multiple and pluriform. Hence, the whole creation represents God's goodness less incompletely than one creature.[12] Aquinas' theology of variety has potential for the valuing of our environment as it points to our interdependence with the cosmos and our fellow creatures.

This account of creation is not merely the claim that God is to be understood as creator and sustainer of everything. Although these notions are included in the doctrine of creation, Aquinas goes much further in stressing the ways in which creation is an action of the Trinity. While it is proper to attribute creation primarily to the Father as the originator, the other two persons are also involved in creation since creation is an action of the undivided divine being.[13] Accordingly, creation also reflects the Son and the Spirit. This has a double significance for the doctrine of creation. The wisdom of the Son permeates the entire created order. Here Aquinas employs the image of the artist. Just as something of the artist can be discerned in the work of art, so we can discern something of God's wisdom in creation. There is no part of the world that cannot express this wisdom in some way, however obscure that may be to our minds. The Spirit brings created things to their end in God's economy of creation and salvation. Consequently, we have to see creation as a continuous action for Aquinas. The world is never without the impression of divine action. The divine Spirit is at work everywhere to bring creation to a *telos* desired by God. Aquinas's account of creation out of nothing is therefore suffused with notions of divine goodness, self-expression and spiritual indwelling. These militate against any construction of a tyrannical relationship between creator and creation in his theology.

Martin Luther

Although it was not a contested doctrine at the time of the Reformation, both Martin Luther and John Calvin lectured extensively on the subject of creation. Their approach is characterized by three distinctive emphases. The first of these is a return to the biblical passages. Each produced commentaries on Genesis – in Luther's case what we now have may be a heavily redacted version of lecture transcripts – in which a more literal approach to the text can be discerned. Second, creation is presented from an existential perspective. It is an article of faith that expresses confidence in the parental care of God. In relation to this, a third emphasis emerges: the link perceived between creation on the one side and preservation and providence on the other.[14]

The Genesis commentary reveals the importance of the opening chapters of the Bible in Luther's exposition of the Christian faith. He re-affirms the *ex nihilo*

12. Thomas Aquinas, *Summa Theologiae*, 1a.47.1.
13. Ibid., 1a.45.
14. For a discussion of Martin Luther and John Calvin on creation cf. Colin Gunton, *The Triune Creator: A Historical and Systematic Study* (Edinburgh: Edinburgh University Press, 1998), pp. 147–54.

doctrine, arguing that it is the sign of the majesty of God in all of God's works. His most famous statement on creation, however, is found in the 'Small Catechism'.

> I believe in God the Father Almighty, Maker of heaven and earth.
> What does this mean? – Answer:
> I believe that God has created me and all that exists; that he has given me and still sustains my body and soul, all my limbs and senses, my reason and all the faculties of my mind, together with food and clothing, house and home, family and property; that he provides me daily and abundantly with all the necessities of life, protects me from all danger, and preserves me from all evil. All this he does out of his pure, fatherly, and divine goodness and mercy, without any merit or worthiness on my part. For all of this I am bound to thank, praise, serve and obey him. This is most certainly true.[15]

Here, Luther links creation to the unmerited mercy of God directed towards sinners. Both of these works are the result of God's grace towards us. Luther also argues that God's great work of resurrection becomes more believable when we behold the wonder of creation itself.

> Since God is able to bring forth from the water the heaven and the stars, the size of which either equals or surpasses that of the earth; likewise, since He is able out of a droplet of water to create sun and moon, could He not also defend my body against enemies … or, after it has been placed in the grave, revive it for a new life.[16]

The strength of this approach to creation lies in its existential stress upon faith in creation. This emphasis connects with biblical and liturgical themes that broaden the theology of creation beyond a hypothesis about the origins of the cosmos. However, such a treatment of the topic can result in an approach which is too human-centred. Those aspects of creation that are more remote from humanity are not registered sufficiently. Hence, the move from creation to salvation is arguably too swift, particularly in Luther's linkage of creation and justification. Nonetheless, Luther could also refer to the ways in which non-human creatures share the struggle of human creatures for life against the devil. By virtue of their very existence, these non-human animals are our co-workers in serving God, the creator of all that is. 'God created all these creatures to be in active military service, to fight for us continually against the devil'.[17] Hence, strong existential and

---

15. Martin Luther, 'Small Catechism', in Theodore G. Tappert, ed., *Book of Concord* (Philadelphia: Fortress, 1959), pp. 344–5.
16. Martin Luther, 'Lectures on Genesis, Chapters 1–5', in idem, *Luther's Works*, vol. 1, ed. Jaroslav Pelikan (Saint Louis: Concordia, 1958), p. 49.
17. Ibid., p. 74. Also cf. Bernhard Lohse, *Martin Luther's Theology: Its Historical and Systematic Development*, trans. R. A. Harrisville (Edinburgh: T&T Clark, 1995), p. 242.

providential concerns emerge in Luther's rendition of creation out of nothing. The love of God for sinners is already attested in the work of creation.

The Relation between Creator and Creation

Despite the unanimity of the tradition in favour of creation out of nothing, there has been some unease around the doctrine in modern theology. At the beginning of the nineteenth century, Friedrich D. E. Schleiermacher seemed relatively uninterested in the *ex nihilo* tradition, tending instead to conflate the ideas of creation and preservation. His notion of God as the one on whom we are conscious of being absolutely dependent leads him to dismiss notions of creation out of nothing as unduly speculative. In *The Christian Faith*, he claims that it is a notion which is remote from Christian religious affections; hence, it is to be treated as a matter of indifference.[18] Later writers have found the doctrine troubling for other reasons. As a free act of the transcendent creator, creation out of nothing has connotations of arbitrariness. These do not properly capture the ways in which creator and creation are bound together. A random creation is not one that is valued. Moreover, the classical tradition appears to intensify the problem of evil. If God freely called the universe into being from out of nothing, then why not produce a better universe than this actual one with all its suffering? Such challenges have influenced process theologians who seek to reinvigorate the notion of creation from out of chaos. Divine creation takes place within matter over which God exercises an influence, rather than control. Divine action takes the form of persuasion, seeking to draw order out of chaos in order to maximize love.[19]

My counter claim is that the interaction of God with creation requires to be cast in more personal as opposed to organic concepts.[20] The necessary condition of a personal interaction of creator and creation is the ontological difference which the traditional doctrine expresses through the *ex nihilo* scheme. Such criticism also works against the idea that the world should be thought of as God's body. While this has the apparent advantage of consolidating the connection between God and God's creation, it tends to depersonalize that relationship. As

---

18. Cf. Friedrich D. E. Schleiermacher, *The Christian Faith*, trans. H. R. Mackintosh and J. S. Stewart (Edinburgh: T&T Clark, 1928), pp. 152-6.

19. Cf. David Ray Griffin, 'Creation Out of Nothing, Creation out of Chaos and the Problem of Evil', in Stephen Evans, ed., *Encountering Evil: Live Options in Theodicy* (Louisville: Westminster John Knox Press, 2001), pp. 108-24.

20. In an important philosophical counterpart to this line of argument, John Macmurray distinguishes between the organic and the personal as requiring different forms of conceptuality and understanding. Cf. John Macmurray, *Persons in Relation* (London: Faber and Faber, 1961). This is further developed with reference to the relationship of God to the world by Frank Kirkpatrick, *Together Bound: God, History and the Religious Community* (New York: Oxford University Press, 1994).

human agents, we do not think of ourselves as having a personal relationship to our bodies. The difference between creator and creation enables patterns of interaction and indwelling that cannot properly characterize the body-mind relationship.

The doctrine of creation out of nothing may continue to express crucial concerns about how we should conceive of God in relation to God's world, not merely in an act of origination but in continuing interaction. When carefully nuanced, we might then see the classical doctrine as the necessary accompaniment of the kind of dialogical or covenantal relationship that the love of God establishes with creatures. The ontological otherness of God is a necessary condition for the particular forms that the love of God takes for creation. Hence, the story of divine love requires as its accompaniment the theoretical shape supplied by the *ex nihilo* doctrine; it is a fitting testimony to the love of God as the divine Other.

29

THE OTHER AND THE INTERRUPTION OF LOVE

Lieven Boeve

Complimenting and Complementing

In dialogue with the contemporary world, Werner G. Jeanrond's theology has profited from conversations with critical theory, hermeneutics, and philosophies of difference. One of the last fruits illustrates Jeanrond's approach quite well: *A Theology of Love* is a theological and hermeneutical study which offers a historical as well as a systematic account of what love means theologically.[1] In my contribution, I aim to participate in this theological endeavour with an attempt to modestly complement the reflections of Jeanrond's theology of love: a complement meant as a compliment.

In order to get started, I connect my argument to my study *Lyotard and Theology: Beyond the Christian Master Narrative of Love*.[2] Assisted by Lyotard's postmodern critical philosophy of difference, I will analyse Christianity as the master narrative of the idea of love. Then I will present Jeanrond's *A Theology of Love*. In responding to the question of how a Christian theology of love can prevent itself from becoming a master narrative, I will show how attention to difference is the key to unlock the closing features of narratives since difference 'interrupts' the Christian master narrative of love (first interruption of love – object genitive). At the same time I will explore how 'love' interrupts not only the Christian temptation to fall back into master narratives, but also engenders a critical consciousness *vis-à-vis* such tendencies in other narratives (second interruption of love – subject genitive). Today, theologies of love, therefore, are called upon to retrieve a notion of love which neither includes nor excludes otherness, but is challenged by it, and even more so, lives by this interrupting challenge.

---

1. Cf. Werner G. Jeanrond, *A Theology of Love* (London: Continuum/T&T Clark, 2010).
2. Cf. Lieven Boeve, *Lyotard and Theology: Beyond the Christian Master Narrative of Love* (London: Bloomsbury/T&T Clark, 2014). For another theological engagement with Lyotard, cf. Phillip E. Davis, 'St Lyotard on the Differend/Difference Love Can Make', in Colby Dickinson, ed., *The Postmodern Saints of France: Refiguring 'the Holy' in Contemporary French Philosophy* (London: Bloomsbury, 2012), pp. 123–37.

Christianity's Master Narrative of the Idea of Love

It may seem strange to us that Jean-François Lyotard mentions Christianity when he criticizes *modern* master narratives after publishing his *La condition postmoderne*.[3] He even qualifies the Christian narrative as the epitome of a master narrative. In his list of modern master narratives in *Le postmoderne expliqué aux enfants*,[4] Lyotard presents the Christian narrative of the 'redemption of original sin through love' as the first master narrative – followed thereafter by the Enlightenment, the Hegelian, the Marxist and the capitalist master narrative:

> the Christian narrative of the redemption of original sin through love; the *Aufklärer* narrative of emancipation from this ignorance and servitude through knowledge and egalitarianism; the speculative narrative of the realization of the universal Idea through the dialectic of the concrete; the Marxist narrative of emancipation from exploitation and alienation through the socialization of work; and the capitalist narrative of emancipation from poverty through techno-industrial development.[5]

All of these master narratives, according to Lyotard, have lost their credibility, because they failed to deliver what they promised: a better world for all.[6] Moreover, they brought about the very opposite of what they had promised: totalitarianism and terror with millions of victims. The emancipation of the few led to the servitude of the many; prosperity in the first world came at the third world's

---

3. Jean-François Lyotard, *La condition postmoderne: Rapport sur le savoir* (Paris: Minuit, 1979). For the English translation, cf. *The Postmodern Condition: a Report on Knowledge*, trans. G. Bennington (Manchester: Manchester University Press, 1984).

4. Jean-François Lyotard, *Le postmoderne expliqué aux enfants. Correspondance 1982–1985* (Paris: Galilée, 1986). For the English translation, cf. *The Postmodern Explained: Correspondence 1982–1985*, trans. D. Barry (Minneapolis: University of Minnesota Press, 1993).

5. Jean-François Lyotard, *The Postmodern Explained*, p. 25.

6. 'In the course of the past fifty years, each grand narrative of emancipation – regardless of the genre it privileges – has, as it were, had its principle invalidated. *All that is real is rational, all that is rational is real*: "Auschwitz" refutes the speculative doctrine. At least this crime, which is real, is not rational. *All that is proletarian is communist, all that is communist is proletarian*: "Berlin 1953," "Budapest 1956," "Czechoslovakia 1968," "Poland 1980" (to name but a few) refute the doctrine of historical materialism: the workers rise up against the Party. *All that is democratic is by the people and for the people, and vice versa*: "May 1968" refutes the doctrine of parliamentary liberalism. Everyday society brings the representative institution to a halt. *Everything that promotes the free flow of supply and demand is good for general prosperity, and vice versa*: the "crises of 1911 and 1929" refute the doctrine of economic liberalism, and the "crisis of 1974–9" refutes the post-Keynesian modification of that doctrine' (Jean-François Lyotard, *The Postmodern Explained*, p. 28–9).

expense; technological mastery over the world resulted in ecological disturbances. These modern projects do not remain unfinished, as Lyotard maintains against Jürgen Habermas; rather they failed.[7] In the case of Christianity, one could add that the master narrative of love turned into structures which, in the name of love, produced the narrative's counterpart: the lack of love, the abuse of power, ideology and indifference. The paedophilia scandal is an all too clear example hereof, on account both of the officials-perpetrators in the Roman Catholic Church and of institutional blindness which prevented a proper handling of the situation.

The main problem with master narratives consists in the observation that they are incapable of respecting difference: whatever does not fit into the narrative. For Lyotard, they fail to bear witness to the occurrence of difference, the '*différend*'. Otherness is either already included in the narrative (as more of the same), or immediately excluded from the narrative (and not seriously taken into account). The interruption presented by otherness to the narrative is easily done away with. Narratives always tend to do so, as Lyotard explains in *Le différend*, because they re-tell the *différend* from the perspective of their own particular finality.[8] They constitute a universe of meaning in which whatever happens finds its place. The Latin American Cashinahua Indians, an example Lyotard gives, construct their cultural world from a multitude of mythological stories related to origins. The narrator is authorized by the story itself, while the same story constitutes the 'we' of the narrative: the narrator, the narrated, and those who listen to the narrative. '[The story] envelops every name; it is always actualizable and always has been; both diachronic and parachronic, it secures mastery over time and therefore over life and death. Narrative is authority itself. It authorizes an infrangible *we*, outside of which there is only *they*'.[9]

Building on Lyotard's analysis, one could first conclude that all narratives – whether pre-modern or modern – make a similar cognitive claim: they presume that they represent the world as it truly is. Secondly, they exhibit a totalizing power by quasi-automatically encapsulating all there is in the narrative (or by excluding what does not fit). In doing so, description and prescription are easily held together. Narratives legitimize individual and communal identities, institutions, politics and ethics; and they do so while grounding their authority on the narrative itself. Along with these general characteristics of narratives, modern master narratives share two explicitly modern characteristics. First, in place of a collection of mythological stories, which call upon a founding origin, a modern master narrative presents itself as a grand narrative of history, legitimized by its end. The second characteristic of modern master narratives

---

7. Cf. Jean-François Lyotard, *Le postmoderne expliqué aux enfants*, pp. 38–9, against Jürgen Habermas, *Die Moderne – ein unvollendetes Projekt: Philosophisch-Politische Aufsätze 1977–1990* (Stuttgart: Reclam, 1990).

8. Jean-François Lyotard, *Le différend* (Paris: Minuit, 1983). For the English translation, cf. *The Differend: Phrases in Dispute*, trans. G. Van Den Abbeele (Manchester: Manchester University Press, 1988), p. 230.

9. Jean-François Lyotard, *The Postmodern Explained*, p. 33.

concerns their universalist pretensions: they speak on behalf of everyone, in the name of humanity. Master narratives strip individual names, places, and events of their particularity and apply them universally to the narrative's end. Hence, what makes modern master narratives specifically modern is that they are driven by an 'idea'. Such an idea serves as the finality of history, universalizing the particulars (modern characteristics). Also, such an idea encompasses whatever is meaningful, while at the same time totalizing whatever happens (narrative characteristics). In Marxism, for instance, the idea of the emancipated proletariat constitutes the end of history; hence, whatever happens in history must be explained in line with that idea. Thus, in the struggle for emancipation, particular episodes are considered to be universally significant because of the idea. It constitutes the basis for the cognitive claim that reality is about the emancipation of the proletariat, so that all are called to further this emancipation. At the same time it legitimizes the inclusion of all into the proletariat ('we'), as well as the exclusion (and eventually the extermination) of the others ('they', the bourgeois).

As mentioned above, the multitude of victims has shown the failure of the modern master narratives. According to Lyotard's analysis, these narratives' insensitivity to the occurrence – to the *différend*, as they construct identity, describe what happens and prescribe what ought to happen – is the precise reason why they cannot keep their promises; indeed, why they realize the very opposite of what they promised.

Lyotard argues that Christianity can be considered as a kind of proto-modern master narrative. Due to its way of narrating, it is a master narrative par excellence.

> [B]etween two narratives belonging to the same genre, one can be judged stronger than the other if it comes nearer to the goal of narratives: to link onto the occurrence as such by signifying it and referring to it. The Christian narrative vanquished the other narratives in Rome because by introducing the love of occurrence into narratives and narrations of narratives, it designated what is at stake in the genre itself. To love what happens as if it were a gift, to love even the *Is it happening?* as the promise of good news, allows for linking onto whatever happens, including other narratives (and, subsequently, even other genres).[10]

By loving from the outset what is to happen, the Christian master narrative determines what can happen. The event of difference never disturbs the course of the narrative, because it is already included from within the dynamics of the idea of love. Although the Christian master narrative also consists of many stories which legitimize it from an origin, its eschatological character forms the basis for a powerful legitimation by the end – namely, love realizing the fulfilment of love in the coming Reign of God. 'Eschatology recounts the experience of a subject affected by a lack, and prophesies that this experience will finish at the end of

---

10. Jean-François Lyotard, *The Differend*, p. 232.

time with the remission of evil, the destruction of death, and the return to the Father's house'.[11]

The legitimization of history from the end by the idea of love is accompanied by the encompassing universalization of the Christian narrative. 'The obligation to love is decreed by the divine Absolute, it is addressed to all creatures (who are none other than His addressees), and it becomes transitive (in an interested sense, because it is conditional): if you are loved, you ought to love; and you shall be loved only if you love'.[12] Love reveals itself to all who open themselves in love to love. Particular histories and stories are universalized and 're'-told from the perspective of the realization of the idea of love. Small narratives, such as those about sin, function as examples of this love. Simultaneously, the Christian master narrative exhibits the cognitive claim of describing reality as it truly is. The narrative enables Christians to legitimately judge concerning what was, what is, and what is to come. It is therefore also a totalizing narrative, bearing its own legitimation in itself and linking description quasi-automatically to prescription: because one is loved, one ought to love. From the outset, the occurrence of difference is stripped of its interruptive otherness. It is registered within the Christian narrative as gracious gift of love. People who do not love are sinful.

However, is the Christian narrative doomed to be a master narrative, held hostage by the idea of love? Must the idea of love enforce the closure of the Christian narrative? What about our theologies of love? In what follows, I will first present Jeanrond's theology of love in order to test whether it escapes the clutches of the Christian master narrative. Then, drawing inspiration from some of Lyotard's intuitions, I will point towards a way of preventing the Christian narrative of love from closing in upon itself.

Werner G. Jeanrond's Theology of Love

In his theology of love, Jeanrond offers a hermeneutical account of the way in which love has been conceived as a core concept within the Christian tradition. Against a particular reception of Augustine's view on love, he offers a position which can be qualified as thoroughly catholic, in line with the dictum: '*gratia non destruit naturam sed perficit*'. Human beings are not completely corrupted

---

11. Jean-François Lyotard, *Postmodern Fables*, trans. G. Van Den Abbeele (Minneapolis: University of Minnesota Press, 1997), p. 96. For the French original, cf. *Moralités postmodernes* (Paris: Galilée, 1993). Christian hope then is the prototype for the modern expectation of the subject's reconciliation with itself at the end of history. Once emancipated from the link to the particular Christian narrativity, modern master narratives are exclusively legitimated by their finality, and love becomes transformed into republican brotherhood or communist solidarity. Cf. Jean-François Lyotard, *The Differend*, p. 235.

12. Ibid., p. 232. Texts from the New Testament could give Lyotard sufficient reason to think so. Cf. Jn 14.21-3 and 1 Jn 4.7-12 for example.

(by original sin), but have a creaturely capacity for love through which they can contribute to the realization of God's love. For Jeanrond, there is no opposition between human love and divine love, no depreciation of human love by divine love; there is no separation between *eros* and *agape*: both are aspects of divine and human love alike.

Because 'love has a history',[13] which is complex and complicated, and forms part of a learning process, Jeanrond develops his point through a hermeneutical reading of the theological history of love. He observes an ambiguity present in the New Testament in the way the term is used between the synoptics, where the love of neighbour receives a universal twist to include others ('who has become neighbour to the other?'), and the Pauline-Johannine approach, where love among Christians forms a distinctive characteristic of the Christian community, differentiating it from others.[14]

Further, to understand Augustine's reflections on love, three elements should be taken into account: Augustine's personal biography, his (Neo-)Platonic intellectual background, and his lineage to the Pauline-Johannine approach. For Augustine, experience shows that the 'interior soul' has no control over the 'exterior body' which is why human beings are not genuine agents of love, but affected by 'original sin'. Real love is divine love, to be distinguished from human self-love. Only by turning to God who is love are humans able to love. When a person loves the other, it is pre-eminently God who is loved. Here, a Platonic heritage, a biblical tradition and a mentality that seeks unity and stability beyond all worldly divisions and conflicts merge.[15]

Although Augustine's influence remains ever-present, Jeanrond points to the fact that in the Middle Ages a renewed attention was paid to the loving subject. With reference to Bernard of Clairvaux, Thomas Aquinas, courtly love, and female mysticism, he underscores the importance of the subject's experiences of love, of the subject as an agent of love, and of love as a concrete praxis. In discussing the female mystics, however, he notices once again the self-negation required from the mystic lover. The rediscovery of the subject thus turns once more into doubt of the subject as an agent of love. Martin Luther – and the reception of Luther – will confirm this doubt. Again, a separation occurs between human love and divine love, transforming the latter into Christian love, to be distinguished from non-Christian kinds of love. Love becomes a Christian virtue. 'Like for Augustine, Luther's anthropological starting point is the fallen human being that must first be transformed by grace before Christ, in him or her, can perform works of love'.[16]

The separation between divine and human love is confirmed by Protestant thinkers such as Søren Kierkegaard and Anders Nygren. Christian love should be purified from all remnants of human self-love. 'Since Christian love has not been produced by us human beings, but has come to us from above, the human

---

13. Werner G. Jeanrond, *A Theology of Love*, p. 9.
14. Ibid., pp. 30–9.
15. Ibid., p. 54.
16. Ibid., p. 102.

being cannot be the subject of this love'.[17] Hence, the 'human being is not a divinely empowered agent of love, but a mere instrument of God's own love'.[18] Only God can be the true subject of love. While Karl Barth and Eberhard Jüngel have their own particular emphases, both also differentiate between Christian and non-Christian love. Paul Tillich, Karl Rahner, and the encyclical letter on Christian love by Pope Benedict XVI, however, develop the unity of divine and human love. For Rahner, the loving and loved subject is the agent of love. At the same time, the fact that 'I can love my neighbour as my neighbour' is already God given; human love and divine love go together.[19] From within Rahner's transcendental approach, this is expressed as follows: 'The act of love of neighbour is the only categorical and original act, in which the human being attains the whole of the given reality, fulfils his or her own self and thus experiences God's transcendental and gracious self-communication'.[20]

Jeanrond further develops the unity of divine and human love. Love characterizes itself as a relationship – a praxis which cannot be reduced to a principle. Reflections on love are grounded in the praxis of love. Love, therefore, is embodied, having both individual and institutional expressions. Politically, love is closely related to justice. Love and the reflection on love are learned in networks of love. All human love flourishes within the horizon of God's love – a horizon which is established by the God who created loving human beings. The God-given human capacity to love is to be learned in order to mature it into concrete love, anticipating its perfection by God. As Jeanrond puts it elsewhere: 'Love is the horizon in which Christians are invited to imagine God's coming reign. Love is not a divine consummation of God's imposition on men, women, and children. Rather it is a divine gift that allows us to hope for the promise, not against, but for and with the participation of humankind'.[21]

The Twofold Interruption of a Theology of Love

In the Christian master narrative, the idea of love serves as the interpretive key for all there is. Hence, the narrative makes a cognitive claim, legitimizes itself from its end, is universalizing and totalizing. However, it seems that Jeanrond's take on love is different: love is not an idea which is to be conceived from a God's eye perspective, but a concrete historical and relational praxis, wherein divine and human love are intertwined. Still, it is a narrative of love, in which love seems to be the ultimate criterion. Theologies of love which separate (impure) human from (pure) divine love, thus making God the sole subject of love, would seem to

17. Ibid., p. 119.
18. Ibid., p. 120.
19. Ibid., p. 146.
20. Karl Rahner, quoted ibid., pp. 146-7.
21. Werner G. Jeanrond, 'Love and Eschatology', *Dialog: A Journal of Theology* 50 (2011), pp. 53-63 (61).

be more vulnerable to a closing of the narrative, for they hold to a love seemingly accessible only to Christians. In such a perspective, the love of others and other loves are not considered true love.

The key of Lyotard's postmodern criticism of modern master narratives concerns their inability to allow for difference to happen: the fact that they, in structuring the narrative, do not in any way bear witness to the *différend*, to that which remains other to the narrative, interrupting its seamless continuation. Otherness is immediately retold from the perspective of the narrative. However, for the Christian narrative of love, the other may be not only a loving subject, but one whose love is not necessarily the same as ours (because it is not Christian). We may not be able to legitimately include or exclude the other love of the other under the heading of what we know of God's love. The other may well interrupt our conceptions of love and push these to their limits. The first interruption of a theology of love, operated by the postmodern critical consciousness, therefore, concerns our all too safe and often all too self-securing notions of love which offer us stable keys for relating to otherness, in symmetrical or asymmetrical ways. These others may well be the victims of our love: those who remain unseen or unheard within the framework of our narrative, although – or precisely because – we 'love' them. Love then serves to close the narrative; it has neither eyes nor ears for the otherness which is too easily included or excluded from the narrative.

Postmodern critical consciousness interrupts the hegemonic features of a Christian narrative of love, criticizing its aspirations to offer a grand narrative of history, its epistemological God's eye perspective along with its ensuing cognitive claim, its too easy universalizations and its totalizing powers. In a religiously pluralized world, the Christian narrative is neither the self-evident response to human aspirations, nor the logical result for all those who think rationally. Nor is it to be profiled as the grand master narrative of Christian love, the only one able to safeguard humankind against a fallen modern context which is univocally analysed in terms of relativism, secularism and nihilism. The consciousness of difference, the *différend*, interrupts our attempts to use a Christian love as a criterion, as if we would know what it is, and as if we would be the ones to use it. When love, or God as love, functions as a criterion for legitimation, the Christian narrative rapidly closes in on itself.

However, do we know what love is? Is love given to Christians as a criterion? Is Christian love self-securing? Perhaps, the first interruption of our theologies of love may point us to a second interruption: the interruption of our theologies by love. The interruption of (our theologies of) love, by the postmodern critical consciousness of difference, makes us aware of the temptation each narrative, and thus also the Christian narrative, experiences to secure itself, to become encompassing. However, on closer inspection, it would seem that such a first interruption of love sets free the interruption by love of the Christian narrative: it is love itself which interrupts our attempts to close the narrative. In the name of love, God enters history to open up closed narratives. Both in words and in deeds, Jesus demonstrated this interruptive power of love: inverting the concept of neighbour in the parable of the Samaritan, showing its active dimension:

the question is not 'which other is my neighbour?', but 'to whom do I become neighbour?'; questioning our belonging to the Christian narrative of love by confronting us, in the parable of the prodigal son, with our position as the eldest son, unable or unwilling to understand the father's abundant love for that other 'son of yours'; dethroning the scribes from Moses' chair when they wanted to stone the adulterous women in the name of God's law, while not condemning but liberating the woman, hereby revealing who God in God's mercifulness really is; opening up the Christian narrative for others. Again and again, our experiencing, understanding and practicing of love are interrupted. Whenever the Christian narrative tends to close, it is God who interrupts it. God opens the horizon of love. Hence, interruptive love becomes a way to try to understand how God relates to history – as well as a way to interrupt all such understanding. Certainly, Jeanrond's retrieval of love as a historical and relational praxis in networks of love is open to both the first and second interruption of love, both enabled and challenged by the always greater God.

30

THE MIDDLE ENGLISH POEM *PEARL*: A STUDY IN THE UNFAMILIAR

Santha Bhattacharji

The Middle English poem *Pearl*,[1] depicting a vision of a paradisal landscape and the heavenly Jerusalem, is usually studied for the beauty of its language and the technical complexity of its verse.[2] Apparently exploring the narrator's grief for a deceased child, it carries an emotional charge that most examples of the dream-vision genre,[3] or of the courtly commissioned elegy,[4] do not. Rightly, scholars of

---

1. Major editions include: Eric V. Gordon, ed., *Pearl* (Oxford: Oxford University Press, 1953); Malcolm Andrew and Ronald A. Waldron, eds, *Poems of the Pearl Manuscript* (London: John Arnold, 1978), the fifth edition of which appeared with Exeter University Press in 2007. All quotations from the poem in this article are from this edition; however, all translations are my own.

2. In a vast field, see the bibliography in Sarah Stanbury, ed., *Pearl* (Kalamazoo, MI: Medieval Institute Publications, 2001).

3. In terms of elegy, the closest parallels are Geoffrey Chaucer's *Book of the Duchess* (in Middle English) and Boccacio's *Olympia* (in Latin). Cf. Geoffrey Chaucer, 'The Book of the Duchess', in *The Riverside Chaucer*, ed. Larry D. Benson (Boston: Houghton Mifflin, 1987), pp. 330-46 (Middle English text); for a modern translation, see Geoffrey Chaucer, *Love Visions*, trans. B. Stone (London: Penguin Books, 1983), pp. 22-57; for Boccaccio's *Olympia*, see Israel Gollancz, ed., *Boccaccio's Olympia* (London: Chatto and Windus, 1913). For the dream vision genre in general, see Anthony C. Spearing, *Medieval Dream Poetry* (Cambridge: Cambridge University Press, 1976); Kathryn L. Lynch, *The High Medieval Dream Vision: Poetry, Philosophy and Literary Form* (Stanford: Stanford University Press, 1988).

4. Scholarship has investigated whether this courtly poem could have been commissioned by an aristocratic patron on the death of a female child or young adult who can be identified from historical records. Suggestions include Margaret Hastings, daughter of the Earl of Pembroke, or Margaret, granddaughter of Edward III: cf. Oscar Cargill and Margaret Schlauch, 'The Pearl and Its Jeweler', *PMLA* 43 (1928), pp. 105-23; another suggestion is Anne of Bohemia: cf. Michael J. Bennett, 'The Historical Background', in Derek Brewer and Jonathan Gibson, eds, *A Companion to the Gawain-Poet* (Cambridge: Brewer, 1997) pp. 71-90 (84).

Middle English, while eager to discuss every aspect of the poet's skilful manipulation of the literary traditions available to him, are cautious when it comes to discussing the poem's theological content. However, in this contribution, I would like to step outside the bounds of my usual discipline, and examine this poem as a profound meditation on difference, revealed, paradoxically, in what was thought to be familiar. In particular, it is the spiritual dimension, both of persons and of doctrine, which is revealed to be strange, untamed, and unrecognized.

In keeping with this overall theme, the poem does not set out a clear narrative. The cause of the narrator's grief only gradually reveals itself, hinted at through guarded language and allegorical details. The narrator revisits a garden where an exquisitely perfect pearl had slipped through his fingers into the grass. It is mid-August, and the warmth and the scent of flowers combine with the exhaustion of grief to cause him to fall asleep on the mound where he had lost the pearl. Immediately, his spirit seems to leave his body and wander in a dazzling landscape, where he encounters a pearl-decked young woman. Gradually he recognizes her as someone 'nearer than aunt or niece' (l. 233). It is only later that the poem suggests that she may have been very young when she died: she was 'full young and tender of age' (l. 412) and had 'lived barely two years in our land' (l. 483); indeed, she could barely utter the Our Father or Creed (l. 485). By inference, she could in no way have accumulated any merit in order to enter heaven.

As is typical of the dream-vision genre, the poem develops into an extended debate, in which the Pearl-Maiden explains her high estate in heaven, where she is now the bride of the Lamb. Far from being delighted that she is alive, honoured and fulfilled, as we might expect, the narrator is baffled and disturbed, and somewhat outraged that she, the cause of both his joy and grief on earth, particularly grief, is herself happy in heaven. What seems to disturb him is the overturning of all his assumptions about the finality of death – at least for a person who has died too young to have in any way earned eternal life through prayer and penance on earth.

The rest of the poem concerns this struggle to accept her ongoing existence, but in a realm which seems to operate according to completely different laws to those governing earthly society. As is typical of dream-vision poems, *Pearl* ends rather abruptly, with the dreamer waking out of his dream when, in an effort to join the Maiden, he jumps into the river which separates him from her. The tone at the end of the poem is one of resignation to the reality of separation and to the heavenly Prince who has decreed it; whether the dreamer will be able to absorb the extraordinary new perspectives he has been given is left open to question.

There is in fact no certainty that the traditional reading of the poem, which deduces that the narrator is grieving for a daughter who died before the age of two, is actually correct, or the only possible reading. The courtly romance vocabulary applied to the Maiden, the perfect pearl the narrator has lost, initially strongly suggests that he is speaking of a lover. Recent studies have therefore offered alternative interpretations. Perhaps the dreamer had fallen in love with an adult convert to Christianity, a foreigner (a pearl 'from the Orient', l.3) who could barely yet say the Our Father or Creed, but had been baptized;[5]

---

5. For a helpful overview of the debate, cf. Jane Beal, 'The Pearl-Maiden's Two Lovers',

or perhaps 'death' might be entrance into a monastic cloister.[6] However, these interpretations focus on the sections of the poem describing the Pearl-Maiden and the dreamer's intense feelings for her. They do not properly take into account the poem's central argument, based on a long retelling of the Parable of the Workers in the Vineyard, on which my contribution will concentrate. For example, someone embracing monastic life is embarking on a whole lifetime of prayer and penance, which would richly 'earn' a place in heaven; moreover, one entering the cloister as a child would presumably be categorized as one of the workers who entered the vineyard at the first hour. Similarly, with an adult convert, although the innocence bestowed in baptism could be that of a recently baptized adult, the interpretation of the Parable of the Vineyard would have to say something about baptism wiping out everything that had been done in the person's previous life; it is also questionable if baptism would have been conferred on an adult who could not say the Creed, the necessary baptismal confession of faith.

Instead, the poem's argument seems to hinge on the assertion that the Maiden has eternal life because she was baptized immediately after birth:

Bot innoghe of grace hatz innocent.
As sone as þay arn borne, by lyne
In þe water of babtem þay dyssente.
Then arne thay boroʒt into the vyne. (ll. 625-9)
(But the innocent have sufficient grace. As soon as they are born, in due order they descend into the water of baptism: at that point they are brought into the vineyard.)

My contribution will therefore keep to the traditional interpretation that the narrator has been devastated by the death of a very young child. A poem on this subject would have resonance in the period in which the poem was probably written, which was sometime between 1348 and 1400, perhaps in the 1380s or 1390s.[7] In the aftermath of the Black Death of 1349, recurrences of the plague killed many children, preventing the recovery of the population of Europe until well into the sixteenth century.[8] So the despair of parents and relatives may well have loomed large in the late fourteenth-century emotional landscape.

Studies in Philology 100/1 (2003), pp. 1-21.

    6. Cf. Lynn Staley, '*Pearl* and the Contingencies of Love and Piety', in David Aers, ed., *Medieval Literature and Historical Enquiry* (Cambridge: Brewer, 2000), pp. 83-114.

    7. Cf. the introduction to Sarah Stanbury, ed., *Pearl*.

    8. For recurrences of the Black Death and the effect on different sections of the population, cf. for example Jim L. Bolton, 'The world turned upside down', in Mark Ormrod and Philip G. Lindley, eds, *The Black Death* (Stamford: Paul Watkins, 1996), pp. 17-78; John Hatcher, *Plague, Population and the English Economy, 1348-1530* (Macmillan: The Economic History Society, 1977); Rosemary Horrox, ed., *The Black Death* (Manchester: Manchester University Press, 1994), pp. 3-13; John F. D. Shrewsbury, *A History of Bubonic Plague* (Cambridge: Cambridge University Press, 1970), pp. 126-33.

Taking up the theme of unfamiliarity, let us begin with the strangeness of the dream-landscape. The dreamer wanders in a land of crystal cliffs, trees with indigo trunks and silver leaves, pearls forming the gravel underfoot and precious stones the bed of the crystal-clear river (ll. 62–120). It is not at all clear how we are to categorize this landscape. Since the river forms an impassable barrier between him and the Maiden, whose abode is the heavenly Jerusalem, it is not heaven as such; but neither is it what would usually be considered a depiction of an earthly paradise, as it lacks some of the characteristics of the *locus amoenus* of medieval literary tradition:[9] there are no soft green banks to sit on, intriguing companions or the invitation to relaxation and play. Although the dreamer finds the scents and beauty of the garden soothing and refreshing, for flesh and blood this is in some ways an uncomfortable landscape, almost harsh in the brilliant light that bathes it. The Maiden sums up the difference by expressing the mode of her existence now compared to what it was on earth:

For þat þou lestez watz bot a rose
Þat flowred and fayled as kynde hyt gef;
Now thur3 kynde of þe kyste þat hyt con close
To a perle of prys hit is put in pref. (ll. 269–72)
(For what you lost was but a rose, which flowered and withered as nature granted it. Now, through the nature of the casket that encloses it, it proves to be a pearl of price.)

The point of interest, for the purposes of my contribution, is that this strange, uncomfortable though healing landscape, bathed in brilliant light, is an *inner* landscape: accessed in a dream, it is, one could argue, a product of the dreamer's own psyche. If it is an objective place, it is one that can only be accessed in spirit, as he had made clear when describing how his spirit 'sprang in space' (l. 61) to enter this mysterious realm.

This place of encounter, then, where he can communicate with the Pearl-Maiden, is within him; and this suggests that human beings contain depths that are stranger, more enduring and less 'organic' than one might suspect, but also less 'private' than one might expect. The dreamer complains bitterly that he has lost his 'privy perle'; she constantly reminds him that she belongs to the Prince, and he comes to realize that so does he. This realm that is ruled by the Prince is the one they share, at least potentially.

The second point of interest is the unrecognizability of the Pearl-Maiden. The little child, the dreamer's very own precious possession, in this strange realm has a totally different appearance: she has her full adult stature; she has full spiritual understanding, so that she can instruct him, the adult (a reversal of roles he takes time to adjust to); she belongs not to him, but the Prince, who is also the slain

---

9. The most formative study of the medieval concept of the *locus amoenus* occurs in Ernst R. Curtius, *European Literature and the Latin Middle Ages*, trans. W. R. Trask (Princeton: Princeton University Press, 1953), pp. 183–202.

Lamb (ll. 161–420). This is a powerful image of the potential encounter between persons who matter a great deal to each other, but hitherto in well-defined earthly roles. The sudden glimpses of the full stature and the spiritual wisdom of another, underpinned by his or her unsuspected intimacy with the slain Lamb, can be strange and disconcerting, plunging us suddenly into a wild and uncomfortable psychological landscape, even while these glimpses are also received as an unexpected gift.

The third area of difference to explore is the doctrinal content of the debate. The dreamer is the one who knows his catechism, as it were, but he does not recognize what he has been taught in what the Maiden is telling him. The different perspectives begin to emerge when he struggles to understand what she means by saying that she is the bride of the Lamb. In our earthly world, we think of positions in exclusive terms, as establishing a uniquely privileged place within a hierarchy. If she is the bride, is she saying that she has supplanted Mary as Queen of Heaven? In language which reflects the simple yet poetic vocabulary of many medieval religious lyrics,[10] with which one might try to instruct a child, he asks:

Art þou þe quene of heuenez blwe,
Þat al þys worlde schal do honour?
We leuen on Marye þat grace of grewe,
Þat ber a barne of vyrgyn flour.
Þe croune fro hyr quo moȝt remwe
Bot ho hir passed in sum fauour? (ll. 423–32)
(Are you the Queen of the blue heavens, whom all this world must honour? We believe in Mary, from whom grace grew, who bore a child of virgin flower; who could remove the crown from her, unless she surpassed her in some favour?)

The language is one of reverence towards the Mother of God, but the dreamer is using it to make an aggressive statement to the Maiden; Mary for him is a concept to deploy in argument, not a reality. For the Maiden, however, inhabiting the spiritual realm on the other side of the river, Mary is an overwhelming spiritual presence; to name her is to acknowledge this presence. The Maiden therefore immediately drops to her knees, takes off her crown, and salutes the Virgin:

'Cortayse quen,' þenne sayde þat gaye,
Knelande to grounde, folde vp hyr face,
'Makelez moder and myryest may,
Blessed bygynner of vch a grace!' (ll. 433–6)
('Courteous queen', then said that fair one, kneeling to the ground; she turned up her face: 'Matchless mother and most beautiful maiden, blessed beginner of every grace!')

---

10. For some examples, cf. Carleton Brown, ed., *English Lyrics of the XIIIth Century* (Oxford: Clarendon Press, 1932), pp. 26; 27; 32; 42; 55; 65; 116; 118.

Then, standing up, she returns to the debate, with a force that shows she perfectly understands that the dreamer is basically attacking what she has told him. She explains that in heaven a place of honour is not exclusive but inclusive; no one 'supplants' another (l. 440). The 'property' of heaven (l. 446) – its 'laws of physics', as it were – means everyone is queen or king of the whole realm, and no one seeks to 'deprive' another (l. 449). Anyone in a place of honour is thereby empowered to *give* honour to everyone else, and each person would like to see the status of all the others raised five-fold, if any enhancement of the perfect joy of heaven were possible. Mary, then, as 'Queen of grace', is necessarily the greatest bestower of honour, and remains 'empress' over all. The dreamer, however, is still put out:

> *What more honour mo3te he acheve*
> *Þat hade endured in worlde stronge,*
> *And lyued in penaunce hys lyvez longe*
> *Wyth bodyly bale hym blysse to byye?* (ll. 475–9)
> (What higher honour could a man achieve, who had endured resolutely in the world, living his whole life in penance and bodily pain in order to buy himself bliss?)

It is the unfairness of it all that upsets him. What is the point of years of service and penance? *'That Cortayse is to fre of dede'* (That Courteous One is too generous in his way of acting) he complains (l. 481). God is too open-handed; he seems to set no limits. The Maiden responds by picking up his concern with limits (*date*, in Middle English), and extends the strangely reversed principles of heaven into her lengthy retelling and interpreting of the Parable of the Vineyard. She identifies herself with the workers who enter the vineyard at the eleventh hour, and do very little work before they are paid.

Her vivid retelling causes the dreamer to object strenuously to the unfairness of the last workers getting the same reward as the first.

> *Me think thy tale unresounable.*
> *Goddez ryzt is redy and evermore rert,*
> *Other Holy Wryt is bot a fable.*
> *On sauter is sayd a verce overte*
> *That spekez a poynt determynable:*
> *'Thou quytez uchon as his desserte,*
> *Thou hyze kyng ay pertermynable.'* (ll. 589–96)
> (Your tale seems to me against reason. God's judgement is swift and always supreme, or Holy Scripture is but a fable. In the Psalter is stated a clear verse that utters a determinable point: 'You reward each one according to his deserts, O high King ever supreme in judgement [or: eternal in judgement; or: predeterminable].')

He wants a determinable system in which God is *'perterminable'*. This unique and much disputed word has been variously interpreted, but the underlying concept is the eternal reliability of God's judgement, which implies a system of divine law in which we can calculate how much reward we are in line for.

She understands that he feels threatened by the vastness of the Lord's generosity, as did the workers in the vineyard. In the parable, the Lord responds to them by first making the point that he can do what he likes with his own wealth, a point which presumably is easier for the workers to accept, in their possession/dispossession-based human thinking. The Lord then goes on to ask them if they are upset because he is good; he perceives that what is really disturbing them emotionally is his generosity. What is threatened is the sense of a system of reward that can be relied on; trusting in the Lord's goodness suggests something of a lottery. The Maiden goes to the core of the narrator's unease by using the word *joparde* (jeopardy, l. 601), which captures the sense of a gamble that can be lost. She then tries to convince him that it is precisely the goodness of the Lord that can be relied upon, not our own efforts. She piles up images of bottomless abundance for God's goodness:

> *He lauez His gyftez as water of dyche,*
> *Oþer gotez of golf þat neuer charde* (ll. 608–9)
> (He lavishes his gifts like water from a ditch, or drops from a spring that never dries up.)

The dreamer is being invited to trust in this abundant grace, and not to structure for himself a tight, apparently safe conceptual universe of humanly predictable cause and effect.

What is being laid bare here is the human urge to be able to control the eternal outcome of one's earthly life: in a sense to dictate to God, through a system of graded rewards which God himself has not initiated or agreed to. In particular, it becomes clear that humans are determined to have a system in which some people get less. The workers of the first hour have the full reward they were expecting; they have nothing to complain about. They are indignant, however, because no one gets less than they do. Similarly, the narrator is upset because the Pearl-Maiden, a tiny child at death, does not get less, as he thinks she should, than someone who has lived a full human life. The subtext, perhaps, is that he feels that by rights he should eventually end up higher in heaven than she, and consequently he feels obscurely cheated and let down.

In contrast, what the Maiden's retelling of the Parable of the Vineyard seems to imply is that, by granting the penny of eternal life to every worker, the life of each worker is retrospectively given value by God, whatever its apparent merit in the eyes of others. In any case, she asks, what is so special about being an adult? The longer one lives, the greater the chance of falling away from one's baptismal purity, and everyone has sins to repent of. In the end, we all have to accept the kingdom of God as a gratuitous gift, like a little child.

The emphasis on childhood means that the poem is not actually drawing a distinction between faith and works in quite the way later centuries were to do. A tiny child cannot have an adult faith, any more than she can perform works.

Rather, salvation in the poem is bestowed through the gift of baptismal innocence. Innocence in a sense 'earns' grace, because it bestows likeness to the sinless Lamb, but this innocence has been purchased for us by the Lamb's own blood. It is therefore the Lamb's act which bestows salvation. In a few intensely lyrical verses, the Maiden describes the Lamb's death in the earthly Jerusalem. This serves to shift the argument from its focus on human beings; from henceforth the poem will focus on the heavenly Jerusalem and on the Lamb himself.

Paradoxically, then, to abandon any sense of what is 'owed' or 'not owed' to each one in heaven and to receive the kingdom of God like a little child is actually the humble position; although it apparently does not focus on sin and unworthiness, it properly recognizes human creatureliness, which can only receive, not claim. The childlike mind is also the one that is large enough to receive the goodness of God with delight and wonder, whereas the narrator's adult mind can only respond to the generosity of God with insecurity and distrust.

Thus, another difference emerges: the infinite goodness of God casts a brilliant light on the fallenness of the human mind. Grudging, self-serving, self-preoccupied, even when apparently lost in grief for another, its overriding need is to be affirmed by having some people be of less worth than itself. This is the mind which is familiar to us, in which we feel at home. In a spiritual perspective, it suddenly emerges as a strange, odd and unlovely sight.

However, this leads to the question, where are we truly comfortable? Where is our true home? Almost the last two hundred lines of the poem, nearly a sixth of the whole work, is taken up with a vision of the heavenly Jerusalem, where the Maiden dwells (ll. 985–1152). Like the dream landscape in which the narrator finds himself, it is a place of dazzling light, built of precious stones, where crowds follow the Lamb to his throne. As we saw, this is not a comfortable environment for perishable flesh and blood, but now the dreamer longs to join the Maiden in that heavenly city. Now able to focus on the Lamb, rather than his own grief, when he wakes up his chief comfort on earth will be beholding Christ in the Eucharist, 'Þat in þe forme of bred and wyn/Þe preste vus shcewez vch a daye' (who in the form of bread and wine/The priest shows us every day).[11]

The dreamer, then, seems to have undergone a transformative process which will fit him eventually to share in the life of the heavenly Jerusalem. The poem, however, has demonstrated that this is not easy. The spiritual realm, which tells us about immortality, offers us profound hope; but this hope so challenges our earthbound thinking that it emerges not as a source of joy, but of discomfort. The vision of heaven has revealed the goodness of God, which it embodies. Like anything else that is perceived as different and unfamiliar, the goodness of God comes to us as something profoundly disturbing and threatening.

11. Malcolm Andrew and Ronald A. Waldron, eds, *Poems of the Pearl Manuscript*, p. 110.

31

FINDING THE OTHERNESS OF GOD IN LITERATURE

David Jasper

I first met Werner G. Jeanrond in September 1984 at Durham University when he spoke at the second of a series of conferences on literature and religion which continue to be held to the present time. The conference was concerned with issues in English and German Romanticism, and Werner Jeanrond's lecture, which was subsequently published in a book which I edited, entitled *The Interpretation of Belief* (1986), explored the impact of Friedrich Schleiermacher's hermeneutics on contemporary interpretation theory. The book as a whole was constructed around Caspar David Friedrich's remarkable painting of 1808, *The Cross in the Mountains*, and the way in which it presents a series of ambivalences which prompt reflection: 'not simply the perception of the sacred in the real world, but the stark contrast between the central image of the Cross and the background of the twilight, between the massive created earth and the sun-shot sky, within one of whose beams rises Christ crucified, interceding between earth and heaven'.[1]

Such ambivalences, set between heaven and earth, lie at the heart of the hermeneutical task. To such a task, caught between two realms, Jeanrond returns in his essay as he seeks a critical theory of interpretation. In his reading of Schleiermacher he rejects that 'sympathetic congeniality' between text and reader that is found in Hans-Georg Gadamer, but rather, drawing upon Schleiermacher himself, insists upon 'the difference between the individuality of the text and the individual reader [that] can only be minimized through efforts of approximation, but never sublated in Hegel's sense'.[2] Schleiermacher's term 'divination' describes the risk involved in an inevitably preliminary grasp of the meaning of the text, and the process of reading as an enterprise which risks 'again and again a deeper grasp

---

1. David Jasper, 'Preface', in idem, ed., *The Interpretation of Belief: Coleridge, Schleiermacher and Romanticism* (London: Macmillan, 1986), pp. vii–ix (vii).
2. Werner G. Jeanrond, 'The Impact of Schleiermacher's Hermeneutics on Contemporary Interpretation Theory', in David Jasper, ed., *The Interpretation of Belief*, pp. 81–96 (85–6).

of sense in history'.[3] Every act of reading is risky, and although the grammatical structure of the text remains constant, the mystery of its sense is appropriated anew time and time again. Thus we can never be said to have moved beyond the 'always preliminary divination of the sense' of the text – the hermeneutical task is always incomplete.

What does this mean for the theological dimension within the texts of literature? The recent Papal Encyclical of Pope Francis, *Lumen Fidei* (*The Light of Faith*),[4] makes a brief reference to the passages in Fyodor Dostoevsky's *The Idiot* (1868/69) which reflect upon the painting by Hans Holbein the Younger (1497–1543) entitled *The Body of the Dead Christ in the Tomb*. The reference is a good example of theology's unwillingness to remain unresolved – open – in the face of the undetermined mystery of literature. Early in Dostoevsky's novel, Prince Myshkin had attempted unavailingly to speak of the picture. Later he sees a reproduction of it in Rogozhin's house and 'struck by a sudden thought' he exclaims, 'Why, some people may lose their faith by looking at that picture'.[5] Much later in the novel, the minor character Ippolit gives an extended account of Holbein's painting which concludes with a question:

> The picture seems to give expression to the idea of a dark, insolent, and senselessly eternal power, to which everything is subordinated, and this idea is suggested to you unconsciously… And if, on the eve of the crucifixion, the Master could have seen what He would look like when taken from the cross, would he have mounted the cross and died as he did? This question too, you can't help asking yourself as you look at the picture.[6]

By contrast, *Lumen Fidei* offers a theological resolution to the painting that is quite other from the never-ending challenge of the novel. In the Encyclical it is clearly stated that 'it is precisely in contemplating Jesus' death that faith grows stronger and receives a dazzling light; then it is revealed as faith in Christ's steadfast love for us, a love capable of embracing death to bring us salvation'.[7]

The more unresolved encounter with Holbein's painting in *The Idiot* is the subject of an essay by Julia Kristeva to be found in her book *Black Sun: Depression and Melancholia* (1987; trans. 1989). Placing it within the context of the image of death in the Renaissance, Kristeva offers a very different vision from that of Pope Francis, nearer to that of Dostoevsky, and linked with Desiderius Erasmus' *In Praise of Folly* (1511). Erasmus and Holbein were close friends. Acknowledging his folly, writes Kristeva, man looks death in the face, 'absorbing it into his very

---

3. Ibid., p. 6
4. *Lumen Fidei (The Light of Faith): Encyclical Letter of the Supreme Pontiff Francis* (Dublin: Veritas Publications, 2013).
5. Fyodor Dostoevsky, *The Idiot*, trans. D. Magarshack (Harmondsworth: Penguin, 1955), p. 251.
6. Ibid., p. 447.
7. *Lumen Fidei (The Light of Faith)*, p. 18.

being, integrating it not as a condition for glory or a consequence of a sinful nature but as the ultimate essence of his desacralized reality, which is the foundation of a new dignity… man achieves a new dimension. Not necessarily that of atheism but definitely that of a disillusioned, serene, and dignified stance'.[8]

What Kristeva calls the 'humanization', 'devoid of pathos and Intimist on account of its very banality'[9] in Holbein, and Dostoevsky's reading of Holbein, links closely with Jeanrond's description of Schleiermacher's term 'divination' which 'describes the courageous risk of an always preliminary grasp of the text's sense. Understanding is a never-ending task'.[10] And in this provisionality and uncertainty as we are confronted with the deliberate openness of the literary text, its immediate question, as we face the reality of death as a cadaver which seems to shatter all our hopes, where is God? Or, more precisely, where in our human being is there space for God in our absorption of death as an end? For here the ready resolution of *Lumen Fidei* is an unwelcome, too ready, presence, without the patience of the necessary dignity of irresolution to be found in the space of literature. It is not that resolution is not to be hoped for, but rather that it cannot be found too quickly. As Maurice Blanchot reminds us, in the space of literature, the work must allow death its space, the divine must allow the human its dignity as the story awaits its end, and God remains 'other' in the uncertainty of our imperfect understanding.[11] Dostoevsky acknowledges this supremely in the conclusion of *Crime and Punishment* (1866) as Raskolnikov waits in the living death of his punishment in Siberia with the hope of a possibility that is the condition of his 'gradual regeneration'. But, in the last words of the book, 'that might be the subject of a new story – our present story is ended'.[12]

Theology and its reassurances must await the painful, necessary dignity of the human, known in the unending, unresolved hermeneutical challenges of literature, challenges which remain even yet when the light of faith begins to shine more brightly. In George Steiner's words, caught between Good Friday and Easter Sunday, we must patiently traverse the paradoxes of the terrible beauty as 'ours is the long day's journey of the Saturday. Between suffering, aloneness, unutterable waste on the one hand and the dream of liberation, of rebirth on the other'.[13] It is art and literature that teaches us the immensity of waiting, the beauty of suffering though not without hope. Only here can we enter, with stumbling steps, the shocking intimacy of human experience that is not yet ready – if it ever will be,

---

8. Julia Kristeva, 'Holbein's Dead Christ', in eadem, *Black Sun: Depression and Melancholia*, trans. L. S. Roudiez (New York: Columbia University Press, 1989), pp. 105–38 (118–19).

9. Ibid., p. 115.

10. Werner G. Jeanrond, 'The Impact of Schleiermacher's Hermeneutics', p. 86.

11. Maurice Blanchot, 'The Work and Death's Space', in idem, *The Space of Literature*, trans. A. Smock (Lincoln: University of Nebraska Press, 1982), pp. 85–159.

12. Fyodor Dostoevsky, *Crime and Punishment*, trans. D Magarshack (Harmondsworth: Penguin, 1966), p. 559.

13. George Steiner, *Real Presences* (London: Faber and Faber, 1989), p. 232.

perhaps – for the narrative of promise that leads to the end. As Jacques Derrida has reminded us, we must not omit to undertake the human, liberating work of mourning in the face of death.[14]

In what sense can we grasp the agonizing, even shocking, ending of Imre Kertész autobiographical novel *Fateless* (1975)? A young Jewish boy survives the horrors of Auschwitz, where so many died, finally returning home to Budapest and his family. 'My mother was waiting and would no doubt greatly rejoice over me'.[15] But neither his mother nor the rest of his family can possibly understand the change that has taken place in him, nor the full nature of the experiences that have prompted it. He speaks in a language that lies outside the structures of those who can only look upon the Holocaust from the outside with horror. And only he knows fully that to live at all, even in a manner that to the rest of us is unimaginable, entails the recognition that nothing is impossible.

> [T]here is nothing impossible that we do not live through naturally, and keeping a watch on me in my journey, like some inescapable trap, I already know there will be happiness. For even there, next to the chimneys, in the intervals between the torments, there was something that resembled happiness. Everyone asks only about the hardships and the 'atrocities,' whereas for me perhaps it is that experience which will remain the most memorable. Yes, the next time I am asked, I ought to speak about that, the happiness of the concentration camps.
> If indeed I am asked. And provided I myself don't forget.[16]

As with Holbein, it is almost impossible for us to look death in the face, but that is exactly what the young boy, Gyuri, has done, and in this utterly desacralized reality is found a new dignity and even 'something that resembled happiness'. As one reads this passage, the attempt to make sense of it is almost defeated. Indeed, we, though bystanders, are almost offended, were it not that Gyuri alone can enter the dark truth of his sayings. And where are God and those patterns of religious thought that try vainly to comprehend the nature of such evil? Perhaps we might put it this way: that God is wise enough to know when to leave the space clear, the unresolved *espace littéraire* which allows the foundation of a new human dignity held within the fragility of memory and enquiry.

The Jewish tradition, perhaps more than any other, knows the divinity of the text, its garments, the ink and paper that hold it before us, challenging our attempts at interpretation, yet sustaining our hope against the blackness of night. Another survivor of the Holocaust, the Italian Primo Levi, while he was a prisoner in Auschwitz, received the precious gift of a letter from home, and he wrote, 'that piece of paper in my hands, which had reached me in such a precarious way and which I would destroy before nightfall, represented a breach, a small gap in the

---

14. Jacques Derrida, *The Work of Mourning*, ed. Pascale-Anne Brault and Michael Naas (Chicago: University of Chicago Press, 2001).
15. Imre Kertész, *Fateless*, trans. T. Wilkinson (London: Vintage Books, 2006), p. 262.
16. Ibid., p. 262.

black universe that closed tightly around us, and through that breach hope could pass'.[17]

From the reading of the text flows a stream of possibilities as, in Schleiermacher's words, 'the hermeneutical task moves constantly'[18] in never-ending, always-preliminary acts of understanding that have their beginning in the dignity of human nature in the face of all that life can suffer. In her essay on Holbein's *Dead Christ*, Kristeva writes of the 'Protestant affliction' of John Calvin and Martin Luther whereby the human will is enslaved to God and the devil.[19] Rather, she suggests, Holbein is closer to the Occamist position of his friend Erasmus whereby human free will provides a way of access to salvation. It is this way which I am identifying here with the space of the text in which the imaginative will of the human enables a process by which God, in God's otherness, may yet be hoped for. At the end of *In Praise of Folly*, Erasmus writes of the imaginative world – the world of the poet – whereby we can deliberately look upon the face of death and yet live, even in happiness, in spite of all. Erasmus writes of theology which looks to articulate the 'future life of heaven toward which the pious aspire with so much endeavour'.[20] Yet it is Folly who leads some, the poets and artists, to find such a transformation in the foretaste of the present: 'They are very few, [and] suffer from something akin to madness. They speak in a manner that is not quite coherent, not in the ordinary manner but with meaningless sounds'.[21] Such a one may indeed be Kertész's survivor Gyuri, as we seek to interpret his words – not quite meaningless sounds but yet, calling from the depths of Gyuri's tormented spirit, almost beyond our comprehension – about the happiness of the concentration camps.

The reference to *In Praise of Folly* has been made quite deliberately, for it is hard in reading that work, especially in translation, to catch the tone and the levels of irony which are throughout employed. Erasmus is of the company of literary men and women, and he is most serious when he flicks words at his reader as challenges, as does Søren Kierkegaard or Franz Kafka, whom Blanchot once compared with the poet Friedrich Hölderlin: 'Kafka's passion is just as purely literary, but it is not always only literary. Salvation is an enormous preoccupation with him, all the stronger because it is hopeless, and all the more hopeless because it is totally uncompromising'.[22] Always in Kafka's writings, God is ever near, but never stated, always 'other'. Another of this company of literary figures is the unjustly forgotten

---

17. Primo Levi, 'A Disciple', in idem, *Moments of Reprieve*, trans. R. Feldman (London: Abacus, 1987), pp. 49–54 (54).

18. Friedrich D. E. Schleiermacher, 'General Hermeneutics', in Kurt Mueller-Vollmer, ed., *The Hermeneutics Reader: Texts of the German Tradition from the Enlightenment to the Present* (Oxford: Blackwell, 1986), pp. 73–86 (73).

19. Julia Kristeva, 'Holbein's Dead Christ', pp. 119–20.

20. Desiderius Erasmus, 'In Praise of Folly', in idem, *The Essential Erasmus*, trans. John P. Dolan (New York: New American Library, 1964), pp. 98–173 (172).

21. Ibid.

22. Maurice Blanchot, 'Kafka and the Work's Demand', in idem, *The Space of Literature*, pp. 57–84 (57).

French writer André Schwarz-Bart, if only for his extraordinary novel *The Last of the Just* (1959). In the last pages of this book, Ernie Levy, the last of the just, that is those 36 Jews in every generation whom God has chosen to bear the burden of the suffering of the world, is travelling in a box car to the death camp with some other adults and a group of frightened children. Setting a little girl on his knees he tells them of the joys in store when they will reach the Kingdom of Israel on their arrival the next day. 'There children can find their parents, and everybody is happy. Because the country we're going to, that's our kingdom, you know. There, the sun never sets, and you may eat anything you can think of. There, an eternal joy will crown your heads; cheerfulness and gaiety will come and greet you, and all the pains and all the moans will run away...'[23] An older woman, a doctor, in the box car, rails at Ernie for telling lies to the children who will face such appalling sufferings and finally death when they reach their journey's end.

> Rocking the child mechanically, Ernie gave way to dry sobs. 'Madame,' he said at last, 'there is no room for truth here.' Then he stopped rocking the child, turned, and saw that the old woman's face had altered.
> 'Then what is there room for?' she began. And taking a closer look at Ernie, registering all the slightest details of his face, she murmured softly, 'Then you don't believe what you're saying at all? Not at all?'[24]

This is literature, where there is no truth but only the telling of stories. Here the truth claims of theology have no part, at least in the first instance, and there is no place yet for God, but there are only stories to comfort the children on their journey to a terrible death the next day. There is only what Jeanrond, writing of Schleiermacher's term 'divination', calls the 'courageous risk' of the one who, even without belief, dares to search for some preliminary grasp upon sense – the making of meaning in an utterly meaningless world. And in this space of fiction may be sensed, even experienced, an absent presence – the otherness of God in literature, the future hope in the darkness of the present. Derrida describes this present hope as a *trace*. 'But this future, this beyond, is not another time, a day after history. It is *present* at the heart of experience. Present not as a total presence but as a *trace*. Therefore, before all dogmas, all conversions, all articles of faith or philosophy, experience itself is eschatological at its origin and in each of its aspects'.[25]

In *The Last of the Just* Ernie Levy, of course, dies, 'dead six million times', a character in fiction who yet remains to haunt our imagination. The novel ends on the same extraordinary note as Kertész's *Fateless* as it speaks of the happiness of the concentration camps: 'And praised be Auschwitz. So be it. Maidanek. The Eternal.

---

23. André Schwarz-Bart, *The Last of the Just*, trans. Stephen Becker (London: Secker & Warburg, 1961), p. 396.
24. Ibid., pp. 397–8.
25. Jacques Derrida, 'Violence and Metaphysics', in idem, *Writing and Difference*, trans. A. Bass (London: Routledge & Kegan Paul, 1981), pp. 79–153 (95).

Treblinka. And praised be Buchenwald. So be it. Mauthausen. The Eternal'.[26] In literature, this grotesque doxology before death itself is finally sanctified and made possible by the figure of Ernie Levy, the teller of children's stories, 'disillusioned, serene and dignified'.[27] And so the novel's narrator concludes, with the hope of Dostoevsky: 'Yesterday, as I stood in the street trembling in despair, rooted to the spot, a drop of pity fell from above upon my face; but there was no breeze in the air, no cloud in the sky... there was only a presence'.[28] And in this trace of a presence, even in the lies of fiction, the uncertainties of sense and the endless search for meaning which is the task of hermeneutics and before that of poetics itself, whose vocation is to find the silence at the heart of all language, is finally to be realized a total presence:

> That silence [which] is the silence of a new solitude, an absolute solitude which has finally negated and reversed every unique and interior ground of consciousness, thereby releasing the totality of consciousness in a total and immediate presence. ... for the only true joy is the joy of loss, the joy of having been wholly lost and thereby wholly found again. Not only is the true paradise the paradise that we have lost, but the only regained paradise is the final loss of paradise itself.[29]

When the 'new atheist' Richard Dawkins was read the story of Ernie Levy's 'lies' to the children in the box car he was asked, 'What would you have said to them?' He replied that he would have said the same thing. He would have told them stories of heaven.

Reading, interpreting, grasping some sense, often in spite of all, in the endless search for meaning in texts, perhaps alone can prepare us for the claims of theology. It is only when, perhaps illicitly, we find innocence and beauty in the darkest places, where neither innocence nor beauty can *be* found, that spaces open up for the impossible. If Ernie's story, and Dostoevsky's, are concerned with the nature of truth, what then of that greatest of all religious virtues, love? George Steiner has written of a late poem on love and freedom, with a glance at the comedic in William Shakespeare, by another survivor, Paul Celan:

> The innocence of obscenity has moved into the last total embarrassment available to us, which is that of prayer. We know this if only by virtue of a supreme word-play and finding at the climax of one of Celan's late poems. He says to, he says of the beloved that she 'beds and prays him free'. The pun does not translate: *bettest/betest*. But the wonder of the congruence is plain. The

---

26. André Schwarz-Bart, *The Last of the Just*, p. 408.
27. Julie Kristeva, 'Holbein's Dead Christ', p. 119.
28. André Schwarz-Bart, *The Last of the Just*, p. 409.
29. Thomas J. J. Altizer, *Total Presence: The Language of Jesus and the Language of Today* (New York: The Seabury Press, 1980), pp. 107-8.

commerce of love finds the as-yet unspoken. Privacy is made new, Eros translates (as in Bottom) into *Logos*. And this translation speaks freedom.[30]

The obscene is found both within the public and the private, the intimate lives of people. In the paradoxes of literature and language even this can become the space in which a divine Otherness suggests light and love.[31]

In his essay in *The Interpretation of Belief* with which we began, Jeanrond reflects upon what he calls the absurdity of Gadamer's accusation of a theological bias in Schleiermacher's hermeneutical reflection. Certainly, we may agree that it is the theological need to interpret texts that constitutes Schleiermacher's hermeneutical point of departure. Yet, as Jeanrond recognizes, 'he always insists that the theological interpreter has no prerogative when he tries to understand texts'.[32] Theology, in other words, must be neither hasty nor haughty in its claims, but await the otherness of God in the textures of the textual, literary world. Schleiermacher maintained that the final goal of interpretation was 'to understand the text at first as well as and then even better than its author'.[33] Yet, as Manfred Frank has pointed out, this constitutes no arrogant claim upon superior competence, 'but it means for the interpreter to risk again and again a deeper grasp of sense in history. The components of the text, its grammatical structure, remain the same, but their sense has to be appropriated anew in every act of reading'.[34]

It is our story-shaped world[35] that affirms the power of human dignity – a profound humanism that radiates from Holbein's almost unbearable painting of Christ's dereliction which, in *The Idiot*, is known and held up as a challenge to theological expectation and its consolations. Perhaps, reflects Ippolit, if Christ had known what horror his followers would have to face as they see his cadaver after the crucifixion, would he even have died as he did? Yet, it is our task to watch, and to persist as patient interpreters in a vocation that seeks to bind earth with heaven, just as Hermes, the messenger of the gods, 'bridged the gap between the divine and the human realm'.[36]

---

30. George Steiner, *Real Presences*, p. 195

31. The theme of love has been prominent in Werner Jeanrond's recent work, culminating in the publication of Werner G. Jeanrond, *A Theology of Love* (London: Continuum/T&T Clark, 2010).

32. Werner G. Jeanrond, 'The Impact of Schleiermacher's Hermeneutics', p. 85.

33. Friedrich Schleiermacher, 'General Hermeneutics', p. 83.

34. Manfred Frank, cited in Werner G. Jeanrond, 'The Impact of Schleiermacher's Hermeneutics', p. 86.

35. Brian Wicker, *The Story-Shaped World: Fiction and Metaphysics: Some Variations on a Theme* (London: The Athlone Press, 1975).

36. Werner G. Jeanrond, *Theological Hermeneutics: Development and Significance* (London: Macmillan, 1991), p. 1.

INDEX OF SUBJECTS

'Abraham's stock' 44
absoluteness 131, 138–44, 244
    Buber, Martin and 128
    Hegel, George F. W. and 55
agape 79–80, 81–2, 83, 85–6
    Christianity and 82, 201
    Good Samaritan, and the 85
aggression 242–3
alien 154
alterity 2, 9–13, 70
    God and 10–11, 13
    radical 10–13, 155
    reduction of 6
animals 148, 213, 215–16
antinomianism 88n. 3
apophatic theology 11
appropriation 99, 101
approximation 3, 10, 293
Arabs 250–2
art 137, 149, 270 *see also Cross on the Mountains, The*; *Body of the Dead Christ in the Tomb, The*
asymmetry 70, 118
autarchy 6
autonomy 6, 141–2, 170

bereavement 191
Bible, the
    interpretation of 52–7
    Ricoeur, Paul and 102
Black Sun: Depression and Melancholia (Kristeva, Julia) 294, 297
body 196, 202
Body of the Dead Christ in the Tomb, The (Holbein, Hans (the Younger)) 294–5, 300
Brothers Karamazov, The (Dostoevsky, Fyodor) 105–6
Buddhism 162, 261–2

caritas 194–5
Cashinahua, the 277
cataphatic theology 11
Catholicism
    Jewish relations and 41–2, 43–6, 50
    gender and 161, 167–71

CEDAW (*Convention on the Elimination of All Forms of Discrimination Against Women*) 170
charity 8n. 38
China 185–8
Christian Faith, The (Schleiermacher, Friedrich D. E.) 272
Christianity
    agape and 82, 201
    China and 187
    community and 200
    faith and 122–3
    gender and 161–71, 173–80, 184–5
    humour and 147–8, 149–52
    identity and 6–7, 8–9
    Islam and 239–46
    Judaism and 233–5, 240
    love and 8, 82, 275–83 *see also Theology of Love, A*
    as a master narrative 275–7, 278–9, 281–3
    sexuality and 185
    South Korea and 187
    theology and 43
    tolerance and 258–60, 261
    traditions and 182
christology 9, 174–6, 202, 205–7
    Dorner, Isaak August and 204
Church Dogmatics (Barth, Karl) 210
churches 181–3
classic, the 3
closure 2, 6, 12–13
collective person, the 202, 205–6
colonialism 109
Common Humanity, A (Gaita, Raimond) 85–6
communication 10, 140–1 *see also* dialogue
communities 89–92, 194–5
    love and 199–207
complementarity 155
Confessions (Augustine, Saint) 191, 192
Convention on the Elimination of All Forms of Discrimination Against Women (CEDAW) 170
cosmos, the 211–14
courageous risk 298
Course of Recognition, The (Ricoeur, Paul) 103
creatio ex nihilo 265–73

creation 99–102, 211–15, 265–73
creatureliness 280, 292
creatures 71–4, 212–13, 215, 269–71, 279–80,
Crime and Punishment (Dostoevsky, Fyodor) 295
critical thinking 97
cross, the 173–80
Cross in the Mountains, The (Friedrich, Caspar David) 293

De Doctrina Christiana (Augustine, Saint) 192–3, 196
De Genesi ad litteram (Augustine, Saint) 163–4
De Trinitate (Augustine, Saint) 192
death 162, 170, 286–7, 294–9 *see also* bereavement
  Jesus Christ and 174–6, 294 *see also* resurrection
demands 80–1
dependence 176–9, 195
Deuxième Sexe, Le (Beauvoir, Simone de) 177
dialogic 105–9, 110
dialogical personalism 115
dialogue 105–13, 248–9
  interreligious 222–7, 231–8, 245–6, 248–9, 257
  philosophy of 125–8
Dialogues on Natural Religion (Hume, David) 107
Die Verbum 51–9
différance 55–6
difference 275, 277
différend, Le 277, 278, 282
dignity 78, 144n. 21, 187–8, 295–7, 300
distance 156
diversity 205, 260–1, 269
divination 293–5, 298
double creation 163
dynamics 2, 10, 13–14, 59, 132

ecclesiology 12, 76, 171, 194, 195
Egypt 20, 232
  Joseph story and 26, 28–30, 32
  Tale of Sinuhe 30–2
Eigenschaft 75
emancipation 143–4, 276, 278
empathy 110, 155, 156, 221–9, 243–4, 245 *see also* feelings
encounters 80–1, 84–5, 115–23 *see also* Pearl
  models of 155–6
enlightenment 142, 143
equality 155
eros 81, 82, 83, 86
  Good Samaritan, and the 85

eschatology 10, 12, 42–3
ethics 65–6, 75
etiske fordring, Den (Løgstrup, Knud E.) 80–1, 85
Evangelii Gaudium (Francis I) 169
exclusion 7, 12, 153, 201, 255, 259
  women and 164, 168–9
existentialism 3–4, 270–2
exodus tradition 25
experience 1, 6, 11, 57, 87–93, 221–9
experiences 88

face 68–9, 177–9
  face of the other 68–9, 177–9
faith 182–3, 224–5, 258–9
familiarity 225, 286, 288
Fateless (Kertész, Imre) 296, 297
feelings 112, 125, 127, 153 *see also* empathy
female 162–71 *see also* gender
feminism 173–80 *see also* gender
foreigner, the 154–6
foreignness 153–9
free will 139, 297
freedom 179
Fremden verstehen, Den (Sundermeier, Theo) 154
friendships 253–4
fundamentalism 242–3

gay 184
Gegenüber 155, 210, 212 *see also* vis-à-vis
gender 161–71, 184–5 *see also* feminism
generosity 249
Germany 182, 231, 233
gift 55, 77, 138, 268, 101
  Buber, Martin and 127, 128
gift of love 8, 11, 279
globalization 6–7
God 10–13
  as absolute person 128
  alterity and 10–11, 13
  encounters and 127–8
  foreignness and 156–7
  Godlikeness and 164–6
  hospitality and 251
  image of 192
  justice and 73–4
  Kingdom of 77
  love and *see* love of God
  Moses and 19–22
  nature of 71–4
  openness 282–3, 290
  otherness and 22, 139, 178, 259–60
  pertermirable 290–1
  relationships and 128, 130–1, 211–15

Index of Subjects

subject, and the 74, 128
   trust and 74
Godlikeness 164-6
Good Samaritan, the 34, 84-5, 199, 201, 206 *see also* neighbour
Gospels, the 151
grace 77, 134, 139, 192, 258-9

Hebrews 42, 157
   Nostra Aetate and 44-6, 50
   hermeneutics and 42, 46-50
hermeneutics 4-6, 13
   Barth, Karl and 4
   Bible, and the 52-7
   dialogue and 110-11
   Die Verbum and 51-9
   foreigner and 154-6
   Hebrews and 42, 46-50
   interreligious 7-8, 10, 221
   Ricoeur, Paul and 97, 99, 112
   Romans and 42
   xenological 155-6, 159
hermeneutics of love 113, 222, 228
hermeneutics of suspicion 112-13
hermeneutics of trust 112-13
Hinduism 162
History of the Development of the Doctrine of the Person of Christ (Dorner, Isaak August) 204
Holocaust, the 296
homeostasis 155
Homilies on the First Epistle of John (Augustine, Saint) 194
Homilies on the Gospels (Bede) 47-8
homo capax 101
homo divinus 74-6
homosexuality 184
hope 12, 49, 243, 279n. 11, 292
   radical hope 12
hopelessness 113, 297
hospitality 248-54
human beings 77-8 *see also homo capax*
   encounters and 80-1, 84-5
   goodness and 85-6
   love and 191-7
   non-human 211-13, 215, 216, 271
   recognition and 85-6
   value of 79
human love 133, 193, 280-1
   Augustine, Saint and 191, 193, 196-7
   Kierkegaard, Søren and 130
human rights 169-71, 187
humanity 201-2, 204, 211-16
   non-human 211-13, 215, 216, 271

humour 145-52

I and Thou (Buber, Martin) 115-17, 126
identification 54, 91, 96, 174-5 *see also* empathy
identify 68
identity 7, 9, 34, 155, 241-2
   intolerance and 256, 260
   mediation and 55
   religious 142, 257
Idiot, The (Dostoevsky, Fyodor) 294-5, 300
ignorance 54, 232
Im-Possibility of Interreligious Dialogue, The (Cornille, Catherine) 225-6
images 73
imagination 225, 227
In Memory of Her (Schüssler Fiorenza, Elisabeth) 184
incarnation, the 152
inclusion 163, 164, 165, 167, 278
incompleteness 139, 144, 294
indifference 256
infinity 139-40
institutions 9, 76-7, 111, 120
instrumentalizations 5
inter-hope dialogue 12
inter-religious translations, theories of 7-8
interpretation 2-6, 58, 293-4, 300
   Bible, and the 52-6
   Paul, Saint and 87-93
Interpretation of Belief, The (Jasper, David) 293, 300
interreligious dialogue 222-7, 231-8, 245-6, 248-9, 257
inter-religious translations, theories of 7-8
interruption 275-83
intolerance 255-6
Iran 236
Islam 169-70, 236-8, 239-46, 249-52 *see also* Muslim
   tolerance and 260-1
Israel 25, 44, 232
Israelites, the 23

Japan 262
Jerusalem 234, 236, 292
Jesus Christ 9, 205 *see also* christology
   death of 157, 174-6, 294 *see also* resurrection
   humour and 146-7, 149-50
   love and 194-5
   maleness and 169
   neighbour and 204, 206
   outsiders and 183

Paul, Saint and 89-93
salvation and 258-9
trust and 122-3
vis-à-vis and 212-13
Jews 296, 298 *see also* Judaism
Catholicism and 41-2, 43-6, 50
Joseph story and 28-9
Johannine Gospel 34-40
Judaism 231, 233-6, 238, 240 *see also* Jews
justice 74, 75-6

kabod 138-9
kenōsis 176, 178
Kingdom of God, the 77
Kjerlighedsgerninger 66

language 6, 54, 55, 72, 102-3
dialogue and 245-6
encounters and 115-23
love and 127
Nygren, Anders and 84
religion and 5, 85, 137-41
symbols and 103
'Language and Proximity' (Levinas, Emmanuel) 119
Last of the Just, The (Schwarz-Bart, André) 298-9
laughter 147 *see also* humour
Laughter: A Scientific Investigation (Provine, Robert R.) 147
lesbian 184
Leviathan (Hobbes, Thomas) 202-3
Life of Jesus, The (Strauss, David) 204
Life Together (Bonhoeffer, Dietrich) 204-5
linguistic communities 6
literature 54, 57-8, 294-300 *see also* texts
style and 150-1
live-entering 225
loss 191
love 1-2, 11-14 *see also agape*; *eros*
aggression and 242-3
Augustine, Saint and 189-97, 280
Christian 8, 82, 275-83 *see also* Theology of Love, A
collective 199-207
community and 91-2
divine love 269, 273, 280-1
empathy and 222
enemies and 130, 201, 258
foreignness and 157
God and *see* love of God
Human and *see* human love
individuals and 199, 201-2
Johannine Gospel and 34-40
Kierkegaard, Søren and 64-6, 68

language and 127
of neighbour *see* love of neighbour
Paul, Saint and 91-3
praxis of *see* praxis of love
relationality and 79
religion and 144
seeing and 66-9
subjectivity and 125-6, 131-3
theology of 128-31, 133 *see also* Theology of Love, A
love of God and 87-93, 128-31, 133, 144, 199
Augustine, Saint and 197
creation and 265, 269, 271, 273
love of neighbour 65, 68, 129-31, 197, 204-6
see also Good Samaritan, the
Lumen Fidei (*The Light of Faith*) (Francis I) 294-5
Lutheran theology 173, 175-6, 258, 270-1

Manichaeism 268-9
Mary, Mother of Jesus 36-7, 289
master 177, 179
master narratives 276-9, 281-3
meaning 53-4, 58, 137-8, 144, 298-9 *see also* interpretation
Bakhtin, Mikhail and 106
Judaism and 45-6
master narratives and 277, 278
Ricoeur, Paul and 100-1, 103
mediation 55
Meeting God on the Cross (Guðmundsdóttir, Arnfríður) 175
Mimesis: The Representation of Reality in Western Literature (Auerbach, Erich) 150-1
mocking 147
modernity 141-4
modesty 244-5
monarchy, the 202
Moses (Michelangelo) 17
Mulieris dignitaten (John Paul II) 167
Muslim 44, 232, 236-8, 239-46, 249-50, 252 *see also* Islam
Mystik des Apostels Paulus, Die (Schweitzer, Albert) 47

naïveté 3-4
narratives 275-8 *see also* master narratives
negative theology 139
neighbour 70, 282-3 *see also* Good Samaritan, the
love of 65, 68, 129-31, 197, 204-6
networks 131, 281, 283
networks of love 131, 281, 283
Norway 83
Nostra Aetate 41-2, 43-4, 50

object 74, 177, 192
  Buber, Martin and 115–17, 120
  community and 199, 202, 205
  individual, and the 199, 205, 207
  interpretation and 3–4, 6, 7, 11
  love and 81–2, 86, 132, 191–3, 196
toleration and 256–7
On the First Principles (Origen) 48–9
Oneself as Another (Ricoeur, Paul) 96, 98, 100
open 106
openness 2–13, 110, 112–13, 226 see also space
  God and 282–3, 290
  interreligious dialogue and 232–3, 248–9
  literature and 295
  reality and 140, 142
'opposite' 212 see also *vis-à-vis*
Ordinatio sacerdotalis (John Paul II) 168
other, the 1–4, 6–7, 80–1, 84–6, 177 see also otherness; outsider, the; stranger, the
  agape and 84–6
  colonialized 109
  cross and the 178
  demand and 80–1
  dialogue and 110–13
  divine Other 152, 273, 300
  encounters with 80, 115–23
  eros and 84–5
  face of the other 68–9, 177–9
  infinity and 140
  love and 8–9, 13, 34, 40, 79
  radical 1, 2, 10–13, 155, 177–80
  Ricoeur, Paul as 95–103
  seeing and 63–70
  total other 8, 10, 34–40
  God as 22
  Moses as 18, 24
otherness 2, 6–9, 12–13, 181, 217 see also and other, the
  empathy and 222–7, 229
  foreignness and 153–9
  God and 139, 178, 259–60
  identity and 241
  Levinas, Emmanuel 117–18
  Moses and 18, 20
  Nicodemus and 39
  power and 178
  radical 177–8
  religion and 139–44
  women and 179, 184
Otherwise than Being (Levinas, Emmanuel) 119
outside 35, 120–1, 154, 156–7, 183 see also fundamentalism
  creation and 101

humanity 214, 216
outsider, the 20–3, 183, 224, 225 see also other, the

Parable of the Vineyard 287, 290–1
patriarchal tradition 25
Paul, Saint 87–93, 235–6 see also Pauline
Pauline 46–7, 168, 280 see also Paul, Saint
Pearl 285–92
performative utterances 119–20, 121
person 81, 84–6, 152 see also collective person; other, the
  first 125, 132
  God as absolute 128,
  grace and the 77, 131
  individual 199, 201–2
  just 74, 75–6
  second 125, 132
  third 118, 120, 125, 132–3
Phenomenology of the Spirit, The (Hegel, Georg F. W.) 55
philosophy 84, 109, 110, 133
  Buber, Martin and 117, 121, 123, 127–8
  dialogue and 125–8
  empathy and see empathy
  Levinas, Emmanuel and 121, 123, 177
  Ricoeur, Paul and 95–103
  Soja, Edward W. and 209
Platonic Renaissance in England, The (Cassirer, Ernst) 148–9
pluralism 231, 255 see also plurality
plurality 53–4, 87, 92–3, 133, 231 see also pluralism
pneumatology 182
poem 137 see also poetry
Poetics (Aristotle) 150
poetry 58, 137–8 see also *Pearl*
postmodernism 1, 106, 210, 282
Praise of Folly (Erasmus, Desiderius) 146, 297
praxis 9, 181
praxis of love 1–2, 8–9, 11–13, 222, 280–1
  Johannine literature and 33–4
prayer 77, 299
promise 23n. 29, 26, 78, 278, 295
prophecy 249
Protestantism
  gender and 161, 167
psychoanalysis 112
public sphere, the 85
  dialogue and 108

Qur'an 170, 237, 239, 240, 243, 244, 246, 249, 250, 260

reading 3, 293–4
    Barth, Karl and 4–5
    texts 18
reality 139–40
reason 74–6, 108–10, 209
    tolerance and 258
recognition 8, 85–6, 155, 188, 217
reconciliation 12, 27, 149, 182, 238
    Paul, Saint and 258
Reflections on Covenant and Mission 45
relationality 6, 8–11, 13–14, 116 *see also* relationships
    love and 1–2, 79–86, 186
relations 1 *see also* relationality *and* relationships
relational anxiety 1
relationality 1–2
relationships 40, 55, 131–2, 197, 199 *see also* encounters; relationality
    Buber, Marin and 116–18, 122, 126–8, 177–9
    creation and 265–73
    dependence and 176–9, 195
    empathy and 221–9, 243–4 *see also* feelings
    God and 128, 130–1, 211–15
    hospitality and 248–54
    love and 281 *see also* love
    religious 239–46 *see also* tolerance
    vis-à-vis 155–6, 212–14
religion 137–44, 181–3
    China and 185–8
    empathy and 224–9
    freedom of 171
    gender and 161–71, 173–80
    in public life 248
    tolerance and 255–62
Renaissance, the 148–9
respect 8, 156, 181, 188, 201, 217 *see also* tolerance
    Barth, Karl and 210, 216
Responsio (Ratzinger, Joseph) 168
resurrection 37, 175
revelation 4, 51–2, 55, 260–1
    Ricoeur, Paul 100
'Révélation sans théologie, théologie sans révélation' (Nault, François) 51
richness 77–8
risk 111–12, 113, 250, 253 *see also* divination
Romans 42

Sages, The (Urbach, Ephraim E.) 234
St. Paul: The Foundation of Universalism (Badiou, Alain) 87–8
salvation 123, 152, 176, 237, 294, 297
    creation and 99–100, 102, 271

    grace and 258–9
    Pearl and 292
sameness 140, 143
Sanctorum Communio (Bonhoeffer, Dietrich) 205
Scivias (Hildegard von Bingen) 166
scripture 52
Scripture Principle, the 259
seeing 63–70
self 11, 74, 76, 126, 133 *see also* identity
    Augustine, Saint and 190
    Buddhism and 262
    dialogue and 110–11, 113, 118
    empathy and 221
self-awareness 71, 242
self-confidence 142
self-consciousness 109–10
self-denial 130
self-distanciation 101, 137
self-esteem 242
self-evident presuppositions 82–4
self-love 81, 280 *see also eros*
self-relativizing 259–60, 261
self-respect 111
self-revelation 54–5, 72–3
self-understanding 110, 113, 245, 258
    Islam and 239
    Israel and 25
separation 25, 29, 96, 115–16, 280
serfdom 75
servant 130, 177
sex 162 *see also* gender
sexuality 184–5
Showings (Julian of Norwich) 166
sin 113
slavery 74–5
solidarity 189–90
South Korea 187
space 209–17
Spain 111
speech 119–21
spirit 127
Spirit, the 182–3, 185–6
spirituality 186–7, 243–44
Sprachgeschehen 123
strangeness 250
stranger, the 23, 154, 159, 249–50 *see also* other, the
subject, the 3, 76, 101, 115–17
    God and 74, 128
    human 141, 143–4, 192–3, 195–6 *see also* human beings
    love and 34, 125–6, 132, 207, 280–2
    other, and the 177–8

spiritual 192
  tolerance and 256
subjectivity 125, 131–3
submission 176
subordination 4
suffering 88–9
Symbolism of Evil, The (Ricoeur, Paul) 102–3
sympathy 149, 155–6, 222–3, 225–6
sympotic dialogue 107–8

Tale of Sinuhe 30–1
texts 3, 4–5, 51, 54, 56–8, 296–7, 299 *see also* interpretation *and* literature
  reading 18
  Ricoeur, Paul and 101
  sacred 244–5
textual paradigms 42–3, 49, 51–2, 57–9
Theological Hermeneutics (Jeanrond, Werner G.) 6
theology 1, 4, 6, 10–11
  apophatic 11
  cataphatic 11
  hermeneutics of 4, 6–7
  negative 139
  Ricoeur, Paul and 95–103
  space and 210
theology of love 128–31, 133
Theology of Love, A (Jeanrond, Werner G.) 128–9, 189, 275, 279–81
theology of the other 238
Thirdspace 209, 216–17
Timaeus (Plato) 266
Time that Remains: A Commentary on the Letter to the Romans, The (Agamben, Giorgio) 87–8
tolerance 255–62
Torah, the 18–19
total 7, 8, 10
totalitarianism 10
'Towards an Interreligious Hermeneutics of Love' (Jeanrond, Werner G.) 222
trace 298
tradition 6, 9, 247–8
transcendence 2, 3, 6, 8–10, 12–14
  Chinese and 186
  creation and 268n. 7
  encounter and 122
  Levinas, Emmanuel and 119
transformation 2, 3, 6, 8–10, 12–14

Christian faith and 200
differences and 240
encounter and 123
fundamentalism and 242
hospitality and 251
love and 131, 279n. 11, 280
Nicodemus and 40
poetry and 137
religion and 142–3
translation 7, 138, 143, 156, 246
travel 250
treatises 106
trust 112–13, 243–4
  faith and 122–3, 258
  freedom and 179–80
  God and 74
  Jews and 235
  language and 120, 121
  other, and the 80–1, 83–5, 110, 115

UK 182
unfamiliarity 250, 288, 292 *see also* stranger
unity 53–4, 78, 132, 195, 205–6
  love and 281
  tolerance and 260–1
universalism 77, 86, 92
  Christ's humanity and 204
  collective person and 201–2, 206
  encounter and 80
  Moses and 23
  narratives and 278–9, 281, 282
  tolerance and 256
US 182
utterances 119–20, 121

vis-à-vis 155–6, 212–14

War and Peace (Tolstoy, Leo) 106
Weggefährten (Schmidt, Helmut) 232–3
Who One Is (Hart, James G.) 132
will 74 *see also* free will
  of God 192, 213, 237, 261, 268
Works of Love (Kierkegaard, Søren) 64–6, 68, 130

xenological hermeneutics 155–6, 159

Zwischen 126, 128, 129

INDEX OF NAMES

Aaron 20, 21–2
Abraham 237–8, 250
Adorno, Theodor W. 107, 137, 142
Agamben, Giorgio
   Time that Remains: A Commentary on the Letter to the Romans, The 87–8
Apinar, Snjezana 251
Arendt, Hannah 189–90, 195
Aristotle 148
   Poetics 150
Auerbach, Erich
   Mimesis: The Representation of Reality in Western Literature 150–1
Augustine, Saint 163
   Christian community and 194
   Confessions 191, 192
   creation and 268–9
   De Doctrina Christiana 192–3, 196
   De Genesi ad litteram 163–4
   De Trinitate 192
   Homilies on the First Epistle of John 194
   loss and 191
   love and 189–97, 280
Austin, John L. 119–21

Badiou, Alain
   St. Paul: The Foundation of Universalism 87–8
Bakhtin, Mikhail 105–9, 110
   humour and 148
Barth, Karl 10, 210–17
   Church Dogmatics 210, 213
   hermeneutics and 4
   Paul, Saint and 90
   reading and 4–5
   Ricoeur, Paul and 99
Bea, Augustin (cardinal) 43
Beauvoir, Simone de
   Deuxième Sexe, Le 177
Bede, The Venerable
   Homilies on the Gospels 47–8
Ben-Chorin, Schalom 233, 234, 238
Benedict XVI (pope); *see also* Ratzinger, Joseph 170, 281
Blixen, Karen 157
   Babette's Feast 157–9

Blundell, Boyd 99
Bonhoeffer, Dietrich 204–6, 215
   Life Together 204
   Sanctorum Communio 205
Boys, Mary C. 46
Breivik, Anders Behring 79
Buber, Martin 122, 177–8
   gift and 127, 128
   I and Thou 115–17, 126–7, 177
   relationships and 116–18, 122, 126–8, 177–9

Cassirer, Ernst
   Platonic Renaissance in England, The 148–9
Celan, Paul 299–300
Cobb, John B. 182
Connelly, John 44, 50
Cornille, Catherine
   Im-Possibility of Interreligious Dialogue, The 225–6
Crüsemann, Frank 27, 28
Cunningham, Philip A. 46

Dawkins, Richard 299
Derrida, Jacques 55–6, 298
Dineson, Isak *see* Blixen, Karen
Dorner, Isaak August
   History of the Development of the Doctrine of the Person of Christ 204
Dostoevsky, Fyodor
   Brothers Karamazov, The 105–6
   Crime and Punishment 295
   Idiot, The 294–5, 300
Dulles, Avery (cardinal) 44–6
Durkheim, Émile 199

Ebeling, Gerhard 258
Eckhart, Meister 71–8
Eichmann, Adolf 44
Erasmus, Desiderius 146
   Praise of Folly 146, 294, 297

Flood, Gavin 224, 225
Francis I (pope)
   Evangelii Gaudium 169

Lumen Fidei (The Light of Faith) 294–5
Frank, Manfred 3, 300
Frei, Hans 98–9
Freud, Sigmund 17–18, 24, 242
Friedrich, Caspar David
   Cross in the Mountains, The 293

Gadamer, Hans-Georg 105, 109–12
Gaita, Raimond 85–6
   Common Humanity, A 85–6
Ghazali, Al- 252–3
Guðmundsdóttir, Arnfríður 175
   Meeting God on the Cross 175

Habermas, Jürgen 7, 105, 108, 143, 277
Hagar 237, 250
Haight, Roger 182
Hart, James G. 132
   Who One Is 132
Hegel, Georg F. W. 55, 149, 177, 293
   Phenomenology of the Spirit, The 55
Heidegger, Martin 69, 117
Hildegard von Bingen 166
   Scivias 166
Hobbes, Thomas
   Leviathan 202–3
Hodgson, Peter C. 182
Holbein, Hans (the Younger)
   Body of the Dead Christ in the Tomb, The 294–5, 300
Hölderlin, Friedrich 297
hooks, bell 216
Hume, David
   Dialogues on Natural Religion 107
Husserl, Edmund 117, 121, 132, 224, 226

Isaac, Jules 43
Ishmael 237 *see also* Ismail
Ismail 250 *see also* Ishmael

Jeanrond, Werner G. 6–14, 33, 247–8, 293
   empathy and 222
   interpretation and 4–6
   Interpretation of Belief, The 293, 300
   Johannine Gospel and 34
   love and 81, 128–31, 195, 222
   otherness and 181
   Theological Hermeneutics 6
   Theology of Love, A 128–9, 189, 275, 279–81
   'Towards an Interreligious Hermeneutics of Love' 222
John Chrysostom, Saint 145
John Paul II (pope)
   Mulieris dignitaten 167

Ordinatio sacerdotalis 168
John XXIII (pope) 43
Johnson, Earl S., Jr. 42–3
Joseph 25–32
Julian of Norwich 166
   Showings 166
Jüngel, Eberhard 5, 98, 102, 281

Kafka, Franz 297
Kertész, Imre
   Fateless 296, 297
Kierkegaard, Søren 129–30, 152
   love and 79
   Works of Love 64–6, 68, 130
Kristeva, Julia
   Black Sun: Depression and Melancholia 294, 297

Lang, Bernard 28–9
Le Goff, Jacques 148
Levi, Primo 296–7
Levinas, Emmanuel 68–70, 117–19, 121, 177–8
   'Language and Proximity' 119
   Otherwise than Being 119
Lindbeck, George R. 5
Løgstrup, Knud E. 80–1
   etiske fordring, Den 85
Luther, Martin 173, 175, 182, 258, 270–2
Lyotard, Jean-Françoise 276–8

McLaughlin, Eleanor 174
Marion, Jean-Luc 11
Meister Eckhart 71–8
Michelangelo
   Moses 17
Min, Anselm K. 182
Moses 18–24
Muhammad 236, 239, 240, 244, 250, 252

Nakashima Brock, Rita 174
Nault, François 51
   'Révélation sans théologie, théologie sans révélation' 51
Nicodemus 33–4, 35–40
Nygren, Anders 79–80, 81–5

Origen
   On the First Principles 48–9

Panikkar, Raimon 224
Paul, Saint 87–93, 235–6 *see also* Pauline
Pawlikowski, John T. 46
Pick, Lucy 111
Plato

Timaeus 266
Polkinghorne, John 182
Provine, Robert R.
   Laughter: A Scientific Investigation 147

Radford Ruether, Rosemary 174
Rahner, Karl 141n. 13, 197, 281
Ratzinger, Joseph 167
   Responsio 168
Reik, Theodor 242
Ricoeur, Paul 3–4, 95–9, 155n. 4
   Course of Recognition, The 103
   Oneself as Another 96, 98, 100
   Symbolism of Evil, The 102–3
Roncalli, Angelo Giuseppe 43
Rose, Gillian 197
Rosenthal, Franz 249–50

Sadat, Anwar El 232
Scheler, Max 116
Schleiermacher, Friedrich D. E. 3, 4, 110, 183, 204, 272, 293, 295, 297, 298, 300
   Christian Faith, The 272
Schlink, Eugen 53
Schmidt, Helmut
   Weggefährten 232–3
Schüssler Fiorenza, Elisabeth
   In Memory of Her 184
Schwarz-Bart, André 298
   Last of the Just, The 298–9
Schweitzer, Albert
   Mystik des Apostels Paulus, Die 47
Searle, John R. 120

Soja, Edward W. 209
   Thirdspace 209, 216–17
Solberg, Mary M. 175
Steiner, George 299–300
Strauss, David
   Life of Jesus, The 204
Sundermeier, Theo
   Fremden verstehen, Den 154

Theobald, Christoph 55
Theophilus of Antioch 266
Theunissen, Michael 125–6, 128
Thomas Aquinas, Saint 269–70
Thompson, Deanna A. 175
Thucydides 108–9
Tolstoy, Leo
   War and Peace 106
Tracy, David 3, 98–9

Urbach, Ephraim E.
   Sages, The 234

Vanhoozer, Kevin 99–101
Volkan, Vamik 242
Von Rad, Gerhard 27

Weil, Simone 223
Welker, Michael 182
Williams, Rowan 8, 189–97
Winch, Peter 84–5
Wollstonecraft, Mary 166

Yong, Amos 182